D1261196

THE CAMBRIDGE COMPANION TO

MAIMONIDES

Moses ben Maimon, known to English-speaking audiences as Maimonides (1138–1204), represents the high point of Jewish rationalism in the Middle Ages and played a pivotal role in the transition of philosophy from the Islamic East to the Christian West. His greatest philosophical work, the *Guide of the Perplexed*, had a decisive impact on all subsequent Jewish thought and is still the subject of intense scholarly debate. An enigmatic figure in his own time, Maimonides continues to defy simple attempts at classification. The twelve essays in this volume, all by leaders in their respective fields, offer a lucid and comprehensive treatment of his life and thought. They cover the sources on which Maimonides drew, his contributions to philosophy, theology, jurisprudence, and Bible commentary, as well as his esoteric writing style and influence on later thinkers.

Kenneth Seeskin is Professor of Philosophy at Northwestern University and winner of the Koret Jewish Book Award. He is the author of *Jewish Philosophy in a Secular Age; Maimonides: A Guide for Today's Perplexed; No Other Gods: The Modern Struggle Against Idolatry; Searching for a Distant God: The Legacy of Maimonides*; and *Autonomy in Jewish Philosophy*.

CAMBRIDGE COMPANIONS TO PHILOSOPHY

OTHER VOLUMES IN THE SERIES OF CAMBRIDGE COMPANIONS:

ABELARD *Edited by* JEFFREY E. BROWER *and* KEVIN GUILFOY
ADORNO *Edited by* TOM HUNN
AQUINAS *Edited by* NORMAN KRETZMANN *and* ELEONORE STUMP
HANNAH ARENDT *Edited by* DANA VILLA
ARISTOTLE *Edited by* JONATHAN BARNES
AUGUSTINE *Edited by* ELEONORE STUMP *and* NORMAN KRETZMANN
BACON *Edited by* MARKKU PELTONEN
SIMONE DE BEAUVOIR *Edited by* CLAUDIA CARD
DARWIN *Edited by* JONATHAN HODGE *and* GREGORY RADICK
DESCARTES *Edited by* JOHN COTTINGHAM
DUNS SCOTUS *Edited by* THOMAS WILLIAMS
EARLY GREEK PHILOSOPHY *Edited by* A. A. LONG
FEMINISM IN PHILOSOPHY *Edited by* MIRANDA FRICKER *and* JENNIFER HORNSBY
FOUCAULT *Edited by* GARY GUTTING
FREUD *Edited by* JEROME NEU
GADAMER *Edited by* ROBERT J. DOSTAL
GALILEO *Edited by* PETER MACHAMER
GERMAN IDEALISM *Edited by* KARL AMERIKS
GREEK AND ROMAN PHILOSOPHY *Edited by* DAVID SEDLEY
HABERMAS *Edited by* STEPHEN K. WHITE
HEGEL *Edited by* FREDERICK BEISER
HEIDEGGER *Edited by* CHARLES GUIGNON
HOBBES *Edited by* TOM SORELL
HUME *Edited by* DAVID FATE NORTON
HUSSERL *Edited by* BARRY SMITH *and* DAVID WOODRUFF SMITH
WILLIAM JAMES *Edited by* RUTH ANNA PUTNAM
KANT *Edited by* PAUL GUYER

KIERKEGAARD *Edited by* ALASTAIR HANNAY *and* GORDON MARINO
LEIBNIZ *Edited by* NICHOLAS JOLLEY
LEVINAS *Edited by* SIMON CRITCHLEY *and* ROBERT BERNASCONI
LOCKE *Edited by* VERE CHAPPELL
MALEBRANCHE *Edited by* STEVEN NADLER
MARX *Edited by* TERRELL CARVER
MEDIEVAL PHILOSOPHY *Edited by* A. S. MCGRADE
MEDIEVAL JEWISH PHILOSOPHY *Edited by* DANIEL H. FRANK *and* OLIVER LEAMAN
MILL *Edited by* JOHN SKORUPSKI
NEWTON *Edited by* I. BERNARD COHEN *and* GEORGE E. SMITH
NIETZSCHE *Edited by* BERND MAGNUS *and* KATHLEEN HIGGINS
OCKHAM *Edited by* PAUL VINCENT SPADE
PASCAL *Edited by* NICHOLAS HAMMOND
PEIRCE *Edited by* CHERI MISAK
PLATO *Edited by* RICHARD KRAUT
PLOTINUS *Edited by* LLOYD P. GERSON
QUINE *Edited by* ROGER F. GIBSON
RAWLS *Edited by* SAMUEL FREEMAN
THOMAS REID *Edited by* TERENCE CUNEO *and* RENÉ VAN WOUDENBERG
ROUSSEAU *Edited by* PATRICK RILEY
BERTRAND RUSSELL *Edited by* NICHOLAS GRIFFIN
SARTRE *Edited by* CHRISTINA HOWELLS
SCHOPENHAUER *Edited by* CHRISTOPHER JANAWAY
THE SCOTTISH ENLIGHTENMENT *Edited by* ALEXANDER BROADIE
SPINOZA *Edited by* DON GARRETT
THE STOICS *Edited by* BRAD INWOOD
WITTGENSTEIN *Edited by* KANS SLUGA *and* DAVID STERN

The Cambridge Companion to MAIMONIDES

Edited by

Kenneth Seeskin

Northwestern University

CAMBRIDGE UNIVERSITY PRESS
Cambridge, New York, Melbourne, Madrid, Cape Town, Singapore, São Paulo

Cambridge University Press
40 West 20th Street, New York, NY 10011-4211, USA

www.cambridge.org
Information on this title: www.cambridge.org/9780521819749

First published 2005

Printed in the United States of America

A catalog record for this publication is available from the British Library.

Library of Congress Cataloging in Publication Data

Cambridge companion to Maimonides / edited by Kenneth Seeskin.
p. cm. – (Cambridge companions to philosophy)
Includes bibliographical references and index.
ISBN 0-521-81974-1 (hardback) – ISBN 0-521-52578-0 (pbk.)
1. Maimonides, Moses, 1135–1204. 2. Maimonides, Moses,
1135–1204 – Teachings. 3. Philosophy, Jewish. I. Seeskin, Kenneth,
1947– II. Title. III. Series.

BM755.M6C36 2005
181′.06 – dc22 2004020376

ISBN-13 978-0-521-81974-9 hardback
ISBN-10 0-521-81974-1 hardback

ISBN-13 978-0-521-52578-7 paperback
ISBN-10 0-521-52578-0 paperback

Contents

Acknowledgment

I would like to thank Michal Zamir-Muehlethaler for valuable assistance in the preparation of this manuscript, especially in the area of checking and systematizing transliteration. In general we have tried to balance the demands of technical accuracy with those of familiarity.

Citations and Abbreviations

The following abbreviations to Maimonides' work are used throughout this volume:

CM *Commentary on the Mishnah*
EC *Eight Chapters*
GP *Guide of the Perplexed*
MT *Mishneh Torah*

Most references to the *Guide of the Perplexed* contain the book, chapter, and then page number to the English translation of Shlomo Pines published by the University of Chicago Press. Thus "*GP* 3.32, p. 529" means that the citation comes from Book Three, Chapter 32, and can be found on page 529 of Pines' text.

References to the *Mishneh Torah* contain the Book, topic, chapter, and section. Thus "*MT* 1, Repentance, 5.1" refers to Book One, Laws of Repentance, Chapter 5, Section 1.

A bibliography of Maimonides' works, related works of other philosophers, and secondary literature can be found at the end.

The following general abbreviations are also used:

B. Babylonian Talmud
M. Mishnah
R. Rabbi
T. Tosefta
Y. Palestinian Talmud

All Talmudic citations are to the Babylonian Talmud unless otherwise noted.

Contributors

SEYMOUR FELDMAN is Professor of Philosophy, Emeritus, at Rutgers University. He is the translator of Gersonides' *The Wars of the Lord*, 3 vols. (1984, 1988, 1999), and the author of *Philosophy in a Time of Crisis: Isaac Abravanel, Defender of the Faith* (2003). He has edited and annotated new translations of Spinoza's *Ethics* and *The Theological–Political Treatise*.

GAD FREUDENTHAL is Permanent Senior Research Fellow at the Centre national de la recherche scientifique (CNRS) in Paris. He is the author of *Aristotle's Theory of Material Substance. Form and Soul, Heat and Pneuma* (1995), coeditor of *Torah et Science: Perspectives historiques et théoriques. Études offertes à Charles Touati* (2001) and *Mélanges d'histoire de la médecine hébraïque. Études choisies de la Revue d'histoire de la médecine hébraïque, 1948–1985* (2003), and author of numerous articles bearing on the intellectual history of Jews in the medieval and early modern periods. He is also the editor of the annual *Aleph: Historical Studies in Science and Judaism*.

ALFRED L. IVRY is Skirball Professor of Jewish Thought and Professor of Middle East and Islamic Studies at New York University. A specialist in medieval Jewish and Islamic philosophy, his most recent publications have been critical Arabic and Hebrew editions of Averroes' *Middle Commentary* on Aristotle's *De anima*.

MENACHEM KELLNER is Wolfson Professor of Jewish Thought at the University of Haifa and the author of *Dogma in Medieval Jewish Thought* (1986), *Maimonides on Judaism and the Jewish People* (1991), and *Maimonides on the "Decline of the Generations" and the*

Nature of Rabbinic Authority (1996) as well as other books and essays in medieval Jewish philosophy and modern Jewish thought.

SARA KLEIN-BRASLAVY is Professor of Jewish Medieval Philosophy at Tel-Aviv University. She is the author of *Maimonides' Interpretation of the Story of Creation* [in Hebrew] (1978), *Maimonides' Interpretation of the Adam Stories in Genesis – A Study in Maimonides' Anthropology* [in Hebrew] (1986), and *King Solomon and Philosophical Esotericism in the Thought of Maimonides* [in Hebrew] (1996). She has published numerous articles on Jewish medieval philosophy and is one of the editors of *Les méthodes de travail de Gersonide et le maniement du savoir chez les scolastiques* (2003).

JOEL L. KRAEMER is John Henry Barrows Professor Emeritus in the Divinity School and Committee on Social Thought at the University of Chicago. He has written on the transmission of the intellectual heritage of Greek antiquity to the world of Islam in *Humanism in the Renaissance of Islam* (1992) and *Philosophy in the Renaissance of Islam* (1986). Kraemer has been investigating Maimonides' life and thought in their Islamic context and has edited *Perspectives on Maimonides: Philosophical and Historical Studies*. He has prepared a collection of Maimonides' letters for the Yale Judaica Series and is writing a biography of Maimonides.

HAIM (HOWARD) KREISEL is Professor of Medieval Jewish Thought at Ben-Gurion University of the Negev. He is the author of *Maimonides' Political Thought* (1999); *Ma'ase Nissim by Nissim of Marseilles* (2000); *Prophecy: The History of an Idea in Medieval Jewish Philosophy* (2001); and *Livyat Hen: The Work of Creation by Levi ben Avraham* (2004). He has published dozens of articles in the field of medieval Jewish thought and is the current Director of the Goldstein–Goren International Center for Jewish Thought at Ben-Gurion University.

DAVID NOVAK is the J. Richard and Dorothy Shiff Professor of Jewish Studies at the University of Toronto. He is the author of eleven books and numerous articles. His latest book is *Covenantal Rights*, and his forthcoming book is *The Jewish Social Contract* (both from Princeton University Press).

AVIEZER RAVITZKY is the Saul Rosenblum Professor of Jewish Philosophy at the Hebrew University of Jerusalem and the Chair of the Department of Jewish Thought. He is the author of *History and Faith: Studies in Jewish Philosophy* (1996); *Messianism, Zionism and Jewish Religious Radicalism* (1996); and several other books and numerous articles on medieval and contemporary Jewish thought. He is the winner of the Israeli Prize (2001).

KENNETH SEESKIN is Professor of Philosophy at Northwestern University. He is the author of *Jewish Philosophy in a Secular Age* (1990), *Maimonides: A Guide for Today's Perplexed* (1991), *Searching for a Distant God* (2000), *Autonomy in Jewish Philosophy* (2001), and *Maimonides on the Origin of the World.*

DAVID SHATZ is Professor of Philosophy at Yeshiva University. His publications in general philosophy focus on the theory of knowledge, free will, ethics, and the philosophy of religion, whereas his work in Jewish philosophy focuses on Maimonides and on twentieth-century rabbinic figures. He is editor, coeditor, or author of ten books, including *Philosophy and Faith* (2002); *Questions About God* (2002); *Mind, Body and Judaism* (2004); and *Peer Review: A Critical Inquiry* (2004).

JOSEF STERN is a professor in the Department of Philosophy and Committee on Jewish Studies and an associate member of the Divinity School at the University of Chicago. He is the author of *Problems and Parables of Law: Maimonides and Nahmanides on Reasons for the Commandments (Ta'amei Ha-Mitzvot)* (1998) and *Metaphor in Context* (2000), and he has published numerous articles in contemporary philosophy of language and medieval Jewish philosophy. He is currently at work on two books, *The Matter and Form of Maimonides' Guide* and *The Unbinding of Isaac: Maimonides on the Aqedah.*

Introduction

It is impossible to overstate Maimonides' influence on Jewish philosophy. Although his predecessor Judah Halevi may have come closer to expressing what most Jews think about God, and his successor Levi ben Gerson (Gersonides) may have been a more rigorous practitioner of scholastic philosophy, neither shaped Jewish self-understanding the way Maimonides did. One reason is the breadth of his contribution: In addition to his standing as a philosopher, Maimonides established a commanding reputation as a rabbi, Talmudic expositor, physician, and social commentator. But the most important reason has to do with intellectual power. By trying to bring Judaism and philosophy closer together, he did not leave either as he found it. If Judaism became more rigorous in defending its central beliefs, philosophy became more willing to face its limitations.

In Maimonides' judgment, Judaism stands or falls on its commitment to an incorporeal God who cannot be represented in bodily form. It is clear, however, that this commitment runs counter to the tendency of most people to think in material terms and deny the existence of anything incorporeal. The problem is acute because for Maimonides to conceive of God in the wrong way is not to conceive of God at all. Thus a person who prays to an image of a king on a throne has not fulfilled the commandments of the religion no matter what else he or she may do. Nor, as far as Maimonides is concerned, has he or she fulfilled the rational potential of a human being.

From a religious perspective, the way to overcome this tendency is to see that behind each and every commandment is the realization that an incorporeal God is the only legitimate object of worship. From a philosophic perspective, it is to prepare oneself for contemplation of a God whose perfection cannot be measured in human terms. Seen in this light, philosophy is not just an academic subject but a sacred obligation. By diverting attention from temporal matters to eternal, it relieves us of the conceit of thinking that everything in the universe reflects our interests or was created for our benefit. According to Maimonides (*MT* 1, Principles of the Torah, 4.12), when a person studies philosophy and realizes the vastness of the universe "his soul will thirst, his very flesh will yearn to love God. He will be filled with fear and trembling, as he becomes conscious of his lowly condition, poverty, and insignificance."

For all its profundity, Maimonides' thought is difficult to classify. There is Maimonides the defender of tradition and Maimonides the thinker who sought to reshape it, Maimonides the student of Aristotle and Maimonides the critic, Maimonides the believer and Maimonides the skeptic. Which is the real Maimonides? In one sense all; in another sense none. All – because each of these descriptions identifies an important theme in his writing; none – because his mind was too active for simple descriptions to do him justice.

We can begin by recognizing that Maimonides was a literary genius who was uncomfortable with the written word and strove to overcome its limitations. The *Mishneh Torah*, his fourteen-volume code of Jewish law, is written in simple, elegant Hebrew in order to make an enormous body of legal literature intelligible to people without technical training. Open to any page and you will hear the patient, methodical voice of someone who wants his readers to understand everything Jewish law asks them to do and why they are asked to do it. By contrast the *Guide of the Perplexed*, written in Judeo–Arabic, is a substitute for the one-on-one discussion that takes place between a teacher and an advanced student. There (*GP* 1, Introduction, p. 8) Maimonides admits that the problems he wants to discuss are so difficult that no one knows the full truth and that even if someone were to be blessed with special insight, he would find it hard "to explain with complete clarity and coherence even the portion that he has apprehended." Accordingly he informs the reader (*GP* 1, Introduction, pp. 6–7) that he intends to contradict himself and write in an esoteric fashion so that truth may be "glimpsed and then again concealed."

There is also the problem of discussing in a public forum ideas much of the public may not accept or understand. In the *Guide*

Maimonides says several times that people incline to the things to which they are accustomed. In most cases this means that they trust only what they can apprehend with the senses. How then can they serve a God who has no visual likeness? Tell them directly that God is immaterial and they will conclude that God is imaginary. Tell them that God does not get angry when people sin and they will conclude that sin is permitted. On the other hand, let them wallow in ignorance and you make spiritual progress all but impossible.

Maimonides' answer to this dilemma was to write in different genres for different audiences revealing truth in piecemeal fashion. Even in the space of the *Guide*, he employs biblical exegesis, philosophic exposition, scientific demonstration, parable, dialogue, and dialectic to get his message across. He admits that he will not limit his remarks on any one subject to a single passage and reserves the right to contradict himself if circumstances warrant. As Aviezer Ravitzky points out, this has led to centuries of debate on what Maimonides meant and allowed any number of interpreters to find their own opinions articulated in his text. Aristotelians saw him as an Aristotelian, believers in miracles and creation saw him as a defender of traditional doctrine, Hermann Cohen saw him as a proto-Kantian, Leo Strauss as a thinker forced to choose between Jerusalem and Athens. Whatever one's predilections, one should be cautious with generalizations. Underneath the labels that occupy historians of philosophy, there is the thinker who struggled with age-old questions and constantly challenged the reader to think for herself.

Consider the facts of his life. Maimonides was born in Cordova, Spain, in 1138. As Joel L. Kraemer indicates, Maimonides came from a distinguished family and grew up in a center of scientific and philosophic learning. Although he was forced to leave his native home, wander through the Middle East for a dozen years fearing for his life, and was devastated by the accidental death of his brother, he established himself as an authority on a wide range of issues and did not shirk from controversy. Kraemer stresses that Maimonides held a Platonic view of teaching. Rather than a way of transmitting authoritative doctrine from teacher to pupil, it is a process of thinking best communicated through dialogue. The result is a philosophy that is not merely intellectual but transformative. Such a philosophy maintains the rigor of its own methods but recognizes the limits of human knowledge and the ability of prophets to shed light on issues that philosophy alone cannot resolve. It culminates in the intellectual love of God, a point at which, in Kraemer's words "rationalism and mysticism intersect."

In his essay on philosophical sources, Alfred L. Ivry challenges the view that the contradictions in the *Guide* are entirely of Maimonides' making. Instead the conflicting desires in Maimonides' heart, and the interests he shared with theological and theosophical traditions, combined to produce a book that is pulled in several directions. That is why it is difficult to say whether Maimonides belongs to the Averroian or the Avicennian school of thought. As Ivry goes on to argue, the *Guide* oscillates between theoretical and practical concerns and shows the influence of rationalists and mystics alike. To take a noteworthy example, Maimonides is sharply critical of the *mutakallimūn* but not above using some of their arguments when it suits his purpose.

My own essay on metaphysics begins by denying that one can treat Maimonides in the way one treats Aristotle and Aquinas. By that I mean one cannot simply say this: Here is the metaphysical system he adopted and list a set of principles. Rather, one has to see that some of his views can be demonstrated whereas others can only be pointed to or hinted at. Although metaphysics frees us from the need to think in material terms, and in that respect is a prerequisite for understanding God, it also shows us that categories such as substance, attribute, and relation or distinctions such as act–potency and cause–effect do not apply to God. In the end Maimonides' view of metaphysics is both respectful and critical; it is both a necessary part of the pathway to God and something that must eventually be overcome.

Maimonides' view of metaphysics is also the focus of Josef Stern's essay. As Stern sees it, there is nothing Maimonides values more than knowledge, especially knowledge of metaphysics or divine science. But when one considers the limitations that Maimonides puts on knowledge, it appears this kind of knowledge is all but unrealizable. What are we to make of this? Stern follows a path similar to Kraemer by suggesting that Maimonides puts more emphasis on the process of acquiring knowledge than on a body of established results. Rather than the exposition of a doctrine, philosophy is a set of intellectual practices that discipline the soul and help one cultivate happiness or perfection. These practices vary and include everything from intellectual apprehension to emotional stability to self-examination to religious observance. Again we are warned not to look for a one-dimensional interpretation.

Maimonides' insistence on the limits of human knowledge is also the focus of Gad Freudenthal's essay on the philosophy of science. Although it is natural to think of epistemological limits as an obstacle in the search for truth, this need not be so. As Freudenthal points out, lack of certainty in science can also give rise to philosophic reflection. This is especially true when we consider Maimonides' critique of Aristotle's astronomy and his rejection of the claim that the world we inhabit is fully knowable. From this Maimonides concludes that the world is not eternal and that there are grounds for believing that God exercises free choice in particularizing certain features of the natural order.

Freudenthal goes on to show that like other aspects of his philosophy, Maimonides' view of knowledge reveals a number of conflicts. He accepts Aristotle's view of the sublunar world but not of the heavens. He upholds the power of the human mind to rise above the data of experience but casts doubt on its ability to extrapolate from that data to the origin of the world. He believed that the properties of various substances can be established by appeal to "experience," but refused to accept the claims of astrologers when they made a similar appeal. In all, science, though indispensable for understanding the world and interpreting Scripture, is not infallible. It too demands the application of specific arguments to specific areas of inquiry.

That brings us to Maimonides' practical philosophy. We have already seen that the distinction between theoretical and practical may not be hard and fast. David Shatz starts from the fact that Maimonides regards the highest form of perfection as intellectual and sees morality as subordinate. According to a common way of reading Maimonides, the purpose of morality is to prepare the way for contemplation. But as Shatz recognizes, this reading is too simple because Maimonides has two conceptions of morality: that which leads to contemplation and that which results from it. If the former is related to *phronēsis* or practical wisdom, the latter is not: It is a consequence or overflow from theoretical wisdom. This distinction enables us to see why Maimonides' conception of *imitatio Dei* is different from Aristotle's and why, at the end of the *Guide*, Maimonides argues that far from taking the place of worship or ethical behavior, contemplation enhances them.

In his analysis of Maimonides' political thought, Haim Kreisel also emphasizes the close connection between theory and praxis. Beyond the goal of establishing order and protecting life and property, society exists in order to facilitate the highest level of human perfection: pursuit of the sciences and worship of God. In this way intellectual perfection is not just something it is good to have but a goal that exists in us by nature and defines us as human beings. This sets Maimonides apart from liberal theorists, who believe that once society recognizes certain basic rights, it is up to each individual to decide what to do with his or her life. For Maimonides a state that takes a hands-off attitude to the spiritual and intellectual development of its citizens neglects the primary reason for its existence. As Kreisel indicates, Maimonides' view of society raises the question of whether liberal theories are as self-evident as their proponents sometimes claim.

Society's duty to promote the development of theoretical reason is also a central theme of David Novak's essay on jurisprudence. This applies not only to Jews and their law but to gentiles and their law as well. Novak therefore argues that Maimonides recognizes three types of practical reason: that of ordinary jurists, who take the laws of their society as given and make no deductions from them, that of philosophically inclined jurists, who base legal decisions on rational principles, and that of true metaphysicians, who bring practical reason and theoretical reason together in a manner that preserves the teleology of the Torah. For all of his emphasis on the limits of reason in resolving theoretical questions like the origin of the world, it is noteworthy that Maimonides extends the range of rabbinic or humanly made law beyond anything that had been done before. As Novak maintains, this assigns vast importance to the role of practical reason in the divinely created order.

Ravitzky's essay not only reviews the history of attempts to explain Maimonides' esotericism but takes up the larger question of his philosophy of education. From Samuel ibn Tibbon, the original translator, to Leo Strauss, generations of commentators have argued that the *Guide* is deeply esoteric, by which they mean that Maimonides goes to great lengths to conceal his views from the average reader and offer enough hints for sophisticated readers to figure out where he really stands. Although he might say that he accepts miracles and creation *ex nihilo*, according to the esotericist tradition, he is really committed to an eternal world governed by natural necessity. In Straussian terms, Athens wins out over Jerusalem.

Although Maimonides was aware that the social fabric relies on myths, conventions, and preconceived notions that may not stand up to philosophic scrutiny, Ravitzky argues that this does not establish the esotericist's case because Maimonides also believed that the human condition is dynamic. The person who relies on myth today may turn to philosophy tomorrow if we take the time to explain why the latter is superior – both spiritually and intellectually. In short Maimonides believed in the possibility of intellectual progress and devoted much of his life to promoting it. If so, the idea that Maimonides divided humanity into two groups and hid his views from one of them is insupportable. Ravitzky sums up his essay by suggesting that Maimonides is willing to employ several argument forms, switch identities, and mediate between cultures if that is what is needed to help the reader understand the problem under discussion. While this approach is incompatible with spoon feeding, it does not necessitate full-blown esotericism.

Sara Klein-Braslavy is more sympathetic with esotericism, especially in regard to Maimonides' Bible commentary. The Bible is an esoteric work that presents the truths of philosophy in a way that reveals them to those able to appreciate their full significance but conceals them from the masses. To accomplish this end, it employs parables, metaphors, equivocal terms, and other literary devices that "speak in the language of human beings" but can be interpreted at a variety of levels. Moreover, Maimonides writes in an esoteric fashion scattering his remarks across a number of passages and conveying meaning through hints or clues that a discerning reader can pick up. Klein-Braslavy indicates how subtle Maimonides' Bible commentary can be and how alert the reader must be to follow it in detail. Although he often remains within the scope of Jewish literary tradition, Maimonides typically finds the truths of Aristotelian philosophy underneath biblical narrative.

Even so, Maimonides' commentary is not systematic in the sense that he discusses the Bible verse by verse. His treatment of parables, metaphors, and equivocal terms is part of a longer philosophic work. In the end, Klein-Braslavy concludes that Maimonides leaves it to each individual reader to digest the commentary, learn the philosophy, and rely on their own efforts to understand the text.

From a religious perspective, the most controversial essay in this collection is Menachem Kellner's discussion of the spiritual life. According to the traditional view, holiness is an internal property of certain people, places, or times. On this view, there is an essential difference between Israel and the other nations, Jerusalem and other cities, the holidays and normal days of the week. The former are holy from the first moment of creation, and their holiness was revealed to Moses and the rest of Israel at Sinai. In Kellner's opinion, this is the view Maimonides seeks to overturn. For Maimonides there is no essential difference between a holy people, place, or time and an unholy one. Apart from God's commandment, the former are no different from other people, places, or times. The difference, as Kellner expresses it, is in status not quality of existence. Thus holiness is a challenge rather than an ontological given. If Jerusalem is a holy city, it is because it plays a prominent place in Jewish law, not because it rests on a special kind of soil. Holiness, as one might say, is conferred rather than discovered.

It follows that the commandments that identify people, places, or times as deserving of special attention are contingent. If the exodus had occurred on another continent, God could have picked other times or places for special attention. If the Jewish people had behaved differently on the exodus, God could have picked different rituals by which to remember it. Put otherwise, the historical circumstances in which the Law was given played an important role in determining its content. It is also important to note that for Maimonides, holiness is not restricted to Jews. Any person who renounces the possibility of a corporeal God, behaves in an appropriate fashion, and devotes himself to the perfection of the intellect is worthy of salvation. Although Maimonides is often accused of being an intellectualist – even an elitist – in religious matters, one consequence of his intellectualism is a rejection of parochialism in all its forms.

The final essay by Seymour Feldman traces Maimonides' influence on subsequent thinkers. It is safe to say that much of Jewish medieval philosophy after Maimonides was a continuing discussion with the master. That is not to say that his conclusions were generally accepted. As is true in the current environment, there were vigorous debates over what Maimonides meant, how deep his esotericism went, and how persuasive his arguments were. As Feldman points out, esotericism is only part of the problem; there is also the question of what to do with doctrines that represent a radical departure from Jewish tradition: the denial of multiple attributes in God, the nature of prophecy, or the scope of divine providence. The fact is, however, that, as late as the seventeenth century, when Spinoza rethought many of these issues, Maimonides was still a central figure. His centrality continues to this day.

Like philosophy itself, great philosophers are not judged on the basis of the problems they solved since many of these problems are such that a decisive resolution is impossible. Rather they are judged by the quality of thought they stimulated. By that standard, Maimonides' place among the greats is assured.

JOEL L. KRAEMER

1 Moses Maimonides

An Intellectual Portrait

1.1. INTRODUCTION

Moses Maimonides was born in Cordova, Spain, in 1138 and died in Cairo in 1204. Cordova was then the capital of Andalusia (Muslim Spain) and the largest and most affluent city in Europe. Under the Spanish Umayyads (756–1031), Cordova thrived as a cultural center and political capital. Andalusia reached a high level of civilization, with art, literature, history, science, music, and jurisprudence flourishing as nowhere else in Europe. The reign of enlightened Caliph ʿAbd ar-Raḥmān III (912–61) marked the beginning of a period of cultural flourishing for Andalusia, including its Jewish communities. The caliph embraced a tolerant policy, integrating the diverse religious communities and ethnic groups in his state. In such an environment, the Jews found a niche and prospered. ʿAbd ar-Raḥmān, a devotee of both religious and secular learning, attracted literati and scientists by giving them generous endowments. A multitude of libraries, mosques, madrasas [colleges], and hospitals enticed scholars from the eastern part of the Islamic world to emigrate to the west, bringing with them intellectual treasures that made Andalusia culturally preeminent for many centuries.

The Jewish Quarter, where Moses and his family lived, was located close to the Great Mosque and the royal palace, in the southwestern section of the city, near the Guadalquivir River and its ancient Roman bridge. Jews passed by the Great Mosque, overwhelmed by its vastness, peering curiously through the gates at the arcades and multiple rows of high double, horseshoe arches, sensing its allure, mystery, and otherness. The Qurʾānic inscriptions over the mosque's gates proclaimed Islam's dominance and superiority over Judaism and Christianity, promising paradise to Muslims who had surrendered themselves to Allah and divine punishment to those who did not take heed.

Maimonides' ancestors were scholars who had served as judges and communal leaders. In the epilogue to his *Commentary on the Mishnah* he lists seven generations of eminent sages and magistrates, and he says that he began the commentary when he was twenty-three and completed it in Egypt when he was about thirty.[1] He was then a newcomer to Egypt, an émigré from the West who needed to establish his identity; by invoking his illustrious ancestry he implied a basis for personal authority.

Maimonides shared the prevailing view that Andalusian Jews were descended from the Jerusalemites exiled after the destruction of the Second Commonwealth in 70 C.E. From his Andalusian heritage he drew a sense of aristocracy and noblesse oblige.[2] The splendor of Andalusia under ʿAbd ar-Raḥmān III and his son was reflected in the brilliance of Jewish learning of the time. The erudite Ḥisday ben Shaprut became court physician and advisor to the caliph thanks to his linguistic competence (in Hebrew, Arabic, Latin, and the Romance dialect) and medical skill. When Emperor Constantine sent the caliph an illuminated Greek manuscript of Dioscorides' *De materia medica*, the classic work on pharmacology, Ḥisday, along with a Byzantine monk, translated it into Arabic. He carried out many diplomatic missions for the dynasty.[3]

The caliph appointed Ḥisday head of the Jewish communities in his realm and authorized him to run their affairs and represent them at court. Jews gave him the title *Nasi* [prince]. He was a patron to intellectuals, and his literary salon became a gathering place for poets, grammarians, scholars, scientists, and philosophers. He was the archetypal Jewish courtier, faithful to his heritage yet ready to adopt the cultural values of the surrounding environment, combining traditional learning in Bible, Talmud, and *Midrash* with proficiency in logic, mathematics, and astronomy. He orchestrated the Jewish cultural renaissance centered in Cordova, making Jewish religious and secular culture in Andalusia independent of the Baghdad academies and the Geonim.

Another Jewish courtier who became a cultural paragon in the collective memory of Andalusian Jewry was Samuel ben Joseph Ibn Naghrila (993–1055), a gifted calligrapher and literary stylist in

Arabic, who in 1013 became vizier to the Zīrid rulers of Granada and head of the Jewish communities of Andalusia with the title *Nagid.* Ibn Naghrila was resourceful and multitalented, a brilliant administrator, poet, and rabbinic scholar. Aside from composing poems on love, wine, and old age, he also wrote war poetry.[4]

The synthesis of traditional Jewish learning with secular knowledge among these courtiers became the hallmark of the educated Andalusian Jew and served as a model for emulation. The courtiers were men for whom the Arabic ideal of *adab,* a cultured refinement, was fundamental in their educational program. They created a cultural identity of their own by writing Hebrew poetry redolent with biblical resonances. Andalusian Jewry celebrated the heroic achievements of these men, and the exemplar of the cosmopolitan and cultured courtier, learned in the secular sciences and in Jewish law and lore, set a precedent for Maimonides as he later fashioned his career.

Maimonides placed himself squarely in an Andalusian tradition of learning and looked to the sages of Sefarad as his authorities in legal matters. His father had been a pupil of Rabbi Joseph Ibn Migash (1077–1141), head of the academy of Lucena. Foremost among the Lucenan masters was Rabbi Isaac Alfasi (1013–1103). Rabbi Maimon transmitted Ibn Migash's teaching to Moses, who called the Lucenan sage "my teacher," though he had never studied with him. Maimon must have brought the precocious lad to visit Lucena – only forty-three miles from Cordova – but Ibn Migash died in 1141 when Moses was just three years old. Maimonides revered these scholars, but he did not hesitate to be critical toward them, including his father, demonstrating early on an independence of authorities evident later in his stance toward Aristotle and Galen.

Lucena was also a center of secular culture for Andalusian Jews. The city welcomed intellectuals, including the poets Moses and Abraham Ibn Ezra, Judah Halevi, Joseph Ibn Sahl, and Joseph ibn Ṣaddīq, as well as the grammarian Jonah Ibn Janāḥ. These were rabbinic sages steeped in secular subjects, imbued with cultivated literary taste, and gifted with poetical talent. Joseph Ibn Ṣaddīq studied Rabbinics in Lucena, then became a judge in Cordova in 1138, and also wrote poetry, a treatise on logic, and a philosophical work praised by Maimonides[5]: "As for the *Book Microcosm,* which R. Joseph Ibn Ṣaddīq composed, I have not seen it. But I knew the man and his discourse,[6] and I recognized his eminence and the value of his book, for he undoubtedly followed the system of the Sincere Brethren."[7]

With the death of Ibn Migash, in 1141, rabbinic learning declined in Andalusia. The historian and philosopher Abraham Ibn Daud wrote that after Ibn Migash "the world became desolate of academies of learning."[8] The decline coincided with political instability in the wake of the Almohad invasion. The sons of Ibn Migash fled to Toledo, and other scholars followed a similar route northward to Christian regions of Spain and southward to Morocco.

1.2. THE ALMOHAD INVASION

Muḥammad Ibn Tūmart founded the fundamentalist Almohad movement in the High Atlas Mountains of Morocco among the *Maṣmūda* Berbers, who recognized him as the *Mahdī*, a divinely guided messianic redeemer. He fought to restore the pristine faith of Islam, based on the Qur'ān and the Sunna, and to enforce the precepts of the sacred law. The Almohads united North Africa and Andalusia under the rule of a single empire.[9] Suddenly, Jews who had been living in Spain for a millenium had to prove that they belonged there, and if they were not willing to embrace Islam, their choice was exile or death. The Almohads invaded Andalusia and occupied Cordova in 1148, and the Maimon family left the city then when Moses was just ten years old.

1.3. ANDALUSIAN YEARS

For a period of some twelve years the Maimon family wandered from place to place in Andalusia. During those years, young Moses became absorbed in the sciences, beginning, as was typical, with logic, mathematics, and astronomy. The first subject he studied was astrology, which he later rejected as baseless and useless.[10] However, astrology was tied in with a knowledge of astronomy. Understanding the calendar required knowledge of astronomy to determine the time of the new moon, to synchronize lunar and solar time, to calculate the periods of seasons, and to compute the Metonic cycle of intercalated months. But studying traditional sources with Talmudists could not provide him with the scientific knowledge he needed, and he realized that he had to study the secular sciences.[11] His scientific curiosity brought him into contact with Muslim intellectuals. He convened with students of the philosopher Abū Bakr Muḥammad ibn aṣ-Ṣā'igh Ibn Bājja and with a son of the astronomer Jābir Ibn Aflaḥ.[12] Later, Maimonides and Joseph ben Judah, his pupil, edited and revised Jābir Ibn Aflaḥ's *Book of Astronomy*, in which the Andalusian astronomer had criticized Ptolemy's *Almagest*.

1.4. THE ANDALUSIAN SCHOOL OF ARISTOTELIAN STUDIES

Maimonides' philosophical orientation places him in the milieu of the twelfth-century Andalusian School of Aristotelian studies.[13] The pioneer of the Aristotelian revival in Spain was Abū Bakr Ibn Bājja (Avempace) (d. 1139), followed by Ibn Ṭufayl (d. 1185) and Ibn Rushd (Averroes, d. 1198). These Spanish Aristotelians were translated into Latin and had made a profound impact on Latin Scholastic philosophy. This school shared a system of ideas, similar sources and terminology, a common set of definitions and problems, and a shared method of discussing the issues. A Neoplatonic component influenced Aristotelian metaphysics, so that the term "Neoaristotelianism" is appropriate.[14] The political philosophy of the Spanish school was Platonic, and was crowned by Averroes' *Commentary on Plato's Republic*.[15]

Like Maimonides, Averroes was born in Cordova. We have no record of an encounter between these two colossi, though legend has them meeting in Lucena. Toward the end of Averroes' life, in 1195, he was banished from Marrakesh to Lucena, his teachings condemned and his philosophical works torched as dangerous to religious faith. In Lucena he certainly met many Jews, as it was mostly a Jewish city, but Maimonides was in Egypt at the time. Some claimed that Averroes' ancestors were of the Jewish faith.[16]

Maimonides knew Averroes' works and admired his commentaries on Aristotle. He wrote to his pupil Joseph ben Judah in 1191, presumably after finishing the *Guide*, that he had recently received all of Averroes' books on Aristotle except for *De Sensu et Sensibili*, adding that in his opinion Averroes "hit the mark well."[17] He had not found time, he says, to study all his books until now.[18] Maimonides later advised Samuel Ibn Tibbon to study Aristotle's works with the commentaries of Alexander, Themistius, or Averroes.[19]

The two gentlemen of Cordova had much in common. Both were descendants of venerable Andalusian families of scholars and judges. Both displayed Andalusian pride, a drive for independence, and a sense of supremacy over past authorities, especially their predecessors in the eastern part of the Islamic world.[20] Both were outstanding jurists and physicians, and both mastered the sciences and wrote philosophy. Both embraced a naturalistic Aristotelianism and taught that the religious law summons us to philosophize.[21] Writings of both Averroes and Maimonides were translated into Latin soon after their demise, introducing Aristotelian rationalism into medieval Christian thought.

Maimonides esteemed Aristotle, but he was not the hard-bitten apostle that Averroes was. Averroes carefully pruned Neoplatonic branches from his Aristotelian tree, discarding emanationism as cryptocreationism, accusing al-Fārābī (Alfarabi) and Ibn Sīnā (Avicenna) of corrupting the true doctrine of Aristotle, "the first philosopher," with whom the sciences reached their summit. Maimonides did not shun the Neoplatonic or mystical sides of Alfarabi and Avicenna, nor did he represent Aristotle as a consummate scientist, but as an earnest seeker of the truth who propounded plausible theories in a tentative way. Maimonides' view of Aristotle as an aporetic philosopher reflected his own view of what philosophy should be.[22]

Later, in the *Guide*, Maimonides continued to ponder scientific problems that he confronted early in life, mainly the conflict between the Aristotelian paradigm of celestial physics and Ptolemy's system with its epicycles and eccentrics. It was necessary to devise a mathematical model to explain the observed movements of the heavenly bodies, such as the retrograde motion of planets, but Maimonides never solved this problem and hoped that in the future some scientist might succeed in doing so.[23] Maimonides did not exaggerate the difficulties of these astronomical conundrums so as to have a weapon in the theological debate with Aristotelianism.[24] The difficulties were, in fact, insurmountable in his day. He would have had to live until the heliocentric astrophysics and laws of planetary motions of Johannes Kepler (1571–1630) and Isaac Newton (1643–1727) to have answers to the astronomical puzzles that occupied him in his youth and throughout his life. He did not acknowledge ignorance to make room for faith but out of intellectual honesty.

Maimonides paid tribute to the philosophical legacy of Andalusian Jews: "As for the Andalusians among the people of our nation, all of them cling to the affirmations of the philosophers and incline to their opinions, in so far as these do not ruin the foundation of the Law. You will not find them in any way taking the paths of the *mutakallimūn*."[25] This is not strictly true, as Baḥya Ibn Paqūda and Joseph Ibn Ṣaddīq were not averse to *kalām* arguments. Despite this general adulation, Maimonides hardly quoted his great Andalusian forebears, such as Abraham Bar Ḥiyya, Solomon Ibn Gabirol, Judah Halevi, Abraham Ibn Ezra, or Abraham Ibn Daud. He also deplored the poetic–didactic *azharot* (liturgical poems enumerating the 613 commandments) written in Spain, such as those by Ibn Gabirol. He finds a mitigating circumstance only in that the authors were poets and not rabbinic scholars.

1.5. FEZ

The Maimon family immigrated to Fez in around 1160 when Maimonides was in his early twenties.[26] Jewish custom required that a man take a wife by the age of eighteen, but there is no evidence that Moses was married at this time. A man might claim that his heart cleaved to the Torah, preventing him from fulfilling his marital obligation. And Moses would have desired to be settled before marrying.[27] He had three sisters, who may have gone to Fez at this time as well. We never meet his mother. Legends have her dying in childbirth.[28] In fact, we know little about women of this period unless they were learned or entered the public sphere in business or trade, which was rare.

The five-year period of Maimonides' residence in Fez, from around 1160 to 1165, came under the shadow of Almohad oppression. Given the alternative of conversion to Islam or death, numerous Jews chose conversion, many becoming pseudo-Muslims, or crypto-Jews, called *anusim* [coerced]. This subterfuge in twelfth-century Morocco prefigures the Marrano phenomenon in late medieval Christian Spain.

About four years after arriving in Fez, Maimonides wrote his *Epistle on Forced Conversion*, reassuring his suffering brethren of divine care and future redemption.[29] He wrote the epistle in reaction to a widely circulated responsum by a rabbinic scholar who had instructed Jews to accept martyrdom rather than submit to Islam. This legal opinion implicitly invited mass martyrdom, as had occurred in the Rhineland during the First Crusade.

Maimonides reacted strongly to the responsum. He believed that if forced converts are no longer Jews, they and their children are lost forever. Like his father, he emphatically instructed them to pray and observe the commandments clandestinely. He did not rely on *halakhah* alone. He appealed also to *aggadah* and to historical precedent, as did the sages of Italy and Ashkenaz in permitting Jews to sacrifice their lives to avoid apostasy.[30] This epistle is a responsum, in which juridical analysis, entailing judgment on the basis of real circumstances and applying the religious law to life situations, outweighed the letter of the law. Later on, in his legal responsa written in Egypt, Maimonides did not consistently follow strict law. He instructed leniency in certain cases in which punctiliousness on legal rules could lead to untoward consequences.[31]

His final advice to Moroccan Jews was to leave the country of persecution for places where one could practice one's faith openly.[32] He included himself among the collective "we" who were forced to convert to Islam, implying that he then lived as a crypto-Jew himself. A Muslim historian, Ibn al-Qifṭī (1172–1248), reports that Maimonides feigned Islam publicly, adhering to its rituals, studying the Qur'ān, and praying in a mosque.[33] Later, when he was in Egypt, a jurist named Abū l-ʿArab Ibn Muʿīsha, who had lived in Fez, met him and accused him of having converted to Islam in Andalus.[34] Abandoning Islam after converting was punishable by death according to Islamic law. Al-Qāḍī al-Fāḍil, Saladin's chief administrator and Maimonides's patron, saved him by contending that conversion under coercion was invalid.[35]

Ibn al-Qifṭī, who gave us this account, was a contemporary of Maimonides and lived in Cairo until 1187. Later, in Aleppo, he befriended Joseph ben Judah, Maimonides' pupil, from Ceuta, who also feigned Islam according to this historian.[36] Although Ibn al-Qifṭī's book has come down to us in a later recension, and contains some errors, we have no reason to doubt the information on Maimonides and Joseph ben Judah. Simulating Islam is explicable under the circumstances. Both Joseph ben Judah Ibn Shimʿon and Joseph ben Judah Ibn ʿAqnīn had done the same.

We must not regard the Maghrib at this time as a cultural and intellectual wasteland. Despite their religious intolerance, the Almohads sponsored the study of philosophy and the sciences. Ibn Tūmart had adopted a theology based on the ideas of al-Ghazālī (Alghazali) and had taken a strong stand against belief in positive divine attributes. The works of Alghazali were popular in the West. Maimonides was familiar with Alghazali's writings, perhaps from this time.[37]

This direction in Almohad intellectual life was congenial to the cultivation of rational discourse. Abū Yūsuf Yaʿqūb, having lived in Seville as a young man, attained literary refinement and an interest in philosophy and poetry, and amassed an impressive library. He welcomed Ibn Ṭufayl and Averroes to his court as physicians and advisors. His son and successor, Abū Yūsuf Yaʿqūb, was receptive to learning as well, though it was under him that Averroes was temporarily banished to Lucena, his books torched.

Maimonides may have been influenced by Ibn Tūmart's theology in his own strong stand against positive divine attributes, in favor of a spiritualized conception of the deity, and in his attempt to formulate the basic beliefs of Judaism in a creed (the thirteen principles of faith). Maimonides' vigorous condemnation of anthropomorphism as superstitious idolatry recalls the reforming zeal of Ibn Tūmart.

1.6. MEDICAL STUDIES

Maimonides began his medical training in Andalusia and continued these studies in the Maghrib. He had high regard for Maghribi physicians, in particular Abū Marwān Ibn Zuhr (Avenzoar of the West, ca. 1092–1162), whose teachings he studied, and he also was in direct contact with his son Abū Bakr (1110–98). Abū Bakr became personal physician to Caliph Abū Yūsuf Yaʿqūb al-Manṣūr (ruled 1184–99). Abū Marwān Ibn Zuhr had served the Almohad ʿAbd al-Mu' min as physician and vizier. He was a friend and collaborator of Averroes and dedicated a medical manual to him, on which basis Averroes wrote his great medical work *al-Kulliyyāt* (*the Book of Generalities, Colliget* in the Latin West). He referred in his medical writings to contacts he had with physicians in the Maghrib, and it is clear that he received formal medical training while residing in Fez.[38]

1.7. EARLY WRITINGS

Maimonides began writing about scientific and philosophic subjects as a young man. He wrote a treatise on the calendar (*Ma'amar ha-'ibbur*) in 4918 A.M. (= 1157–58 C.E.). It was a practical guide for teaching a novice rather than a theoretical discussion. He therefore wrote briefly and gave tables for easy comprehension.[39] His zeal for order already expressed itself here in systemization and organization of knowledge, in simplifying complicated topics, making them easy to grasp and memorize. There are two sections of seven and three parts, in which he discussed lunations [*moladot*] and seasons of the year [*tequfot*].

His serious application to the calendar and mathematical astronomy came later in his *Laws of the Sanctification of the Moon* in the *Mishneh Torah*.[40] In his *Commentary on the Mishnah* he announced his intention to write a treatise on the calendar, with demonstrative proofs that no one could refute.[41] As the *Treatise on the Calendar* was an elementary booklet, he had no reason to regard it as fulfilling the urgent need for authoritative guidance on calendar issues, which went to the heart of Judaism. By 1166 he was busy writing the *Laws of the Sanctification of the Moon*, which is the eighth treatise of the *Book of Seasons* in the *Mishneh Torah*. This brief treatise was written over a period of twelve years and consisted of nineteen brilliant chapters, in which he distinguished himself as a master of the subject.[42] The second part of *Sanctification of the New Moon* (Chapters 6–10), written in 1166, is an elaboration and enhancement of the brief *Treatise on the Calendar* and fulfillment of the promise he had made in his *Commentary on the Mishnah*.[43]

The numerical values he assigns to astronomical and calendar phenomena are the same in the *Treatise on the Calendar* and the *Sanctification of the New Moon*. He posits in both that daylight and night are each 12 hours all year long. These were "seasonal hours," meaning that an hour's length varied depending on the season of the year. An hour has 1,080 parts, a number divisible by all integers from 1 to 10 except 7. The interval between successive solar–lunar conjunctions is 29d, 12h, 793 parts.[44] The seasons are 91d, 7h, and 540 parts. A lunar year is 354d, 8h, 876 parts, a solar year 365d, 6h. The first cycle began at 1 A.M., on Monday evening 1 Tishre, 5h, 204 parts. These values are ancient, and therefore it is not surprising that they show up in Maimonides' writings, but the total concurrence is significant.

One of Maimonides' early scientific works was a revision of a mathematical and optical work, *al-Istikmāl wa-l-manāẓir*, by Yūsuf al-Mu'tamin of the Hūdid dynasty in Saragossa (reigned 1081–5).[45] Members of the family of Ibn Hūd al-Mu'tamin taught the *Guide* to a circle of Jews in Damascus.[46]

It was probably during these early years, perhaps in Fez, that Maimonides composed his *Treatise on the Art of Logic*.[47] He addressed the work to a Muslim, and gave no hint of his own religious identity, nor did he cite the Bible or Talmud. The addressee, real or fictional, had requested a concise explanation of logical terminology, a first step in studying logic. This is an introductory work depending much on Alfarabi, whose logical works he recommended to Ibn Tibbon. In the final (fourteenth) chapter of the treatise, Maimonides discussed the philosophic sciences. In the section on political philosophy, he distinguished between the secular laws of the philosophers and the divine commandments in force "in our time." The language implies that he did not restrict "divine commandments" to Judaism but included Christianity and Islam as well.[48]

He showed here his fondness for number symbolism. He noted at the end that the treatise has fourteen chapters, in which 175 terms are discussed (7 × 25). Chapter 2 treats 2 × 7 terms, and Chapter 10 studies the ten categories. In Chapter 7 he discussed the fourteen moods of the valid syllogism. Philosophy or science has seven parts. Each chapter repeats the terms studied, except Chapter 10, giving the last four a kind of independence.[49] His numerology is a mnemonic device and an aid for scribes, but it also reveals an absorption in numerical symbolism and partiality for heptads, which we find later in the *Mishneh Torah* and the *Guide of the Perplexed*. It is also a kind of identification mark identity, a "numerical signature" (as Gad Freudenthal expresses it).

While writing on scientific subjects, Maimonides did not neglect traditional studies. He wrote a commentary on three of the six orders of the Babylonian Talmud, omitting four tractates that he could not finish for lack of time, and he wrote a commentary on Tractate *Ḥullin*, dealing with issues of ritual purity, and glosses over difficult passages in the entire Talmudic corpus. More significant was his *Precepts of the Jerusalem Talmud*, done along the lines of Isaac

Alfasi's *Book of Precepts*.[50] The Jerusalem Talmud is more concise than its Babylonian counterpart and contains less nonlegal material. Rabbinic scholars used the Babylonian Talmud, which came later, as the official source for legal instruction, and the Jerusalem Talmud was therefore not studied as much. Maimonides praised it for explaining the reasons for normative legal decisions, whereas the Babylonian Talmud merely stated decisions without giving their rationale.

1.8. *COMMENTARY ON THE MISHNAH*

Maimonides began his *Commentary on the Mishnah* shortly after arriving in Fez. It was an overwhelming task that absorbed much of his time and energy, as he reproduced the entire text of the Mishnah to which he appended his commentary. It is written in Judaeo–Arabic, and various translators rendered it into Hebrew. Much of it is preserved in a fair autograph copy in neat semicursive script with corrections.[51] His son Abraham added corrections, following his father's instructions, and even his descendants added their comments. There are also autograph draft copies written in a cursive script preserved in the Genizah, showing many deletions and corrections. He even added passages to his *Commentary on the Mishnah* (completed 1168) after finishing the *Guide* in 1190.[52] Because Maimonides was constantly refining his thoughts and correcting his works throughout his life, and they were copied at different times, various versions were put into circulation.

In his introduction to the *Commentary on the Mishnah*, he discussed the nature of the Oral Law and prophecy and explained the history and sources of the religious law. Elucidating the Oral Law was critical because the Karaites denied its validity and rejected the Talmud as an authoritative text.

In the introduction to Tractate *Sanhedrin*, Chapter 10 of the Babylonian Talmud, called *Pereq Ḥeleq*, Maimonides outlined the fundamental principles of Judaism.[53] He defined the true meaning of monotheism, prophecy, revelation, providence, reward and punishment, the messianic era, and resurrection of the dead. Defining Judaism was an innovation that may have been influenced by the precedent of the Almohad creed [*ʿaqīda*] (see Section 1.2). In the Introduction to Tractate *Avot*, known as the *Eight Chapters*, Maimonides discussed philosophic ethics, thereby inserting Greek philosophy into the very bosom of Judaism.[54]

1.9. THE BEAUTIFUL LAND

Maimonides and his family departed from Morocco on 4 April 1165. During the voyage, on 18 April 1165, the sea became stormy and an enormous wave almost inundated the ship.[55] He vowed that he, his family, household, and descendants would fast annually to mark the event, and that he would remain in solitude on that anniversary every year, praying and studying all day long in privacy. Just as on that day at sea he found only the divine presence, so he vowed not to see anyone on that day every year unless absolutely necessary. His natural tendency was for solitude and private meditative prayer, the highest form of worship (*GP* 3.51). In the midst of a terrifying storm at sea, his life trembling in the balance, he felt the divine presence.

The voyage from Morocco to the Holy Land lasted a month until the family finally disembarked safely in Acre: "And thus," he says, "I was saved from the forced apostasy."

Acre was the capital of the Crusader towns of Syro-Palestine. The city was a European enclave with many Christian quarters named for its residents. All of the city's mosques except one had been converted into churches. The Maimon family remained in Acre through the summer of 1165. Then in October, Maimon ben Joseph, along with his sons Moses and David, accompanied by a local scholar named Japheth ben Elijah, made a pilgrimage to Jerusalem, where they remained for three days. Maimonides wrote that they traveled from Acre to Jerusalem "at a time of danger," alluding to the ongoing hostilities between the Crusaders and Muslims. They worshiped in the vicinity of the Temple Mount, the esplanade where the Second Temple stood until 70 C.E. It was customary for Jews at such a moment to lament the ruins and to rend their garments while reciting Isaiah 64:9–10.

After visiting Jerusalem, the small group traveled to Hebron, the site of the tomb of the Patriarchs at the Cave of Makhpelah, sacred to Christians and Muslims as the tomb of Abraham. They then returned to Acre, remaining there until May 1166, when they left for Egypt. They must have traveled by sea, with all its dangers, for traveling overland through the desert was expensive and even more perilous.

1.10. EGYPT

In 1166, Maimonides and his family arrived in Alexandria, where they resided briefly before traveling to Fusṭāṭ (Old Cairo). The Maimon family settled in the Mamsusa Quarter of Fusṭāṭ, bordering on Qaṣr ash-Shamʿ just outside its walls, a short walk from the two main Rabbanite synagogues.[56] Mamsusa had many Christian residents and some Muslims living alongside Jews.

Three Jewish communities coexisted in Fustat, each with its own synagogue. The sectarian Karaites were the more affluent members of Jewish society. Two Rabbanite communities were organized around their places of worship – the Synagogue of the Iraqians and the Synagogue of the Palestinians. The Synagogue of the Iraqians supported the academies in Iraq, followed their ritual, and came under the authority of their Gaonate. The Synagogue of the Palestinians adhered to the Palestinian rite – the triennial lectionary cycle for instance – and supported the Palestinian academy. The Palestinian Synagogue controlled matters of official authority in Egypt and was institutionally under the jurisdiction of the Jewish centers of learning of Syro-Palestine. But by this time, the Palestinian academy had relocated to Fustat along with many of its scholars. The two main Rabbanite synagogues were located within the walls of Qasr ash-Shamʿ on the same street. As Maimonides followed the Babylonian rite, he would have worshiped in the Synagogue of the Iraqians. When he achieved authority in Egypt, he tried to unify the rites by eradicating the customs of the Palestinians. Moses Maimonides and his son Abraham tried unsuccessfully to introduce synagogue reforms in the direction of decorum and piety. Abraham says that his father did not attend either of the synagogues on a regular basis but rather held prayer services in his own study hall [*bet midrash*].

The Synagogue of the Palestinians, called the Ben Ezra Synagogue, has survived the ravages of time and is still standing today. This is fortunate, as the building contains a store chamber where discarded manuscripts were deposited. Untouched for centuries, these records survived very much intact because of the dry climate. The collection, when rediscovered, became a scholar's treasure, known as the Cairo Genizah (from the Hebrew word *ganaz*, meaning "to hide," "to store away").[57]

Maimonides's first five years in Egypt, from 1166 to 1171, were the twilight period of the Fāṭimid dynasty (969–1171), a phase marked by chaos and upheaval, with regents or viziers replacing young and weak caliphs.[58] Under the Fāṭimids, Egypt had enjoyed great economic prosperity despite the usual disasters of famine and urban unrest. Egypt was favorably located at the junction of two international trade routes, having access to the Mediterranean Sea and the Indian Ocean. The dynasty stimulated Mediterranean trade and restored the ancient trade routes between Egypt and the Far East through the Red Sea. This route was of vital importance for the India trade, in which many Jewish merchants were involved, including Moses Maimonides and his family.

The Fāṭimids were relatively liberal rulers, and Maimonides benefited from the open and tolerant atmosphere of Fāṭimid Egypt. Under the Fāṭimids, Cairo became a cosmopolitan center of religious and secular knowledge. Caliph al-Muʿizz (d. 975) established the al-Azhar Mosque in Cairo (972) shortly after the conquest of Egypt. It was an institution of religious learning and training for Ismāʿīlī missionaries, and it offered free public education and even classes for women.

The Ismāʿīlī belief in a single philosophic truth at the heart of different religions opened the door to the study of philosophy and the sciences, and an ethos of free inquiry and unrestricted scientific thought lured intellectuals to the Fāṭimid court. The life of the intellect was accessible to all religious groups, and scientists could exercise their powers freely and contribute to the advancement of knowledge. The caliphs encouraged literary activity, wrote poetry, and sponsored the decorative arts. Under their rule Cairo became a resplendent cultural metropolis along with Baghdad in the East and Cordova in the West.

The Ismāʿīlī chief missionary taught Ismāʿīlī doctrine in secret sessions in a special room in the caliphal palace reserved for the intellectual elite and spiritually qualified. The royal palace also housed the magnificent Fāṭimid library. An institution called the Academy of Science [*Dār al-ʿilm*] was devoted to the sciences and religious subjects. Books from palace libraries were transferred to the institute, where people could read, and study and copy texts. Experts gave lectures there on language, religious disciplines, and the natural sciences.

1.11. ISMAʿILISM AND NEOPLATONISM

During Maimonides's six years under Fāṭimid rule he had access to Ismāʿīlī writings and to lectures by Ismāʿīlī missionaries. There is an affinity between Ismāʿīlī thought and Maimonides' philosophic theology. Maimonides' extreme formulation of an apophatic theology was apparently influenced by Neoplatonic writings.[59] His vocabulary is close to the terminology of Ismāʿīlī missionary and philosopher Ḥamīd-ad-Dīn al-Kirmānī (d. sometime after). His statement that by a series of negations we achieve positive knowledge about something resembles al-Kirmānī's "affirming by the method of negation."[60] Alfred L. Ivry has stressed Maimonides' dependence on Ismāʿīlī and Neoplatonic doctrines.[61] Maimonides' familiarity with Neoplatonic and Ismāʿīlī texts need not have begun with his arrival in Fāṭimid Egypt. He may have been acquainted with this literature already in Andalusia and the Maghrib. Muḥammad ibn ʿAbd Allāh Ibn Masarra (883–931) had introduced a kind of Neoplatonic Gnosticism into Andalusia in the tenth century, and the Epistles of the Ikhwān aṣ-Ṣafāʾ were widely disseminated there and in the Maghrib.[62]

Ismaʿilism embodied Jewish and Judeo–Christian motifs, making it attractive to Jews and Christians. Some Jews converted to this version of Islam, whereas others wrote in an Ismāʿīlī mode.[63] Jewish Ismaʿilism was, however, a bridge to apostasy. A negative reference to Ismāʿīlī doctrine occurs in the *Guide*, in which Maimonides criticized those who interpret miracles figuratively (by *taʾwīl*), citing the Islamic esotericists [*ahl al-bāṭin*].[64] His disapproval may have been qualified, however, for he used the term *taʾwīl* in the same context to describe his *own* system of interpreting biblical texts.[65]

Maimonides rejected the astrology of Jewish Ismaʿilism, popular in Yemen and in Nethanel Fayyūmī's *Bustān al-ʿuqūl*, particularly predictions about the coming of the Messiah.[66] He may have linked this aspect of Ismaʿilism with the astral mysticism of the Sabians, which he rejected.[67]

1.12. COMMERCE AND TEACHING

Maimonides came to the attention of the ruling Fāṭimid dynasty as a protégé of the talented administrator al-Qāḍī al-Fāḍil, then serving Caliph al-ʿĀḍid (reigned 1160–71) and his vizier, Shāwar. Ibn al-Qifṭī says that during the last days of the Fāṭimids Maimonides taught the ancient sciences, such as mathematics, logic, and astronomy.[68] These sciences were taught at the caliphal palace and at the Academy of Sciences, but we do not know where he actually lectured.

Ibn al-Qifṭī reports that Moses engaged in commerce in precious gems and the like. The family may have traded in jewelry already in Spain and Morocco. Because they traveled from place to place, it was expedient to sell small articles that were valuable and portable. Most precious gems were imported from India and the Far East. He maintained an interest in the India trade as a sedentary merchant throughout his life. In a letter to his pupil Joseph ben Judah, written in 1191, when Joseph was in Aleppo and about to travel to Baghdad, Moses instructed him to settle accounts with a certain Ibn al-Amshāṭī when the man arrives from India.[69] Members of the Amshāṭī family were great merchants active in the India trade.[70] In the same letter, Moses advised Joseph not to teach professionally and neglect his business affairs, but rather put his main effort into business and medical studies and study the Torah for its own sake, not for income. Joseph followed this advice, and, after traveling to Baghdad with merchandise, he went on to India, returning safely, and then invested in real estate. He became a physician at the court of Sulṭān aẓ-Ẓāhir Ghāzī, a son of Saladin (Ṣalāḥ ad-Dīn), in Aleppo.

It was not uncommon for physicians to engage in commerce. The successful ones had extensive contacts with members of the merchant class. Those who were affluent had capital to invest, and they had a vested interest in commerce, especially in pharmaceuticals and precious stones. The illustrious poet–philosopher Judah Halevi (d. 1140), also a physician, had close contacts with merchants and engaged in trade. In fact, many traders were scholars, the merchant–scholar becoming an ideal type in this age – men such as ha-Levi's friend, the India trader Ḥalfon ben Nethan'el, the eleventh-century merchant–banker Nahray ben Nissim, and Abraham ben Yiju.[71]

Maimonides disapproved of using religious office or teaching Torah for a livelihood, an unpopular view then as today. People were routinely remunerated for religious offices, and they raised funds to support communal officials and academies. Opposing this, Maimonides invoked an unimpeachable precedent. The Talmudic sages, he pointed out, did not seek money from people or raise funds for their academies and for their exilarchs, judges, or teachers of Torah. They maintained themselves from ordinary employment. They were hewers of wood and drawers of water, and some were even blind, but they devoted themselves to the study of Torah without remuneration.[72]

During Maimonides's early years in Egypt he solidified his reputation as a religious authority by finishing his *Commentary on the Mishnah* (1168). Travel and hardships had delayed completion of the commentary. In a postscript, he excused its defects and explained how hard it had been to achieve. He was aware of its flaws and invited his critics to judge him gently, for what he embarked on was not a minor thing, and to carry it out was not easy for someone whose heart was constantly preoccupied with adversities because of exile and wandering *from one end of heaven to the other* (Deuteronomy 4:32). While traveling overland and at sea, he continued studying secular sciences as well. Throughout his life he bore aloft these two beacons, Torah and science, and they were a consolation for him in stressful times.[73]

1.13. HARD TIMES

During his early years in Egypt, Maimonides suffered several disasters, including his father's death and the Crusader invasion of Egypt that led to the burning of Fustat in 1168. But the worst disaster of Moses' life until then was the death of his beloved brother David, who drowned at sea on his way to India, while in possession of much money belonging to Moses, to himself, and to others, leaving a young daughter and his widow in Moses' care.[74] For about a year after the evil tidings reached him, Moses remained "prostrate in bed[75] with a severe inflammation, fever and numbness of heart,[76] and well nigh perished." He wrote eight years later that from then on he has been in a state of disconsolate mourning: "How can I be consoled? For he was my son; he grew up upon my knees; he was my brother, my pupil. It was he who did business in the market place, earning a livelihood, while I dwelled in security." David has gone on to eternal life, leaving Moses "dismayed in a foreign land."[77] "Were it not for the Torah, which is my delight, and for scientific matters, which let me forget his sorrow, *I would have perished in my affliction*" (Psalm 119:92).

Maimonides suffered a physical breakdown and mental anguish after his brother's death. He was overwhelmed with grief and a sense of irretrievable loss as though his own life had ended. His paralyzing illness and protracted sorrow point unmistakably to a severe depression, the kind that occurs when a person sensitized by stressful life events, especially traumatic separation, suffers the loss of a loved one.[78] Such an episode makes the victim susceptible to recurrences of depression throughout life.

Biographers have written that as result of David's death Maimonides had to relinquish the life of a scholar and take up medicine as a profession, but there is no evidence for such a transition. Maimonides had studied medicine in North Africa before coming to Egypt and attained prominence as a physician in his early days in Egypt even before David's demise.

1.14. ASCENT TO POWER

Nevertheless, there was a momentous transformation in Maimonides' life after the tragedy. About a year later Maimonides became *ra'īs al-yahūd* [Head of the Jews], the supreme religious authority over Egyptian Jewry.[79] He was then thirty-three years old and had been in Egypt for five eventful years. He became Head of the Jews in August–September 1171, at the time Saladin became sultan over Egypt and founded the Ayyūbid dynasty. We cannot prove a link between the two events, but al-Qāḍī al-Fāḍil, Saladin's chief administrator and Maimonides's patron, was instrumental in the Ayyūbid success. During the first years of Ayyūbid rule, al-Fāḍil gave Moses a stipend, evidently for medical services to the dynasty and to his own household. Ascending the rungs of Egypt's social hierarchy required the protection of a powerful patron, and Maimonides's career hinged on the meteoric ascent of his benefactor. Attaining this position required rare skill for overcoming the shoals of Egyptian politics and the rapids of Jewish affairs. Evidence points to his having been Head of the Jews for short periods of time, in 1171–3, and later in the 1190s.[80]

The Head of the Jews was the highest judicial authority in the community. He appointed chief judges and they in turn appointed and supervised communal officials outside Cairo with his concurrence. His power in the community depended on his weight with the government. As Head of the Jews in Egypt, Maimonides had broad communal responsibilities – supervising marriage, divorce, and inheritance;

overseeing synagogues and public property; and administering the poll tax. The Head was sometimes called *Nagid*, but Maimonides did not assume this title, though he was given this epithet in letters. After the headship of Samuel ben Ḥananyah (1140–59) the title *Nagid* was not used until Abraham, son of Moses, took over.[81] In general, Maimonides looked on exalted titles held by his Jewish contemporaries – the Geonim in Iraq, for instance – with ironic disdain.

Even when Moses was not officially Head of the Jews, his role as a respondent (*rav* = *muftī*) to legal queries from Egypt and elsewhere – North Africa, Sicily, Syro-Palestine, Baghdad, and Yemen – made him the leading Jewish religious authority in Egypt and beyond. People addressed him by the title *ha-rav ha-gadol be-yisra'el* [the great teacher in Israel]. He was the president of a council, called *majlis* or *yeshivah*, an institution for study and instruction in the law, in which he made legal decisions in consultation with colleagues. The council deliberated cases brought from lower courts, thereby acting as a kind of supreme court. People appealing the judgment of a lower court would submit petitions to Maimonides and his *yeshivah*, and he and his colleagues instructed the court or local community on how to respond to the situation. They also issued legal ordinances [*taqqanot*] to reform communal practices.

Moses married into a prestigious Egyptian family renowned for its learning and piety. As a newcomer to Egypt, this was a way of gaining acceptability and status. His wife was a daughter of a government official, Abū l-Maḥāsin Misha'el.[82] Moses' brother-in-law, Abū l-Maʿālī, married Moses' sister, becoming thereby his brother-in-law twice over.[83] A son of this sister, Abū r-Riḍā', assisted Maimonides with his medical writing and later became a famous physician in his own right, serving Sultan Qilij Arslan in Seljuq Anatolia. A letter of congratulations on Moses' marriage, from the Cairo Genizah, describes the bride as being from an aristocratic family [*bat tovim*]. The wedding took place after Moses was thirty-three, as he is called in the letter "the great *rav*," a title he assumed in 1171.[84] The marriage connected Maimonides with Egypt's elite society. Abū l-Maʿālī was secretary to Saladin's wife, mother of Saladin's oldest son, al-Malik al-Afḍal. Maimonides later administered to al-Malik al-Afḍal as physician, and his patron, al-Qāḍī al-Fāḍil, served as chief administrator to al-Afḍal.

Abraham ben Moses (1186–1237), his only son, was born when Moses was forty-six. People theorize that Abraham was the offspring of a second marriage, that a first wife died, but there is no evidence for this. He may have married many years before Abraham was born and had daughters about whom we hear nothing.

Abraham studied with his father, emulated him, and carried on his struggle to unify and regulate religious practice. Moses groomed his son for leadership by having him observe as he carried out communal supervision. Abraham studied philosophy and medicine and became a well-known physician, but the mainspring of his character was his devotion to Sufism. He followed his father's career as physician and communal leader, succeeding him as head of Egyptian Jewry.[85]

Abraham married into a family of learning and wealth. He married the daughter of Ḥananel, a pious judge and learned merchant, son of Samuel ben Joseph, who served in Maimonides's court. Samuel's uncle was the great India trader Abraham ben Yiju.[86] Abraham ben Yiju, of al-Mahdiyya, Tunisia, was the quintessential learned merchant of the time. A scribe by profession, known for his fine calligraphy, he also wrote and collected poetry and composed responsa on legal issues. He was "the most important single individual of the India papers preserved in the Genizah."[87] Maimonides certainly knew ben Yiju, who spent time in Fustat, and may even have helped him with legal problems ensuing from his marriage to a freed Indian slave woman (Ashu, renamed Berakhah [Blessing]).[88] Abraham Maimonides' marriage to the daughter of a learned man was vital for the financial autonomy of the spiritual leader, which his father stressed, and it united the House of Maimonides with the House of ben Yiju.

Abraham served as a physician in the Nasiri hospital, founded by Sultan Saladin. There, he met the famous Muslim doctor and historian of medicine, Ibn Abī Uṣaybiʿa, who gave a brief biography of Abraham in his history of physicians.[89] Ibn Abī Uṣaybiʿa's father had been a pupil of Maimonides, an instance of the general collegiality and collaboration that took place among physicians of diverse religious backgrounds.

1.15. THE AYYŪBIDS

Maimonides lived through a dramatic turning point in Egyptian history, marked by a Sunnī restoration after two centuries of Shīʿī

(Ismāʿīlī) rule. A foreign Kurdish–Turkish and Syrian army became the mainstay of the dynasty, and the Shāfiʿī and Malikī legal schools replaced the Ismāʿīlī rite and the Ayyūbid dynasty favored the Ashʿarī school of theology.[90] Maimonides was therefore closer ideologically to the deposed Fāṭimids than to the reigning Ayyūbids. A rhymed epitome of this theology dedicated to Saladin was made a textbook in schools. The Ashʿarīs espoused a doctrine of occasionalism in nature, believing that God creates events anew every moment. Maimonides criticized the denial of natural causation as undermining the possibility of science.[91] His own views were thus at variance with the prevailing doctrines of the Ayyūbid religious establishment.

Dedicated Sunnīs, the Ayyūbids relentlessly stamped out vestiges of Fāṭimid Ismāʿīlism and other forms of heresy. The most striking event of this kind was the execution of the philosopher Shihāb ad-Dīn as-Suhrawardī in Aleppo (1191) by Saladin's son al-Malik aẓ-Ẓāhir Ghāzī, with orders coming from Saladin himself in a letter that was probably drafted by al-Qāḍī al-Fāḍil.[92] The execution of as-Suhrawardī was a cause célèbre. Bahā' ad-Dīn Ibn Shaddād, a biographer of Saladin, commended Saladin's deed as an act of piety. Saladin, he wrote, believed in resurrection of the body and despised philosophers and deniers of the divine attributes.[93] Under these circumstances, we can understand Maimonides's discretion in the *Guide* and elsewhere.

1.15.1. Al-Qāḍī al-Fāḍil

Al-Qāḍī al-Fāḍil [The Excellent Judge] al-Baysani (1135–1200), Maimonides's patron, was poet, litterateur, administrator, statesman, model stylist, and avid bibliophile.[94] Maimonides dedicated his book *On Poisons and Antidotes* to al-Fāḍil, who had requested first aid advice for poisonous bites or stings and precautions against poisons. Al-Fāḍil requested that ingredients for preparing certain antidotes, like the *theriaca*, lacking in Egypt, be imported from distant countries, for aside from opium none of the necessary ingredients for compounding them were available in Egypt. Jews were prominent importers of pharmaceuticals, and Maimonides could help obtain the required ingredients.

Al-Fāḍil amassed a great library in his palace, which he later transferred to the madrasas [college] he established. Maimonides' profound knowledge of Arabic philosophy, science, theology, and jurisprudence presupposes contact with a first-class library of this sort.

1.15.2. Ibn Sanā' al-Mulk

Maimonides had ties of friendship with the poet al-Qāḍī as-Saʿīd Ibn Sanā' al-Mulk (ca. 1155–1211), also a protégé of al-Qāḍi al-Fāḍil. Ibn Sanā' al-Mulk wrote a famous book on strophic poetry and was the first to import this Andalusian–Maghribi genre into Egypt, where it gained popularity in raffiné circles. His laudatory poem on Maimonides was included by Ibn Abī Uṣaybiʿa in his history of physicians.[95]

Ibn Sanā' al-Mulk's circle of companions, described as "lovers of discussion," included our Mūsā ibn Maymūn. Ibn Sanā' recorded a discussion of theology involving a Shīʿī scholar from Aleppo and ar-Ra'īs Abū ʿImrān Mūsā al-Yahūdī. And so we find an Egyptian Sunnī, along with a Shīʿī from Aleppo and an Andalusian Jew, convening in Cairo to engage in an intellectual interchange.[96]

1.16. DEALING WITH AFFAIRS OF EVERYDAY LIFE

As the highest religious authority in Egypt, Maimonides received many queries on aspects of Jewish law. Over 500 of his responsa survive. They are priceless witnesses to the way his mind worked as he applied the law to actual life situations.[97] We have his opinions on a broad spectrum of issues – synagogue decorum, business partnerships, marriage, divorce, inheritance, orphans and widows, ownership and rental of property, trusteeship, debts, conversion to Judaism and apostasy, circumcision, menstruation, charity, court procedure, legal documents, and so on. We also have documents illustrating his personal involvement in release of captives and care of synagogues.

Pursuing communal responsibilities was for Maimonides a pious activity, a form of *imitatio Dei*. As God is governor and sustainer of the universe, bestower of providential care and justice, so the leader of the community embodies these attributes in his guidance of his people.

1.17. EPISTLE TO YEMEN

In 1172, Maimonides – then thirty-four and *ra'īs al-yahūd* for one year – wrote an epistle to the Jews of Yemen, who were suffering the torment of forced apostasy, as had the Jews in Spain and North Africa.[98] It is one of his best-known writings, and it endeared him to Yemenite Jews forever. He placed their anguish within a divine plan, assuring them that their trials will end, that a messianic advent awaits them in the near future. We know that the Yemenites included his name in the Kaddish prayer, but this was not a special privilege, as they did the same with other Egyptian Heads of the Jews.

The formal addressee of the epistle was Jacob son of Nethanel Fayyūmī, who had written a letter to Maimonides describing the plight of the Yemenite Jews, but it was also addressed to all "our brothers, our scholars, all the disciples of the communities in Yemen." Although he wrote to Jacob and other scholars, Maimonides wanted the epistle to be read with ease by all men, women, and children, and he wished the message to be understood by all the communities in Yemen. He therefore wrote in Arabic, bidding the recipients to instill his message in the youths, children, and women, to reinforce their weakened and unsettled faith.

The "forced apostasy at the two ends of the world, east and west" – the Maghrib and Yemen – impelled Maimonides to utter a harsh judgment on the Islamic nation [*umma*]: "Never has a people arisen against Israel more hurtful than it, nor one which went so far to debase and humiliate us and to instill hatred toward us as they have."[99] In speaking of the Islamic nation and its hurtful legislation, he uses a word – *nikāya* – that connotes "spiteful harm," suggesting hatred springing from envy.

Maimonides writes as a physician, a healer, who sends a pharmacopoeia, a medicine of the soul, a restorative, relieving pain and distress.

Maimonides worked out a philosophy of history to explain the supremacy of Islam and the humiliation of Jews and Judaism. He quoted biblical verses, mainly from the Book of Daniel, anticipating all the vicissitudes that came to pass, predicting the contemporary suffering. He applied the prefiguration verses as a soothing balm on aching hearts, for if the anguish and grievous ordeals can be viewed as the unfolding of a grand design, they are easier to comprehend and endure. Moreover, there are divine promises of ultimate triumph and vindication.

Like others before him, Maimonides perceived catastrophe, wars, upheavals, and apostasy as presentiments of the footsteps of the Messiah. He viewed the Crusades as the ultimate showdown between the two great world powers, Christendom and Islam, and as a prelude to the final redemption of the Jewish people. He saw these events as messianic travails, "the pangs of the Messiah," harbingers of the restoration of prophecy and a messianic advent in the near future.

Despite the rabbinic prohibition against calculating the End of Days, Maimonides claimed to possess an extraordinary family tradition, going back to "the beginning of our exile from Jerusalem," according to which the prediction of Balaam in Numbers 23:23 alludes to the future restoration of prophecy to Israel in 4970 A.M. (1209–10 C.E.).[100] The restoration of prophecy to Israel is one of the preliminaries of the messianic advent. This, said Maimonides, is the most valid calculation of the End communicated to us, but we have been forbidden to promulgate it so that people do not think that the Messiah has tarried unduly long. Maimonides ends with qualified assent: "God is the best knower of the truth," leaving room for error.[101]

The prediction of a messianic advent was intended to raise the spirits of the Yemenite audience. Yet the anticipation of such an occurrence in the near future drove his historical outlook. He perceived his role as precursor of the restoration of prophecy. He saw himself as a Moses *redivivus*, a redeemer and savior of his people. A mainspring of his personality was this identification with the biblical Moses. Maimonides wrote the *Mishneh Torah* and the *Guide of the Perplexed* to reconstitute the Jewish people as strong, wise, and understanding, to prepare it for the anticipated messianic age. This was an active Messianism built on natural preparation, not a passive Messianism based on eschatological visions of divine interventions.[102]

1.18. *MISHNEH TORAH*

In the years 1168–77, Maimonides, then in his thirties, compiled his monumental compendium of Jewish law, the *Mishneh Torah* [*Repetition of the Torah*] in fourteen books, the numerical value of the Hebrew word for "hand," and therefore called *ha-Yad ha-ḥazaqah* [the *Mighty Hand*].[103]

The *Mishneh Torah* established Maimonides's reputation worldwide and for all time as the authority par excellence on Jewish law. Whereas at the end of the *Commentary on the Mishnah* he was diffident and apprehensive of criticism, he was now confident, knowing that his great work on jurisprudence was in its form, method, style, scope, and structure absolutely unprecedented, in fact revolutionary. The *Mishneh Torah* was also unsurpassed and altered the whole realm of rabbinic literature. It became the benchmark for all subsequent writing on Jewish jurisprudence.

Maimonides elucidated the motivations, methods, aims, and general stylistic features of the *Mishneh Torah* in many texts and in various ways.[104] One motivation for compiling a totally new legal compendium was his sense of collective intellectual decline resulting from grueling and stressful times, causing difficulties in comprehending the interpretations, responsa, and legal precepts that the Geonim composed, not to mention the two Talmuds and *Midrashim*, all of which demand sufficient wisdom to understand the laws of the Torah correctly. This motivation, based on cultural pessimism, parallels Maimonides' account of Judah ha-Nasi's motives in reducing the Oral Law to writing when he compiled the *Mishnah*. Judah ha-Nasi realized that the number of disciples was diminishing because of the overwhelming expansion and power of the Roman Empire and Jews taking flight to the ends of the earth.[105] Maimonides wanted to justify in both cases the necessity for writing down oral traditions. For him, as for Socrates in the *Phaedrus*, all teaching should be oral, the written word serving as a mnemonic. He discerned that the community lacked a true legal compendium with correct, precisely formulated opinions.[106] The vicissitudes of the times and loss of knowledge made imperative a compendium that would be concise and serve as an *aide-mémoire*.

Along with the collective need for a legal compendium there was a private need, as Maimonides explained to Joseph ben Judah. In fact, he put the private need first, saying that he composed the *Mishneh Torah* in the first place for himself so as to be released from study and research and for the time of old age when his memory would fail him. Old age and the prospect of a feeble memory is a perennial motif for justifying writing, but he seems to have meant this literally.

Along with external troubles and a decline in intellectual power, he anticipated personal anxieties, infirmities, and weakness.

Although the *Mishneh Torah* is a legalistic study, it also contains passages on philosophical theology, systemizing principles of faith, ethics, and even medicine. The first part, the Book of Knowledge, contains sections on the Foundations of the Law, Ethics, and Laws of Repentance.[107]

Maimonides intended his legal work to serve as a compendium of the entire Oral Law up to the redaction of the Talmud and the interpretations of the Geonim. Hence he titled the work *Mishneh Torah*, because when a person first reads the Written Law and then this compendium he will know the entire Oral Law without needing to consult any other book. A "Repetition of the Law" is ascribed to the first Moses in the Book of Deuteronomy (17:18).

The *Mishneh Torah* is a comprehensive digest of the religious law, its prospect determined not by the actual historical situation, wherein the amplitude of the religious law was constricted by conditions of Exile, but by the vista of a restored national sovereignty. In the messianic age, all the ancient laws will be reinstituted. Significantly, the last book of the entire *Mishneh Torah*, the Book of Judges, contains regulations concerning the jurisdiction of the supreme court, treatment of rebels, and precepts pertaining to kings and wars, that is, communal obligations that are pertinent only under a reborn sovereignty in a messianic age.[108] The Book of Judges appropriately culminates with a vision of the messianic era. There, Maimonides represents Jesus and Muḥammad as paving the way for the Messiah and preparing all mankind to worship the Lord, "for they fill the entire world with talk of the Messiah, the Torah, and the commandments."

Above all, Maimonides intended to facilitate and simplify the law, to make it comprehensible and intelligible. The governing passion of Maimonides's mind was order and harmony, clarity and simplicity. He tried to arrive at first principles to explain diverse facts, precepts, and regulations. He strived to control complex material and make it accessible to inquiring minds. The *Mishneh Torah* exemplifies his drive for simplicity and order by topically arranging the scattered statements in the Talmud into groups of laws arranged under rubrics – The Laws of the Sabbath, The Laws of the Tabernacle, The Laws of Civil Damages, The Laws of the Murderer, and so on.

Without benefit of concordances, databases, and electronic texts, he combed all of rabbinic literature, the Talmuds and Midrashim, for references to a specific topic. He was justifiably proud of this feat of memory and organization.

He wanted the *Mishneh Torah* to serve as a basis for repetition, contemplation, and spiritual exercises that deepen one's devotion to the right way of life. He directed his pupil Joseph ben Judah to persevere in studying the *Mishneh Torah* by heart. Memorization was a spiritual exercise of assimilating and internalizing teachings and deepening their effect in such a way as to transform a person's consciousness.[109] Maimonides' literary technique here, as in his medical works, was to divide the text to be remembered into short pieces [*halakhot* or *fuṣūl*] easy to memorize. His was a memory culture, as ours is documentary and electronic.[110]

1.19. COURT PHYSICIAN

Maimonides moved in the highest intellectual and political circles in Cairo thanks to his skill as a physician, his learning, and his savoir faire. In a letter written in 1191,[111] he boasted to his pupil Joseph ben Judah that he had acquired a very great reputation in medicine among the distinguished men of the realm, such as the chief judge,[112] the army officers [amirs], the court of al-Qāḍi al-Fāḍil, and other leaders of the country, from whom he does not receive any payment.

In the same year, the Baghdadian physician–philosopher ʿAbd al-Laṭīf al-Baghdādī came to Cairo and asked to meet only three people, among them the *ra'īs* Mūsā ibn Maymūn al-Yahūdī.[113] Al-Baghdādī says that Mūsā came to see him, and he described the Jewish sage this way: "He was of superior merit, but love of authority and serving powerful people prevailed over him." In a different version of his autobiography, ʿAbd al-Laṭīf relates that he found in Cairo only two scholars studying the ancients, one a Maghribi Jew, called Mūsā ben Maymūn, "who has extensive knowledge and great intellectual gifts, but was too much concerned with worldly success and frequenting the great [as their physician]."[114] This is intriguing testimony of an eyewitness, but al-Baghdādī tended to be hypercritical in evaluating his contemporaries. In his description he added a comment on the *Guide*: "He [Mūsā ibn Maymūn] wrote a book for the Jews and called it *Kitāb ad-dalāla*, and cursed whoever would write it in a non-Hebrew script. I read it and found it to be a bad book which destroys the foundations of religious laws and beliefs, whereas he thought that he was restoring them." This testimony may indicate that the *Guide* was available in Arabic script shortly after its completion (ca. 1190).

The other Cairene intellectual al-Baghdādī met, Abū l-Qāsim ash-Shāʿirī, a man whom Maimonides would have known, introduced the visitor to the books of Alfarabi, Alexander of Aphrodisias, and Themistius. Ash-Shaʿārī's philosophical orientation was therefore close to that of Maimonides.

Outstanding physicians customarily served in royal courts, as did Galen and the Muslim physicians Abū Bakr ar-Rāzī, Avicenna, Abū Marwān Ibn Zuhr, and Averroes. Jewish physicians followed this pattern, but they also served as representatives of their community, as did Maimonides' predecessors, Samuel ben-Ḥananyah ha-Nagid, Nethanel ben Moses, and his brother Sar Shalom. The status of courtier–physician demanded an array of talents – medical expertise, linguistic versatility, political shrewdness, and tact. The courtier–physicians were distinguished by an aristocratic lineage and a sense of noblesse oblige, and they cultivated an intellectual heritage of Jewish learning united with Greek wisdom.

According to the historian Ibn Abī Uṣaybiʿa, Maimonides served as court physician to Saladin, and we have no reason to doubt this, although we lack independent evidence.[115] Maimonides definitely served Saladin's eldest son, al-Malik al-Afḍal and dedicated two of his medical works to him – *On the Regimen of Health* and *On the Cause of Symptoms*. Al-Malik al-Afḍal held power in Egypt briefly, for about two years (1198–1200). Maimonides wrote his *Regimen of Health* in 1198 during the first year of al-Afḍal's reign, and he composed *On the Cause of Symptoms* in 1200 when he was confined by an illness. He explained that his own infirmities and weak constitution prevented him from visiting the prince in person. He therefore wrote his opinions, answering medical questions and assessing counsel given by other physicians. Al-Malik al-Afḍal, a young and frivolous profligate, was subject to attacks of depression and indigestion. In these two works, written for this despondent hedonist, Maimonides was acting as physician of the soul.

Serving royalty was not an unalloyed blessing. Maimonides complained in his correspondence that attending the imperial entourage was an exasperating responsibility. He described his taxing daily routine in a famous letter to Samuel Ibn Tibbon, translator of the *Guide*.[116]

Members of the royal family made assorted demands. Saladin's nephew, Taqī ad-Dīn Ibn ʿUmar, beset by a bevy of young maidens, aspired to have his ardor enhanced, yet his overexertion had drained him to the point of febrile emaciation. In response to a request, Maimonides wrote a medical work *On Cohabitation* for the prince, prescribing aphrodisiac concoctions but also counseling temperance in erotic pursuits. These, he claimed, debilitate, enfeeble, and attenuate the body. Here we find the Sage of Fustat, the Great Eagle, applying his vast medical skills to the awesome task of resuscitating the waning vigor of an impotent potentate.

1.20. MEDICAL PRACTICE

Medicine in the Arab–Islamic milieu was based mainly on the Greek Hippocratic Corpus and the works of the Roman physician Galen of Pergamum (129–216/17 C.E.). The classical medical library was translated into Arabic in the ninth and tenth centuries and became accessible to the great Muslim physicians, who added their own experience and wisdom. In medicine, as in other fields, Maimonides strived to reduce complexity to system and order. He chafed under Galen's prolixity and reduced the Roman physician's massive literary output to a single book of extracts that a physician could carry around in his pocket. He also wrote a work called *Medical Aphorisms*, containing about 1,500 passages culled mainly from Galen, with critical comments, providing the physician with a handy desk manual, reducing Galen's 129 books to one. Again, he wanted people to be able to master a field by learning its essentials by heart. He cited Galen often and regarded him as a great medical authority, but had little use for him as a philosopher. Even on medical issues, he was not a mere follower of Galen's authority. He had a way of dismissing physicians as not philosophical enough, as he did also with Abū Bakr ar-Rāzī.

Maimonides' medical writings contain no references to Talmudic medicine, nor is there a hint of magic, superstition, or astrology, widespread at the time in medical practice. In his *Medical Aphorisms*, he disapproved of magic medicaments that he found in works of Abū Marwān Ibn Zuhr, whom he otherwise admired. He was understanding, however, when the power of suggestion assists the patient, as when women in childbirth used amulets.[117] In principle, Maimonides divorced medicine and science from religion. For al-Malik al-Afḍal's melancholy he prescribed wine and music, both strictly forbidden to Muslims.[118] He asked his patient not to censure him for recommending what the Islamic law prohibits, for he has not ordered that it be done, but merely prescribed what medicine dictates. The physician, *qua* physician, must advocate a beneficial regime regardless of the religious law, and the patient has the option to accept or decline. If the physician does not prescribe what is medically beneficial, he deceives by not offering his true counsel. The religious law, Maimonides explains, is for the next world, whereas medicine aids the body in this world.[119] When dealing with medicine, he viewed religion from the perspective of a scientist.

1.21. THE *GUIDE OF THE PERPLEXED*

Maimonides began his celebrated masterpiece, the *Guide of the Perplexed*, in 1185, when he was forty-seven, and completed it in around 1190, when he was fifty-two. This is the third and last volume of his trilogy, following the *Commentary on the Mishnah* and the *Mishneh Torah*. He wrote the *Guide* in Judaeo–Arabic, and it was translated in his lifetime into Hebrew and then into Latin and other European languages.[120]

1.21.1. The Addressee

Maimonides dedicated the work to Joseph ben Judah Ibn Simeon, who had studied philosophy previously with a Muslim teacher. Joseph had survived as a forced convert during the Almohad persecutions until he found an opportunity to escape to Alexandria. From there he sent letters and poetic compositions to Maimonides, who was impressed and invited Joseph to be his pupil.[121] Eventually, Joseph left Fustat for Aleppo, Syria, in 1185, and remained in touch with his teacher by correspondence. Maimonides went on teaching him by sending chapters of the *Guide* in the form of an extended epistle, addressed to Joseph and to those like him.

He sent the parts of the *Guide* by installments. Maimonides says in a letter to Joseph that he is sending (or has sent) him six quires of the *Guide*.[122]

In a witty allegorical letter of rebuke,[123] Joseph complained that he had legally married Maimonides' daughter Pleiades (= the *Guide of the Perplexed*),[124] but that his bride (the *Guide*) was faithless even under the bridal canopy – others possessed her before Joseph himself: "All of this was before two firm witnesses,/ Ibn 'Ubaydallah and Averroes, friends./ While still in the bridal canopy she was unfaithful to me/and turned to other lovers."[125] Joseph says that the father–author abetted this. In his response, Maimonides spurned this as a false allegation made out of envy. He calls Joseph *kesil*, meaning both Orion and fool. As for Averroes, he writes, "Contrary to the law[126] he summoned two mixed kinds to witness."[127] Maimonides denied a connection of Averroes with the *Guide*. His letter is humorous and irreverent, and scholars doubt its attribution to Maimonides, as though he were incapable of levity.[128] Consider this riposte in his letter to Joseph: "She [the *Guide*] was reared to be steady/ in the [heavenly] sphere/[129] *and he took her for a harlot,/ for she had covered her face*" (Genesis 38:15).[130] But I suggest that we not view Maimonides as though he were an Eastern European rabbi from a Lithuanian *yeshivah*. He was, after all, a Sefaradi. A man who could write that if we ascribe anger to God, He will be angry with us,[131] was not the austere humorless figure we often encounter in Maimonidean scholarship.

1.21.2. Style of the Guide

We must note the *Guide*'s form of discourse and the parameters of genre, convention, and audience that affected its creation. Maimonides does not call it a book [*kitāb*] or epistolary essay [*risāla*], but *maqāla*, which means "statement" or "utterance." The *Guide* is recorded discourse and the style intimate and conversational. Maimonides speaks to the addressee as "you," as he did in previous works, thereby making the reader feel that the author is speaking directly to him or her.

As Maimonides is communicating oral discourse in writing, the reader of the *Guide* should not expect anything beyond intimations, and these are dispersed among other subjects. The message of the

Guide is scattered throughout its chapters, and the reader must pick up hints and join them to form a coherent account.[132] Maimonides gave keys for unlocking its secrets throughout the text. He guided by allusion rather than by imparting an authoritative body of teachings, as Plato saw knowledge not as information transmitted from teacher to pupil but as a manner of being and thinking communicated through dialogue. Maimonides claimed total authorial control, claiming that nothing in the text is arbitrary and you must read it with keen care.[133]

Medieval commentators appreciated the *Guide's* esotericism, but it was Leo Strauss in modern times who rediscovered esoteric writing and called attention to the obscure nature of the *Guide*, including its number symbolism.[134] Maimonides wrote as a pedagogue, wanting the reader to discover the truth on his or her own.[135] Strauss writes, "The *Guide* as a whole is not merely a key to a forest but is itself a forest, an enchanted forest, and hence also an enchanting forest: it is a delight to the eyes. For the tree of life is a delight to the eyes."[136] Strauss's approach has alienated some readers who plunge into "The Literary Character of the *Guide for the Perplexed*" without reading the superscription from Aristotle and wind up in difficulties and knots.[137]

The numerical symbolism, playful and serious, persists in the *Guide* and helps us follow its message. Aside from the structure of the whole, seven is vital to the most important discourses of the *Guide*, such as the causes of contradiction, Jacob's ladder, and the parable of the palace (*GP* 3.51). He divides the scriptural commandments into classes different from the classification of the *Mishneh Torah*, yet the number remains fourteen.[138] The account of the chariot, which is the *Guide's* main theme, has seven sections, beginning with 1.1–70. The middle section of these *Heptameres*, the account of the chariot, the deepest secret, has seven chapters.[139] Maimonides alerts us to the significance of seven when he says that the Hebrews often use seven,[140] and that the Law uses seven in the case of Passover because it imitates natural things and brings them to perfection in a way.[141]

The number seven was regarded in antiquity as a symbol of completeness and perfection. It underlies the creation narrative in Genesis 1:2–3.[142] It is also built into a cosmic plan of seven planets, seven days, and seven stars of Pleiades and Orion.[143] The idea that numbers are constitutive of the structure of the universe goes back Plato and to Pythagoreanism and was used by the Ikhwān aṣ-Ṣafā'.[144]

1.21.3. The Purpose of the Guide

Maimonides began and ended the *Guide of the Perplexed* with poems. A manuscript leaf with the first poem in what appears to be his handwriting exists in the Cairo Genizah, originally bound, it appears, as the cover of the work.[145]

Maimonides wants to raise the reader from imaginary and superstitious beliefs that cause fear to a rational consciousness that brings equanimity. The reward is a new vision of the world, intellectual serenity, self-transformation, and spiritual conversion. The aim of the *Guide* is to enlighten and to give peace and tranquility to body and soul: "And when these gates are opened and these places are entered into, the souls will find rest therein, the eyes will be delighted, and the bodies will be eased of their toil and of their labor."[146]

It teaches philosophical truths without hindering religious commitment, showing that philosophy need not disrupt social norms or destroy religious beliefs. Religion conveys the abstract truths of philosophy in the form of images and symbols, Maimonides argues, but religion is not merely a mythic representation of rational verities; it also takes over where science reaches its limits. No philosophical system can give a rational account of the universe as a whole. Maimonides believed that human intelligence is limited, that there is a transcendental mystery beyond reason, and that we find traces of this mystery shimmering through the beauty and harmony of nature.

The *Guide* urges human beings to become fully human by perfecting their reason and living in accordance with wisdom. Beyond this, Maimonides instructs us to contemplate the beauty and harmony of the universe and to experience the divine presence everywhere, in a silent room, in a storm at sea, or in the starry sky above, so that we come to a "passionate love of God."[147] The horizon of the ordinary human world, he wrote, is transformed by revelatory moments. "We are like someone in a very dark night over whom lightning flashes time and time again."[148]

Aware of how easily governments and peoples, and with them, individuals, can be brought to ruin, Maimonides held aloft, amid the chaos and turmoil of his epoch, a love of order, restraint, and moderation. His ethical system is a form of therapy, a cure for excessive desires, illusions, false standards, and extreme tendencies. If people live by reason and in harmony with nature, following ethical and religious precepts and adhering to a regimen of health, they can escape "the sea of chance" as far as humanly possible.

This kind of philosophy, which is not merely intellectual but transformative, leading to a life of wisdom, emerges from ancient thought, from the writings of Plato, Aristotle, and the Stoics. Pierre Hadot, the French historian of philosophy, has shown that ancient philosophy was not merely the study of philosophic systems but philosophy as "a way of life," a life focused on the pursuit of wisdom. It is in this philosophic tradition that Maimonides takes his bearings. The *Guide* resumes the psychagogical (the art of leading souls) character of Socrates' speeches, which were aimed at the spiritual edification of interlocutors. The philosopher in the Hellenistic period is a compassionate physician, a person who heals human suffering and whose main concern is "care of the soul." Philosophy as therapy treats not only cognitive issues but also irrational fears and anxieties. This is precisely what Maimonides does in the *Guide* and the reason why its influence has been so formidable.

Maimonides, the foremost exponent of Jewish rationalism, was convinced of the limitations of human reason. In the realm of nature reason can produce scientific knowledge. There are, however, matters that the intellect is totally incapable of apprehending, as reason has an absolute limit.[149] We are like someone in a deep dark night, only intermittently illumined by lightning flashes. Sometimes the truth flashes as though it were day, and afterward matter and habit conceal it as though it were night. We must stop at this limit and contemplate the revealed doctrines taught by the prophets that we cannot comprehend by ourselves or prove scientifically.

He had a belief in the order and harmony of the universe and a conviction that there is a supreme intellect that manifests itself in nature. He saw in nature a marvelous structure that we can understand only very imperfectly, and that must fill us with a feeling of humility. To know that what is mysterious for us really exists and shows itself as the highest wisdom and the most radiant beauty is the essence of true religious feeling. This is the *amor dei intellectualis*, which he speaks of as a rapturous obsession.[150] It is at a point where rationalism and mysticism intersect.

1.22. *TREATISE ON RESURRECTION*

Maimonides wrote his *Treatise on Resurrection* in 1191 in reaction to a letter that Samuel ben Eli, head of the Baghdad academy, wrote to Yemen, claiming that Maimonides did not believe in the resurrection of the dead.[151] The ensuing debate on resurrection was a battle in a war between Maimonides and the Baghdadian scholars. These battles had usually been fought on legal grounds, but here the field is philosophical–theological. At stake was leadership of the Jewish communities in the Middle East.

Samuel ben Eli's allegation could have embroiled Maimonides with the Ayyūbid political and religious authorities. The philosopher Shihāb ad-Dīn as-Suhrawardī had been executed in the same year for heresy, including denial of resurrection (see Section 1.15).

In a letter to Joseph ben Judah, Maimonides asserted that people distorted his views on resurrection.[152] He had to convince his audience that he believed in it, and explained that resurrection is a generally accepted belief among the religious community and that it should not be interpreted symbolically. By "generally accepted belief" Maimonides meant a commonly accepted opinion, unproven but believed by broad consensus and worthy of consent. Resurrection of the dead is a foundation of the religious law by consensus within the religious community. All who adhere to the community are obligated to believe in it, but it falls short of being a philosophic truth.

1.23. *LETTER ON ASTROLOGY*

Maimonides wrote his *Letter on Astrology* in 1195 in response to a query by sages in Montpellier in southern France concerning the validity of astrology.[153] At this time, most philosophers and scientists accepted astrology as a valid science. Maimonides replied curtly that obviously the *Mishneh Torah* has not reached these sages, for if it had, they would have known his opinion about all those things they asked, as he had explained this entire question in Laws Concerning Idolatry.

In this letter, Maimonides gave an original interpretation of the reason for the destruction of the Second Commonwealth in 70 C.E. What annihilated the kingdom, destroyed the temple, and brought Jews to their condition of exile was that their forefathers imagined books of astrology to be illustrious sciences having great utility, and consequently did not study the art of war or the conquest of lands but imagined that those things would help them. No other Jewish thinker gave such a naturalistic explanation for the destruction of the Second Temple, one that offered also a prognosis for the future: The Jewish commonwealth could not be reestablished unless the people learn the art of war.

The *Letter on Astrology* initiated a long correspondence with the sages of southern France, leading to his sending replies to questions on the *Mishneh Torah* and copies of the *Guide* for a local scholar, Samuel Ibn Tibbon, to translate into Hebrew. His letter to Samuel Ibn Tibbon (dated 30 September 1199) indicates that he was not satisfied with the translation. He offered general advice not to translate literally but by sense, and he made many suggestions on specific passages.[154] In this letter, he discouraged Ibn Tibbon from visiting him and even said that, if he comes, he would not be able to spend even an hour with him. There has been much speculation about this rejection. A daring theory holds that Maimonides was displeased that Ibn Tibbon had revealed the secrets of the *Guide* (a radical Aristotelianism).[155]

We now have an autograph letter by Maimonides, which appears to be to Samuel Ibn Tibbon, in which he speaks of his incapacity[156]:

> I request of his honor, R. Samuel the sage, the pious (may his Rock preserve him), that he judge me in the scale of merit in everything, whether to a great or lesser extent. He is surely aware that I esteem him, and his stature is eminent in my heart. But my capacity is limited, and time presses, nor can a man reveal all the circumstances for various reasons. In any case, the merciful one desires the heart. May his peace increase.

Again he speaks of pressure and lack of time, adding tantalizingly that he cannot reveal all the (extenuating) circumstances. Friedman suggests tentatively that he may be alluding to political rivalry. He became once again Head of the Jews in the 1190s, and he was occupied with his service as physician to the royal entourage, while his own health was delicate.

1.24. DEMISE

Maimonides refers often in his letters to his fragile health, his complaints becoming more frequent during the last decade of the twelfth century when he was burdened with obligations to the royal court and the community. According to his grandson David, Maimonides died on 13 December 1204. Given his age and infirmities, it is likely that this date, at least the year, is correct. When his nephew Abū r-Riḍā' copied his *Commentary on Hippocrates' Aphorisms* in 1205, he wrote that his illustrious uncle was dead. According to Ibn al-Qifṭī, Maimonides requested that his descendants have him buried in Tiberias. A tombstone marks the gravesite where he is believed to be interred. However, we cannot be sure, and, like the biblical Moses, "no one knows his burial place to this day" (Deuteronomy 34:6).

NOTES

1. Maimonides gives the year as 1479 S.E. (Seleucid Era) = 4928 A.M., beginning 16 September 1167. He was born then in 4898, beginning 18 September 1137, and so in 1137–8. See Havlin 1972, 1985; Friedman 1993, pp. 540–1. The conventional date 1135 is based on his grandson's statement that he was born on Passover, 30 March 1135. A later embellishment gave the exact hour of his birth – 1:00 P.M.
2. *Epistle to Yemen*, Shailat 1988, *Letters*, p. 105; trans. Kraemer, in Lerner 2000, p. 124; Hebrew letter accompanying the *Guide*, ed. Baneth, *Epistles*, p. 12; and see Friedman 2002, p. 68, n. 98.
3. On Ḥisday ben Shaprut, see Ashtor 1973–9, Chap. 5.
4. See Brann 2002, pp. 24–90, with ample bibliography.
5. In his letter to Samuel Ibn Tibbon, Shailat 1988, p. 552.
6. See 2 Kings 9:11.
7. The famous Ikhwān aṣ-Ṣafa', whose tenth-century encyclopedia was current in Spain; see Fierro 1996. Cf. Pines 1963, p. lx.
8. Abraham ibn Daud, 1967. *The Book of Tradition*, ed. and trans. G.D. Cohen, Philadelphia: Jewish Publication Society.
9. Le Tourneau 1969; Halkin 1953; Corcos-Abulafia 1967; Hirschberg 1974, pp. 37, 123–27.
10. *Letter on Astrology*, ed. Shailat 1988, *Letters*, pp. 480–81; trans. Lerner, 2000, p. 180.
11. In his *Commentary on Rosh ha-Shanah* 22b (p. 18), he wrote that the moon can be seen in the East before sunrise and the same day in the West after sunset, but in *CM*, Rosh ha-Shanah, 2.9, he said that whoever

thinks this is "nothing but an utterly ignorant man, who has no more sense of the celestial sphere than an ox or an ass" (cf. 1 Sam 12:3). Lieberman, *Hilkhot ha-Yerushalmi*, pp. 13–14, suggested that Maimonides wrote the *Commentary on Rosh ha-Shanah* when he was young before studying astronomy and that later he was self-deprecating. In the early work, he spoke of ten celestial spheres, whereas his later view was that there were nine (as in Ptolemy's *Planetary Hypotheses*); see Tanenbaum 1996; but cf. Davidson 2001, pp. 114–17, denying attribution to Maimonides. However, a superscript indicates that Rabbi Samuel ben R. Abraham Skeil copied it from the writing of Maimonides. The vocabulary and presentation of astronomical and calendrical data with illustrations bear the earmarks of Maimonides' writing, as does a reference to our master Joseph ha-Levi (Ibn Migash) (p. 4).

12. *GP* 2.9, p. 268.
13. Pines 1963, p. ciii; Kraemer 1999.
14. See Merlan 1963.
15. Ed. and trans. E. I. J. Rosenthal 1956; trans. Lerner 1974. Strauss (1936) was the first to point out the Platonic influence in the political thought of these Aristotelians.
16. Urvoy 1998, p. 18.
17. Averroes' epitome of the *Parva Naturalia* includes six of the nine Aristotelian treatises, the first being *De sensu et sensibili*. See Peters 1968, p. 46.
18. Baneth, *Epistles*, p. 70. The phrase "all his books" may mean books aside from the commentaries. This may imply that he had studied some of Averroes' books before this time. A. Altmann and H. A. Wolfson believed that when Maimonides wrote the *Guide* he did not know Averroes' writings. See Altmann 1953, p. 294, n. 3; 1969, 109, n. 3. Wolfson 1929, p. 323.
19. Shailat, *Letters*, p. 552. See S. Harvey 1992.
20. See Sabra 1984, pp. 143–4, for Averroes.
21. W. Z. Harvey 1989.
22. Kraemer 1989.
23. This issue has been much discussed, e.g. by Pines 1963, pp. lxxi–lxxii, cix–cxi; Kraemer 1989; Langermann 1991a, 1996, 1999; Kellner 1991b, 1993c; W. Z. Harvey 1997.
24. See Pines 1963, p. cx. He also notes that Maimonides was concerned with the requirements of scientific theory as well. Pines 1979, p. 29, makes a stronger statement, that Maimonides' emphasis on the limitations of human science, perhaps his greatest contribution to philosophical thought, was aimed at making room for faith, anticipating Kant.

25. See *GP* 1.71, p. 177. Before this passage Maimonides criticized some Geonim, placing them in the dubious company of the Karaites as having adopted theological arguments from the Islamic *mutakallimūn* (p. 176).
26. Maimon ben Joseph wrote his *Epistle of Consolation* in Fez in 1471 S.E., corresponding to 1159–60 C.E.; ed. and trans. L. M. Simmons, 1890.
27. See *MT* 1, Character Traits, 5.11; 1, Study of the Torah, 1.5; 4, Marriage, 15.2.
28. Avishur 1998, p. 54 and see Index, p. 381.
29. *Iggeret ha-Shemad* is also called *Ma'amar Qiddush ha-Shem* (*Treatise on Martyrdom*); ed. Shailat, 30–59; trans. and discussion of Halkin and Hartman in Maimonides 1985b, pp. 13–90; see Soloveitchik 1980; Hartman 1982–3; Abumalham 1985. Davidson 2001 rejects this epistle as inauthentic, as he does Maimonides' commentary on BT Rosh ha-Shanah, his composition on the calendar, and *Treatise on Logic*. Such a rejection would seem to require assigning these not inconsequential works to some other author.
30. See Grossman 1992; Hartman 1982–3.
31. See, for instance, *Responsa*, 1986, ed. Blau, no. 22, p. 15.
32. He gives similar advice in the *Epistle to Yemen*, ed. Shailat, p. 92; trans. Kraemer in Fine, 2001, p. 111; and see *MT* 1, Character Traits, 6.1; 1, Study of the Torah, 5.4.
33. *Tārīkh al-ḥukamā'*, p. 318; trans. Kraemer in Fine, 2001, p. 424. Ibn al-Qifṭī says that this happened toward the end of Maimonides' life.
34. It should be the Maghrib instead of Andalus, though Andalus could be used in that sense. For the jurist–theologian–poet Abū l-ʿArab Ibn Muʿīsha al-Kinānī as-Sabtī (d. 585/1189), see al-Maqqarī, *Nafḥ at-ṭīb*, (1988) III, 326; Ibn al-ʿAdīm, *Bughyat aṭ-Ṭalab fī tārīkh Ḥalab*, IV, 1827–28. And see Munk 1851, p. 329, who cites the Muslim historian adh-Dhahabī.
35. Based on the principle that there is no coercion in religion [*lā ikrāha fī d-dīn*] in Qur'an 2.256.
36. *Tarīkh al-ḥukamā'*, p. 392. See also Ibn Abī Uṣaybiʿa (1965), *'Uyūn al-anbā'*, p. 582. Ibn Abī Uṣaybiʿa knew Abraham, son of Maimonides. There are other sources as well, but these are contemporary.
37. Gileadi (1984) claims that the *Guide*'s title, *Dalālat al-ḥā'irīn*, is taken from Alghazali: and see Lazarus-Yafeh 1997 on Alghazali's influence on Maimonides. Pines omitted Alghazali as a source for Maimonides in his "Translator's Introduction" (1963) and discounted the influence of Ibn Ṭufayl.
38. See Maimonides, *On Asthma*, ed. and trans. G. Bos 2002, xxv–xxvi. This is the first of the medical writings since Meyerhof to be edited and translated in a scholarly fashion.

39. Ed. Lichtenberg 1859, II, 17a–20b; trans. Dünner 1959; ed. and trans. Weil and Gerstenkorn 1988; and see Baneth 1908–14. The treatise was written in Arabic, but all we have is a Hebrew version.
40. See Maimonides 1956a; and see Obermann, Introduction, pp. xliv–xlv. For previous works, see Obermann's Introduction, p. xlv, n. 35. And see Langermann 1999, I, 8, 16. See in general S. Stern 2001.
41. CM Rosh ha-Shanah 2:7 and Sukkah 4:2. In the *Treatise of the Calendar* he did not explain the causes for phenomena but set out only premises and principles. In CM 'Arakhin 2.2, he praised someone in Andalusia who had composed a fine composition on the calendar, possibly alluding to Abraham bar Ḥiyya, whose *Book on the Calendar* he evidently used in Sanctification, Chapters 6–10; see Maimonides 1956a; Obermann, Introduction, xliv–xlv. Cf. Davidson 2001, p. 118.
42. O. Neugebauer, in his commentary on Sanctification, said that it shows "the great personality of the author and supreme mastery of a subject, worthy of our greatest admiration"; Neugebauer 1983, 324 [384]. As for the number of chapters, notice that 19 = 12 Zodiacal signs + 7 planets (*GP* 3.29, pp. 519–20) and is also the number of years of the Metonic cycle.
43. See also Maimonides 1956a; Obermann, Introduction, pp. xxxi–xxxiii.
44. Neugebauer 1983, 327 [387].
45. See J. P. Hogendijk 1986, cited by Langermann 1996, p. 107, n. 2. And see the discussion in Langermann 1984, pp. 59–65, accompanied by treatment of a treatise he assigns to Maimonides titled *Notes on Some of the Propositions of the Book of Conics* [of Apollonius of Perga (241–197 B.C.E.)]; see *GP* 1.73, p. 210. The treatise contains a commentary on *Conics*, Book VIII, based on Ibn al-Haytham's restoration of the book. See also Rashed 1987. Freudenthal 1988, p. 114, n. 3, raised doubts about its authorship by Maimonides, a skepticism he still holds and that is shared by Roshdi Rashed, as he informed me (personal communication July 21, 2003).
46. This was the Sufi scholar Abū ʿAlī al-Ḥasan ibn ʿAdūd ad-Dawla ibn Hūd al-Judhāmī (d. 1300), a nephew of al-Mu'tamin. See Kraemer 1992.
47. To the editions and translations mentioned in Kraemer 1991b, p. 77, n. 1, add Brague 1996 (Arabic text with French translation).
48. The treatise is philosophical (his only philosophical writing), and as such is universal. He introduces the first chapter speaking of "we" (logicians) (Strauss 1983, p. 208). He uses the Qur'ānic form for the name of Jesus and uses as an example of a writer Isḥāq the Sabian, the great epistolary stylist (see also Brague 1996, 17–18, but note that Maimonides uses the

Islamic term *ṣalāt* for prayer throughout his writings, as well as *duʿā'* for individual prayer). Maimonides does not hesitate to use Qur'anic locutions even in purely Jewish writings, as the epithet *kālim Allah* [God's spokesman] for Moses in the *Epistle to Yemen*; ed. Shailat, p. 90; trans. Kraemer in Fine 2001, p. 108. Giving as an example of temporal priority Moses and preceding Jesus (which disturbed Davidson) was commonplace, and was simply chronological without any theological implications.

49. See Strauss 1959, p. 165; Brague 1996, p. 13. As Strauss says, these considerations are "necessarily somewhat playful. But they are not so playful to be incompatible with the seriousness of scholarship."
50. Ed. Lieberman 1947.
51. The fair copy is given in facsimile in Maimonides 1956b. The text was edited and translated into Hebrew by Qāfiḥ 1963; and see for autographs Blau and Scheiber 1981; Hopkins 2001.
52. See the text in ed. Shailat, *Letters*, p. 370 and p. 142, n. 18. Maimonides says there that the greatest principle of the Torah is that the world is created [*muḥdath*] by God *ex nihilo*, and that he only had recourse to the idea of eternity according to the philosophers so that the demonstration [*burhān*] of God's existence should be absolute, as he has explained in the *Guide*. This addition is a denial of the view, apparently already current, that Maimonides actually accepted the Aristotelian position. See also Kellner 1986, p. 544.
53. Hyman 1967; Kellner 1986, pp. 10–17.
54. *Ethical Writings of Maimonides*, trans. Weiss and Butterworth 1975, pp. 59–104; Weiss 1991.
55. Ed. Shailat, *Letters*, pp. 224–5; trans. Kraemer in Fine 2001, pp. 421–2 (correct 12 October 1166 to 1165 C.E.). Not all scholars accept this text as authentic.
56. For Qasr ash-Shamʿ (also called the Fortress of Babylon), see Lambert 1994; and see Goitein 1967–93, Index, 38.
57. For the synagogue, see Lambert, 1994; and for the Genizah, see Goitein, 1967–93, I, pp. 1–28; Reif 2000.
58. On the Fāṭimids, see Sanders 1998; Walker 1998.
59. Pines 1963, p. xcvi.
60. *GP* 1.59, pp. 138–9, and 1.60; see Pines 1980, pp. 296–7, citing al-Kirmānī's *Raḥat al-ʿaql.*
61. Ivry 1986, 1991, 1995.
62. See n. 9 in this chapter.
63. Pines 1947; S. M. Stern 1983; Kiener 1984.
64. Pines translates: "Islamic internalists" in *GP* 2.25, p. 328.

65. Pines 1980, Appendix VI, p. 294.
66. See *Epistle to Yemen*, ed. Shailat, *Letters*, p. 100, trans. Kraemer in Lerner 2000, p. 120.
67. See Corbin 1986.
68. Ibn al-Qifṭī, *Tārīḥ al-ḥukamā'*, p. 318; trans. Kraemer in Fine 2001, p. 423.
69. Maimonides 1985a, p. 70.
70. See Goitein 1980, p. 163 and n. 32. M. A. Friedman suggests that he is Samuel Ibn al-Amshāṭī; Friedman 1988–9, pp. 182–3.
71. For Halevi, see Gil and Fleischer 2001; and for India traders, see Goitein 1973. Goitein's *India Book* is being edited by M. A. Friedman.
72. *CM*, Avot, 4.7, ed. Qāfiḥ, pp. 441–2; *MT* 1, Study of the Torah, 1.9, 3.10–11. And see *MT* 7, Gifts to the Poor, 10.18.
73. See his letter to Japheth ben Elijah, ed. Shailat p. 230; trans. Kraemer in Fine 2001, p. 425; and his letter on his son Abraham; ed. Baneth, *Epistles*, p. 95; trans. Kraemer in Fine 2001, p. 427; and see *MT* 1, Repentance, 10.6.
74. David's letter to Moses before his journey has been miraculously preserved; see Goitein 1973, pp. 207–9; and Moses describes his reaction in his letter to Japheth ben Eli; ed. Shailat, 228–30; trans. Kraemer in Fine 2001, pp. 424–5.
75. In *MT* 12, Property and Presents, 8.2, Maimonides uses the expression "prostrate in bed" in the sense of "dangerously ill."
76. He weaves verses from Scripture to describe symptoms of melancholia, viz. Deuteronomy 28:22, 28, 35 and Job 2:7.
77. Cf. Exodus 2:22, 18:3, in which the biblical Moses says, "I have been a stranger in a foreign land," meaning Egypt. A foreign land as opposed to eternal life also suggests life in this world.
78. See Freud 1937.
79. Goitein 1966, 1980; Friedman 1988–9; Cohen 1989; Ben-Sasson 1991. Both Ibn al-Qifṭī (1903, p. 392) and Ibn Abī Uṣaybiʿa (1965, p. 582) report that he was Head of the Jews [*ra'īs al-yahūd*] in Egypt. This was a title conferred by the government. And in Genizah documents he is called *ra'īs* (or *rayyīs*) in contexts in which it implies "head" in this sense. But cf. Levinger 1990 (also in 1989) and Davidson 1997, who denies that Maimonides was ever Head of the Jews.
80. I have found evidence in the Genizah papers that Sar Shalom Halevi, whom Maimonides replaced, was again Head of the Jews in 1173, that is, if we can assume that documents written under his jurisdiction [*bi-reshuteh*] imply this. See Mss. Or 1080 J 7 and Or 1080 J 8 from March–April, 1173.

81. Descendants of Maimonides for two centuries were Nagids in Egypt, from his son Abraham (1186–1237) to his great-great-great grandson David ben Joshua (1335–1415).
82. This is reported by Ibn al-Qifṭī 318–19; see trans. Kraemer in Fine, 2001, p. 423.
83. It is known in Arabic as a *mubādala* [exchange] marriage.
84. Friedman 2001, pp. 194–211.
85. On Abraham, see the brilliant portrait by Goitein in 1967–93, Vol. 5, pp. 476–96. See also Avrom Udovitch's reference to the concluding paragraph in his Foreword to the volume, p. xv.
86. Friedman, "The 'Family of Scholars' and the House of Maimonides," "Ibn al-Amshati – A Family of Merchants, Philanthropists, Sages and Pietists" [Heb.], appendices to the *India Book* (published).
87. Goitein 1973, p. 186. Goitein and Friedman 1999. Ibn Yiju is featured in a lovely novel by Amitav Ghosh 1993; and see also Ghosh 1992. He resided in India for a long time, from 1137 through 1149. The earliest document in Ben Yiju's records is a bill of manumission for the female slave Ashu, written in 1132 in Mangalore, on the Malabar Coast of India. Ben Yiju married her and named her Berakhah [Blessing], daughter of Abraham.
88. See *Responsa*, 1986, ed. Blau, no. 211, pp. 373–5, in which he flexes the law in cases in which a man marries a female slave with whom he lived before her release and conversion. Ben Yiju himself had written a responsum on the subject, which is included in Goitein's *India Book*.
89. He writes, "I met [Abraham] in the year 631 or 632 [October 1231–September 1233], while working in the hospital there, and found him to be a tall sheikh of lean body, pleasant manners, refined speech, and distinguished in medicine"; Goitein 1967–93, 5. 477.
90. On the Ayyūbids, see Chamberlain 1998.
91. See especially *GP* 1.73, pp. 202–3.
92. See Ziai 1992.
93. Bahā' ad-Dīn Ibn Shaddād 2002, *an-Nawādir as-sulṭāniyya*, trans. Richards, p. 20.
94. Helbig 1908; Dajani-Shakil 1993.
95. *ʿUyūn al-anbā'*, 582–83; trans. Rosenthal in Fine 2001, p. 427.
96. Rosenthal 1981.
97. 1986, ed. Blau 1986.
98. Ed. Shailat, *Letters*, pp. 82–111; 1985b, trans. and discussion in Maimonides 1985b, pp. 91–207; trans. Kraemer in Fine 2001, pp. 14–27. See Friedman 2002.

99. Maimonides alludes to Qur'ān 2:61, which says, speaking of the people of Moses, "And humilation and wretchedness were stamped upon them."
100. He mentions Balaam's prophecy regarding the advent of King David and the Messiah in *MT* 14, Kings and Wars, 11.1. He discusses Balaam's role as prophet in *GP* 2.41, pp. 42, 45 and 3.22.
101. Hartman 1985, pp. 202–10, doubts that Maimonides believed in the tradition. For a thorough discussion, see Friedman 2002, pp. 50–63.
102. Kraemer 1984.
103. Even its parts are numerologically significant. The Book of Knowledge, for instance, is divided into five parts, two of seven chapters, two of ten, and one (Laws of Idolatry) of twelve (see Foundations of the Torah 3.6). For the view that fourteen is "sheer coincidence," see Fox 1990, p. 15.
104. See especially Twersky 1980.
105. *MT* Introduction, trans. Lerner 2000, 139–40.
106. Letter to Joseph ben Judah, ed. Baneth, *Epistles*, pp. 50–54; see trans. Kraemer in Fine 2001, p. 425.
107. Alghazali began his *Revivication of the Religious Sciences* with a Book of Knowledge. It has been shown (Kraemer 1979) that Maimonides follows, especially in Foundations of the Torah, Alfarabi's scheme (based ultimately on Plato) of the opinions that ought to be posited in the virtuous, or excellent, city. The correspondence may be detected both in order of presentation and in the themes themselves.
108. Blidstein 2001.
109. Hadot 1995.
110. See Carruthers 1992, pp. 7–8.
111. Baneth, *Epistles*, p. 69; 1975, *Ethical Writings of Maimonides*, trans. Weiss and Butterworth, p. 122.
112. The chief judge (not identified by Baneth) was ʿAbd al-Malik ibn ʿĪsā Ṣadr ad-Dīn Ibn Dirbas (Durbas) (d. 605/began July 1208), an Ashʿarī and Shāfiʿī of Kurdish background, who replaced a Shīʿite judge on 23 Jumādā II, 566 = 3 March 1171. He served until 18 Rabīʿ I, 590 = 13 March 1194, when he was replaced with Zayn ad-Din ʿAlī ibn Yūsuf ad-Dimashqī. Maimonides' proximity to the Muslim chief judge relates to his role as a judicial authority. He refers about ten times to Muslim judges in his responsa; see Blau, *Responsa*, 3.219.
113. See Ibn Abī Uṣaybiʿa 1965, pp. 687–88; trans. Kraemer in Fine 2001, p. 427. For two other meetings with Maimonides, see Fenton 1982, and Isaacs 1993.
114. S. M. Stern 1962, p. 64.
115. *ʿUyūn al-anbāʾ*, p. 582.
116. Shailat, *Letters*, pp. 550–51; trans. Kraemer in Fine 2001, p. 428.

117. And see *MT* 1, Idolatry, 11.11.
118. 1974b, *On the Cause of Symptoms*, ed. and trans. J. O. Leibowitz and S. Marcus, pp. 15–3.
119. Cf. *MT 1*, Idolatry, 11.12, on the Torah being medicine for the soul.
120. The *Guide* remains unedited in a critical edition based on available manuscripts; see Hill 1985; Sirat 2000; and Langermann 2000.
121. Munk 1842; Yahalom 1997.
122. Baneth, *Epistles*, pp. 67–68.
123. Baneth, *Epistles*, p. 23.
124. Pleiades has seven stars and is known to be a guide at night.
125. Ibn ʿUbaydallāh is the name of Maimonides' family after his eponymous ancestor. This is the first time Averroes is connected with the *Guide*.
126. Cf. Esther 4:16.
127. Cf. Leviticus 19:19 and Deuteronomy 22:9. The two kinds to witness are Maimonides with Averroes, who is not permitted to be a witness according to Jewish law.
128. Baneth, *Epistles*, 17–30.
129. Combines Lamentations 4:5 and Exodus 17:12, in which the stem *'-m-n* is used in two different senses, and alluding to a third, faithfulness, thus a triple paronomasia.
130. Tamar had covered her face, and so her father-in-law Judah took her for a cult prostitute. Maimonides signals that whereas his daughter was modest and covered her face, Joseph son of Judah took her for a prostitute. (He may also be alluding to the veiled character of the *Guide*.)
131. *GP* 1.36, p. 84.
132. We find the method dispersal [*tabdīd*] in alchemical writings, which were highly esoteric and depended on this style along with alphanumeric symbolism; see *GP* Introduction, p. 607; Kraus 1986, 32, 42–3, 49, and 336.
133. Strauss 1958, p. 121; 1962, p. 60 (re Plato). He uses the expression, "the law of logographic necessity." We may see in this an application of Talmudic hermeneutics.
134. "How To Begin To Study" (1963).
135. Strauss, in teaching the *Guide*, used the same method. Lenzner stresses this in his fine dissertation (2003) and in 2002. Others are less circumspect and wish to reveal esoteric teachings, perceiving hidden doctrines from radical Aristotelianism to extreme skepticism, just as the "real" Strauss is supposed to be a Nietzschean anarchist or an archconservative (or both). Scholars assume that Strauss intimated that Maimonides was an Aristotelian in cosmogonic questions (eternal

universe), and that this was his own view, but nothing could be further from the truth.

136. Strauss 1963, pp. xiii–xiv, alluding to (aside from Heidegger and Weber) *GP* Introduction, p. 20; and cf. p. lvi, where he quotes it again differently. Cf. Genesis 3:6 and Proverbs 3:18.
137. See the review of Strauss (1963) by Fox (1965), in which he criticizes Strauss's own veiled writing.
138. Strauss 1952, p. 87, n. 143; 1959, pp. 165–66; 1963, p. xxx.
139. The number four is vital for the chariot; see *GP* 2.10, p. 272 ("the number four is wondrous").
140. *GP* 2.29, p. 339.
141. *GP* 3.43, p. 571.
142. For the remarkable use of seven and its multiples throughout Genesis 1:1–2:3, see Levenson 1988, citing U. Cassuto.
143. Langermann 1999, I, 33, discusses Abraham Ibn Ezra's numerical symbolism; and see Giora 1988.
144. Netton 1982, pp. 9–16; Schimmel 1993, p. 18. And see Kraus (1986), Chapter 5. The number seven is fundamental for the Ismāʿīlīs, but also for Islam in general. The *shahāda* [declaration of faith] has seven words and so does the *Fātiḥa* [the opening Surah of the Qur'an, used in liturgy]; and see Surah 15:87. Ibn Tufayl, in *Ḥayy ibn Yaqẓān*, as is well known, has his hero pass through seven-year stages toward perfection (Schimmel 1993, p. 128).
145. Ms. J 2.39 recto. The verso has the beginning of the "Epistle Dedicatory." A card in the volume is signed P[aul] F[enton], who had noted this document. The *Guide* also ends with a poem. L. Strauss, in a letter to S. Pines (August 20, 1956, in the Strauss archives at the University of Chicago, called to my attention by Ralph Lerner), which I am publishing, suggests an improved translation of the Epistle Dedicatory, and raises the question why Pines omitted the prior Hebrew verses, "which, incidentally, consist of twenty-six words."
146. *GP* Introduction, p. 20.
147. See S. Harvey 1997.
148. *GP* Introduction, p. 7.
149. *GP* 1.31.
150. *MT* 1, Principles of the Torah, 2.2, 4.12; 1, Repentance, 10.3; *Guide* 3.51.
151. Ed. Finkel (1939); ed. Shailat, *Letters*, pp. 319–76; ed. Halkin and Hartman 1985b, 209–92; trans. Fradkin in Lerner 2000c, pp. 154–77; and see Lerner 2000, pp. 42–55; Stroumsa 1999; and Langermann 2000. The texts published by Stroumsa and Langermann have put to rest any doubts about the authenticity of the treatise.

152. Ed. Baneth, *Epistles*, pp. 66–67.
153. Text in Marx 1926; Shailat, *Letters*, pp. 478–90; trans. Lerner 2000, pp. 178–87; and see studies by Langermann 1991b; Freudenthal 1993; Fixler 1999; Kreisel 1994; Sela 2001b; Lerner 2000, pp. 56–64.
154. Shailat, *Letters*, pp. 511–54.
155. See the discusssion in Fraenkel 2002, pp. 36–7. This had been proposed by A. Ravitzky, but (as Fraenkel shows) it was based on a poor text of Abraham Maimonides' *Wars of the Lord* rather than on the Margaliyot edition.
156. The document is preserved in TS AS 149.41. See Friedman 2001, pp. 191–4.

ALFRED L. IVRY

2 The *Guide* and Maimonides' Philosophical Sources

Maimonides lived in the Islamicate civilization of twelfth-century Spain/Andalusia, Morocco, and Egypt. He was heir to a rich body of philosophical, theological, and theosophical literature, traditions that converged and diverged at different points, depending on their origins and target audiences. Following in the footsteps of Christian theology, the Muslim theologians or *mutakallimūn* began within a hundred years of Muhammad's death. By the tenth century, Muslim philosophy and theosophy had appropriated their largely pagan Greek origins and established themselves as distinctive systems of thought. Arabic translations were made of the Greek philosophical corpus available in the ninth century: all of Aristotle with the possible exception of his *Politics*, and little directly of Plato except for his *Timaeus*, *Republic*, and *Laws*. Commentaries on Aristotle were also translated, as were works by Plotinus and Proclus that were passed off as Aristotle's.[1] *Falāsifa*, like the tenth-century Alfarabi, the eleventh-century Avicenna, and the twelfth-century Averroes, incorporated so much of these teachings that Maimonides felt he could rely on them for his knowledge of Aristotle.

Faced with competing intellectual and religious approaches, Maimonides embraced philosophy, opposed *kalām* theology, and shunned theosophy and mysticism in general – or so it seems, from a first reading of the *Guide of the Perplexed*. The truth is, however, that Maimonides' thought contains contradictions, not all of his own making. The Muslim sources he used had already given Aristotelian thought a Neoplatonic gloss, making labeling problematic. Given conflicting desires in Maimonides' heart and the common interests he shared with theological and theosophical perspectives, it is not surprising that those perspectives insinuated themselves into his writing.

Many of the challenges in identifying Maimonides' philosophic sources were surmounted by Shlomo Pines in a magisterial essay on this theme that he wrote as an introduction to his translation of the *Guide*.[2] In the forty years that have passed since publication of this book there have been some further discoveries, and a number of further conjectures, indicating sources that may have influenced Maimonides in composing his masterpiece.[3] Notwithstanding these additions, Pines' monograph remains a point of reference for any study of this sort.[4]

In this chapter I approach the topic somewhat differently than Pines did. Where he structured his monograph according to individual authors and schools of thought, the first section of this chapter does that only in part, and in brief. The remaining sections of this chapter then examine a few select themes of the *Guide* only and attempt to illustrate the divergent sources on which Maimonides' work is constructed.

2.1. AUTHORS ACKNOWLEDGED AND OTHERWISE

Maimonides mentions many of his sources in the *Guide* itself and offers a partial evaluation of them and of others in a letter to his Hebrew translator, Samuel Ibn Tibbon.[5] Aristotle heads the list of philosophical authorities that Maimonides admires and quotes or paraphrases most often. As he tells Samuel, however, Aristotle needs to be studied with commentaries, specifically those of Alexander Aphrodisias, Themistius, or Averroes.

In addition to his commentaries, the second-century (C.E.) Alexander is very important to Maimonides for three separate treatises that received Arabic translation. Alexander's *De Anima* (and a falsely attributed *De Intellectu*) helped shape Maimonides' understanding of the potential or material intellect, even as Maimonides accepted, together with everyone else, Alexander's positing of Aristotle's active intellect as a universal Agent Intellect.[6]

Two other treatises of Alexander are lost in Greek but extant in Arabic translation. They are *On Providence* [*Fī l-ʿināya*], also known as *On Governance* [*Maqāla fī t-tadbīr*],[7] and a treatise called *On the*

Principles of the All [*Fī mabādī al-kull*].[8] The former treatise expresses the view, to which Maimonides is sympathetic, that Aristotle believed in a divine providence that devolved on only the celestial spheres and the species of existing beings, not on individuals per se[9]; whereas the latter treatise contributed greatly to both Maimonides' appreciation of Aristotle as offering a coherent picture of the physical universe, as well as to Maimonides' empathy, in *Guide* 1.31, with the difficulties facing such an attempt.[10] It is from this latter treatise too that Alexander is enlisted, in *Guide* 2. 3, to support Maimonides' view that Aristotle himself was not convinced of the demonstrative nature of his proofs for the eternity of the universe. This claim made it easier for Maimonides to press his own arguments for the possibility of creation.[11]

Maimonides' commendation of the study of Averroes' commentaries yields intriguing similarities and differences in the two men's philosophies. Both were Aristotelians at heart, convinced of the scientific priority of physics to metaphysics; even more than Maimonides, Averroes determined to avoid a priori theological assumptions and arguments. The God of Averroes is Aristotle's God, who is not the deity Maimonides wishes to endorse (certainly not publicly). Yet Maimonides appears to share much else with Averroes, including that portion of his doctrine of monopsychism that views intellectual conjunction as a loss of individual identity. Judgments about Averroes' influence on Maimonides are difficult, however, as it is not clear how much of Averroes Maimonides had read when composing the *Guide*, especially because Averroes is never mentioned in it. Even so, comparisons with Averroes are inescapable.

Maimonides is not silent about his admiration for the writings of the tenth-century Muslim philosopher Alfarabi. Quite the contrary, Maimonides praises his books highly to Samuel, saying that one need not study anyone else for logic, and that everything he wrote is "wheat without chaff." As a young man Maimonides used treatises of Alfarabi as his model when composing a brief though comprehensive logical manual.[12]

Maimonides' treatise follows Alfarabi at times quite closely, not only in its discussion of logical terms, but also in the concluding chapter, which classifies all the sciences included in philosophy, ending with political philosophy.[13] "True happiness" is to be found in this sphere of activity, Maimonides says, in governing a city, educating its citizens, and creating just laws for them. The influence of Alfarabi is apparent, showing that, from an early age, Maimonides was taken with his political philosophy as well as with his logic.

Alfarabi figures prominently in the *Guide* and is referred to on subjects dealing with logic, the *kalām*, the eternity of the world, the intellect, and providence.[14] His importance goes beyond these citations, however; to a considerable degree he may be seen as the *éminence grise* of the text, providing a subtext that Leo Strauss, Lawrence Berman, and others have explicated. For Alfarabi is the author of a number of works extolling political philosophy as the path to human fulfillment and happiness, a path that requires astute and manipulative leadership by philosophers. He portrays religious law as a philosophically inspired, human instrument by which a society is organized, and regards the narratives of the canons of religion as symbols and parables of philosophical truths, conveyed in the conventional beliefs of a given society. Seen in this light, the *Guide* appears to explicate Alfarabi's teachings.[15]

In his letter to Samuel, Maimonides also gives high marks to Abū Bakr Ibn Bājja (Avempace), an earlier twelfth-century Andalusian philosopher (d. 1139). He is mentioned in the *Guide* a number of times and figures as one of the conduits through which Maimonides formed his opinions about the intellect and conjunction, as well as astronomy and the challenge it posed to acceptance of Aristotelian metaphysics.[16]

Unlike Alfarabi, Ibn Bājja had a negative attitude to political life and sought happiness in personal intellectual perfection. This attitude was shared by another Andalusian, Ibn Ṭufayl, and attracted Maimonides to some degree. Happiness is expressed in terms of conjunction with the universal Agent Intellect, the total essence of sublunar reality. In this conjunction, Ibn Bājja held, as Averroes did after him, that man loses his personal individual immortality. Although Maimonides is reluctant to discuss this subject in any depth, he agrees in passing with Ibn Bājja on this sensitive and controversial point.[17]

The *Guide* thus oscillates between practical or political philosophy and metaphysics. Biblical Law is presented along rational lines that have their ethical principles grounded as much in Aristotle's *Nicomachaean Ethics* as in the rabbinic tradition. Maimonides refers a number of times in the *Guide* to this work[18] and patterned the major portion of his *Eight Chapters* treatise on ethics on an Alfarabian treatise that relied heavily on Aristotle.[19]

Although separated since adolescence from Andalusia physically, Maimonides considered himself within the tradition of its Peripatetic philosophers, who saw themselves as following Alfarabi. Thus in his letter to Samuel he offers unstinting praise only to those whom he sees as Aristotelians. Plato's books are "dispensable for an intelligent man," the style – enigmatic and parabolic – not to be recommended even though Maimonides' own work is eminently parabolic and enigmatic. Avicenna's books, though admittedly "accurate," "subtle," and "useful," cannot compare with those of Alfarabi even though there are many Avicennian traces in Maimonides' composition. Many other philosophers, Greek and Muslim, are not mentioned at all, though their presence informs Maimonides' thought and inhabits the *Guide*.

In addition to the favorite authors whom he praises in the letter to Samuel, Maimonides refers by name and often by composition in the *Guide* to (in descending order of frequency) Plato, Ptolemy, Galen, Epicurus, Euclid, John Philoponus, and Pythagoras, among the ancient authors, and to an equal though less famous number of Christian Arab and Muslim writers.[20] After Aristotle, the greatest number of references in the *Guide* belong to the two competing schools of Muslim theology or *kalām*, the Ashʿarites and Muʿtazilites. Notwithstanding their personal anonymity, the *mutakallimūn* are identified and treated seriously, which is more than can be said for Neoplatonic and Shīʿite authors of Maimonides' acquaintance. He studiously avoids mentioning them, though they too should figure in any account of the philosophical sources of his thought.

Plotinus and Proclus were absorbed into Islamic and medieval Jewish philosophy through Arabic paraphrases of the *Enneads* and *Elements of Theology*. Isolated statements of theirs, sometimes attributed to others, also circulated and had their impact. The earliest expressions of Islamic philosophy, the *Encyclopedia* of the "Brethren of Purity" and the compositions of the first philosopher of Islam, the ninth-century Al-Kindī, already exhibit familiarity with various aspects of Neoplatonism. These include its emphasis on the transcendent One, a being who is unknowable and yet identified with goodness and an intelligent providential concern that extends to individuals only as members of their species, thus leaving room for human freedom; a doctrine of creation expressed through emanation, giving ontic superiority to immaterial forms; a view of matter as the locus of the lowest level of reality, approaching nonbeing in its indeterminancy and viewed as a doctrine of human cognition through which a person's intellect can (re)join intellectually with the supernal intelligible world.[21]

These themes and attitudes are strongly represented in the *Guide,* and though they may have reached Maimonides in part through Avicenna and other sources, they should be recognized for their Neoplatonic, particularly Plotinian, provenance. Maimonides' indebtedness to this perspective is reflected in his view of God as well as emanation, matter, and Divine providence.[22]

Neoplatonic views found greater receptivity among Shīʿī, particularly Ismāʿīlī, theologians than among their Sunni counterparts. This may be due to affinities between the hierarchic structures of Shīʿī theosophy and the hypostatic realms of Neoplatonic cosmogony. In any event, Shīʿī theologians like Abū l-Ḥasan an-Nasafī (d. 943), Abū Ḥātim ar-Rāzī (d. 993–4), Abū Yaʿqūb as-Sijistānī (d. 975), and Ḥamīd ad-Dīn al-Kirmānī (d. ca. 1021) adapted this philosophy to their theology. In their writings, God creates the world from nothing by His will, emanating the classical triad of Universal Mind, Soul, and Nature. The individual strives to unite his soul with these universal hypostases, helped by the immortal prophets and imāms of Shīʿī belief.[23]

Shīʿī thought thus contains certain elements peculiar to its own tradition as well as a general endorsement of mystical ideas that would not have attracted Maimonides. Other elements of their thought, however, would have had a seductive appeal for him. He could not have objected to their heavy reliance on allegory in using the Qurʾān for their doctrines or for their strong stand against predicating attributes to God. The Shīʿites in general were known as supreme esotericists, the laws of Islam having meaning on both the literal level, commanding observance, and on a deeper spiritual level that was known only to the educated initiates.

Maimonides would have found the last major Ismāʿīlī theologian, al-Kirmānī, particularly attractive, for he added the spherical cosmic structures of the Aristotelian philosophers to the triadic scheme of Neoplatonic hypostases. Al-Kirmānī also held both to the idea of a voluntaristic creation from nothing, and a universe that, though created, will last forever. Moreover, al-Kirmānī expresses his opposition to predicating attributes of God in the same language that Maimonides later adopts. Although Avicenna is thought to have influenced Maimonides' view of negative theology, al-Kirmānī may also be an important source for it. Last, though Maimonides would have been uncomfortable to admit it, his understanding of Moses as a unique individual with superhuman intelligence, a prophetic lawgiver combining both intellectual and political skills, has many similarities with Ismāʿīlī teachings of their occulted leaders.[24]

Taking all of this into account, Samuel would have been well advised to take Maimonides' advice on what to read in order to understand the *Guide* with a grain of salt. Philosophical currents other than that represented by Aristotle and his followers influenced Maimonides, though he could not admit that to his correspondent, nor probably to himself.

2.2. HERMENEUTICS AND SOCIETY

Maimonides' first concern in the *Guide* is to educate the reader how to read the Bible. He does so forcefully and dogmatically, for the first seventy(!) chapters of the book. This section of the *Guide* is primarily devoted to an unorthodox hermeneutic of the biblical text. Maimonides' basic conviction is that the canon is not to be taken literally when it speaks of God. In as thorough a manner as possible, Maimonides removes every human and personal aspect of the Deity, every attribute by which He is conceived and depicted.

Maimonides does this in the belief that predicating attributes of God introduces plurality and corporeality into the unique simplicity of God, thereby returning Judaism to the pagan world from which it came. Maimonides has a philosophical animus against idolatry,[25] which for him equals false beliefs about God. This animus drives his exegetical engine ruthlessly and for the most part turns the historic God of Israel into an ahistoric Deity.

Metaphor and allegory are the devices that Maimonides employs to reconfigure the Bible. These were literary techniques commonly found in the Islamic theological and philosophical literature with which Maimonides was familiar, as well as in Jewish theological texts. Among medieval Jewish predecessors, Saadia Gaon in the tenth century follows the *Muʿtazila* branch of *kalām* in not reading biblical anthropomorphisms literally. Yet neither Saadia nor those who followed him in the rabbinic tradition were prepared for the thoroughgoing deconstruction of the biblical text that Maimonides undertook.

Nor does an exact precedent for this appear among the Muslim philosophers. Although Avicenna has some Qurʾānic exegesis, he mainly wrote full-scale allegories that are literary gems in their own right, even if tantalizingly ambiguous. It is not this form of allegory that Maimonides adopts, however. He utilizes only one allegory of his own in the *Guide*, toward the end of the book (3.51); the parable of a ruler in his castle and the various classes of subjects surrounding him. Maimonides' use of allegory in the *Guide* is not confined to set pieces; rather, it is employed throughout the work wherever the Bible describes God anthropomorphically.

This extensive use of the Bible as the prime example of philosophical teachings is foreign to the philosophers' methodology and sense of prudence. It is more to be found among the writings of the theologians of Islam, both Sunnī and Shīʿī. They customarily explicate Qurʾānic verses to bring out their nonapparent meanings and hidden truth. Among the Shīʿites al-Kirmānī even used biblical as well as Qurʾānic sources in this way, it being an Ismaili understanding that all religions contain the same essential truth. Like other Ismāʿīlī teachers, he saw it as his mission to convert the world to the true faith.

Maimonides did not see himself as addressing non-Jews, but did feel a similar compunction to use the Bible to impress his philosophy on his own community. For the most part, the Muslim philosophers refrained from doing this with the Qurʾān. However much Alfarabi was concerned with enlightening his powerful patrons to lead their states along principles of justice and prudence that dictated conforming to the religious norms of their faith, he avoided using the Qurʾān as a proof text for that purpose. He writes of the ideal state in a discreet and relatively impartial way, without explicitly privileging the Islamic creed or people.

This approach did not keep other Muslim *falāsifa* out of trouble with their conservative critics, who used the traditional literal readings of the Qurʾān to attack the philosophers for their denial of such fundamental beliefs as creation from nothing, God's knowledge of particulars, and the belief in a physical resurrection and afterlife. More basically, the philosophers were challenged to prove the very legitimacy of their discipline.

This was the challenge thrown down by the formidable foe of the philosophers, the theologian and mystic Alghazali (d. 1111). Averroes responded to this challenge in his famous *Kitāb Faṣl al-maqāl* [*The Decisive Treatise*].[26] There he defends the right to interpret the Qur'ān allegorically, where its statements would otherwise contradict "reason," that is, the philosopher's understanding of what is possible in a natural, that is, scientifically understood, universe.

For his part, Averroes would limit the use of allegory to strictly philosophical works, intended for an educated audience only. In his own philosophical corpus, however, he uses allegory very seldom, preferring to argue from the data of the senses and not from appeals to authority. To Maimonides, though, allegory opens the door to appreciating the Bible as a philosophical document. This does not mean that the Bible offers philosophical arguments, simply that it assumes and exemplifies the conclusions of such arguments. When read correctly, the Bible for Maimonides is compatible with philosophy, or rather with that portion of philosophy that has established itself as incontrovertible. In this way, the *Guide* not only legitimates philosophy for the believer, it legitimates the Bible for the philosopher.

Maimonides' concern in writing this book is twofold: to uphold philosophy and to uphold the Jewish faith. This latter goal can also be formulated as a desire to strengthen the ties that bind a people to their tradition and community. This sense of national responsibility is less apparent in the Muslim philosophers whom Maimonides admired; their political allegiance was to the particular prince or caliph who patronized them. While not wishing to offend the sensibilities of their coreligionists, the Muslim *falāsifa* did not see themselves as being called to defend their faith or to reformulate it; hence they did so only reluctantly, and only when forced. Ibn Ṭufayl even had his autodidact hero Ḥayy ibn Yaqẓān returning to his isolated island, after a futile attempt to enlighten society.

This is not Maimonides' way. His passion to reform his society and to educate those capable of understanding him to the path he believed led to happiness required him to expose the esoteric dimension of the Bible as much as he dared. Maimonides' allegorical treatment of the Bible extends beyond treating depictions of God's actions as metaphors; it extends toward understanding the entire text as an imaginative human construct, not to be taken literally as God's spoken word. "The Torah speaks in the language of man," he frequently declares, meaning that Moses and the prophets who followed him express in striking yet conventional language the abstract truths that metaphysics seeks. These truths, which center on God's nature and relation to the world, derive from God, which is why the prophets depict them as divinely "revealed."

For Maimonides, the biblical text is sacred because it represents the most perfect, specific, and concrete representation of abstract universal truths possible. It does this in historical and legal terms, congruent with the circumstances and beliefs of ancient Israel. Accordingly, Maimonides' God is particularized and personalized in keeping with the Bible's own presentation, and he makes little attempt to disabuse his reader of this partisan view. As he proceeds, it becomes clear that for him the Law of Moses is critical for establishing the people's identity. The law not only binds the people of Israel to God, it makes Him their God, defining Him in their terms. Consequently, Maimonides insists upon the integrity of the biblical text and on Jewish law, appearing to take Sinai and its antecedent history literally.

In this manner, Maimonides practiced what Alfarabi, following Plato, taught: that it is incumbent on a philosopher who would influence his society to conform to the accepted beliefs and traditions of the people.[27] These philosophers also taught the necessity of occasionally inventing fictions to solidify society. Maimonides does not do this; his approach is rather to treat the historic dimension of the Bible as essentially factual. His concern for the unity and welfare of the Jewish people (and perhaps also an awareness of the personal danger to which he would otherwise be exposed) limits the extent to which he explicitly allegorizes the Bible.

Maimonides' interpretation of the biblical text as a popular expression of philosophical truths is facilitated by his admiration for Alfarabi. It is Alfarabi who claimed that in an indigenous society, philosophical awareness must precede the structures of religious belief. Maimonides echoes that view in his presentation of Abraham who, as an accomplished philosopher, preceded Moses the Lawgiver. For Alfarabi, moreover, it is the philosopher who ideally assumes the role of prophet, statesman, and religious leader, effectively translating his universal insights into particular laws for his community. This naturalization of prophecy and revelation may have been too much for Maimonides, who distinguishes between prophet and statesman and between Moses and every other prophet. Without these disclaimers, however, Maimonides' Moses may be seen as cut from Alfarabi's cloth.

In any event, Maimonides regards the Torah as a political document as much as a metaphysical one; its concern with the practical side of life is significant, or nearly as significant, as its pursuit of theoretical truth. Alfarabi was reputed to have given up his belief in some of the claims for metaphysical knowledge, like the possibility of achieving complete mastery of the subject and thereby attaining immortality. He is said to have affirmed that true happiness is to be found in the political sphere, affecting and governing society. This too may have influenced Maimonides, who shows a somewhat less but still marked degree of skepticism regarding metaphysics, but is unreservedly enthusiastic in his attempt to persuade his readers of the efficacy of Jewish law.[28]

2.3. ALTERNATIVE PHILOSOPHIES

As Maimonides makes clear in the introduction to the *Guide*, he wishes to reconcile Judaism and philosophy, to show that they are generally compatible, albeit with some differences. These differences are highlighted in the text, so that the *Guide* appears to many to be a critique of philosophy rather than an endorsement. As such, it becomes, in the eyes of many readers, a philosophically informed defense of Judaism.

Critiquing philosophy from within is a genre that Alghazali perfected in his *Tahāfut al-falāsifa* [*The Incoherence of the Philosophers*], a century before Maimonides. It is hard to believe Maimonides was unfamiliar with this text and others of the man who was and often still is considered the most informed and influential critic of philosophy that Islam ever produced.

This is especially true of Alghazali's celebrated *Iḥyāʾ ʿulūm ad-dīn* [*The Revivification of the Religious Sciences*], with its detailed explanation and endorsement of Islamic law. For both men, religious law was to be strictly observed. Maimonides' *Mishneh Torah*, his *Code of*

Jewish Law, is similar to Alghazali's *Ihyā'* in that it too teaches that ultimately one is brought through the law to proper appreciation of the love of God. As Maimonides specifies in the *Guide*, however, this love is proportional to one's knowledge, an intellectual standard that is foreign to Alghazali's conception. In the *Iḥyā'*, he endorses a Ṣūfī-style mystical love, far removed from the philosophical constructs to which Maimonides was attracted.

Still Alghazali's *Incoherence of the Philosophers* contains many of the themes that Maimonides engages in the *Guide*. The *Incoherence* follows his *Maqāṣid al-falāsifa* [*The Intentions of the Philosophers*], and like it presents an essentially Avicennian perspective on philosophy, only now to rebut it point by point. Maimonides would have learned much philosophy from these texts and may have pondered Alghazali's critique of Avicenna's thought in preparing his own views. The *Incoherence* takes up such questions as the nature of an eternal versus a created universe, the nature of Divine and human knowledge, the nature of the Deity, the human soul and intellect, and the efficacy of causal explanation. With the exception of the human soul and intellect, these are some of Maimonides' major concerns in the *Guide*.

Maimonides also searches for weak links in Alghazali's armor and finds many of them in their cosmology. Both men are critical of arguments for the eternity of the world and present counter arguments for creation. For both men the will of God is the determining factor in a generally inexplicable cosmos.[29] Further similarities can be found in their attraction to Neoplatonic themes and images, to esoteric teachings, and to condescending attitudes toward their contemporary coreligionists.[30]

Yet for all their personal and intellectual similarities, a great chasm separates Maimonides from Alghazali, which may account for the fact that Maimonides never mentions his name. For all his philosophical acumen, Alghazali was a *mutakallim* turned Ṣūfī, whereas Maimonides was opposed to both *kalām* and Sufism. Alghazali was a moderate Occasionalist and had written in support of *kalām* atomism. Maimonides presents these positions in the *Guide* as fundamental theses of *kalām* and takes strong exception to them. Notwithstanding his criticism of certain metaphysical views held by the philosophers, he is quite comfortable with all the other areas of the philosophers' concerns. Alghazali would have seemed to him to be a philosophical naysayer. The closeness of many of their views may have posed a problem for Maimonides, who wished to go further down the road Alghazali had spurned. Therefore, rather than mention his name, Maimonides chose to debate with him (and other *mutakallimūn*) in the extensive critique of *kalām* that he offers in the *Guide*.[31]

More troubling than Maimonides' ignoring of Alghazali is his ignoring of Averroes' defense of philosophy, the *Tahāfut at-tahāfut*, [*The Incoherence of the Incoherence*]. Maimonides would have found much in this work to agree with, though perhaps it would have also forced him to choose between Averroes and Avicenna. Despite his avowed preference for his fellow Andalusian, Maimonides' own thought is deeply indebted to both.

In the *Incoherence of the Incoherence*, Averroes strives to defend an essentially Aristotelian conception of metaphysics, minimizing the Neoplatonic accretions that Avicenna had introduced. Thus God is the first mover of the outermost sphere, the efficient as well as final cause of the world's motion. Nor does Averroes distinguish between essence and existence, as had Avicenna, who used this distinction to portray a world of essences dependent on an external cause – God – for their existence. The Averroian God is a prime mover, not a bestower of existence, and his world is described sufficiently through Aristotelian causal theory, without requiring any further explanatory scheme.[32]

These teachings of Averroes may have been too much for Maimonides. He may not have read the *Tahāfut at-tahāfut*, and if he did he was not fully persuaded by it. He is not averse to adopting aspects of Avicenna's metaphysics and uses the distinction between necessary and possible existence in one of his proofs for the existence of God. In *Guide* 2.4 Maimonides is also partial to the Avicennian view of God as an indirect first cause, whose being, through an emanative power, stimulates the intelligence of the outermost sphere, thereby setting the dynamics of the world into play. In this way Maimonides distances God from the material entailment that Averroes' view would force on God.

Actually Maimonides is inconsistent in regard to God's relation to the world, and in *Guide* 1.72 and 2.1 appears to assert that God is the first mover of the world, a view that would align him with Averroes. Maimonides' view of the centrality of physics for establishing our notion of God is also closer to Averroes' approach than to Avicenna's.[33]

The mixture of diverse elements of both Averroes' and Avicenna's thought on Maimonides is clear, and it becomes increasingly difficult to put Maimonides in either an Aristotelian–Averroian or modified Aristotelian–Avicennian box.[34] Either Maimonides combines elements of both or he shared much of Averroes' naturalistic perspective without being aware of the kinship.

2.4. *KALĀM* AND PHILOSOPHY

Maimonides may have viewed *kalām* as the siren song for Jewish intellectuals of his day. His student Joseph ben Judah, the addressee of the *Guide*, wished to be informed of the methods and intentions of the *mutakallimūn*,[35] and his perplexity may well have derived from the divergent approaches of *kalām* and philosophy. It is thus not surprising that Maimonides' first philosophical discussion in the *Guide*, following his explanation of biblical terms, is devoted to a detailed exposition and then refutation of the principal tenets of *kalām*.

Both before and after Maimonides presents the premises of *kalām*, however, he informs the reader of principal beliefs of the philosophers, beliefs with which he concurs. First mentioned, in *Guide* 1.68, is a statement that is "generally admitted" by the philosophers and which also, he says, is "one of the foundations of our Law." It is "that He is the intellect as well as the intellectually cognizing subject and the intellectually cognized object, and that those three notions form in Him, may He be exalted, one single notion in which there is no multiplicity."[36]

Repeating this statement later in the chapter, Maimonides emphasizes that this unity of subject, object, and intellectual act obtains for the human intellect when in action. Human beings and God thus have significant similarity, indicating that these terms are not absolutely equivocal. This is a point he made in the opening chapter of the *Guide*, and it is central to his concept of God and our relation to Him. Maimonides' debt to Aristotle's *Metaphysics* 12.7 and *De Anima* 3.5 is transparent.[37]

The next philosophical belief Maimonides emphasizes is causation. The philosophers generally recognize God as first cause.[38] This, Maimonides explains, is part of their fourfold understanding of causality, which he correctly identifies as having been propounded in Aristotle's *Physics*. Maimonides says he himself does not disagree with "one of the opinions of the philosophers," namely, that God is the efficient, formal, and final cause of the universe. This is a view Maimonides could well have learned from Avicenna, who goes beyond Aristotle's (remotely) efficient and final cause to view God as a form of forms and bestower of all formal reality, through the process of emanation.[39]

A further Avicennian note is sounded in discussing God as a final cause when Maimonides claims that the will of God provides the reason why things exist as they do.[40] Maimonides qualifies this view immediately, offering another opinion – one more strictly Aristotelian – in which Divine wisdom is considered as the final cause. His own view is that both will and wisdom, being identical in God, are equal.

This view may seem to diminish the significance of positing a separate Divine will. Nevertheless, Maimonides here is eager to mention the theme of Divine volition, which for him is the major distinction between Aristotle's philosophy and his own. In equivocating on the nature of God's will, Maimonides may be seen as vacillating between the views of Avicenna and those of Averroes because the former is more disposed to predicating volition of God whereas the latter collaspses it into wisdom.

Before detailing the premises of the *mutakallimūn*, Maimonides (*Guide* 1.72) deems it appropriate to present a précis of the philosophers' view of the world as a whole. As he says, he wishes to explain "that which exists as a whole by informing you of what is demonstrated and is indubitably correct."[41] Accordingly, he summarizes a great deal of the accepted scientific truths of his day, viewing the universe as a harmonious organic whole.

He begins with a description of the heavens, outlining their unique ethereal matter and spherical configurations. He follows Ptolemy rather than Aristotle (and Alfarabi) in accepting the existence of nonconcentric and irregularly moving spheres, though otherwise his description follows Aristotle.[42] Maimonides sees the spheres as animated by both a soul and intellect, together influencing both their own movement and that of the spheres below them. The souls on earth, which are the moving principles of every animated being, also derive from "the soul of heaven," with God as remote cause and the soul of the lunar sphere as proximate cause.

The matter of earthly existence is a product of heavenly motion as well, the four elements formed, mixed about, and evolving into the diverse species that are the permanent features of changing matter. Both in the heavens and on earth, the physical world is governed by immaterial forces, and ultimately by a uniquely intelligent being: God. The immanent nature of God's involvement in the physics of the universe is circumscribed by Maimonides' remark to the effect that God is unaffected by the world He governs and that the mechanism for this governance is emanation. This description of the universe is heavily indebted to the views put forth by Aristotle and his commentators and to Avicenna's adaptations of these views in his various philosophical compendia, particularly in his *Shifāʾ* and *Najāt*.[43]

Having presented these philosophical notions without argument, Maimonides proceeds to grapple with the *mutakallimūn*'s views of the world and its maker. Here another set of authorities is called on, though not identified individually. In *Guide* 1.71, Maimonides had offered an historical overview of the development of this body of theological teaching, collapsing its divergent strands into an earlier and later stage, that of the Muʿtazila and Ashʿariyya respectively, extending from the ninth century to Maimonides' own day. Whatever their subdivisions, all *mutakallimūn* have the same method, Maimonides claims, and that is to disregard how everything is, seeing its existence as merely a divinely ordained "custom" (or "habit," *ʿāda* in Arabic), with no physical necessity attached to its existence.

In *Guide* 1.73, Maimonides lays down what he claims to be the twelve "common premises" of the *mutakallimūn*, a summary that for many years has been taken as definitive of their views. With the greater availability of primary *kalām* texts and the formidable scholarship of Shlomo Pines, Joseph van Ess, and (most recently) Michael Schwarz, it now appears more likely that Maimonides has constructed a composite picture of *kalām* principles, only some of which can be confirmed in the sources in the manner he describes. Maimonides may thus be seen as having shaped a large body of disparate theological teachings according to an internal logic he discerns in them. In so proceeding, he could have been influenced by the approach he adopted in writing the *Mishneh Torah*, culling a dominant tradition from the competing voices of the rabbis of an earlier age.

Several of the *kalām* tenets Maimonides describes are found in the writings of Alghazali's Ash'arite teacher, Imām al-Ḥaramayn al-Juwaynī (1028–85). These include the fundamental belief in the existence of atoms and accidents (a belief shared by almost all the *mutakallimūn*)[44]; a conviction that the accidents (and hence atoms) have no intrinsic endurance, perishing by themselves when not re-created by God (a view reported as well by Alghazali in his *Incoherence*)[45]; and the belief in God as the sole responsible agent for every action. For them a self-sustaining, causally determined natural world is a delusion. What passes for nature is rather the product of "custom" or a "habit" that God has chosen to give us.[46]

The Tenth Premise of the *mutakallimūn* is considered by Maimonides to be their main proposition. It is the "affirmation of admissibility" (or possibility, *tajwīz* in Arabic), wherein they allege that anything that may be imagined "is an admissible notion for the intellect." That is, the Muslim theologians believe the intellect or reason cannot reject anything the imagination presents to it, so that anything that can be imagined is possible. Maimonides acknowledges that the *mutakallimūn* draw a line at the imagining of self-contradictory statements because they are nonsensical and hence unimaginable. Concerning the physical world, however, there is nothing they see that cannot be imagined otherwise, no laws of nature, indeed no nature at all.

Maimonides is right in seeing this premise as central to the *Kalām* worldview, supported by the entire doctrine of atomism and occasionalism. Yet Schwarz does not find the doctrine as such given priority in the *kalām* sources.[47] It would appear Maimonides emphasizes the contrast between the intellect and imagination more than the theologians themselves do, perhaps because they saw the doctrine of admissibility as eminently rational.[48] Because Alghazali's *Incoherence* attack on the doctrine of causal efficacy, which antedates that of David Hume, is entirely reasonable,[49] it may be that the logic of this argument led Maimonides to acknowledge that he has not refuted it.[50]

Maimonides rests his case on the reliability of the senses and the conviction they attest to a stable and predictable natural world. He is confident in the intellect's ability to classify and order at least the sublunar world, to comprehend it through the creation of universal notions, and to distinguish between essential and accidental predicates. The logical distinctions created by the intellect are for him apt and adequate expressions of an external natural reality. This is an article of faith for Maimonides, buttressed by faith in a rational God, the Creator (in one sense or another) of a rational universe.

2.5. PROOFS AND COUNTERPROOFS OF CREATION

The major challenge to Maimonides in the *Guide* is to establish, with as much certainty as is possible, that the God whose existence, unity, and incorporeality he believes have already been demonstrated, is also the God of creation and of revelation. Toward that end, he must show that Aristotelian physics and metaphysics do not necessarily contradict this goal. To do this, he reviews the premises that Aristotle and his followers think have already been demonstrated and then critiques them. These premises, as given in the introduction to Part Two of the *Guide,* number twenty-six. Maimonides concurs with all but one, that which assumes the eternity of motion and time, and hence of the universe as a whole. He is prepared to accept this premise as an a fortiori argument: If God's existence within an eternal universe can be proved, so much the more can it be assumed within a created universe.

The premises with which Maimonides agrees involve the impossibility of an infinite magnitude, and endorse Aristotle's conceptions of potentiality and actuality, change, essence and accident, time, motion and body, matter and form, and causation (as previously delimited). They are taken from Aristotle's *Physics* and commentaries to it, as well as from the *Metaphysics* "and its commentary."[51]

If Maimonides is referring to the Greek commentaries on the *Physics* available in Arabic translation, he could have in mind the commentaries of John Philoponus and Alexander Aphrodisias. If, however, he is using the term "commentary" loosely, he might also be thinking of Themistius' paraphrase of the *Physics*. As for the *Metaphysics*, Maimonides could have had access only to the partial commentary of Alexander to Book Lambda, or again, though it is not strictly speaking a commentary, to Themistius' paraphrase.[52] Themistius and Alexander of Aphrodisias are the two Greek commentators whom Maimonides recommends to Samuel Ibn Tibbon, alongside the commentaries of Averroes (who wrote no less than three commentaries to both works of Aristotle). However, the numerous metaphysical compositions of Alfarabi, Avicenna, and Ibn Bājja may also be considered as commentaries on Aristotle's text, and Maimonides was familiar with each.

Indeed, Themistius and Alexander are not the only sources Maimonides drew on in detailing Aristotle's premises. As Schwarz, following Davidson, has noted, a number of these premises and the demonstrations built upon them are employed by Avicenna in his *Shifāʾ* and *Najāt*, as well as in his other encyclopedic works. Moreover, Alghazali in *Intentions of the Philosophers* mentions many of these same premises and arguments by way of summary. Even more striking is the fact that Maimonides' premises 19–21 are based on Avicenna's own distinction between necessary and possible existence, a distinction Maimonides adopts to distinguish between God and everything else in the universe.

Thus Maimonides' core physical and metaphysical beliefs are mostly, though not entirely, Aristotelian. Likewise, the consequences of these premises – that there must be a first mover and cause of the motion and hence existence of the world – are drawn from both Aristotelian and Avicennian sources. This mover must be neither a body or a force in a body, hence not moving or changing; a single, purely actual being whose existence is necessary, and thus uncaused.

As noted, the critical mechanism that allows God to relate to the world is that of emanation, a concept adumbrated in *Guide* 1.72, and expanded on in 2.12. Maimonides does not actually develop this concept in detail, which may account for Pines' consistent choice of "overflow" for emanation, though the Arabic term (*fayḍ*) is quite standard in Neoplatonic texts. Maimonides borrows this term without the hypostatic structures that surround it in classical Neoplatonic texts, probably again going to Avicenna for a precedent.

The world is moved and governed by God through natural intermediaries in the heavens. In *Guide* 2.9 Maimonides proceeds to describe the bodies of the heavens, their material and formal principles, motions, and effects. In *Guide* 2.24 he shows a keen familiarity with past and current astronomical theory, and with the problems and challenges astronomy faced in his day. Averroes (and before him Ibn Bājja) expresses a similar awareness in his *Long Commentary* on the *Metaphysics*.[53] Indeed, it is in the anomalous nature of the movement of the heavenly spheres, as well as the irregular distribution of stars in their spheres, that Maimonides finds an argument for a volitional Creator, one who arranges matters with no compulsion guiding His will.[54]

Maimonides' stated goal is to argue for a God who creates the universe, and his tactic is to attempt to show, as did Alghazali, weaknesses in the philosophers' proofs for eternity. To do this, he offers in *Guide* 2.14 a summary of the philosophers' proofs for an eternal universe, proofs that assume an Aristotelian conception of God. Indeed, Maimonides states at first that only Aristotle's opinions ought to be considered in this matter.[55] Following *Physics* 8:1 and 1: 9, the first two arguments assume that there cannot be a beginning to the motion and hence existence of the heavenly bodies and of prime matter without assuming the existence of extraneous causes.[56] A third argument follows Aristotle in claiming that the (presumed) circular motion of the heavens can never cease, and hence could never have begun, given that circular motion has no contrary to change its nature.[57]

Maimonides' fourth argument for an eternal universe is from the concept of possibility, which he has already defended against the *mutakallimūn* as linked to the real potentialities of an actual material object. Here he argues that the world could not have had the possibility of being generated without a prior material substratum from which this possibility could be realized. Although this argument is also attributed to Aristotle, it owes its particular formulation to Avicenna.[58]

Maimonides next presents arguments that are post-Aristotelian, but that he claims to be derived from Aristotle's philosophy. Although they are arguments that "start from the Deity," as opposed to the world or nature, it is a deity congruent with the philosophical principles by which nature is construed. Thus, Maimonides reasons, to suppose God to have created the world after not having created it would require that His being would have changed from that of a possible to an actual agent, the possibility requiring a cause to be realized. Maimonides calls this notion "a great difficulty,"[59] thinking that it would introduce multiplicity and contingency into God. Other post-Aristotelian arguments Maimonides presents explicitly preclude God from acting or changing in any way. Because God is perfect, wise, and unchanging, so are the acts that issue from Him, and the world as a whole. If so, it must exist perpetually, as does He.[60]

Although Maimonides would have Peripatetic philosophers responsible for all the arguments for an eternal universe based on the nature of the cause of the world, some have been traced to Proclus, who composed a list of eighteen such proofs, which John Philoponus recorded for purposes of rebuttal. Some of this list was translated into Arabic and attracted considerable attention.[61] Maimonides probably received the proofs secondhand, from Alfarabi.[62] Alfarabi is also likely to have been the source for whatever knowledge Maimonides may have had of Philoponus' counterarguments, though his appreciation of them was greater than Alfarabi's. In a work no longer extant called *On Changeable Beings*, Alfarabi is known to have attempted to refute Philoponus' rebuttals of Proclus.[63]

Maimonides' own rebuttals against the arguments for eternity reflect those advanced by Philoponus, Alghazali, and others.[64] As Maimonides asserts in *Guide* 2.18, God's action cannot be subjected to the analysis of change that applies to material beings. For God, creation would not be a movement from potentiality to actuality. Nor is God's will affected by anything external to it, such that it may be said to undergo change. All the arguments of the philosophers who assume a univocal meaning to human and divine will are to be rejected, certainly insofar as creation is at issue; for before the creation of the world there are no physical constraints on that will or commitments that God has made to the world. God is free to will and not to will, Maimonides says, and this is "the true reality and the quiddity of (divine) will."[65]

As Maimonides admits at the end of *Guide* 2.17, his counterarguments have not proved that God did create the world, but only that there is a possibility that He could have. The very notion of possibility used here has slipped its Aristotelian moorings and is no longer tied to actual material existence. In effect, Maimonides has returned to a *kalām* notion of possibility, which renders his entire advocacy of creation suspect.[66]

In conclusion, the issues previously discussed show that Maimonides moves ably among the many sources available to him, in the process weaving a philosophical *cum* theological tapestry of his own.

NOTES

1. Walzer 1962; Peters 1973, pp. 286–331.
2. Pines 1963, pp. lvii–cxxxiv.
3. Many scholars who are accomplished Judaists and Arabists have contributed to this research. A short list must include the pioneering work of the late Lawrence Berman and the many contributions of Herbert Davidson and Joel L. Kraemer. Cf. now Kraemer 1999, pp. 40–68.
4. Nearly all of the sources identified by Pines, as well as those disclosed by the extraordinary nineteenth-century Orientalist Salomon Munk, and by more recent scholars, are now to be found in the thorough annotation that Michael Schwarz has provided alongside his modern Hebrew translation of this work. Besides copious annotation of sources given in the secondary literature, Schwarz provides detailed indices of Greek and Muslim authors referred to in the text and notes. Schwarz 2002, 2:826–32.
5. A fresh translation of this letter can be found in Kraemer 1999, pp. 43–4. It is forthcoming in a collection of Maimonides' letters to be published by Yale University Press.
6. A. P. Fotinis 1979; Altmann 1987, pp. 60–129.
7. Silvia Fazzo and Mauro Zonta 1999.
8. Badawi 1947, pp. 253–77. This work is ascribed to Aristotle in the full title.
9. *GP* 3.17. Some of Maimonides' other descriptions in this chapter of the various types of providence, and his identifications of them, also appear to derive from Alexander's treatise. Pines 1963, p. lxv. Maimonides would have found his views on providence, synonymous with God's relation to the world, expressed in Avicenna as well. Cf. Avicenna 1960, Vol. 2, Books 8:6, 9:6 and Avicenna 1985, pp. 95–100, 149–56.
10. Pines 1979, pp. 100–4. Reprinted in Buijs 1988, pp. 111–15.
11. Pines 1963, pp. lxviii–lxxi.
12. Efros 1938; Brague 1996.
13. Dunlop 1957, 224–35; Kraemer 1991b, pp. 77–104.
14. Pines 1963, pp. lxxviii–xcii.
15. Strauss 1987; Berman 1974, pp. 155–78.
16. Pines 1963, II: 9, p. 268; II: 24, p. 326; Langermann 1991a, pp. 159–71.
17. Pines 1963, *GP* 1.74, p. 221.
18. Pines 1963, pp. 371, 476, 572, 601, 608.
19. Davidson 1963, pp. 33–50.
20. Cf. the index in Pines 1963, p. 657.
21. Ivry 1991a, pp. 117–26.

22. Ivry 1991a, pp. 127–39. As given there, cf. for emanation, *GP* 1.58 and 69; 2.12; for matter, 3.8, 9, and 16; and for providence, 3.17–21.
23. Ivry 1995, pp. 274–6, 281.
24. Ivry 1995, pp. 289–99.
25. Cf. *MT* 1, Idolatry, 2.3–9.
26. Butterworth 2001; formerly translated by Hourani 1967.
27. Maimonides has God subscribing to this principle, in *Guide* 3.32. Pines 1963, p. lxxii, thinks Alexander may have contributed to Maimonides' formulation of this idea. For a comprehensive summation of Alfarabi's political philosophy, see now Mahdi 2001.
28. Pines 1979; Altmann 1987.
29. Marmura 1997, pp. 92, 131.
30. Lazarus-Yafeh 1975.
31. *GP* 1.71–76.
32. Van Den Bergh 1969.
33. Pines 1963, p. cxiv–cxv.
34. Kraemer 1999, pp. 56–8.
35. Pines 1963, p. 4.
36. Pines 1963, p. 163.
37. Pines 1963, p. 165, n. 8.
38. Pines 1963, 1.69, p. 166.
39. Avicenna 1960, Vol. 2, Book 9. Avicenna 1985, pp. 37–148.
40. Pines 1963, 1.69, p. 170. Janssens 1997, pp. 455–77.
41. Pines 1963, 1.71, p. 183.
42. Schwarz (Maimonides 2002), p. 195, nn. 8 and 10.
43. The various areas of this philosophy are discussed by Avicenna in the separate volumes that comprise his *Shifāʾ*, following Aristotle's teachings on the whole in his *Physics*, *Metaphysics*, *On the Soul*, *On the Heavens*, and *Meteorology*. Cf. too Avicenna's summary of his views in his *Najāt*, ed. Fakhry 1985.
44. Schwarz (Maimonides 2002) 1991, pp. 162, 187.
45. Schwarz (Maimonides 2002), p. 195f. Al-Juwaynī is also a main reference for Maimonides' ninth *kalāmic* premise, in which it is asserted that an accident does not serve as the substratum for another accident. Schwarz 1991, p. 195.
46. Schwarz 1991, p. 205.
47. Schwarz 1992–3, p. 155.
48. Cf. the extended reasoning of al-Juwaynī brought by Schwarz 1992–3, p. 60.
49. Marmura 1997, pp. 170–81.
50. Pines 1963, p. 211.
51. Pines 1963, p. 239.

52. Munk (Maimonides 1960) 2.23, n. 3; followed by Schwarz (Maimonides 2002), p. 255, n. 4.
53. Genequand 1984, pp. 170–88.
54. *GP* 2.19. Maimonides' reasoning is a philosophical version of the theological argument from particularization of the sort that Alghazali also used. Davidson 1987b, pp. 194–201.
55. Pines 1963, p. 285.
56. Cf. the full exposition of this and of Maimonides' other arguments for eternity in Davidson 1987b, pp. 13, 17–23.
57. *On the Heavens* I: 3,4. Davidson 1987b, pp. 28, 29.
58. Davidson 1987b, pp. 16–17.
59. Pines 1963, p. 288.
60. Davidson 1987b, pp. 51–6 (the argument that nothing could have led a creator to create the universe at a particular moment); pp. 61–4 (arguments from God's eternal attributes).
61. Davidson 1987b, p. 51. The extant Arabic portion of Proclus' arguments is found in Badawi 1955, pp. 34–42. John Philoponus presents this list, and responds to it, in his *De aeternitate mundi contra proclum*, Rabe 1899. Philoponus' rebuttals are known in Arabic indirectly, and appear among Muslim philosophers already in the time of the first philosopher of Islam, the ninth-century Yaʿqūb ibn Isḥāq al-Kindī.
62. Pines 1963, p. lxxviii.
63. Davidson 1987b, p. 43, n. 68.
64. Davidson 1987b, pp. 67–85.
65. Pines 1963, p. 301.
66. Ivry 1985, pp. 143–59. Reprinted in Buijs 1988, pp. 175–91.

KENNETH SEESKIN

3 Metaphysics and Its Transcendence

According to Aristotle, first philosophy or, as he sometimes calls it, theology, investigates being as being, which is to say the highest principles and causes of all things. In dealing with Maimonides, it is important to see that, unlike Aristotle, he did not write a systematic treatise on the nature of being. The subject matter of the *Guide of the Perplexed* is identified as natural science (the Account of the Beginning) and metaphysics or divine science (the Account of Ezekiel's Chariot). In Maimonides' view mastery of these subjects is needed for human perfection, and it is impossible to fulfill the commandments without them. Simply put: One cannot love God in ignorance.[1] But instead of making an original contribution to physics and metaphysics, Maimonides claims (*GP* 2.2) that his purpose is to explain the meaning of key terms in the Torah.

There are two reasons for this hesitation. From a religious perspective, Jewish law forbids one to discuss the Account of the Beginning or the Account of the Chariot in a public setting.[2] Thus all Maimonides can do is offer hints or clues that point readers in the right direction and encourage them to reach their own conclusions. From a philosophic perspective, once we get beyond the existence and unity of God, Maimonides doubts that anyone can achieve more than a few momentary insights about the metaphysical realm so that much of what people take to be certain is really a form of conjecture. Although conjecture can be well founded or ill, Maimonides does not regard human knowledge as a seamless web of causes and principles but rather as a patchwork of established truths, educated guesses, and admissions of ignorance. We will see that, in some cases, the third component is as important as the first two.

From the time it was published, the *Guide* became the subject of vigorous debate.[3] Some see it as a disguised defense of the neoplatonized Aristotelianism that reigned in the Middle Ages.[4] Others see it as a defense of traditional Jewish teachings like creation and providence.[5] Still others see it as a skeptical philosophy that rejects large portions of metaphysics and tells us how to cope with the limited knowledge available to us.[6] I will resist the temptation to say there is a kernel of truth in each. My own view is that Maimonides was sympathetic to the Aristotelianism of his day when he wrote the *Mishneh Torah* and tried to minimize the difference between it and Judaism. But by the time he wrote the *Guide*, he began to see cracks in the Aristotelian worldview and tried to formulate something different. For the sake of simplicity, I concentrate on his position as expressed in the *Guide*.

3.1. THE EXISTENCE AND UNIQUENESS OF GOD

Let us begin with Maimonides' conception of God. Like many of his contemporaries, Maimonides claims God's essence is beyond our comprehension, so that we can know *that* God is but not *what* God is. There is then no possibility of inferring God's existence from a definition of what it is to be a perfect being. Instead Maimonides offers four arguments for God's existence based on inferences drawn from the world. Here is a schematic version of the first argument: (1) The existence of an infinite body or infinite number of finite bodies is impossible; (2) whatever force is contained in a finite body is finite; (3) the world is eternal; (4) therefore motion is eternal; (5) only something whose power is infinite can be the cause of eternal motion for, if its power were finite, the most it could explain is motion over a finite period of time; (6) therefore an infinite source of power exists. This source is neither a body nor a force in a body because both imply finitude. Because it is not material, it is not subject to division or change. If it is not subject to division or change, it is outside of time. Because its power is infinite, it cannot derive its power from something else. From this Maimonides concludes that it is one and simple and identical with God.

Although I have left out a number of steps, it is clear that Maimonides' argument derives from Aristotle because it relies on the supposition that the world is eternal. According to his admission (*GP* 2, Introduction) eternity is introduced as a hypothesis even though it does not represent his real view. The reason is that Maimonides is presenting a constructive dilemma. If the world is eternal, God exists because no finite thing can be the source of eternal motion. If the world is not eternal but created, God exists because crea*tion* presupposes a crea*tor*. Therefore God exists.[7]

If this were all Maimonides had to say about God, his position would be little more than a footnote in the history of philosophy. What makes it more than that is the rigor with which he interprets the unity of God. Not only is there one God as opposed to many but that God cannot admit complexity in any sense. According to *Guide* 1.51, p. 113,

> There is no oneness at all except in believing that there is one simple essence in which there is no complexity or multiplicity of notions, but one notion only; so that from whatever angle you regard it and from whatever point of view you consider it, you will find that it is one, not divided in any way and by any cause into two notions.

This is more than rhetoric. From the fact that God is one and simple, Maimonides concludes that there can be no plurality of faculties, moral dispositions, or essential attributes in God. He even goes so far as to say that a Jew who affirms the unity of God but thinks that such unity is compatible with multiple attributes is no better than a Christian who says that God is one and three (*GP* 1.50, p. 111).

To understand his point, we must look at his treatment of attributes. According to Maimonides every attribute falls into one of five classes. The first class is easy to understand: the definition of a thing is predicated on it, for example, man is a rational animal. Maimonides objects that if there were an essential attribute predicated on God in this way, there would be a cause anterior to God, which means a wider concept under which God is subsumed or through which God is defined. Just as man is defined by the concept *rational animal*, God would be defined by the concept *necessary being*. The problem is that, once God is defined by any concept, the essence of God would be dependent on something else and limited in exactly the way the concept is limited. In either case, God's uniqueness and simplicity would be lost.

If there is no essential attribute by which to describe God, then God cannot be subject to definition. Because a definition tells us what something is, there is no whatness connected with God, nothing that allows us to classify God as a member of this species rather than that. This is true even if we characterize the species in such a way that it is limited to a single member, that is, the most powerful thing in the universe, most intelligent thing in the universe, or cause of everything else. It is true even if we admit that each of these descriptions refers to the same thing. The simple fact is that once we have specification of any kind we lose divinity.

The second group of attributes involves the predication of part of a definition, for example, man is rational. This too will not work because it implies that God has an essence that is composite and can be broken into genus and species. The third group involves accidental predicates and fails because it implies that God is a substratum of qualities, quantities, and other attributes that attach to or are derived from an essence. This rules out impressions, affections, dispositions, and habits. To say that God has a tendency to grant mercy or feel gracious is therefore false.

The fourth group involves relations. Following Aristotle, Maimonides conceives of relation as an attribute that inheres in two things at once, in effect a bridge that links one thing to another. On this view, relation implies mutuality: If *x* is the father of *y*, by that very fact, *y* is the son of *x*.[8] Take away either term of the relation, and you will take away the other. Maimonides concludes that relation is a connection that can join only things that resemble each other (*GP* 1.52, p. 118). To use his examples, one finite intellect can be greater than another, and one color can be darker than another. But there is no possibility of a relation between the intellect and color because they have nothing in common, nor between a hundred cubits and the heat of a pepper, nor between clemency and the taste of bitterness.

If this is true, neither is there a possibility of a relation between a necessary being and a contingent one for if there were, there would be an attribute that inheres in God and links God to something else. This would mean that God is affected by and in some sense dependent on another thing. Just as a father's nature is changed and partially determined by his relation to the son, God would be changed and partially determined by a relation to the world. Maimonides wants us to see that, as soon as we begin to talk this way, we compromise divinity once again.

No doubt someone will object that God is better than, more powerful than, and wiser than human beings. Are these not relations? A normal thinker in the Aristotelian tradition would answer yes and try to make sense of a vertical connection linking something in one world to something in the other. At *Guide* 1.56, p. 130, Maimonides takes the harder road and says that God is *not* better than, more powerful than, or wiser than human beings in any respect. For if God were more powerful than us, both God and humans would belong to the class of powerful things, with God occupying a preeminent position and us a secondary one. Such a scheme is possible only if there is a measure of comparison between God and us so that both can be grouped in the same class or included under the same definition.

The suggestion that there is a measure of comparison between God and us is exactly what Maimonides rejects. Rather than being more powerful than us, God's power is completely unlike ours. To say, for example, that the ability to create whole galaxies out of nothing is greater than the ability to lift a book off a shelf overlooks the fact that one is not an enhanced version of the other; rather, the two have nothing in common. By the same token, necessary existence is not a forceful or extended version of contingent existence, and divine simplicity is not a purified form of the simplicity exhibited by material things. On this matter, Maimonides is adamant. According to *Guide* 1.35, p. 80, "There is absolutely no likeness in any respect whatever between Him and the things created by Him." Lest there be any charge of esotericism, he claims that this belief is so important the multitude should accept it on traditional authority if they do not understand the reasons behind it.

The result is that words like *power, intelligence*, and *existence* are completely equivocal when used of God and us, a conclusion Maimonides repeats several times. Even if a creature were to manifest power so enormous that it dominated everything else on earth, *powerful* would still be an attribute that attaches to its essence, making it a powerful force or thing. In that respect, it would be unlike God, whose power is neither separate nor derivative nor measurable in foot-pounds. What is true of power is also true of existence, intelligence, and life. As Maimonides puts it (*GP* 1.57, p. 132), "He exists, but not through an existence other than His essence; and similarly He lives, but not through life; He is powerful, but not through power;

He knows, but not through knowledge." Again God cannot derive power or existence *from* something. This is another way of saying that categories like essence–accident and genus–species do not apply to God. In God everything boils down to a radical unity incomparable with anything else.

The only kind of attribute Maimonides allows is the fifth class, which he terms attributes of action. In dealing with attributes of action, we must keep in mind that they are not descriptions of God but descriptions of what God has made or done. According to Maimonides (*GP* 1.54, p. 124) they are moral terms that refer to the things of which it is said, "And God saw every thing that He had made, and, behold, it was very good." The point is that, when we say God is gracious, we should not think that God has a disposition to act in a certain way but that the world God has fashioned is such that animals receive faculties protecting them from destruction. When we say God is merciful, we should not think that God sits in a heavenly court passing judgment on people but that God has given the gift of existence to things that have no right to claim it on their own. If there is a comparison to be made, it is not between God and us but between the results of our actions and the results of God's. So even though a statement like "God is gracious" seems to be predicating an attribute of a subject, it is really predicating an attribute of something that proceeds from the subject and is separate from it: the act*ion* rather than the act*or*.

Because the things God has made are separate from God, Maimonides claims there is no difficulty in having multiple attributes of action. Just as a single fire can harden some things, soften others, bleach, and blacken without being complex, so it is possible for God to manifest multiple attributes *if* we realize we are talking about the effects of divine activity rather than its source. In his words (*GP* 1.53, p. 121):

> It accordingly should not be regarded as inadmissible in reference to God... that the diverse actions proceed from one simple essence in which no multiplicity is posited and to which no notion is superadded. Every attribute that is found in the books of the deity... is therefore an attribute of His action and not an attribute of His essence.

Although the essence of God remains a mystery, Maimonides is able to say that we can praise God for being gracious, merciful, and the like as long as we are conscious of what we are doing. This allows him to claim that the language of prayer is not nonsense. It can be explained by saying that what we are praising is not God considered as a substance possessing attributes but the glory of God's creation.

The danger is in thinking that every time we offer praise we are calling attention to another aspect of God's persona. There is no force, internal or external, that rouses God into activity and no faculties or dispositions by which to distinguish one divine trait from another. Instead God is simple and purely active. Although we can observe the consequences or effects that proceed from God, we will never be in a position to say what God is or how these consequences or effects are produced. As we see in the next section, our chief way of knowing God is to *deny* that the consequences or effects resemble their source.

Quoting Isaiah 40:18 ("To whom then will you liken God?"), Maimonides insists that any resemblance between God and other things must fail. The simple way of expressing this is to say that God is in a category by himself. We saw, however, that even this formulation is misleading if it implies that God falls under a description. The alternative is to say that God falls under no description and, from our standpoint, will always be behind a veil of ignorance. Maimonides confirms this result by citing Exodus 33, in which Moses asks to see the face of God but is told that no mortal can see God's face and live. Instead Moses is able to see God's goodness, the ways and works of God, things that proceed from God but are not part of God. That takes us back to attributes of action, the one type of attribute Maimonides allows.

3.2. THE *VIA NEGATIVA*

What then do we do with statements like "God lives," "God is powerful," or "God exists"? Clearly they have some meaning. Maimonides responds with the *via negativa*. We have already seen that God is not a body, or a force in a body, or complex, or a being comparable with other beings. Beyond that Maimonides argues that "God lives" should be taken as "God does not lack vitality," "God is powerful" as "God does not lack the ability to produce other things," "God exists" as "God's nonexistence is impossible." Important as it is, this analysis is often subject to misinterpretation. In normal speech, a double negative is no different from a positive. To say "*X* does not lack power" is to say that *X* has at least a moderate amount of it and possibly more. If this is the only point Maimonides is making, his position would be trivial.

To see what he is getting at, one has to understand the kind of negation he is using. Consider an example. The ability to run is a perfection commonly associated with horses. If I say that this horse does not lack the ability to run, you would be justified in concluding that its running ability is unimpaired. As we saw, this cannot be what Maimonides says about God because even if God is superlatively powerful, we would still be assigning God to the class of powerful things. Instead what Maimonides means is that God is not in the class of things that are *either* powerful *or* weak in the normal sense of the term. God does not lack power, but neither is God's power comparable with other things. Maimonides makes this point by referring to a wall that does not see (*GP* 1.58, p. 136), the point being that the wall neither sees nor lacks the attribute of sight because it is in a different category altogether.

In sum God is neither deficient as we normally understand it nor excellent as we normally understand it. God neither lacks the ability to move a book off a shelf nor possesses it in a conventional way; rather God's power is infinite and of a completely different sort. The advantage of negation is that rather than subsume God under a concept and ascribe an essence to God, it indicates that God is outside any of the concepts to which we have access. Still Maimonides argues that even negative predicates are suspect because they introduce some degree of specification: God is the thing about which neither power nor deficiency apply. What then?

Maimonides' answer (*GP* 1.58, pp. 135) is that the purpose of negative predicates is not to provide literal truth but to "conduct the mind toward that which must be believed with regard to Him."[9] I take this to mean that even they are not a true representation of divine simplicity because it is incapable of being represented. Rather, negative predicates are a device for getting us to the point where we realize that all linguistic formulations contain a measure of distortion.[10] In the end, Maimonides argues (*GP* 1.59, p. 139) that the only legitimate response to God is silence. For God and God alone, silence is praise.

Unfortunately Maimonides' remarks about silence are often misunderstood. How can you do philosophy if you cannot say anything? The way to understand Maimonides is to think of his philosophy as a hierarchy of approaches to God. We begin with the Torah and the prayer book with their many descriptions of God as gracious, merciful, slow to anger, and so forth. The first step is to avoid the temptation to think of God as a man sitting on a throne. We see that these attributes refer to features of the world God has created rather than to aspects of God himself. The next step is to see that metaphysical attributes like power, intelligence, and existence cannot mean the same thing when applied to God and us and rather than to affirmations. The final step is to see that even negations introduce problems so that, in the end, even the most rigorous discourse falls short of its subject.

These transitions cannot be completed overnight. According to Maimonides, it may take years of study to understand that the terms of a science like physics or astronomy do not apply to God and have to be negated. Silence then should be taken in the sense of learned ignorance rather than inarticulateness. To be silent is to recognize that (*GP* I.59, p. 139) "None but He himself can apprehend what He is."

It is often said that, although Maimonides praises silence, this can hardly be the end of the matter. What about his proof for the existence of God? What about the claim that God exists, that God is one and simple, or that God is all powerful? Do these not give us the foundation of a traditional metaphysics? The answer is that they do and in that respect are essential parts of human understanding. To deny God's existence in the way that we deny the existence of unicorns is folly. Better to view God as one and simple than to pile on attributes as if they were merit badges. Better to see that God's power cannot be measured in foot-pounds than to compare it to the engine in a car.

Yet helpful as these claims are, they too are limited. To say that something is an important part of our attempt to grasp divinity is not to say that its truth is unassailable. As Maimonides points out in the Introduction, statements instructive at one level of understanding may not be instructive at another. There is much to be gained by denying that God's power, existence, or intelligence are not comparable with ours. Although these denials may be the last step one takes before arriving at silent contemplation, Maimonides' point is that they cannot take the place of that contemplation. To use Wittgenstein's analogy, they are like a ladder we use to climb a building; once we get to the top, we realize they are fallible and are in a position to throw them away. It is in that sense that metaphysics points to its own transcendence.

We saw that, according to Aristotle, first philosophy is a discursive science that expresses itself in a body of propositions culminating in knowledge of God.[11] At *Metaphysics* 12.7, he claims that God thinks, exists in actuality, is unmoved, lives, enjoys eternal and continuous duration, and is completely good. For Aristotle God sits at the top of a metaphysical hierarchy as the substance par excellence. At no point does he suggest that multiple attributes pose a problem or that the essence of God is unknowable. On the contrary, God's essence is supremely knowable: to think.

For Maimonides the picture is more complicated. If substance implies form, essence, and definition, then God is not a substance. In this context the highest achievement is not mastery of a demonstrative science of God but the recognition that the human effort to know God is destined to fail. It follows that "closeness" to God is not a matter of bridging the gap between heaven and earth but of coming to grips with the fact that the gap is infinite and will never be bridged. Accordingly (*GP* 1.59, p. 137),

> Glory then to Him who is such that when the intellects contemplate His essence, their apprehension turns into incapacity; and when they contemplate the proceeding of His actions from His will, their knowledge turns into ignorance; and when the tongues aspire to magnify Him by means of attributive qualifications, all eloquence turns into weariness and incapacity!

Rather than occupy a position at the top of a hierarchy, Maimonides' God is separate from the world and totally unlike it. One way of accounting for such radical separation is to say that God is the *creator* and everything else is part of crea*tion*. Throughout the *Guide*, Maimonides claims that belief in creation is a pillar of the Law second in importance only to belief in the unity of God.[12] It is to the subject of creation that we now turn.

3.3. CREATION: THE THREE ALTERNATIVES

Maimonides never doubts that the world depends on God; the question is how. At *Guide* 2.13, he suggests three ways. The first he attributes to Moses and all those who believe in the Law. God created the world out of nothing in a free and spontaneous act that constituted the first moment in history. For the sake of brevity, I refer to this as creation *ex nihilo* [*min al-ʿadam*] and creation *de novo* [*ḥudūth*]. Unfortunately both are subject to misinterpretation. The claim that something cannot come from nothing [*ex nihilo nihil fit*] derives from Parmenides. But creation *ex nihilo* does not assert that nothing becomes something; rather it asserts that God's act of creation does not require a material cause. Put otherwise, God alone is a sufficient cause for the existence of everything including the material component of the world. By the same token, creation *de novo* does not mean that God exists in time and picks a particular moment at which to start creating. For Maimonides, as for most medievals, time is the measure of motion and cannot exist without it. Because there is no motion before creation, there cannot be any time before creation either. The claim of creation *de novo* is that time and motion came to be together so that, before the first moment, the question "What was God doing?" makes no sense.

The second way is attributed to Plato. The world was created *de novo* but not *ex nihilo*. In other words, God brought the world into existence in the way a potter shapes clay: by imposing form on preexistent matter. According to this view the world is a like a material object: Because it is subject to generation, it must also be subject to destruction. Maimonides takes this to mean that eventually the order and structure of the world will disintegrate so that all that is left will be the matter from which the world emerged.

The third way is attributed to Aristotle and says that creation is neither *ex nihilo* nor *de novo*. What we call creation is really eternal emanation. The crux of the Aristotelian position is that divine causality is not the result of something God does but of what God is. It is in the nature of a perfect being not to remain unto itself but to produce offspring or effects.[13] These effects flow from God in a manner that is both continuous and necessary. God cannot start or stop the process nor exercise control over it by producing at one time something different from what is produced at another.[14] The most immediate consequence of this view is that the world has always existed and will always exist in the form in which it is now.

From a historical standpoint, Maimonides' reading of Moses, Plato, and Aristotle is open to question. Although the first sentence of Genesis is often translated "In the beginning, God created the heavens and the earth," this reading has long been disputed.[15] An alternative reading proposed by Rashi renders it thus: "In the beginning of God's creation of the heavens and the earth, the earth was unformed and void, darkness was on the face of the deep, and the spirit of God hovered over the face of the waters." On one reading the verse describes a radical act that constitutes the first instant of time, on the other it describes an early act (not necessarily the first) in which God shapes the world from a preexistent and formless matter. As Maimonides indicates (*GP* 2.26 and 30), rabbinic commentary reached no definitive conclusion on how it was to be interpreted. Some rabbis sided with Plato; some even sided with Aristotle. So the claim that Genesis is committed to a creation that is *de novo* and *ex nihilo* is reasonable but by no means compelling.

Although Plato talks about a Demiurge or creating force, it is not clear that he believed in creation in the biblical sense. Even in antiquity, many of his followers argued that the creation story in the *Timaeus* is a teaching device used to clarify eternal relationships, much as a mathematician constructs a figure on a blackboard to clarify the properties of a triangle.[16] Not only is there no evidence Plato thought the heavens would perish, there is clear evidence he thought they would not.[17] As for Aristotle, there is no evidence that he believed in emanation. The position Maimonides ascribes to him is a version of the Aristotelianism worked out by Alfarabi and Avicenna, in effect a synthesis of Aristotle and Plotinus. As Maimonides points out, it is not just the view of Aristotle but of his followers and commentators as well.

Historical considerations aside, the three views of creation form a neat pattern: creation *de novo* and *ex nihilo*, creation *de novo* but not *ex nihilo*, eternal emanation that is neither *de novo* nor *ex nihilo*. For reasons that will become clear, Maimonides spends most of his time discussing the Aristotelian view but finds he cannot offer decisive objections against it. Having restricted knowledge of God as severely as he does, he cannot claim certainty about how God is responsible for the world. By his own admission (*GP* 2.17, p. 294), all one can do is tip the balance in favor of Moses. Although some take this as an honest statement of his predicament, others take it as a sign that he does not accept the Mosaic position and secretly favors Aristotle.[18] Again I argue that, although he respects Aristotle, he raises questions about the application of Aristotelian categories beyond the realm of normal experience. If these categories break down, Aristotle's arguments for eternity cannot be trusted.

3.4. THE POSSIBILITY OF CREATION

The arguments for eternity can be divided into two groups: those that proceed from the nature of the world and those that proceed from the nature of God. The first group seeks to show that the idea of a first motion is absurd. According to Aristotle, motion involves the actualization of what is potential. For something to move from potency to act, there must be an agent responsible for the transition. For wood to actualize its potential to burn, there must be something already burning that serves to ignite it. Because the agent responsible for taking something from potency to act must itself be actual, there would have to be motion before the first motion. Therefore the idea of a first motion is absurd. Aristotle holds a similar view in regard to the generation of substances. When a plant or animal is generated, there is a seed whose potential to grow is actualized by something else. It follows that if the world were generated in a similar way, there would have to be a substratum from which the act of generation proceeds. If this is true, creation *ex nihilo* is impossible.

Now consider God. If God created the world after a period of inactivity, two things would be true: (1) Before creation God's activity was merely potential, and (2) at the moment of creation, something superior to God would be needed to instigate the transition from potency the act. Both suggestions are incompatible with the idea of a perfect being because to be perfect means to be fully actual. So it is absurd to suppose that a perfect being can do at one moment something it did not do at another such as bring the world into existence. Therefore, if God is eternal, the world must be eternal as well.

Although none of these arguments is foolish, they all make a crucial assumption: Categories that apply to natural processes also apply to creation. The reason for this assumption is clear. As Norbert Samuelson points out, for someone who is neither a prophet nor heir to a prophetic tradition, the only place to start is with premises derived from experience.[19] If the application of these premises is valid, creation as Maimonides understands it is absurd. If, however, one is heir to a prophetic tradition, their application begs an important question: Why should we think we can understand the origin of a thing by examining its present state and extrapolating backward?

Against this assumption Maimonides asks us to consider a male child taken from its mother at birth and raised by other men on an island. If the child reached maturity and examined his body, there would be no inference by which he could deduce the facts of reproduction or gestation. Told that he spent the first nine months of his life upside down in the body of another human being, he might well respond with disbelief because nothing in his experience would have prepared him for this possibility. Thus extrapolation from the present will not work. If we are going to take the question of origin seriously, we have to recognize that the moment of origin may not be like the other moments in a thing's history. To enter the world is one thing, to pass from one stage of development to the next another.

To return to the arguments for eternity, it may be true that a material substratum is needed to explain a natural process like the production of one existing thing from another. But it does not follow that one is needed to explain how things came to exist in the first place. In one case we have change, in the other creation. Maimonides' argument is that we have to keep them separate. Thus no argument derived from the growth of plants or animals can be used to overturn creation *ex nihilo* without begging the question. In fact when Maimonides takes up logical possibility and impossibility at *Guide* 3.15, he says quite clearly that the bringing into being of a corporeal thing out of no matter is not impossible, assuming that the agent in question is God. It follows that, if God created the world *ex nihilo*, creation is a unique event with no parallel in human experience.

Maimonides employs a similar strategy with respect to God. A finite agent who is inactive over a period of time and suddenly desires to obtain an external object like a drink of water moves from potency to act. For this agent, to will one thing now and a different thing later is evidence of imperfection. But there is no reason to suppose that this analysis applies to God's decision to create the world. According to Maimonides, it is possible for a being separate from matter to will one thing now and a different thing later without undergoing change. How can this be? Although Maimonides is not as explicit as we might like, it appears that at *Guide* 2.18 he invokes what is sometimes referred to as the Principle of Delayed Effect. According to that principle, an agent can will now something that will not happen until later.

Suppose a person has a child. She may will one thing for the child when it is 5 years old, another when it is 15, and another still when it is 25. Although it may be true that the parent wills something different at each point, it is not necessarily true that her plans have been altered because she may have willed the whole sequence of events simultaneously. Aquinas, who was greatly influenced by Maimonides, makes this point by distinguishing between willing change and changing one's will.[20] The parent wills change for her child at the moment of its birth because what is appropriate at one stage of development is not appropriate at another. This is altogether different from someone who becomes thirsty and suddenly reaches for a drink of water. In one case we have a consistent plan that involves no change in attitude on the part of the agent; in the other a change in attitude brought on by a change in material circumstances.

Applying this distinction to God, we can say that God could will to create the world at one point, reveal something to it at another, and redeem it at a third. This does not mean that God undergoes a series of changes requiring the transition from potency to act. That would be true only if God were affected by external forces like incentives or impediments. The only thing affecting God's will is the will itself. In this way God's will is constant even though the object willed is temporal. Given Maimonides' negative theology, he cannot claim to know that God has a will; all he can claim is possibility. Once the possibility is granted, however, the argument for eternity based on the nature of God falls apart.

To soften the blow of his criticism, Maimonides claims (*GP* 2.15) that Aristotle himself did not think his arguments for eternity were decisive. Although I am inclined to believe he is wrong about this, either way he has revealed a number of weaknesses in the Aristotelian position. If God's will does not change in the way the will of a finite creature does, the picture of God as idle and then springing into activity is misconceived. Instead we have a God whose will is free but eternal, a God who chooses a plan for the world that may take all of history to work itself out. Although the unfolding of that plan makes it seem as if God wills things serially, in truth everything was willed at the moment of creation.[21]

3.5. THE LIKELIHOOD OF CREATION

In addition to arguments for the possibility of creation, Maimonides offers several arguments for why creation is more likely than eternity. These arguments can be difficult for modern readers to appreciate because they involve aspects of medieval astronomy that are no longer accepted. According to Aristotle anything that is eternal is necessary.[22] The idea behind this claim is that if something has existed for all time, there must be a reason why it has to exist. Because experience confirms that the heavenly bodies neither come to be nor pass away, Aristotle's view implied that their order and motion is set in the nature of things and cannot be otherwise. If they cannot be otherwise, their existence is not the result of free choice but a causal process. By contrast, if there is no law that explains their order and motion, it would follow that they are not set in the nature of things and alternatives are available. Once there are alternatives, the way is open to claim that God chose one over others.

Because Maimonides' philosophy of science is covered in another chapter, let me simply say that, from his perspective, science cannot provide a credible explanation for why one planet moves this way and another that, why they move at different speeds, and why bodies relatively close to the earth move faster than those further off. The failure to come up with a suitable explanation and, in his opinion, the unlikely prospect of finding one, suggest that the order and motion of the heavenly bodies are contingent, so that (*GP* 3.13, p. 452), "What exists, its causes, and its effects, could be different from what they are." To the objection that someone may come up with a new astronomical theory showing that the order and motion of the heavenly bodies can be explained by causal laws, Maimonides replies (*GP* 2.25, p. 327) that such a development is possible but that no satisfactory theory is known to him, and, until one comes along, he has no choice but to favor creation.

In assessing this remark, we should keep in mind that Maimonides is not talking about a scientific revolution like that of Copernicus, Galileo, or Newton. Conceptual upheavals of this magnitude were unknown in the Middle Ages. His question is whether someone will be able to explain heavenly motion assuming constant circular motion around a fixed point. The problem is that when it comes to heavenly bodies, all we have are inferences drawn from our vantage point on earth. That is why Maimonides is skeptical that a better explanation will be found. Citing Psalm 115:16 ("The heavens are the heavens of the Lord"), he argues that the heavens are too far away for us to know their true nature and that when it comes to the details of their motion, what little knowledge we have is all we are likely to get.[23] This does not mean that we have no knowledge at all but that we do not have enough to make the claim of necessity plausible.

Although history proved Maimonides wrong about astronomy, given the information at his disposal, the lesson he drew is essentially right: Aristotle's philosophy works well for the phenomena it was designed to explain – the generation and destruction of things in the earthly realm. When it comes to heavenly phenomena, which belong to a different order of existence, Maimonides thought that most of what was available to him amounted to conjecture rather than to genuine science.[24]

It is not just the motion of the heavenly bodies that raises questions but their separate identities as well. According to the standard account, the heavens consist of ten pure intelligences, nine transparent spheres, the bodies situated in them (i.e., the bodies we see emitting light), and a large number of secondary spheres needed to explain the orbits of the planets, sun, and moon. Every intelligence possesses a different form, whereas the spheres and their respective bodies are composites of form and matter. If God is one and simple, Maimonides argues, anything that proceeds from God by necessity should be one and simple as well.[25] How then can we account for the generation and interaction of so many different things?

Avicenna's answer was that God's self-conscious reflection produced the first intelligence. The first intelligence is aware of its source, whose existence is necessary, itself as a being necessitated by its source, and itself as a possible being. From the first thought we get the second intelligence, from the second thought the form of a sphere, from the third the matter of the sphere. The process continues until all intelligences and spheres are accounted for. By the time we get to the tenth intelligence, the degree of perfection is so slight that no further intelligences or spheres are generated. Instead it rules over the earthly realm. In this way, God is directly responsible for the existence of only one thing.

Unfortunately there are still problems. How can an intellectual being like a heavenly intelligence produce something made of matter? Even if it could, the intelligences would have to produce both the form and matter of a sphere and the form and matter of the body within it. How can one intelligence produce so many different things? Why do spheres consisting of the same kind of matter rotate in different directions? Why are some parts of heaven crowded with stars while other parts are relatively sparse? Although there were attempts to answer these questions, Maimonides' argument is that the answers are speculative and will never achieve the certainty of natural science, in which demonstration and direct observation are possible.

As he admits, these arguments are versions of the particularity argument of the *mutakallimūn*.[26] That argument asks why, of equally possible alternatives, things are one way rather than another. If no convincing reason can be found, it concludes that there must be an agent who chose one alternative over the other. The problem is that the *mutakallimūn* extend this argument to include all of nature, rejecting natural causation of any kind in favor of God's will.[27] One such argument asks why the sun is a sphere rather than a cube, another asks why an elephant is larger than a flea. In both cases, the *mutakallimūn* conclude that, in the absence of a natural explanation, the only response is to say that God wanted it that way.

Between a world governed by necessity and a world governed by will alone, Maimonides tries to steer a middle course. There are causes that operate in nature in just the way Aristotle thought, but we should not be so bold as to think we can move from knowledge of them to knowledge of God and the origin of the world. The least Maimonides has shown is that no argument compels us to accept eternity; the most is that the biblical conception of God is preferable to a God who is incapable of starting or stopping anything. At bottom the world does not present itself to us as the effect of an eternal process that can only produce one result but as the object of a free and benevolent will. Thus the world is contingent in the sense that God could have created a different world or no world at all.

As I mentioned earlier, most of Maimonides' discussion of creation is directed to Aristotle. In regard to Plato, he says (*GP* 2.13, pp. 243–84) that, although he does not accept this theory, it is permissible for someone to hold it because it does not destroy the foundation of the Law. I take this to mean that because it accepts creation *de novo*, the Platonic theory upholds free choice in God. He even admits that many obscure texts in the Torah and elsewhere can be interpreted in light of it.[28] Still, the Platonic theory is committed to preexistent matter. As we saw, Maimonides argues that the need for a material cause holds only if the creation of the world is a natural process resembling the generation of individual things within it, an assumption that is unproven and open to doubt.

We are left with the conclusion that if the Mosaic view raises doubts, the alternatives raise greater doubts. To someone who insists on certainty, this is a disquieting result because it says that all we can have is a strong presumption that the world was created. Recall that belief in creation is a pillar of the Law second in importance only to belief in the unity of God. Although we might have expected Maimonides to claim that both of these beliefs can be known with certainty, intellectual honesty prevents him from doing so. Again we face the limits of human knowledge. Because creation is a unique event in the history of the world, anyone who claims to know exactly how God is responsible for the world is fooling himself.

Unlike Aquinas, Maimonides does not ask his reader to accept creation *de novo* on faith if that means a mode of awareness that supercedes rational thought.[29] Although belief in creation has prophetic authority behind it, we have seen that prophetic authority does not speak with a single voice. Maimonides therefore admits (*GP* 2.25, p. 327) that if someone could demonstrate the eternity of the world, he would accept it and interpret Scripture accordingly. The fact is, however, that there is no demonstration and, in his opinion, little prospect of finding one. In the end, we are in the position Job was in when he heard the voice from the whirlwind. Reflecting on this passage, Maimonides writes (*GP* 3.23, p. 496)

> Our intellects do not reach the point of apprehending how these natural things that exist in the world of generation and corruption are produced in time and of conceiving how the existence of the natural force within has originated them. They are not things that resemble what we make.

If this is true of things in the world of generation and corruption, it is all the more true of things in the heavens.

3.6. CONCLUSION

Maimonides' attitude to metaphysics is both respectful and critical. Its chief virtue is that it allows us to get beyond the imagination, which can conceive of things only as embodied, and in Maimonides' opinion is the root of idolatry. It is metaphysics that allows us to see that God is one and simple, that God is neither a body nor a force in a body, that God cannot be conceived under a description. Without metaphysics, monotheism as Maimonides understands it would be impossible. Beyond that, metaphysics relieves us of the conceit of thinking that the world reflects our interests and was created for our benefit. Note, however, that most of these functions are negative: The knowledge we gain frees us from an anthropocentric view of the world and teaches us what God is not. Although all this is important, metaphysics is more heuristic than demonstrative, pointing rather than proving. Although Maimonides' book is called *Guide of the Perplexed*, we have seen that it neither resolves every perplexity nor claims to.

Where does that leave us? The answer is it leaves us with a profound sense of humility. In the *Mishneh Torah*, Maimonides offers a brief description of what happens to a person who has pursued physics and metaphysics as far as they go and seen that something lies beyond[30]:

> When a man reflects on these things, studies all these created beings, from the angels and spheres down to human beings and so on, and realizes the divine wisdom manifested in them all, his love for God will increase, his soul will thirst, his very flesh will yearn to love God. He will be filled with fear and trembling, as he becomes conscious of his lowly condition, poverty, and insignificance, and compares himself with any of the great and holy bodies; still more when he compares himself with any one of the pure forms that are incorporeal and have never had association with any corporeal substance. He will then realize that he is a vessel full of shame, dishonor, and reproach, empty and deficient.

Does all this talk of silence, negation, and emptiness imply that our idea of God has no content?

The answer is yes if that means that God has no content that we can describe. As we saw God is not susceptible to definition. But the answer is no if it means that we can understand the rest of the world without God. To see this, let us follow Maimonides and a long tradition of religious thinkers by comparing God to the sun. The sun is hidden from us not because it emits no light but because it emits so much that, when we try to look at it, we are dazzled by its intensity. By the same token, God is unknowable not because the divine essence has no content but because it contains so much that we cannot comprehend it.

To continue with this metaphor, we can see reflections of the sun in pools of water and infer from that we owe our existence to the its heat and light. Similarly, we can observe what God has made and infer that God is responsible for everything that is. But we cannot search for a definition of God and hope to succeed.[31] This makes God inaccessible not because God is cold and aloof but because the difference between God and us is too great for us to fathom.

Since the work of Leo Strauss, many people view the *Guide* as a tug of war between the philosophic tradition and the prophetic. If the approach taken in this essay is right, the strength of Maimonides' philosophy is that it shows how both traditions correct and compliment each other. Note, for example, that the sources on which he draws are varied and range from logic to metaphysics to natural science to biblical commentary. He is just as willing to point out the shortcomings of Aristotelian philosophy as to call attention to the ambiguities in the sacred literature of Judaism. Although each tradition can assist the other, neither is in a position to undermine the other. In the last analysis, neither can do more than point the mind toward God and hope that it will recognize its fallibility in the face of something vastly greater. By directing our minds to a reality beyond the physical, metaphysics enables us to understand how vast.

NOTES

1. *GP* 3.51, pp. 618–28.
2. *Ḥagigah* 11b, 13a.
3. For the history of esoteric interpretation, see the essay by Aviezer Ravitzky in this volume as well as Strauss 1952, pp. 38–94.
4. For a classic defense of this view, see Pines 1963.
5. For an example of this view, see Fox 1990.
6. For an example of this view, see Pines 1979. Pines' interpretation has been challenged by Davidson 1992–3. For a more recent defense of the skeptical interpretation, see Stern in press.
7. For Maimonides' account of this strategy, see *GP* 1.71, pp. 181–2.
8. Aristotle, *Categories* 7.3.
9. Cf. *GP* 1.57, p. 133: "For this reason, we give the gist of the notion and give the mind the correct direction toward the true reality of the matter when we say, one but not through oneness."
10. The only exception Maimonides allows is the *Tetragrammaton*: YHVH. But this is a name that is not supposed to be pronounced. For Maimonides' discussion of it, see *GP* 1.61.

11. See Aristotle, *Metaphysics* 1026a19–23, 1064b1–6.
12. In addition to *GP* 2.25, see 2.13, p. 282; 2.27, p. 332; 3.29, p. 516; 3.50 p. 613.
13. For the origin of this principle, see Plato, *Timaeus* 29e–30a.
14. It is true that Maimonides characterizes the Aristotelian position by saying, "All that exists has been brought into existence, in the state in which it is at present, by God through His volition." It may well be that he has in mind Avicenna, who believed that God has a will but that it is eternal and cannot undergo change. Thus Maimonides concludes his presentation of the Aristotelian position by saying that it offers us a deity in whom "it is impossible that a volition should undergo a change . . . or a new volition arise." Because Maimonides rejects the idea of a will that cannot change at *GP* 2.18 and criticizes Aristotle's followers for altering the plain sense of *necessary* at 2.21, it would be best to say, with Davidson 1987b, p. 2, n. 3, that, in Maimonides' opinion, the Aristotelians use *will* in a Pickwickian sense.
15. The problem is that it is difficult to know what the word (*be-reshit*) is modifying. According to Maimonides (*GP* 2.30, pp. 349–50; 3.10, p. 438), it implies creation out of nothing and should be understood in a way that is compatible with creation *de novo*. Unfortunately his usual word for nothing (*ʿadam*) is ambiguous and can mean either radical nothingness or privation, the primary instance of which is matter. At 2.13, he says that the Mosaic position holds that the world was created from "pure and absolute nothingness," but by 2.30 and 3.10, this qualification drops out. Is the difference significant or simply a case in which, having explained his meaning once, he does not feel the need to explain it again? I opt for the latter. For further discussion and a different viewpoint, see Klein-Braslavy 1986a as well as Samuelson 1991.
16. See Cornford 1966, pp. 23–9.
17. See *Timaeus* 38c, 41a–b.
18. Recent proponents of this view include Shlomo Pines 1963, pp. cxxvii–cxxxi, and W. Z. Harvey 1981a. Defenders of a Platonic interpretation include Davidson 1979, Ivry 1986a, and Samuelson 1991. Finally Klein-Braslavy 1986a argues that Maimonides ends up with a skeptical *epoche*. People with views closer to my own include Wolfson 1973, pp. 207–21, Hyman 1988, and Fox 1990, pp. 251–96.
19. Samuelson 1991, p. 255.
20. Aquinas, *Summa Theologica* 1.46.1.
21. This conclusion sheds additional light on Maimonides' view of miracles as expressed in *EC* (8) and *GP* 2.29, pp. 344–5: Miracles are not last-minute attempts to remedy a desperate situation but extraordinary events that were provided for during creation.

22. *On Generation and Corruption* 338a1–4, *Physics* 203b 29, *Metaphysics* 1050b8–15.
23. For more on Maimonides' skepticism about astronomy, see Kellner 1991b, 1993c, and Stern in press.
24. According to *GP* 2.11, p. 273, one thing that has been demonstrated is that the movement of the sun is inclined to the equator. For the lack of certainty in astronomy, also see *GP* 2.24. For Aristotle's own reservations about astronomy, see *De caelo* 286a4–7, 287b31–288a2, 291b25–8, 292a14–18; *Metaphysics* 1074a14–16.
25. *GP* 2.22, p. 317. For the history of this principle, see Plotinus *Enneads* 5.1.6 and 5.3.15. For further discussion, see Hyman 1992.
26. *GP* 1.74, pp. 218–19; 2.19, p. 303.
27. See *GP* 1.73, p. 202: "They assert that that when a man moves a pen, it is not the man who moves it; for the motion occurring in the pen is an accident created by God in the pen."
28. *GP* 2.25, p. 329; 2.26, pp. 330–1.
29. Aquinas, *Summa Theologica* 1.46.2. The closest Maimonides comes to Aquinas is *GP* 2.17, p. 294. I take this as a preliminary statement that is refined and extended by the chapters that follow.
30. *MT* 1, Principles of the Torah, 4.12.
31. Cf. Aquinas, *Summa Theologica* 1.12.1: "Since everything is knowable according as it is actual, God, Who is pure act without any admixture of potentiality, is in Himself supremely knowable. But what is supremely knowable in itself may not be knowable to a particular intellect, because of the excess of the intelligible object above the intellect; as, for example, the sun, which is supremely visible, cannot be seen by a bat by reason of its excess of light."

JOSEF STERN

4 Maimonides' Epistemology

There is nothing Maimonides values more than knowledge, especially knowledge of metaphysics or, in medieval terminology, "divine science." The *Mishneh Torah* opens with the basic metaphysical and scientific truths everyone is obligated to know and ends with a depiction of the messianic age as an era in which the whole world is engaged exclusively in the pursuit of knowledge. The *Guide of the Perplexed* opens and closes with two parables that depict the "true human perfection," not as the moral or ritual life but as "the acquisition of the rational virtues... true opinions concerning the divine things" (*GP* 3.54, p. 635). And throughout the *Guide*, Maimonides reconstructs traditional religious concepts in epistemic terms: To love God is to know Him (*GP* 3.51, p. 621), and the worst form of idolatry is a cognitive error, "believing [God] to be different from what He really is" (*GP* 1.36, p. 84).

Yet Maimonides' philosophical corpus contains no systematic discussion of the concept of knowledge. One reason may be, as Maimonides says about the plan of the *Guide*, that his "purpose... was not to compose something on natural science, or to make an epitome of divine science," that is, to explain sublunar physics, cosmology, or metaphysics. Writing within the context of Arabic Aristotelianism, Maimonides could take many theoretical notions for granted. Even where he must engage in its explication, he says his aim is never the idea itself but to give a "key to the understanding" of a parable or "secret" in the books of prophecy (*GP* 2.2, p. 254). To piece together a picture of Maimonides' epistemology, one must therefore look to his accounts of divine attributes, prophecy, divine providence, and cosmology. Maimonides' comment also hints at a second possible reason: *Because* these topics are bound up with "secrets," he provides no explicit discussion of them. But in the case of knowledge, what could that secret be?

Although almost everyone acknowledges that Maimonides takes the ideal of human perfection to consist in knowledge including cosmology and metaphysics, the most contested arena in recent scholarship has centered on the question of whether he also believed in limitations on human intellectual capacity that preclude the same knowledge, making the ideal all but unrealizable. Although this chapter is not the place to settle the dispute, I set forth both sides of the argument because the issues take us to the core of his epistemology. In Section 4.1 I lay out the rudiments of Maimonides' general theory of the intellect, in Section 4.2 the controversy over metaphysical knowledge, and in Section 4.3 its implications.

Before I turn to the theory of intellect, some introductory words about the term "knowledge" will be helpful. In Greek and Arabic the term most often used for knowledge (*epistēmē* in Greek, *ʿilm* in Arabic) can refer to the cognitive state of an individual or to a body of systematically organized truths about a particular domain – a science.[1] Most of Maimonides' examples of knowledge that refer to a cognitive state focus on the apprehension of essential forms or what he calls intelligibles. But he also tells us that the individual's ultimate perfection consists of "opinions toward which speculation has led and that investigation has rendered compulsory" (*GP* 3.27, p. 511), that is, what Aristotle calls *epistēmē* or scientific knowledge. Analogously, the question of whether it is possible for humans to have knowledge of metaphysics can be understood as either the question of whether an individual can apprehend the essences of immaterial beings (such as God or the separate intellects) or whether it is possible to produce a metaphysics that meets the standards of an Aristotelian science. Most of the *Guide* deals with the second question. In some chapters, Maimonides presents demonstrations of, say, the existence of God (*GP* 2.1–2); in others he attacks the claims of Aristotelian celestial physics (*GP* 2.19–24). However, he then draws conclusions from the evidence of the possibility or impossibility (as the case may be) of a science of metaphysics that addresses the first question of whether the human has the capacity to achieve the cognitive state.

4.1. THE THEORY OF THE INTELLECT

Maimonides' idea of intellect is the product of considerations drawn both from his psychology, his account of the soul, and his cosmology and metaphysics, his account of the heavens and their immaterial causes. Both stories ultimately derive from Aristotle, although they reached Maimonides only after being filtered through centuries of Hellenistic and Arabic commentators who presented rich, detailed theories.[2] In contrast, Maimonides presents only a brief overview of these ideas in *Eight Chapters* (*EC*) and in scattered remarks in the *Guide*. He assumes his reader is familiar with the Aristotelian repertoire of "intellects" and generally ignores differences among Aristotle and his commentators. In this section I situate Maimonides' sketchy and at times not totally consistent remarks in their broader philosophical contexts. I begin with his psychology, the range of powers that enable living things to engage in their characteristic activities, nutrition (for plants), perception (for animals), and thought (for humans).

Like Aristotle and most of his Arabic Aristotelian counterparts, Maimonides takes the soul to be the form of a body possessing life, without which the body would have only the potential for life. Unlike Plato, who took the soul to be a separate substance from the body, Maimonides takes it to be something inseparable from body in the way that form is inseparable from matter (*GP* 1.72, p. 192).[3] Although each soul of an individual possesses multiple powers, it is indivisible and specific to its species. From this Maimonides concludes that, say, human powers and actions are entirely different from those of other species so that even our words for those powers, for example, "appetitive," are completely equivocal (*EC* 1). Although it is not clear that it is valid, this reasoning is typical of his strategy to transform metaphysical distinctions into semantic ones.

Among the powers of the human soul, two are of special significance: the imaginative and the rational. The imagination is a power both to store "the impressions of sensibly perceived objects" when they are not currently perceived and to combine and separate these impressions into representations of things never perceived (*GP* 2.36, p. 370). This power has an ambiguous status. On the one hand, its images provide the input to intellectual processes and the imaginative faculty is also crucial for the activity of the prophet who, using it, translates abstract philosophical truths into figurative representations that can be grasped by the community-at-large and laws on which the community can act (*GP* 2.36. p. 369ff.). On the other hand, Maimonides is suspicious of the interference of the imagination with reason. Its representations are always of composite particular things, never of the universals, essential or accidental, of which demonstrations are composed. Worse, its powers to combine and separate images are unconstrained by reality, so that what the imagination finds admissible or inadmissible conflicts with what the intellect determines to be possible and necessary. Finally, as a bodily faculty that cannot avoid representing things as bodies, the imagination misrepresents immaterial things like God (*GP* 1.73, pp. 206–12; 1.52, p. 114). For these reasons, Maimonides attacks the *kalām* for its reliance on the imagination and discovers the source of widespread error in the failure to distinguish the imagination from the intellect (*GP* 1.73, p. 209; 2.12, p. 280; 3.15, p. 460).

Under reason, Maimonides includes both theoretical and practical powers by which one "perceives intelligibles, deliberates, acquires the sciences, and distinguishes between base and noble actions" (*EC* 1; see also *GP* 1.53, p. 121; 1.72, p. 191). Unlike most of his Arabic counterparts, Maimonides does not posit distinct intellects corresponding to these powers; in particular, he never explicitly refers to a practical intellect. Some think this is because Maimonides means to disassociate the practical from the intellect and to identify it with the appetites and imagination (as he suggests in *GP* 1.2). Others claim that the practical is a rational activity but, by omitting reference to a practical intellect, Maimonides underscores the unity of the intellect and the superiority of the theoretical.[4] Whatever the explanation, I am concerned with the theoretical power of the intellect whose stages of development Maimonides, following Aristotle, describes as different intellects corresponding to differences of potentiality and actuality.

Maimonides describes the initial stage of the rational faculty – which he also calls the "material," "hylic," or "potential" intellect – as "a faculty consisting in preparedness" (*GP* 1.70, p. 174): that is, a predisposition or capacity to apprehend intelligibles (See *GP* 1.72, p. 190; 1.68, p. 165; 1.72, p. 190; 2.4, p. 257).[5] In other words, the rational faculty is almost the pure potential to know. I say *almost* because Maimonides also holds that even this faculty, or potential intellect, possesses first intelligibles, for example, that the whole is greater than a part or that two things equal to a third are equal to each other (*Logic*, Chapter 8).

Given its nearly unlimited potential to think, such an intellect becomes actual by abstracting individual forms, universal intelligible characteristics, from sensible images.[6] Ultimately, by abstraction and apprehension of *all* intelligible forms, and by demonstration of truths composed of intelligibles, the potential intellect becomes the fully actualized intellect, or "intellect in actu." At its completely mature stage, the fully actualized intellect no longer needs the senses to abstract new forms; all its thinking is of forms that have already been acquired. Not only does it possess all forms in its repertoire, it is constantly engaged in apprehending them. At this stage, the Arabic Aristotelians introduce a term for yet a third intellect, the "acquired" intellect, although opinions vary over whether it is identical with the fully actual intellect or something yet higher. To work out this part of Maimonides' story, I turn now to the cosmological background.

To explain the eternal motion of heavenly bodies, Aristotle posited the existence of a first unmoved mover whom he characterizes as a divine intellect (*nous*) constantly thinking itself.[7] Because he initially assumed that the heavens are enclosed by one sphere, he also assumed that there is a unique prime mover. By the twelfth century, however, the received cosmology recognized a hierarchy of movers, or separate (i.e., immaterial) intellects, each the cause of the being and motion of one of ten spheres that was posited to account for the motions of planets. Each sphere, in turn, was thought to have its own embodied intellect by which it represents to itself the separate intellect associated with it. In addition to human intellects then there also exist these immaterial and spheric intellects. The main difference between them is that the human intellect changes, or undergoes motion.

Like all Aristotelian motion, that of the intellect is a matter of actualization of its potential and, for there to be motion, it must have an agent, or active cause. To play this role, Aristotle posited what came to be known as the active (or agent) intellect whose manner of functioning he compared to that of "light [that] makes potential colors into actual colors" (*De Anima* 3.430a10–15. However, in the Arabic Aristotelian tradition, following Alexander, the active intellect was taken to be a transcendent rather than imminent being, the lowest of the separate intellects, and was given two roles. As Maimonides puts it, its

> existence is indicated by the facts that our intellects pass from potentiality to actuality and that the forms of the existents that are subject to generation and corruption are actualized after they have been in their matter only in potentia. Now everything that passes from potentiality to actuality must have necessarily something that causes it to pass and that is outside it. And this cause must belong to the species of that which it causes to pass from potentiality to actuality. (*GP* 2.4, p. 257)

Here the active intellect has two functions: a cosmological one to explain why generated material substances have their actual forms and an epistemological one to explain how the human intellect actualizes its potential to apprehend intelligible concepts. Two competing models in Arabic Aristotelianism explained how the active intellect plays the epistemological role.

One model, defended by Alfarabi, is that the active intellect is or casts a kind of light (as in Aristotle's image) that simultaneously illuminates the material intellect and the sensible images stored in the imaginative faculty, thus enabling the intellect to discern and actualize intelligible characteristics found in sensible images. Here the active intellect functions as a general condition that enables the native human mind to abstract and apprehend universal features. By itself it donates no knowledge that the human intellect does not acquire on its own. On this model, the acquired intellect is simply the culmination of the fully actualized human intellect. To convey some weak sense of conjunction, Alfarabi sometimes describes the relations of both the acquired to actual intellect and of the active to potential intellect as form to matter.[8] In any case, although the acquired intellect directly apprehends the active intellect, even at this stage the latter does not seem to emanate any knowledge of forms that the human intellect has not already acquired on its own.

On the second model, whose main proponent is Avicenna, the human intellect can never abstract an intelligible form from sensible images by its own powers because intelligible forms must be truly universal, hence applicable to an infinite number of instances. But no finite human faculty can abstract an infinitely instantiable concept from the finite number of sensible images at its disposal. Instead it is the active intellect that, in addition to emanating the material intellect with its first principles, is "the giver of forms," the real source, the continuous donator of each intelligible form apprehended by the material intellect. At each moment when an intelligible form is apprehended by the material intellect, the material intellect conjoins with the active intellect that emanates that form. The function of abstraction is merely to predispose the material intellect to receive the intelligible form emanated by the active intellect. In addition, Avicenna recognizes an advanced state of conjunction when the human intellect has acquired all or most of the intelligible forms that constitute the active intellect and enters into its company. But he denies that even at this stage the acquired intellect unites with the active intellect or has it as a direct object of thought.[9]

Which of these two views is Maimonides'? Not surprisingly, different passages in the *Guide* can be adduced in support of either position.[10] In support of Alfarabi's claim that the active intellect is simply a condition for the actualization of the human intellect, consider Maimonides' illustration of abstraction by the example of someone who "has intellectually cognized this piece of wood to which one can point, has stripped its form from its matter, and has represented to himself the pure form" (*GP* 1.68, pp. 163–4). Elsewhere he elaborates on how the intellect operates in this process:

> The intellect divides the composite [things] and differentiates their parts and makes abstractions of them, represents them to itself in their true reality and with their causes, and apprehends from one thing very many notions. (*GP* 1.73, p. 209)

Three points should be kept in mind. First, the intellect is described as abstracting forms directly from sensible objects, but in fact it operates on composite, particular "sensible forms" stored in memory or imagination that the senses deliver to the mind. Second, its functioning is divided into three steps: (1) abstraction of the forms that can be differentiated in each composite particular sensible form, (2) representation of those forms with their causes, that is, by articulating how the forms should be understood, and (3) apprehension of the abstracted and represented forms.

The word translated in these passages as "representation" (and sometimes as "mental representation") is the Arabic term *taṣawwur*, which can also be translated as (either the act or object of) conception or conceptualization. Although there is considerable debate about its origin, *taṣawwur* refers in its basic case to the formation or grasp of simple concepts as wholes, typically essences. Its most distinctive feature arises from its contrast with *taṣdīq*, which refers to (either the act or object) of assenting to or judging something as true. Thus *taṣawwur* is any cognitive act that does not involve the actual assignment of a truth value. In contemporary terms, it is closer to what we think of as grasping a meaning or entertaining a proposition. I return to this notion in the next section, but it should be noted that such representation involves a further dimension beyond the passive reception by the intellect of the abstracted form.[11]

Third, and most important, despite their lack of detail, the descriptions of abstraction and apprehension in these passages are entirely in terms of the native powers of the human intellect, with no mention of an emanation from the active intellect. Maimonides' silence cannot be dismissed by saying that these passages are preliminary versions of the more complicated Avicennean picture because the claim that it is the native human intellect that is the generator of the apprehended form is required for the argument of 1.68. It is precisely because the abstraction and representation of the form of the piece of wood "is the action of the intellect," that is, the subject's human intellect, that the

> intellect in actu is nothing but that which has been intellectually cognized; and the thing by means of which the form of wood was intellectually cognized and made abstract, that thing being the intellectually cognizing subject, is also indubitably identical with the intellect realized in actu. (*GP* 1.68, p. 164)

If, as Avicenna claims, the acts of abstraction and representation are merely predispositions for the emanation of forms by the active intellect, and if the material intellect is a mere recipient of those forms, there would be a difference between the "intellectually cognizing subject" and its acts of abstraction and thinking, on the one hand, and the intellectually cognized object, the emanated form, on the other. This state is not the identity that results when the abstracted intelligible form *is* the action of the intellect.

Nonetheless this account cannot be the whole story. First, the forms apprehended in the passages in Chapters 1.68 and 73 are material intelligibles because they are abstracted from sensible images of composite material things. This raises the question of how one comes to apprehend immaterial forms like those of God or the separate intellects.[12] Furthermore, it is arguable that it is not only *im*material forms that the intellect cannot abstract and apprehend if all its concepts must be derived from sense impressions. In the example of 1.68 Maimonides says that the intellect "strips" its form from the particular piece of wood, implying that the form (conjoined with matter) already exists "in" the composite material object. Elsewhere he seems to contradict this:

> It is known that no species exists outside the mind, but that the species and the other universals are . . . mental notions and that every existent outside the mind is an individual or a group of individuals. (*GP* 3.18, p. 474)

If the form of the substance wood does not exist outside the mind, it cannot be perceived and abstracted.[13] Indeed it is not clear how we can ever abstract a substantial form like that of wood from sensible forms (like colors or textures) that are the proper objects of sense perception. Some scholars therefore propose that Aristotle introduces the active intellect precisely to account for the intellectual apprehension of such forms.[14]

For similar reasons, one might argue that when Maimonides introduces the active intellect, it is an Avicennean active intellect. Because the forms of composite material substances cannot be explained simply as a mixture of their constituent elements, Maimonides posits the active intellect as their external cause, which he designates by the Avicennean title "giver of forms" (*GP* 2.12, p. 278). In another passage, after explaining that it is the form in the mind of an artisan that causes an artifact to have a particular form and causes that form to be actualized in the artifact, Maimonides concludes, "the giver of a form is indubitably a separate form, and that which brings intellect into existence is an intellect, the active intellect" (*GP* 2.4, p. 258). What Maimonides is arguing here is that the active intellect is what brings the human actualized intellect into existence, but the only way it can do this is by emanating a form whose apprehension by the human intellect constitutes its actualization. This is again Avicenna's model of the active intellect that itself emanates forms. Finally, Maimonides concludes this passage by comparing the human actualized intellect to the embodied intellects of the spheres. Just as the latter derive their being by emanation from their respective separate intellects, so the human actualized intellect derives its being from an emanation of a form from the active intellect, "through which we apprehend the active intellect" (*GP* 2.4, p. 258; cf. 3.8, p. 432). Here, again, the active intellect is the source from which the being of the human intellect derives, not simply a condition for its existence.

In sum, Maimonides' theory of intellect needs something that works like an Avicennean active intellect, and a number of his descriptions fit that model.[15] It should be noted, however, that the passages in question fall in Maimonides' exposition of the "opinion of the later philosophers" about cosmology and about the separate intellects in Part II of the *Guide*. He does not explicitly disavow the views he presents in the philosophers' name but (as we will see in Section 4.2) he subjects their celestial physics and metaphysics to so much criticism that it is hard to think that he commits himself to their whole theory. Furthermore, by emphasizing the parallels between the active intellect and other separate intellects, Maimonides seems to imply that the two accounts hang or fall together. It remains an open question, then, of whether and to what degree Maimonides detaches the Avicennean conception of the active intellect from his critique of the theory of separate intellects as a whole.

A similar remark applies to Maimonides' stance toward the acquired intellect. He takes the ultimate perfection of a human being to consist in being a totally actualized intellect "knowing everything concerning all the beings that it is within the capacity of man to know in accordance with his ultimate perfection" (*GP* 3.27, p. 511). Only in one passage does he explicitly refer to the acquired intellect, which is "not a faculty in the body but is truly separate from the organic body and overflows toward it" (*GP* 1.72, p. 193; cf. *EC*, Chapter 2). But whether and how he distinguishes it from a fully actual intellect is not clear. By saying that it is "separate from the organic body" he may mean that as a fully actual intellect that has abstracted all the material forms there are to be apprehended, it no longer needs the bodily senses. However, Maimonides also seems to endow the acquired intellect with emanational powers of its own, suggesting that this state results from a conjunction or union with the active intellect. Thus he describes "the end of man *qua* man" as undisrupted "mental representation of the intelligibles" that culminates in "union [*ittiṣāl*] with the divine [i.e., active] intellect, which lets overflow toward them that *through which* that form exists" (*GP* 3.8, p. 432, my emphasis). Although he does not explicitly say so, this is a description of an acquired intellect, which includes apprehension of the active intellect characterized in Avicennean terms.

Nonetheless, although it may be the ideal, Maimonides also seems to question whether the state of the acquired intellect is attainable. At the end of the *Guide*, he describes the Patriarchs and Moses as if they were living acquired intellects, in a state of Avicennean "union of their intellects through apprehension of Him" (3.51, p. 623). But after depicting their state of apprehension, he adds, "[their] rank is not a rank that, with a view to the attainment of which, someone like myself may aspire for guidance" (*GP* 3.54, p. 624). That is, Maimonides first presents their state as a regulative ideal by which people should orient their lives. But then he states that no one like him – namely, any human being – may be able to realize that ideal. Unfortunately he gives no reason why this is so. In the next section, I suggest some possible reasons.

4.2. LIMITATIONS OF KNOWLEDGE

No topic in contemporary Maimonidean scholarship has elicited as much controversy as the the question of whether Maimonides believed in the possibility of human knowledge of metaphysics. The "traditional" interpretation of the *Guide* holds that he did believe in the possibility of metaphysical knowledge; what I call the "skeptical" interpretation challenges that assumption.[16] The controversy revolves around three poles. The first concerns sources for a skeptical interpretation in writings of Alfarabi and Ibn Bājja. Because this involves textual issues that go beyond the purview of this volume, I do not pursue them here. The second consists of individual passages in the *Guide* that have been adduced in support of one or the other of these positions. Because of Maimonides' ambiguous manner of writing, each of these lends itself to either interpretation. The moral is that, although these passages cannot be ignored, neither can they be read apart from sustained arguments that furnish a context.

The third pole consists of Maimonides' arguments for one position over the other. The skeptical interpreter's basic argument is that if all apprehension of forms must be abstracted from sensible images, there can be no apprehension of the forms of purely immaterial beings, such as the active intellect or God (or even the spheres of which we have no sensible experience [*GP* 1.58, pp. 136–7]).[17] Traditional interpreters counter that, although true, this argument is incomplete. Although we cannot directly apprehend the form of God or of another immaterial being, this does not preclude the possibility of metaphysical knowledge by inference.

Suppose one apprehends first principles and, by abstraction, acquires the forms of material things. From these intelligibles and certain logical notions (e.g. the derivation of a privation from an affirmative attribute), one can form more general intelligibles such *unity*, *cause*, *corporeal*, *simple*, and *incorporeal*. One can then combine them into propositions, from the propositions build syllogisms, from the syllogisms a science, and begin to demonstrate general propositions, say, that exactly one simple, incorporeal, first cause exists. Without directly apprehending the form of God, one can still demonstrate propositions that assert the existence of a thing under a description that refers to God. Although many details of this story are obscure, the general outline is clear enough.

To buttress their position, traditional interpreters offer two supporting considerations. First, if, as Maimonides says many times, knowledge of metaphysics is needed for human perfection, it would be "bizarre" if he believed it is unattainable. Second, Maimonides gives demonstrations of metaphysical propositions such as the existence, incorporeality, and unity of God. If the skeptical interpretation is right, how could he do this and why would he take credit for it?[18]

In response to the traditional interpretation, skeptical interpreters face two tasks. They must show that Maimonides' metaphysical demonstrations do not meet Aristotelian standards of scientific knowledge and reconcile that lack of knowledge with Maimonides' view of theoretical contemplation as human perfection. To address the first task, I review four arguments in the skeptical interpreter's arsenal; in the next section, I address the second task. For the present, three preliminary comments are in order.

1. Maimonides' skeptical arguments are directed exclusively at claims of knowledge of metaphysics (including cosmology), not at claims of empirical knowledge. He attacks the *mutakallimūn* who, using classical skeptical objections, attempt to show "that the senses do not always procure certain knowledge" (*GP* 1.73, p. 213) and

repeatedly states that everything Aristotle has said about the sublunar sphere "is indubitably correct" (*GP* 2.22, p. 319; cf. 2.24, p. 326).[19] Indeed Maimonides' skeptical arguments about metaphysics and cosmology presuppose knowledge of the sublunar realm. Thus one of his objections to Aristotelian astronomy is that the same principle by which we *successfully* explain why sublunar things have different attributes despite their common matter cannot also explain the different motions and velocities of the heavenly spheres that share a common matter.[20] Borrowing a term from the *kalām*, Maimonides concludes that God "particularizes" the motions of the spheres by which he means that the motions have a cause but we do not know it (*GP* 2.19, pp. 310–12). Just as God responds to Moses' request to know His essence by revealing His divine actions, that is, the lawful processes of the sublunar world (*GP* 1.54, pp. 124–5), so Maimonides' skepticism is not meant to "close the gate of speculation" and "deprive the intellect of the apprehension of things that it is possible to apprehend." Rather it redirects the "intellect [to] move about only within the domain of things that man is able to grasp," namely, the sublunar world, and shows "that the intellects of human beings have a limit at which they stop" (*GP* 1.32, pp. 69–70).[21]

2. Maimonides' skeptical arguments are directed against claims of scientific knowledge (in particular domains like metaphysics) of the caliber that would enable one to become an acquired intellect and conjoin with the active intellect. They are not directed against weaker cognitive states such as belief, which Maimonides defines as the (mental) "affirmation that what has been represented is outside of the mind just as it has been represented in the mind," nor against beliefs held with certainty, that is, an affirmation one realizes cannot possibly be false (*GP* 1.50, p. 111). Unlike later types of skepticism, Maimonides' arguments do not undertake to show that it is possible to doubt the purported knowledge claim in order to unseat it.[22] Instead the model for Maimonides' idea of scientific knowledge and the target for his skepticism are truths meeting Aristotle's standards for demonstration, that is, truths derived from premises that are certain, primary or nondemonstrable, immediate, before, and causes of their conclusions.

As examples of the claim that demonstrative premises be primary or nondemonstrable, Maimonides offers perceptual judgments or first intelligibles. By contrast, the generally accepted opinions that serve as premises of dialectical syllogisms, and their implications, are excluded from scientific knowledge.[23] This is important because, following the lead of recent scholars who have argued that Aristotle's scientific practice employs dialectical argument more than demonstration, some traditional interpreters have argued that Maimonides does the same.[24] Even if one cannot demonstrate metaphysical propositions, one can dialectically prove them – which also yields knowledge. In response, suffice it to say that even if Maimonides gives dialectical argument greater cognitive status in the practice of science, it cannot yield the caliber of apprehension required for an acquired intellect and conjunction with the active intellect. For Maimonides it is this desideratum that must be satisfied by the knowledge that the traditional interpretation requires.

The most important requirement for the caliber of demonstrative knowledge Maimonides seeks, and what his skeptical arguments aim to show is not delivered, is given in the condition that the premises must contain the cause of the conclusion, in which "a cause" means an answer to this question: Why? For in order to have scientific knowledge, one must understand the claim and "we only understand when we know the explanation" (*Post An.* I. 2, 70b:30–1), that is, the cause. Recall here that, in order to apprehend intelligibles, the intellect must represent them *"in their true reality and with their causes"* (*GP* 1.73, p. 209, my emphasis). Therefore only when we have knowledge of causes are we in a position to grasp the phenomena according to their "true reality" rather than as they sensibly appear or according to common opinion.[25] Because this is the standard Maimonides demands, his skeptical project will succeed if he can show that purported demonstrations do not meet it.

3. In his image of intellectual illumination as lightning flashes of different frequencies and intensities, Maimonides asserts that the secrets of the Law are not "fully and completely known to anyone among us" because, even when the truth "flashes out," "matter and habit in their various forms conceal it" (*GP* 1.Introduction, p. 7). Again, "Matter is a strong veil preventing the apprehension of that which is separate from matter as it truly is, ... [namely,] the deity or one of the intellects" (*GP* 3.9, pp. 436–7).[26] Matter, then, is the culprit and can block the acquisition of complete knowledge in two ways: as an obstruction either to *concentration* on God and contemplation of divine science or to *apprehension* of the divine. Matter

prevents concentration through its demands to satisfy one's bodily needs and desires. When they are excessive, matter is also a source of moral imperfection. But even where its demands are minimal, any attention to basic needs is an obstacle to the total concentration required for intellectual perfection. And because it is not possible for there to be form without matter (*GP* 3.8), or intellect without body, the absolute concentration necessary for the complete knowledge of an actualized or acquired intellect is hardly possible.

Matter also serves as a veil obstructing apprehension of the content of the knowledge claim. Among the subjects about which Maimonides makes this claim, we can distinguish two types of argument. The first delineates *limitations* of the human intellect, subjects that do not admit of demonstration but only of a weaker kind of proof, for example, certain claims in astronomy. The second type, which involves antinomies that follow from purported demonstrations, leads to the conclusion that it is humanly *impossible* to have such knowledge, not simply that there are limitations on our intellectual capacity. For the rest of this section, I set out these two types of arguments with examples of each.

1. In 2.24 of the *Guide*, Maimonides sketches the "crisis" over Ptolemaic astronomy and Aristotelian cosmology that raged in twelfth-century Spain.[27] Ptolemaic astronomy posits epicycles and eccentrics that enable the astronomer to make precise predictions of planetary motions. By contrast, Aristotelian cosmology requires all heavenly motion to be uniform, circular, and about the center of the earth. Because of these incompatibilities, some of Maimonides' near-contemporaries rejected Ptolemaic astronomy and some tried to construct alternative theories. Maimonides, by contrast, exploits the conflict in order to motivate "the true perplexity" of Aristotelian cosmology, that is, the irresolvable disagreement that is symptomatic of the lack of demonstrative knowledge and hence the limitations of the intellect (*GP* 1.31, p. 66):

> regarding all that is in the heavens, man grasps nothing but a small measure of what is mathematical;... [T]he deity alone fully knows the true reality, the nature, the substance, the form, the motions, and the causes of the heavens. But He has enabled man to have knowledge of what is beneath the heavens... For it is impossible for us to accede to the points starting from which conclusions may be drawn about the heavens; for the

latter are too far away from and too high in place and in rank. (*GP* 2.24, p. 327)

The barrier to our knowledge of cosmology is not a deep metaphysical fact but rather that we are limited by our place – on earth "far away" from the heavens – and "rank," as creatures of "low and turbid" matter compared with the "noblest and purest matter" of the spheres (*GP* 3.9, p. 436). The moral Maimonides draws is not to cease all inquiry but to master the science God *has* enabled man to have, namely sublunar physics. Nor do these limitations absolutely rule out the possibility of scientific knowledge of cosmology. Maimonides concludes his discussion of the true perplexity by saying that "it is possible that someone else may find a demonstration by means of which the true reality of what is obscure for me will become clear to him" (*GP* 2.24, p. 327).[28]

2. Maimonides argues that astronomy is immune to the doubts that apply to Aristotelian cosmology because it does not attempt to produce "cogent demonstrations" (sing: *burhān qāṭiʿ*; literally: "a cutting demonstration") but only possible hypotheses consistent with general cosmological truths that "agree with what is observed" (*GP* 2.11, pp. 273–4). Here Maimonides assumes an Aristotelian distinction between two types of demonstration based on the condition that the premises must contain the cause, or explanation, of the conclusion. Demonstrations that meet this condition are, in Aristotle's terminology, "of the reason why" [*to dioti*] and, in scholastic terminology, demonstrations *propter quid*. In contrast, syllogistic deductions that argue from effects to the existence of possible causes merely establish *that* the conclusion is true, knowledge of the fact (*to hoti*; in scholastic terminology: *quia*), not *why* it is.[29]

This distinction was developed in various directions by Aristotle's successors. Of particular importance is that Alexander of Aphrodisias and Avicenna both argued that only a demonstration *propter quid* is a real demonstration; a demonstration *quia* constitutes only weaker evidence or proof [*dalīl*] and does not furnish the stuff of scientific knowledge. In contrast Aquinas draws the distinction in order to legitimate demonstrations *quia* as scientific demonstrations.[30] Although Maimonides nowhere explicitly draws the *propter quid*/*quia* distinction and uses the term "demonstration" in multiple senses, his medieval commentator Moses of Narbonne understood the phrase *burhān qāṭiʿ* as a "demonstration of the cause and the fact," that is, a demonstration *propter quid*.[31] Maimonides also seems to follow Avicenna in denying that *quia* arguments are demonstrations, that is, the stuff of scientific knowledge. Thus the astronomer draws his inferences from effects, namely the observed motions of the stars, to possible hypotheses as to their causes "regardless of whether or not things are thus in fact" (*GP* 2.24, p. 326). This is what Maimonides means when he says that the astronomer does not provide a "cogent demonstration"; *quia* proofs that do not give "a precise account of the true reality" (*GP* 2.11, p. 274) are sufficient for his predictive purposes.

The *propter quid/quia* distinction also has implications for the status of metaphysical propositions such as the existence of God. All of the philosophers' demonstrations of the existence of God (*GP* 2.1–2), as well as Maimonides' own dilemma argument (*GP* 1.71, 2.2), begin from observations of empirical effects; likewise, the arguments for, or "indications" of, the existence of the active intellect (in *GP* 2.4, p. 257, cited in the previous section) reason from effects. None of these, even the ones he calls demonstrations (meaning demonstrations *quia*) furnish the stuff of scientific knowledge.

Furthermore, Maimonides' own statements about these proofs indicate that he saw a difference between them and the scientific knowledge supplied by a demonstration *propter quid*. In two chapters he distinguishes between "guidance leading to the existence of a thing and an investigation of the true reality of the essence and substance of that thing" (*GP* 1.46, p. 97). The "immense difference" (*GP* 1.46, p. 97) between these is not between existence and essence but between "guidance" and "investigation of the true reality" of the thing. "Guidance" can come from parables and traditions (*GP* 1.33, p. 71) or "through the accidents of the thing or through its acts or through a relation – which may be very remote from the thing" (*GP* 1.46, p. 97) – that is, from effects. By contrast, "investigation of the true reality" is a scientific inquiry that would uncover the explanation as well as the fact. Maimonides illustrates the distinction by a parable about different ways in which we can make known the existence of a ruler – either through his effects (e.g., law and order in his realm) or through his essence and true reality. The ruler prefigures "the deity who moves the highest heaven" (*GP* 1.70, p. 175) whose existence is proven in the first argument of *Guide* 2.1. Maimonides' point in calling these arguments "guidance" is that demonstrations *quia* do not constitute scientific knowledge.

A similar point applies to a controversial remark Maimonides makes at *Guide* 2.24 (cited earlier): "And even the general conclusion that may be drawn from [the heavens], namely, that they prove the existence of their Mover, is a matter the knowledge of which cannot be reached by human intellects" (*GP* 2.24, p. 327).[32] This is puzzling because it seems to contradict his statements elsewhere in the *Guide* that the "revolution of the heaven" is "the greatest proof through which one can know the existence of the deity" (*GP* 1.70, p. 175; 1.9, pp. 34–5; 2.18, p. 302). However, once we distinguish between *propter quid* and *quia* demonstrations, it is evident that the proof for the existence of the deity from the revolution of the sphere is a demonstration *quia* and does not furnish an explanation of God's existence even if it guides us to what we ought to believe (*GP* 1.34, p. 74). Hence it is not scientific knowledge.

I now turn to two arguments for the stronger claim that it is impossible to have knowledge of certain metaphysical propositions. This type of argument focuses on representations of God in speech and thought and the relation between the intellect and imagination in forming these representations.

3. According to Maimonides, it is demonstrable (*quia*) that

(1) God is one

meaning that He is not only numerically single but an absolute unity who is simple and incomposite. This follows from the Avicennean conception of the deity as the being who is necessarily existent in itself and causally independent of any other being. If such a being were composed of attributes, its existence would be dependent on them. Hence, any such being must have no parts and no attributes. To this Maimonides adds that not only must God *be* incomposite, our knowledge must *represent* Him so. There can be no true representations of God in which He is represented compositely: as a subject with attributes or a substratum for forms. With this constraint in place, Maimonides argues that there can be no representation of God by which we can know that (1) is true.

Recall that, when describing the apprehension of intelligible forms, Maimonides distinguishes a stage in which the intellect makes a representation [*taṣawwur*] of the form (*GP* 1.68, p. 73). Those passages do not say how the representations differ (if they do) from forms themselves. However, elsewhere Maimonides characterizes these representations by using linguistic terms. For example, the representations of their respective separate intellects formed by the embodied intellects of the spheres constitute, according to Maimonides, an autonomous language to which the Psalmist *literally* refers when he writes, "The heavens *tell* of the glory of God" (Psalm 19:2, my emphasis); indeed, he continues, "the true praise" is the "very representation" whereas "speech of lip and tongue" serve merely to "instruct someone else" of, or to communicate externally, the mental representation (*GP* 2.5, p. 260; cf. 1.65). Similarly, in the opening chapter of his discussion of divine attributes, Maimonides draws a distinction between "the notion that is uttered" and "the notion represented in the soul" and then claims that what is believed and known with certainty is the latter (*GP* 1.50, p. 111). In both passages, Maimonides appears to be reading into the term "representation" [*taṣawwur*] what, in his *Logic*, he calls "inner speech" as opposed to the utterances "of the lip and tongue" of external speech.[33] Although there remain many questions about Maimonides' use of this term, what is clear is that these representations, although distinct from external speech, constitute a language, the language of thought.

The most important linguistic dimension of the representations of Chapters 2.5 and 1.50, in contrast to those of Chapters 1.68 and 1.73 that were of simple forms, is that they are syntactically complex like the sentences of external speech. Their syntax is not the conventional grammar of external speech but a universal logical form, which Maimonides says is a more perspicuous structure that guides one to knowledge in the sciences.[34] Nevertheless, however superior they are to external speech, because the inner speech representations are composed of elements according to a syntax, Maimonides finds them problematic – especially when one claims to demonstrate the unity of God.

According to Maimonides, what we claim to know cannot be truly expressed by (1) for three reasons. First, it attributes to God the attribute of being one, whose meaning is "a perfection only with reference to us" (*GP* 1.59, p. 139). To solve this semantic problem, Maimonides proposes that we negate the meaning of the attribute, that is, treat the predicate as if it were completely equivocal (*GP* 1:56, p. 131). Yet even after having negated its content, a second metaphysical problem remains: God "does not possess a thing other than His essence, which ... is identical with His perfections" (*GP* 1.59, p. 139). If God has attributes that compose His essence, He would be dependent on them (*GP* 1.52, p. 115), which contradicts the assumption that He is necessarily existent in himself. Alternatively, if an affirmative attribute indicates "a *part* of the thing the knowledge of which is sought, that *part* being either a part of its substance or one of its accidents" (*GP* 1.58, p. 135, my emphasis), God must be composite rather than simple. Moreeover, having parts, He is also divisible, hence, a body.

To solve this problem, Maimonides proposes to read the affirmative proposition (1) of external speech as the negation of a privation expressed in internal speech as

(2) Not (God is composite).

Furthermore, (2) should be understood as the denial not only of the privation of composition but of the categorial condition (Q) required to be *either* composite *or* one, that is, to fall under the category of quantity. Thus (2) is short for (3):

(3) Not (God is Q).

Here negative attributes avoid the metaphysical problem because they say nothing about the essence of the thing we seek to know (*GP* 1.58, p. 135), hence nothing about a *part* of the essence.[35]

Although better than (1), (2) and (3) nonetheless suffer from a third problem. Their subject–predicate syntax of *attribution* implies that there exists an attribute (signified by the predicate) that is structurally distinguishable from the substance (signified by the subject), and this division holds even if the attribute is privative and negated. As Maimonides emphasizes (*GP* 1.57–9), a privation is no less of an attribute than something affirmative. Put otherwise, privations signify *something* – even though it is not actually present – in a subject in which it ought to exist. Hence, they are attributes and require a substance to which they belong. But this very differentiation of substance and attribute entailed by the subject–predicate syntax of the representation compromises divine simplicity:

For there is no oneness at all except in *believing that there is one simple essence in which there is no complexity or multiplication of notions, but one notion only;* so that from whatever angle you regard it . . . , you will find that it is one, . . . and you will not find therein any multiplicity either in the thing as it is outside of the mind or *as it is in the mind.* (*GP* 1.51, p. 113, my emphasis)

Maimonides' term for complexity, or composition, *tarkīb,* is the same term used for the syntax, or mode of composition, of language. Thus the true oneness in the mental representation of God that Maimonides demands is breached by any representation that contains even the simplest syntactic structure (cf. *GP* 1.60, p. 145). In sum, negated privations avoid problems specific to affirmative attributes but they are subject to any problem of attribution *simpliciter.* Let's call this the syntactic problem of divine attributes.[36]

It follows that if we can demonstrate that God is one or, in inner speech, that God does not possess (the categorial condition) Q, it also follows from the syntactic form of the demonstrated proposition that He is composite. Hence, God is both composite and not. Thus *how* we represent what we know misrepresents *what* we know: God's unity. Contrary to those who take Maimonides to be an advocate of the *via negativa,* it seems that *neither* affirmative *nor* negative attributions furnish knowledge about God. Negative attributes are "better" than affirmative ones, making fewer false presuppositions and "conducting" us in the right direction (*GP* 1.57, p. 133; 1.58, p. 135). But better is not good enough: Negative divine attributes are still false and descriptions formed from them fail to represent the deity. Indeed Maimonides argues that if one represents God in subject–predicate form, "if we say that this essence, which for the sake of example shall be called the deity, is an essence in which subsist many notions that are predicated of it, we apply this term to absolute nonexistence" (*GP* 1.58, p. 135). The speaker does not have a false belief *about* God, an "apprehension that is different from what He really is" (*GP* 1.60, p. 144); he has no belief *about* God, period. The position to which Maimonides' argument leads him is one in which we are prevented from ever forming true representations about God. This is an example not just of a limitation but of the complete impossibility of metaphysical knowledge.[37]

4. The root of the syntactic problem of divine attributes is that the intellects of composite substances (like humans or spheres) must apprehend God through representations that necessarily employ

subject–predicate syntax even in inner speech. Why *necessarily*? Because as embodied intellects, we can never free our representation of an existent from the influence of the body, forced by our "wish to preserve the conception of the imagination" (*GP* 1.51, p. 114). For Maimonides, the representational role of the imagination is a general obstacle to knowledge of immaterial beings. Not only God is conceived in corporeal terms as an essence with attributes (*GP* 1.51, p. 114); the separate intellects are said to "move" and from a "local position in relation to the spheres" (*GP* 1.49, p. 109; 2.12, pp. 279–80). Similar qualifications apply to the idea of emanation [*fayḍ*] that Maimonides regards as the best available figure to express the causality of an immaterial being even though it is also inadequate to capture

> the true reality.... For the mental representation of the action of one who is separate from matter is very difficult, in a way similar to the difficulty of the mental representation of the existence of one who is separate from matter. (*GP* 2.12, p. 279)

Again, this is so difficult because the imagination cannot represent any existent except as a body or any action except as a spatiotemporal event. Maimonides' objection, however, is not simply, as Aristotle said (*De Anima* ii 7 431a16), that there is no thinking, or representation, without imagination but that, despite the need, we have no principled way to distinguish the two. For example, for there to be scientific knowledge based on demonstration, we must be able to distinguish between the necessary, the possible, and the impossible. But both the intellect and imagination claim to discern these modalities. Therefore we need a criterion "that would enable us to distinguish the things cognized intellectually from those imagined" (*GP* 1.73, p. 211). Yet, when he is pushed to produce it, Maimonides concedes that he knows no principle "that permits differentiation between the imaginative faculty and the intellect" (*GP* 3.15, p. 460). If there were one, would it be "something altogether outside both the intellect and the imagination, or is it by the intellect itself that one distinguishes between that which is cognized by the intellect and that which is imagined?" (*GP* 3.15, p. 461).[38] Of course, this conclusion is no surprise. If our matter prevents our intellects from apprehending the immaterial, it will prevent us from clearly distinguishing the actualized intellect from bodily faculties like the imagination. And without a principled method of differentiation, there can be no principled scientific knowledge. Maimonides concludes, "these are points for investigation which may lead very far" (*GP* 3.15, p. 461), indeed *too* far for knowledge of metaphysics.

4.3. INTELLECTUAL PERFECTION WITHOUT METAPHYSICS

A major consideration in support of the traditional interpretation is Maimonides' repeated affirmation of the ideal of a life of contemplation culminating with knowledge of metaphysics. By the same token the greatest challenge to the skeptical interpretation is to square Maimonides' commitment to this ideal with his view of the narrow limits of human understanding, limits that exclude knowledge of metaphysics.

One response to this challenge is to deny the ideal.[39] Because of the constraints on the intellect, some skeptical interpreters argue that, following Alfarabi, Maimonides abandons his earlier belief in the possibility of metaphysical knowledge and, like Kant, gives primacy to the life of action over contemplation. Proponents of this view point out that, in the last sentences of the *Guide*, after saying that human perfection consists in apprehension of God, divine providence, and governance, Maimonides announces that "the way of life" of the perfected individual "will always have in view *loving-kindness, righteousness*, and *judgment* through assimilation to His actions" (*GP* 3.54, p. 638) – apparently shifting the true perfection, a type of *imitatio Dei*, to the ethical and practical.

Traditional interpreters counter that in this passage Maimonides does not abandon his preference for the contemplative life. On the contrary, he says that "the perfection of man" *is* the apprehension of God, His providence, and governance; only afterward does he describe what this way of life leads to: dispassionate Godlike behavior (*GP* 1.54). This does not mean that the behavior is identical with the perfection, only that it accompanies or follows from it.[40] In fact, earlier in the chapter Maimonides explicitly identifies the practical as a lower, nonultimate perfection (*GP* 1.54). Yet there remains a difficulty if we agree that the traditional interpretation of this passage is correct: How can it be reconciled with Maimonides' skeptical arguments? To conclude this chapter, I therefore want to sketch some ways in which Maimonides endorses the theoretical life that take into account his skepticism about metaphysical knowledge.

First, while circumscribing the boundaries of human knowledge, Maimonides redirects us to the teleological study of sublunar nature. In his parable of the palace, the perfected individuals in the inner chamber of the ruler are engaged in "an examination of [*iʿtibārāt*] the beings," that is, the study of natural science, with the aim of "drawing up proofs [*li-l-istidlāl*] about God" (*GP* 3.51, p. 620).[41] This is a contemplative ideal other than metaphysics that is nonetheless focused on God.

Second, in this passage Maimonides uses the verbal noun *istidlāl* [the drawing up of proofs], shifting the focus from the product, the proof, or its conclusion, to the process, the activity of proving it.[42] This shift is an instance of a general motif that finds the value of theoretical inquiry not in the truth demonstrated but in the "spiritual exercise" in which it engages the inquirer.[43] The idea is based on the theme that philosophy is not the exposition of a doctrine but a practically oriented way of life: a set of intellectual practices, including demonstration and dialectic, that aim to cultivate a set of attitudes that engage the individual's entire psychology with the goal of achieving his happiness or perfection. The practices vary. Some involve training that develops intellectual and emotional dispositions, skills, and abilities such as concentration, attention, or self-examination. Other exercises lead one through the investigation of nature to worship of God. Yet others aim to cure the sources of unhappiness. This conception of philosophy was common among Hellenistic schools, and Maimonides, I suggest, holds a similar view.[44]

Among the spiritual exercises, Maimonides includes cosmological and metaphysical inquiry. He transforms these traditional disciplines into routes one follows to perplexities induced by difficulties in their subject matter. In some cases, the perplexities issue in awe and praise of God as the inquirer recognizes his own intellectual inadequacy.[45] At other times, the individual's recognition of his intellectual limits is therapeutic, curing him of unobtainable intellectual passions that lead to unhappiness. Maimonides' example of this kind of intellectual sickness is the fact that we are anxiously driven by longings to have metaphysical and cosmological knowledge we cannot obtain (*GP* 1.31, p. 66). Through the rabbinic story of Rabbi Akiva in *Pardes* (*Ḥagigah* 14b), Maimonides shows how study of the heavens can disabuse us of such unsatisfiable longing. By recognizing, and then respecting, the limitations of his intellect of which he becomes aware through cosmological inquiry, Rabbi Akiva ultimately ceases even to *long* for what he realizes it is not possible for him to know, freeing himself from his unobtainable epistemic passion. According to Maimonides, the tranquility, or peace of mind, he achieves by "refraining and holding back" at the limit of his intellect is the meaning of the talmudic statement that Akiva "entered in peace and went out in peace" (*GP* 1.32, pp. 68–70; cf. *GP* 2.30, p. 353).

Finally, Maimonides proposes that we employ parables as the appropriate verbal medium to express what we limited human inquirers can try to say about metaphysics, barred from scientific knowledge of the subject that would enable us to give an explicit literal discursive exposition.[46] In the Introduction to the *Guide* he explains that the Sages employed the parable to articulate their own intellectual experience of apprehending metaphysics because its allusive, figurative form matches the metaphysical subject matter that "appears, flashes, and then is hidden again" (*GP* 1, p. 8). In a similar way, through the practice of interpreting scriptural, rabbinic, and his own parables, Maimonides tries to guide his reader to and through the same kind of intellectual experience of metaphysics: "that the truths be glimpsed and then again be concealed" (*GP* 1.Introduction, pp. 6–7).

ACKNOWLEDGMENTS

I wish to acknowledge the material support of the Israel Science Foundation (Grant 951/01-2) while this essay was composed, and my thanks to Kenneth Seeskin, Gad Freudenthal, Charles Manekin, and Zev Harvey for comments on an earlier draft.

NOTES

1. For the Aristotelian background, see Burnyeat 1981, Kahn 1981. Maimonides' use of *ʿilm* for the cognitive state in *GP* 1.31, p. 65, can be contrasted with *GP* 2.12, p. 276, where it refers to a science; his other main term for knowledge, *maʿrifa*, usually refers to the cognitive state. On Maimonides' Hebrew terminology, see now Septimus 2001.

2. For Arabic theories of the intellect and Maimonides' place among them, see Davidson 1992–3, Altmann 1987, Kogan 1989.
3. Aristotle holds out the possibility that the actual intellect may be separable from the body, and this idea is seized upon by medieval thinkers in order to account for the immortality of the soul.
4. For the first position, see Pines 1990; for the second, Kreisel 1999, Altmann 1987.
5. Here Maimonides follows Alfarabi, rather than Avicenna, for whom the rational faculty is a substance.
6. Following Aristotle (*De Anima* 3, 4, 429b 6–10), Maimonides acknowledges an intermediate stage of the intellect, called the "habitual" intellect by Alexander, after it has apprehended an intelligible form but is not actively engaged in reflecting on it, a state he compares to "a skillful scribe at the time when he is not writing" (*GP* 3.51, p. 625. I argue (Stern forthcoming) that this notion is central to Maimonides' theodicy.
7. Aristotle uses the term "motion" to refer to all change, not only as it applies to the heavens and, as we use the term nowadays, to locomotion.
8. For example, Alfarabi, *Risāla fī l-ʿaql* ["*Letter on the Intellect*"], in Hyman and Walsh 1973, p. 217.
9. For detailed discussion of Avicenna's views, see Davidson 1992–3, pp. 83–94.
10. The two main parties in this controversy are as follows: for the Alfarabian conditionlike interpretation, Altmann 1987 and Pines 1979 and, for the Avicennean interpretation, Kogan 1989 and Davidson 1992–3.
11. On *taṣawwur* and *taṣdīq*, see Wolfson 1973, Sabra 1980, Manekin 1990, and Ivry 1998. For a parallel three-stage account in Alexander (in which the second stage is purely passive reception of the form), see Altmann 1987, p. 73.
12. For additional passages that attribute to the human intellect the ability to apprehend immaterial forms, see *CM*, *Avot* 3, 20; *GP* 1.62, p. 152; and *GP* 2.12, p. 280 (end); for passages that deny the ability, see *GP* 1.37, p. 86 (in contrast to *GP* 1.38, p. 87) and *GP* 3.9, pp. 436–7. For competing analyses of these passages, see Altmann 1987, pp. 76–7, 118; Davidson 1992–3, pp. 94–7; Kogan 1989; Stern forthcoming.
13. Kogan 1989.
14. Kahn 1981.
15. It remains unclear how, even on Avicenna's account, one apprehends immaterial forms for which there is no predisposing abstraction.
16. The main players in the controversy are, on the traditional side, Altmann 1987, Davidson 1992–3, Hyman 1989, Ivry 1998, Kellner 1990,

Kogan 1989, Kraemer 1989, Kreisel 1999, and Manekin 1990; on the skeptical side, Pines 1979, Seeskin 2000, and Stern 2000, 2001, 2004, and forthcoming; and, on specific issues, Harvey 1990, 1997, and Klein-Braslavy 1986a. It should be noted that Pines characterized Maimonides as a critical philosopher in the Kantian sense; Stern 2004 and forthcoming attempts to highlight parallels between Maimonides' position and classical and Humean skepticism. It should also be noted that Pines' critical reading was part of a broader esotericist interpretive stance, often associated with Leo Strauss, that reads all ancient and medieval philosophy through political lenses. The intensity of some responses to Pines' thesis may be directed against this larger program with which, at least in their minds, it is associated.

17. See Pines 1979.
18. For the most detailed presentation of the traditional interpretation see Davidson 1992–3, pp. 54, 86–7. For the expression in quotes, see p. 54.
19. Maimonides' skepticism does not touch mathematics, where the "perplexity" symptomatic of the limitations of knowledge is "nonexistent" (*GP* 1.31, p. 66). Significantly (and remarkably for his time), Maimonides recognizes certain mathematical notions, for example, the exact value of pi, which will never be known, not because of a "deficiency of knowledge on our part," but because they are "unknown by [their] own nature" (*CM Eruvin* 1.5; cf. *CM Eruvin* 2.5 on irrational numbers). Because not even God could know the exact value of pi, the fact that humans do not entails nothing for the scope of human knowledge. See Langermann 1991a.
20. I am indebted here to Joshua Schwartz.
21. On the importance of knowledge of nature for knowledge of God, see Ivry 1998, Kraemer 2001a.
22. This, despite the fact that certainty is a condition for the premises of a demonstration. That mere dubitability is not sufficient grounds for skepticism is clear from Maimonides' use of Alexander's rules (*GP* 2.3, p. 254; 2.23, p. 321) for accepting belief according to least doubt. On doubt in Maimonides, see Langermann 2002 and on skepticism in Islam in general, van Ess 1968.
23. See *Logic*, Chapter VIII, 48; Hyman 1989; Stern 2000.
24. Kraemer 1989, 2000; cf. also Hyman 1989, Ivry 1998. On Aristotle, see, e.g., Owen 1961 and Nussbaum 1982. Note that it is Aristotelian dialectic that is in question, as opposed to *kalām* dialectic, which Maimonides rejects.
25. The Arabic term *ḥaqīqa*, translated here by Pines as "true reality," is sometimes synonymous or interchangeable with Arabic *dhāt*,

"essence" and sometimes means the reality (including the existence of something) established and explained by a scientific inquiry. A philosophical examination of the term remains to be done.

26. On the image of the veil, see *EC* 7; on habit, *GP* 1.31, p. 67.
27. Pines 1963, pp. cix–cxii; Sabra 1984; Langermann, 1999, pp. 199–202; see also the chapter in this volume by G. Freudenthal.
28. Langermann (1991a). It should also be noted that Maimonides depicts Aristotle not only as the successful scientist of the sublunar realm, but as the cautious doubter who recognized the limitations of his intellect with respect to cosmology; see, e.g., Maimonides' interpretation of *De Caelo* 2.12, cited in 2.19, p. 307ff (and with a different intepretation in 1.5, p. 29). On this image of Aristotle, see Stern in press and Langermann 2002.
29. *Post. An.* I, 13, 78^{b}22–79^{a}15; on the distinction, see Wallace 1972; Freudenthal 2003; Stern 2001, 2004.
30. Alexander (1989) flatly states that "there is no demonstration through what is posterior" (13.30, p. 34); Avicenna 1972, p. 76; Aquinas, *Summa Theologica,* I, 2, 2; Pines 1963, p. lxixf; Altmann 1987, p. 116; Davidson 1987b, pp. 298–9 and references therein.
31. Narbonne 1852, 15b–16a. On Maimonides' ambiguous use of the term "demonstration" [*burhān*], see the entry in the glossary of his Hebrew translator, Samuel Ibn Tibbon, 1987. Other uses of the term *burhān qāṭiʿ* (e.g., in *GP* 2.15, p. 290 and in 2.2, p. 252) require further investigation.
32. On the controversy over this passage, see Kraemer 1989; Davidson 1992–3, 2000; Harvey 1997; Stern 2001, 2004. See also *MT* 1, Principles of the Torah, 1.5, p. 7 for further *quia* demonstrations of the existence, incorporeality, and unity of God.
33. Maimonides, *Logic,* Chapter 14.1–2. On the term "notion [represented in the soul]," see Michael Blaustein 1986 for possible influence of ibn Bajja on Maimonides.
34. *Logic,* Chapter 14. On Alfarabi's influence on Maimonides' conception of logic here, see Stern 1989, 2000, and for the Alfarabian background, the superb introduction in Zimmermann 1981.
35. On Maimonides' general theory of divine attributes, see the chapter in this volume by K. Seeskin.
36. In Chapters 1.61–3 Maimonides attempts to find names of God (e.g., the Tetragrammaton and "I am that I am") whose *syntax* circumvents the duality of subject and predicate; syntax and its metaphysical implications; but even these names do not allows us to form propositions about God. For detailed discussion, see Stern 1989, 2000.

37. For another example of the impossibility of metaphysical knowledge, see the antinomy on *GP* 1.72, p. 193.
38. Fackenheim 1946/7, p. 60, n. 61.
39. Pines 1979.
40. Davidson 1992–3.
41. On the term *iʿtibār*, which is used by Averroes with the same meaning in his *Decisive Treatise* [*Kitāb faṣl al-maqāl*], see Harvey 1998a.
42. On the term *istidlāl* and its importance for key passages in the *Guide*, see Davidson 2000.
43. Hadot 1995.
44. Stern 2001, in press, forthcoming. Maimonides describes the commandments as exercises of this kind in *GP* 3.51, p. 622.
45. See, e.g., the expressions of awe, dazzlement, glory, and praise in the following contexts: *GP* 1.2, p. 26; 1.58, p. 137; 1.59, p. 139; 1.72, p. 193; and Harvey 1990, 1997; Stern forthcoming.
46. On Maimonides' use of parable, see Stern 1998, forthcoming, and Y. Lorberbaum 2001.

GAD FREUDENTHAL

5 Maimonides' Philosophy of Science

5.1. INTRODUCTORY REMARK

Philosophy of science is a metascientific discipline. It takes existing scientific knowledge for its point of departure and reflects on it, asking questions such as this: What is meant by saying that a scientific theory is true, that it has been verified, or confirmed, by experience, that it explains phenomena, that science makes progress? It also reflects on the implications of scientific theories for metaphysics. Only rarely is the philosopher of science a scientist, and most scientists are not much interested in the philosophy of science.

Maimonides was neither a scientist nor a philosopher of science. Rather, he was very well acquainted with the most up-to-date science in the medieval Greek–Arabic tradition and drew on it in his theological investigations, whose results he addressed to a Jewish readership. He aimed to bring together, or accommodate, two bodies of thought, which at the outset were entirely unrelated: the Jewish revelation and tradition, handed down in a body of authoritative texts, and Greek–Arabic rational thought, as systematized by the great representatives of Arabic Aristotelianism. There were a number of issues discussed in both traditions, such as these: the cosmogonic question (how did the world originate?), the nature of God, the relationship of God to the world, especially to man, reward and punishment, and "life" after death. Because the two traditions greatly differed in their ways of construing these issues, and because both claimed to be true, Maimonides had to assess the strength of those claims. For him (as for most thinkers of his time) it was inconceivable to doubt either the validity of revelation and tradition or the truth of what had been demonstrated by philosophy, which he largely identified with the work of Aristotle as interpreted by the Arabic tradition. How can both be true? In an effort to find an answer to this problem, Maimonides came to reflect on the limits of scientific truth, on the one hand, and of scriptural truth, on the other. By carefully defining these limits, he believed he would be able to show that, if the knowledge claims made within both traditions are interpreted correctly, it will turn out that they do not conflict. Thus, willy-nilly he had to delve into questions that belong to the philosophy of natural science and to the philosophy of textual or scriptural science. Lack of certitude within science often gives rise to philosophic reflection.

We should be aware that, as a philosophical subdiscipline, philosophy of science is a late invention. The question "What was Maimonides' philosophy of science?" is thus anachronistic, imposing a present-day category on a thinker who wrote more than eight centuries ago. Still, inasmuch as Maimonides devoted much thought to issues that we classify as belonging to this discipline, it is legitimate to piece together his position, consisting of a mosaic of his views on several issues that I will try to place in their proper contexts.

Two final preliminary remarks: (1) Although the *Treatise of Logic* is not a treatise on epistemology, parts of it bear on issues to be discussed here, and I will draw on it occasionally.[1] (2) I will concentrate exclusively on Maimonides' overt, "exoteric" argument. Whether he in secret held esoteric opinions, for example, that the world is eternal, need not concern us.

5.2. MAIMONIDES' PHILOSOPHY OF THE MATHEMATICAL AND NATURAL SCIENCES

The central question of the philosophy of science concerns the foundations of knowledge. Faced with knowledge claims, one seeks to know: Is this or that claim trustworthy? Should I assume it to be true when planning future actions? In the Middle Ages the stake was even greater than it is today, because philosophers believed that the immortality of one's soul depends on the acquisition of knowledge – that is, *true* knowledge – during one's lifetime. Thus scientific errors could be fatal not only to one's earthly life but to the eternal bliss of one's soul as well.

What, then, is true or trustworthy knowledge? How can it be distinguished from knowledge claims that seem founded but which further investigation shows to be groundless? Here is Maimonides' answer to the question of what knowledge is reliable:

Know, my masters, that it is not proper for a man to hold for true anything other than one of these three things. The first is a thing for which there is a clear proof deriving from man's reasoning – such as arithmetic, geometry, and the reckoning of the periods [= mathematical astronomy]. The second is a thing man perceives through one of the five senses – such as when he knows with certainty that this is red and this is black and the like through the sight of the eye; as when he tastes that this is bitter and this is sweet.... The third is a thing that a man receives from the prophets or from the righteous. Every man endowed with reason ought to distinguish in his mind and thought all the things that he accepts as trustworthy, and say: "This I accept as trustworthy because of tradition, and this because of sense-perception, and this on grounds of reason." Anyone who accepts as trustworthy anything that is not of these three species, of him it is said: "The simple believeth everything" [Proverbs 14:15].[2]

Maimonides makes this statement in the context of an attempt to discredit astrology. He replies (in ca. 1195) to a letter addressed to him by the rabbis of Montpellier in southern France, who (under the influence of Abraham Ibn Ezra) were taken in by the appeal of astrology (still as vivid as ever in our own day). In continuity with Arab Aristotelianism, Maimonides held astrology to be utterly chimerical, a pseudoscience, all of whose claims are unfounded and false. He also opposed it for theological reasons, namely that it could lead to star worship, the worst form of idolatry. It is in the context of his attempt to subvert astrology's claim to be a science that he adduced the view of knowledge just quoted.

According to Maimonides' letter, then, the sources of reliable knowledge are three: man's reason, as exemplified in the mathematical sciences, sense–perception, and reliable tradition. (A very similar statement is made in the *Treatise on Logic*, Chapter 8.) Let us consider how these sources of knowledge give rise to the different kinds of science.

5.2.1. Maimonides' Epistemology of the Mathematical Sciences

Since Antiquity, mathematics – notably Euclidean geometry – has been considered the paradigm of certain knowledge, deriving from man's reason alone. Maimonides, too, cites mathematics to highlight the capacities of human reason. In the *Treatise on Logic*, the following examples are given: The whole is greater than the part, things that are equal to the same thing are also equal to each other, the number two is even.[3] Elsewhere[4] Maimonides adduces more impressive instances of the capacities of mathematical reasoning: Someone who has not studied astronomy will be unable to accept as true the statement that the sun, which we see as a tiny disk, is 166 3/8 times greater in size than the earth. How, he will wonder, can this possibly be known with such a great precision? In our terms, the statement is counterintuitive. But, Maimonides says, the study of mathematical astronomy (whose fundamental text was Ptolemy's *Almagest*, which Maimonides knew in its Arabic translation) provides one with an "apodictic proof" [*burhān*] of this statement, rendering it an indubitable truth. Mathematical science thus proves the power of human reason to go beyond the phenomena and discover truths which may seem unlikely at first blush.

A different argument to the same effect takes its cue from mathematical science and makes the point that reason, specifically mathematical reason, is superior to imagination:

> Hear what the mathematical sciences have taught us and how capital are the premises we obtained from them. Know that there are things that a man, if he considers them with his imagination, is unable to represent to himself in any respect, but finds it impossible to imagine them as it is impossible for two contraries to agree; and that afterwards the existence of a thing that is impossible to imagine is established by demonstration as true. . . . It has been made clear in the second book of the *Conic Sections* that two lines, between which there is a certain distance at the outset, may go forth in such a way that the farther they go, this distance diminishes and they come nearer to one another, but without it ever being possible for them to meet even if they are drawn forth to infinity and even though they come nearer to one another the farther they go. This cannot be imagined and can in no way enter within the net of imagination. Of these two lines, one is straight and the other curved, as has been made clear there in the above-mentioned book.[5]

The notion of the asymptote, which is so counterintuitive but whose existence is proved in mathematics, establishes that human knowledge is not coextensive with imagination (as the *kalām* school of Muslim theology claimed).[6] Maimonides makes a similar point also by adducing the notion of the antipodes: Their existence has been scientifically demonstrated, but cannot be imagined.[7] Both arguments underscore the power of human reason, which not only transcends experience, but even what imagination regards as a possible experience.[8] Inasmuch as these arguments reflect on the power and limits of kinds of knowledge, they are characteristically epistemological arguments.[9]

5.2.2. *Maimonides' Philosophy of Aristotelian Science*

In the letter to his philosophically uneducated correspondents in Montpellier, Maimonides passed in deliberate silence over a rather important point: Information from sense-perception ("this is red and this is black") is only the starting point and the basis for more general statements about physical reality. But how does one demarcate information that is *reliably* grounded in experience from claims that are only seemingly so? To identify the rules by which one passes from secure truths based on sense-perception to more general truths (which can be said to follow from experience) is the business of the theory of inference. Like his contemporaries, Maimonides adhered to Aristotle's views of demonstration, which are thus an essential component of his philosophy of science. To condense in a few pages the entire history of the theory of science in the medieval tradition over some two millennia is not possible, and here we must content ourselves with a few very summary notions.

Aristotle discussed modes of scientific reasoning in his *Posterior Analytics*. He distinguished two kinds of "primary" knowledge[10]: (1) Things better known "to us" are the *particular* things known through perception; (2) things better known "in themselves" are the *universal* things, which as such are closest to reason, but furthest away from perception. Aristotle accordingly distinguished two kinds of explanations employed in science, depending on the kind of "primary" knowledge from which they proceed: (1) The epistemologically most "noble" ones proceed from premises that are true, primary and indemonstrable, immediate, and better known to the intellect than the conclusion that follows from them.[11] These explanations are *demonstrations*, whose premises are the *cause* of the conclusion. Note that "cause" must not be taken – as it is in modern science – as an event that brings about another event. Rather, a cause is one of the four causes distinguished by Aristotle (material, moving, formal, and final[12]), something that answers the question "Why?" These explanations thus afford an understanding of *why* the fact described in the conclusion was necessary. (2) If, for want of suitable primary principles, the explanation proceeds inversely, that is, from perceptible facts, which are better known to us but less well known "in themselves" (i.e., to the intellect), then the cause is not indicated and we gain merely an understanding *that* this or that is the case, but without being told why.[13]

Another kind of argument studied by Aristotle (in the *Topics*) are dialectical arguments, whose premises are views accepted by consensus and, as such, are not productive of scientific knowledge. This, at least, was the theory, although in practice Aristotle himself drew on dialectical arguments in his scientific works, so that his own scientific theories do not always conform to the strict methodological rules he laid down in his logical writings.[14]

The primary principles qualifying as premises for demonstrations and thus as answers to the "Why?" question are the basic tenets of Aristotelian science: for instance, that there are four sublunar elements endowed with rectilinear upward and downward natural motions and a fifth, celestial, element whose natural motion is circular. The facts (or supposed facts) derived from such primary principles were considered as *demonstrated by reasoning* (Arabic, *qiyās*; Hebrew, *heqqesh*). This was the highest sort of scientific knowledge. It is important to realize that when a thinker held certain knowledge claims to have been established by "reasoning," he construed them as certain, invariant knowledge, ruling out the possibility that they might be overthrown. To be sure, one could argue that some allegedly demonstrated statement has not, as a matter of fact, been demonstrated and was therefore subject to doubt. We shall see indeed that Maimonides raised questions about some of Aristotle's own claims to have provided demonstrations of certain facts. But once a demonstration has been acknowledged as such, the possibility of doubt is foreclosed.

These conceptions are largely shared by Maimonides, who follows the scholarly consensus of the Aristotelian philosophy of his day.[15] The notions of things known "through reason" and things known "by experience" were thus by far less intuitive than Maimonides would have his correspondents in Montpellier believe. Thus, in addition to observable facts and the claims of mathematics (including mathematical astronomy), he also held much of the entrenched Aristotelian science of his day to be true. How much? This question brings us straight to Maimonides' original contributions to epistemology. As will be seen, it is precisely when Maimonides defends positions running against the contemporary scientific consensus that he has to deal creatively with epistemological questions; it is at these junctures that his philosophy of science treads off the beaten path.

Aristotle famously held the world to consist of two almost unrelated realms – the sublunar and the supralunar – and elaborated separate physical theories for them. Maimonides unreservedly embraced the Aristotelian physics for the sublunar world and considered it as having been established once and for all: "All that Aristotle states about that which is beneath the sphere of the moon is in accordance *with reasoning* [i.e., has been demonstrated]; these are things that have a known *cause* [i.e., an answer to the "Why?" question]"; Aristotle's theory of the sublunar world is "indubitably correct and no one will deviate from it unless he does not understand it or unless he has preconceived opinions that he wishes to defend."[16] In the Introduction to the second part of the *Guide*, he presents twenty-five postulates that summarize the Aristotelian physics, commenting that they "are *demonstrated* without there being a doubt as to any point concerning them. For Aristotle and the Peripatetics after him have come forward with a *demonstration* [*burhān*] for every one of them."[17]

With respect to Aristotle's views of the supralunar realm, Maimonides' stance was very different. Aristotle himself believed that his theory of the heavens was as well established as the rest of his physics. In his view, the structure ascribed to them was "according to reasoning": They existed by virtue of necessity, and therefore eternally. Maimonides, for his part, rejects this tenet as unfounded. Having fully embraced both Aristotle's theory of science and his sublunar physics, Maimonides dissociates himself from the supralunar part of Aristotle's world picture, offering two lines of reasoning, one scientific, the other epistemological.

1. On the scientific plane, Maimonides adduces two arguments to refute Aristotle's theory. The first[18] proceeds on incontrovertible, theory-independent, astronomical facts. Aristotle's necessitarian

theory implies that the structure of the heavens should be "in accordance with reason," that is, simple, with the celestial bodies fixed on concentric spheres moved by the uppermost sphere. We would expect them to revolve uniformly in the same direction around the earth at the center. But this, Maimonides observes, is not the case. The planets usually move from west to east, but occasionally they move from east to west, so that their motions are not uniform: Maimonides points out that this so-called retrograde motion is incompatible with Aristotle's necessitarian supralunar physics. Similarly, in the eighth celestial sphere the fixed stars are not evenly distributed – some zones are empty, whereas others are densely populated with stars, a fact that again is incompatible with Aristotle's necessitarian view. In Maimonides' view, then, the celestial phenomena are anomalous – or, in his term, they are *particular* – and their irregularity is at variance with Aristotle's celestial physics. Considering these manifold "particularities" of the heavenly phenomena, Maimonides says, "All this and everything that is of this sort would be very unlikely or rather would come near to being impossible if it should be believed that all this proceeds obligatory and of necessity from the deity, as is the opinion of Aristotle."[19]

Maimonides draws two metascientific consequences from the preceding scientific considerations. The first establishes a notion of God (whose existence is presupposed) as a Particularizer. Particular phenomena, Maimonides argues, indicate that the heavens are not the outcome of natural necessity, but rather were created by the Deity as He saw fit.[20] On this construal, if one asks why the heavenly phenomena were purposed as they were, then the only answer is this: "All this has been produced for an object that we do not know."[21] This entire development draws on scientific arguments to establish a philosophy of nature offering a basis for the metaphysical doctrine of the Deity whose action is visible in "pockets" of contingency, or indeterminacy existing within natural necessity[22]; this doctrine in turn allows Maimonides to counter the Aristotelian eternity thesis and to credit the Deity with creation.[23]

The second consequence Maimonides draws from the preceding scientific considerations is epistemological: Because God created the celestial region full of "particularities," that is, phenomena not following from natural necessity, *ipso facto* heavenly phenomena are not subsumable under a scientific explanation (which would derive them from the primary principles). In other words: The Particularizer has created the world in a way that makes it in part *intrinsically unknowable to man* except through revelation. Note that this epistemological stance follows not from considerations related to man's cognitive capacities, but takes its cue from the very structure of the world, which, not being regular, is not fully knowable.

What then of mathematical astronomy? Did Maimonides himself not adduce it as the very example of knowledge that is certain, on a par with mathematics? Does not Maimonides say in the *Guide* that "what is calculated" by astronomers, for example, eclipses, "is not at fault even by a minute"[24]? Maimonides is aware that the stunning exactness of mathematical astronomy may lead one to think that, after all, a scientific theory of the heavens *is* possible, that is, that the heavens resulted necessarily (with the consequence that the world is eternal): "Know with regard to astronomical matters mentioned that if an exclusively mathematically-minded man reads and understands them, he will [or: may] think that they form a cogent [i.e., decisive] demonstration that the form and number of the spheres is as stated."[25] Mathematical astronomy thus poses to his theory of the principled unknowability of the heavens a possible threat that he must find a way to avert.

Suitable arguments were readily at hand. It was Maimonides' good fortune that the mathematical astronomy of his time was very problematic from the vantage point of Aristotelian theory of science and philosophy. To put a complicated matter into a nutshell, astronomers postulated various mathematical devices that posited rotatory motions of the spheres carrying the planets, whose centers of rotation were not the center of the world (located at the center of the earth). The epicycle, for instance, described a rotatory motion around a center that itself was in circular motion around the earth; and the eccentric sphere was one that rotated around a fixed center that was not the center of the earth. Now this kind of structure is incompatible with Aristotelian physics, which considers as *demonstrated* the notion that the earth is the center of all natural rotatory motions. This incompatibility of mathematical astronomy and Aristotelian supralunar physics had been widely debated in the Arabic scientific and philosophical literature, of which Maimonides was very well informed.[26]

For Maimonides, the fact that mathematical astronomy, whose premises run against the most entrenched assumptions of Aristotelian science, still possesses such a striking exactness is a "true perplexity."[27] Indeed Maimonides surmises that Aristotle himself, had he been acquainted with Ptolemaic astronomy, would have regarded it as "established as true" and (like himself) "would have become most perplexed," a speculation that has much to recommend itself.[28] Maimonides now seeks to enlist this "perplexity" in the service of his argument against the Aristotelian claims concerning the necessitarian structure of the supralunar realm.

To this effect, Maimonides offers a characterization of astronomy – or, if you will, a philosophy of astronomy – that denies it the status of demonstrated science. Against the wrong ideas of the "exclusively mathematically-minded man," mentioned in the preceding extract, who tends to think that astronomy provides "a cogent [i.e., decisive] demonstration that the form and number of the spheres is as stated" Maimonides explains:

> Now things are not like this, and this is not what is sought in the science of astronomy. Some of these matters [the claims of astronomy] are indeed founded on the demonstration that they are that way. Thus it has been demonstrated that the path of the sun is inclined against the equator. About this there is no doubt. But there has been no demonstration whether the sun has an eccentric sphere or an epicycle. Now the master of astronomy does not mind this, for the object of that science is to suppose an arrangement [or configuration: *hay'a*] that renders it possible for the motion of the star to be uniform and circular . . . and have the inferences necessarily following from the assumption of that motion agree with what is observed.[29]

A more concise and less nuanced statement is made in the following passage that has become celebrated:

> [A]ll this [i.e., the incompatibility of physics and astronomy] does not obligate the master of astronomy. For his purpose is not to tell us in which way the spheres truly are, but to posit an astronomical system [or configuration] in which it would be possible for the motions to be circular and uniform and to correspond to what is apprehended through sight, regardless of whether or not things are thus in fact.[30]

Both passages have been considered as concise and apt descriptions of an epistemological posture called "instrumentalism," and

Maimonides has indeed been described as the most remarkable medieval "precursor" of this philosophical position.[31] This statement is true, but has often been misunderstood. In modern philosophy of science, the term "instrumentalism" denotes a general, both descriptive and normative, position on the epistemological status of scientific knowledge as such, that is, all possible scientific theories, past, present, and future.[32] By contrast, Maimonides, for his part, is interested in the validity of the knowledge claims of only one particular theory – the mathematical astronomy of his days. Moreover, Maimonides makes a merely descriptive statement. He takes note of what astronomers do *in point of fact*, and urges that their body of knowledge is not "science" in the Aristotelian sense. His observation is not so much philosophical as it is "sociological," in the sense that it describes an actually existing social division of scientific labor: Natural philosophers have to do with demonstrations, and therefore with reality, whereas astronomers have to do with calculations and predictions, that, while highly useful, have no claim to bear on physical reality. It follows – and for Maimonides this is the crux of the argument – that the successes of astronomy give no reason to think that the heavens are knowable after all. This epistemological claim is in continuity with the former, physical argument that, owing to their particularities, the heavens are not subsumable under a scientific theory in the Aristotelian sense.

Maimonides held Aristotle's intellect to have been the greatest possible one.[33] How then is it possible that Aristotle considered as demonstrations arguments – namely those concerning the structure of the heavens – that, as Maimonides has shown, are invalid? Maimonides' answer is the suggestion that Aristotle himself "knows that he possesses no *demonstration* with regard to this point." "Aristotle cannot be supposed to have believed that these statements [concerning the heavens and the eternity of the world] were demonstrations, for it was Aristotle who taught mankind the methods, the rules, and the conditions of demonstration."[34] This false affirmation must thus have been ascribed to him by later philosophers only. What Aristotle offers are mere arguments, which, though appealing, are not apodictic. To buttress this suggestion, Maimonides notes that, to confirm his view, Aristotle pointed out that many peoples "accept as true" the eternity thesis and (consequently) the divinity of the heavens. Now in Aristotle's theory of science, arguments whose premises are merely "generally accepted" principles are "dialectical arguments," which, although at times unavoidable (because no better knowledge is available), are not demonstrative, and thus are of a lesser epistemological validity. The fact that Aristotle sought to strengthen his doctrine of the heavens by adducing dialectical arguments, Maimonides reasons, reveals that he himself did not really think that his other arguments were demonstrative.[35]

Maimonides concludes that the heavens are, as a matter of principle, unknowable, and will forever remain so.[36] This stance can be described as one of "epistemological pessimism," and it is highlighted by contrasting it with the views of some of Maimonides' near contemporaries. Thus, whereas Maimonides uses the difficulties of contemporary celestial science to cast doubt on the capacities of reason, his immediate predecessors in the Spanish Aristotelian school sought to solve these difficulties and advance science. The same holds also of the greatest medieval Jewish scientist, Gersonides (1288–1344): Although an admirer of Maimonides, he strongly opposed the latter's epistemology, following instead Aristotle (and Averroes) in embracing a decidedly optimistic epistemology, which goes hand in hand with his commitment to astronomical research.[37] Maimonides' posture of epistemological skepticism contrasts with the epistemological optimism of great practicing scientists such as Aristotle, Averroes, or Gersonides.

To sum up: Maimonides refutes Aristotle's theory of the celestial realm by adducing the "particularization" argument. This inner-scientific argument establishes the notion of the Deity as a Particularizer, a characteristically philosophical argument. Correlatively, Maimonides uses the *skandalon* of twelfth-century celestial science, the incompatibility of mathematical astronomy and Aristotelian cosmology, to cast further doubt on the latter. Along the way, he offers a concise definition of the "instrumentalist" construal of astronomy, through which he entered the annals of the history of the philosophy of science.

2. Maimonides attacks Aristotle's theory of the eternity of the world also on a second, epistemological, plane: He argues that human cognitive capacities are such that they do no allow man to decide the issue scientifically. In believing that he had established the eternity of the world, Aristotle had made an epistemologically unwarranted claim.

Maimonides' discussion is important and deserves to be quoted in full. His argument consists of a parable (*mashal* in classic Hebrew sources, a literary device of which Maimonides was very fond):

Assume... that a man of a most perfect natural disposition was born and that his mother died after she has suckled him for several months. And the men [the father and his male servants], alone in an isolated island, took upon themselves the entire upbringing of him who was born, until he grew up, became intelligent, and acquired knowledge. Now this child had never seen a woman or female of one of the species of the other animals. Accordingly he puts a question, saying to a man who is with him: How did we come to exist, and in what way were we generated? Thereupon the man to whom the question was put replied: Every individual among us was generated in the belly of an individual belonging like us to our species, an individual who is female and has such and such a form. Every individual among us was – being small in body – within the belly, was moved and fed there, and grew up little by little – being alive – until it reached such and such a limit in size. Thereupon an opening was opened up for him in the lower part of the body, from which he issued and came forth. Thereupon he does not cease growing until he becomes such as you see that we are. Now the orphaned child must of necessity put the question: Did every individual among us – when he was little, contained within a belly, but alive and moving and growing – did he eat, drink, breathe through the mouth and nose, produce excrements? He is answered: No.

Thereupon he indubitably will hasten to set this down as a lie and will produce a *demonstration* that all these true statements are impossible, drawing inferences from perfect things that have achieved stability. He will say: If any individual among us were deprived of breath for the fraction of an hour, he would die and his movements would cease. How then can one conceive that an individual among us could be for months within a thick vessel surrounding him, which is within a body, and yet be alive and in motion? If one of us were to swallow a sparrow, that sparrow would die immediately upon entering the stomach, and all the more the underbelly. Every individual among us would undoubtedly perish within a few days if he did not eat food with his mouth and drink water; how then can an individual remain alive for months without eating and drinking?... If the belly of one of us were perforated, he would die after some days; how then can it be supposed that the naval of the fetus in question was open?... Similarly all the analogies [logical inferences] will be carried on in order to show that it is in no respect possible that man should be generated in that manner.[38]

Like Plato's boy-slave in the *Meno*, Maimonides' boy is devoid of any individual particularities (and even of a name) – he represents human intelligence as such. He is born with "a most perfect natural disposition," that is, with the greatest possible human intelligence: His failure to understand the explanations he is given is thus not due to his personal shortcomings, but to the limits of human intelligence *per se*. Now no one will blame the child, who has never seen a female animal, for not having been able to construe that living beings are generated the way they are: The child is rational and judges on the basis of what he knows. This knowledge rules out the possibility of an animal living and growing in a "belly," with no food or air; this idea appears to run against the laws of nature.

But we, the onlookers, know better: This *is* possible; what the child justly takes for a natural impossibility in truth *is* possible. The discrepancy between the child's and our knowledge allows us, *qua* onlookers, to reflect on the limits of the child's cognitive powers: We know he errs, and he errs because he infers, or extrapolates, from the *existing* state of affairs to an *anterior* state, of which he can have no knowledge. "No inference can be drawn in any respect from the nature of a thing after it has been generated, has attained its final state, and has achieved stability in its most perfect state, to the state of that thing while it moved toward being generated," Maimonides urges[39]; "a being's state of perfection and completion furnishes no indication of the state of that being preceding its perfection."[40]

Through this parable Maimonides wishes to drive home the point that Aristotle's claim to have demonstrated the eternity of the world is unfounded. Aristotle committed the error of extrapolating from the final state of the world, that is, from the known, existing laws of nature, to conclude that a beginning in time of the world was impossible. He unwarrantedly assumed that nature has remained unchanged since all eternity, not taking into account the possibility that "at" or "during" creation other natural laws obtained (as in the female's womb). Maimonides thus holds that Aristotle has not come up with a demonstration of the eternity of the world. Conceding that creation cannot be scientifically proven either, Maimonides concludes that the question how the world came into being is strictly *undecidable by scientific means*. Because we cannot infer the past state from the present state, it follows that our reason does not enable us to investigate rationally the cosmogonic question.

What then is one to believe? Maimonides holds that, because the question cannot be decided scientifically, one's position is a matter for choice, a choice that must be made on theological, or political, grounds. Because this decision has nothing to do with science or epistemology, it does not concern us here.

Maimonides' argument is a perfect instance of an epistemological analysis. He reflects on man's cognitive capacities, or, more precisely, on the *bounds* of man's cognitive capacities. It is a reflection on the *conditions of possibility* of attaining knowledge. This is an epistemological self-reflexive argument, pointing toward a critical theory of knowledge: One realizes one cannot know all one thinks one can know; reason allows man to investigate its own limitations. The late Shlomo Pines, the translator of Maimonides' *Guide* into English and the great interpreter of his thought, made this comment: "Maimonides' emphasis on the limitations of human science is perhaps his most significant contribution to general – as distinct from Jewish – philosophical thought. Like Kant, he pointed out these limitations in order to make room for belief."[41]

Maimonides' philosophy of science, let us now note, is an integral part of his attitude toward science and its study, which I think can be characterized as ambivalent. For although Maimonides strongly emphasizes the cardinal religious importance of scientific knowledge and of the study of science, he also sets limits on the possible scope of science.

Maimonides regarded science as a key to sound knowledge of the Deity and stressed that its study was a religious obligation.[42] The first precept stated by Maimonides in the *Mishneh Torah* is "to *know* that there is a God," that is, "a First Being who brought every existing thing into being."[43] Note that the precept explicitly refers to *knowledge*, not to (mere) belief. In the famous Parable of the Palace, in which Maimonides describes the course of study one should follow in order to approach the Deity, he clearly states that the first steps are the study of logic, of mathematics and of the natural sciences, culminating in that of metaphysics.[44] In fact, Maimonides' conceptual armory – the notions of form and matter, of separately existing forms, of causality, of emanation, and so forth – is wholly grounded in Aristotelian science and philosophy, and the entire venture of the *Guide of the Perplexed* is inconceivable without it.[45] Maimonides indeed made the original claim that the *Ma'aseh Bereshit*, the Account of the Beginning, as given in Genesis and interpreted in various rabbinical (notably mystical) texts, is nothing else than Aristotelian physics, and he similarly identified

Ma'aseh Merkavah, the Account of the Chariot, with Aristotelian metaphysics.[46] These two domains of esoteric Jewish investigations were traditionally ascribed a great religious significance (although open to only the select few), and by identifying them with the secular scientific and philosophical theories, Maimonides obviously sought to endow what were originally pagan bodies of knowledge with legitimacy. Maimonides indeed urges time and again that we should "hear the truth from whoever says it." This emphatic affirmation of the importance of science certainly gave a decisive impetus to the introduction of this initially "alien wisdom" into Judaism from the thirteenth century onward. Were it not for Maimonides' immense authority (nurtured mainly by his status as a foremost authority on Jewish Law [*Halakhah*]), the study of the sciences in medieval Jewish communities would in all likelihood have been by far less pervasive.[47] Even in the early modern period, Jewish thinkers who sought to introduce the study of science into Judaism (which was then devoted mainly to study of the Talmud) enlisted Maimonides in their battles against the traditionalists.

But Maimonides' endorsement of the sciences is not full and unqualified. For one thing, for Maimonides it is the study of metaphysics that is the goal of human existence. Consequently, the study of the sciences, although indispensable as a preparation for it, has a subordinate value only. It is this role of science that is reflected in Maimonides' well-known and apparently frank comment, in a letter addressed to R. Jonathan ha-Cohen of Lunel, that all the "foreign" sciences are mere "apothecaries, cooks and bakers," maids in the service of the Torah.[48] Similarly, it must not be forgotten that Maimonides also sets limits on the scope of scientific research. Maimonides' discussion of the impossibility of investigating the cosmogonic question scientifically, coupled with his insistence on the impossibility of arriving at a scientific account of the heavens, broadcasts the message that certain questions concerning physical reality are not, and as a matter of principle *cannot* be, decided by science. Certain "pockets" in reality are such that they cannot possibly be known to man through a scientific (demonstrative) theory. For these parts of reality, Maimonides implies, faith must step in. Now this move runs against the very spirit of the scientific enterprise, one of whose guiding postulates has been that all reality can and indeed should be scientifically investigated. In fact, the very idea of a science of nature is grounded in the assumption (among others) that nature is constant – that natural necessity is invariable in time and space. This is precisely the assumption denied by Maimonides, who thereby rejects a belief that conditions the very possibility of scientific investigation. Although this stance is logically irrefutable, it is tantamount to rejecting the universal applicability of science.[49]

Maimonides' message was thus inherently ambivalent: Along with the explicit and insisting affirmations concerning the importance of science, there is the view that it is only ancillary to metaphysics and that some questions cannot be subjected to scientific inquiry. This ambivalence can be perceived in the conflicting, even antagonistic effects Maimonides' philosophy of science had on the centuries to come. Consider the following two opposed instances.

Gersonides, who saw himself as a faithful follower of Maimonides, is the scientistic[50] hero: He upheld and loudly proclaimed the view that human reason is capable of investigating all reality. Specifically, he held not only that man can and should investigate the cosmogonic question, but believed he had solved it definitely, that is, that he discovered the demonstrative, scientific theory of creation. He also devoted the greater part of his life to astronomical research whose goal was to describe scientifically the nature of the heavens – exactly the project of which Maimonides had affirmed that it was in principle beyond human reach.[51] An independent mind like Gersonides' thus had no difficulty accommodating his scientific investigations within the Maimonidean program as he construed it.

But Maimonides, or at least his arguments, could also be enlisted in the service of fundamentalist thinkers upholding an ideology of antiscience. In his attempt to salvage the thesis that the world was created in six days (the term "day" being understood in its ordinary everyday meaning!), Menachem Mendel Schneersohn, the last rabbi of Lubavitch, rejects the relevance of all scientific knowledge (geology and theoretical physics) having implications for the question of the age of the universe. To this effect, he argues that we have no way of knowing the laws of nature that obtained "before" or "at" the creation, so that any extrapolation from the present state to the past is invalid.[52] This is precisely the argument that had been adduced by Maimonides some eight centuries earlier, and in all likelihood Schneersohn borrowed it directly from him. The philosophy of science of a twelfth-century thinker, we see, is not necessarily of purely antiquarian interest.

Maimonides, in sum, saw in science a cornerstone of human and Jewish thought and thereby legitimized its study in Judaism once and for all. But in contradistinction to Gersonides, he did not view it as an end in itself, and he also sought to restrict its applicability. His ambivalence toward science is reflected in the immediately following centuries,[53] arguably to this very day, when Judaism's attitude to science remains under continuous debate.

5.2.3. Maimonides' Philosophy of Empirical Knowledge

Aristotle offered a theory of matter, at whose core were the notions of the four elements (earth, water, air, fire) and the four qualities (hot, cold, dry, moist), which was to explain all material properties of substances. It followed that the action of drugs should be deducible from the theory. On Aristotelian premises, if a patient is, say, hot, then administering to him or her a drug whose cold quality is strong will be beneficial as it will help his or her body get back to a healthy state, one in which all components are in equilibrium. Such an action was considered as having been explained "demonstratively" by "reasoning" [*qiyās*] inasmuch as it was shown to follow from the Aristotelian principles, according to which the effects of the drug depend on, and only on, its qualities. The Rationalist school in Hellenistic medicine defended this line of thought.[54] Maimonides himself elegantly formulates its rationale:

> [T]he Empiricists, who do not follow [the method of logical] reasoning [*qiyās*], commit errors, so that occasionally [their treatment] succeeds, [namely] by mere chance, but at other times it does not succeed. Therefore, someone who places himself in the hands of an Empiricist physician, who does not know the rules of [logical] reasoning [*qiyās*], is like a sailor who surrenders himself to the blowing of the wind, which is not according to [logical] reasoning [i.e., cannot be deduced logically from the theory]. Occasionally the blowing of the wind brings the sailor to his destination in the best possible way, but at other times it is the cause of his drowning. I have drawn your attention to this merely because people are often duped by the empirical treatment of the Empiricists. Some escape unharmed, others die, [everything] by mere chance.[55]

Not all material properties could be deduced from the Aristotelian principles, however. In medicine, specifically, certain substances were believed to have effects that were not subsumable under the Aristotelian principles. Their action, it was therefore held, was due not to their qualities (or matter), but to a "form," superadded over and above the properties following from the components. This sort of power of a substance was referred to as its "specific property" (Arabic, *khāṣṣa*; Hebrew, *segulah*).[56] The paradigmatic example of a specific property was the attractive power of the magnet. The existence of specific properties was one of the arguments that proponents of the Empiricist school adduced against the Rationalists.

In the *Commentary on Hippocrates' "Aphorisms,"* one of his medical writings, Maimonides emphasizes that specific properties of substances cannot be inferred from their composition – this, in fact, is their very definition.[57] How, then, does one come to know these properties, whose existence is not allowed for by the Aristotelian theory (so that it cannot be inferred from it)? Maimonides has to reason against the Aristotelian theory of science: "observe by yourself and you'll witness that many drugs are of one and the same force with respect, say, to heat and dryness [i.e., according to the Aristotelian theory they should have had the same effects], and yet each one of them has [specific] effects not shared by the others." How, then, does one know these effects? Because these effects cannot be known by reason, it follows that they are known merely by experience: "concerning the action of a drug by virtue of its specific property... we have no demonstration thereof,... and there is no way of knowing it except by experience."[58] In the *Treatise on Logic*, too, Maimonides briefly says that "what has been found out by experience, as e.g. the purgative virtue of scammony,... is reliable."[59] Maimonides, as the other Aristotelians, therefore considered medicine to be an art rather than a science.

The modern reader may be tempted to rejoice at such statements, viewing in them a Baconian, empirical attitude to science. This would be too hasty, however. For what do Maimonides and his contemporaries mean by *experience*? Classic examples are the poisonous effects of certain plants and fruits, the deadly effects of a snake's venom, and the undeniable virtues of scammony. Although one would readily concur that these are verifiable empirical generalizations, Maimonides also opines: "those bitten by crocodile, if they put the crocodile-fat on the wound, they heal instantly. This has been shown by ocular experience."[60] Maimonides similarly says of the "hanging of a peony on a epileptic and the giving of a dog's excrements in cases of swelling of the throat" that "experience has shown [them] to be valid even if reasoning does not imply them."[61] With respect to the efficiency of peony Maimonides assures his reader: "this has been tried out."[62] Many similar statements that few readers would wish to try out on themselves can be found in Maimonides' medical works, as in those of his contemporaries.

Obviously, the notion of "experience" as used by Maimonides has little to do with our own notion of experience. Indeed, ever since Hippocrates, physicians were aware that gaining medical experience takes a long time. Many illnesses are rare, so that occasions to see how a given drug affects them may not offer themselves to every physician during his lifetime. Moreover, because experiments on animal models were not known, "experience" often involved danger for the patients. It was thus agreed that beliefs concerning the specific properties of various substances cannot be tested anew by every physician.[63] As Maimonides himself stresses, "all this has been established by experience over a long time."[64] The "experience" of the medical tradition thus included accumulated, purportedly empirical know-how that was transmitted from one generation of physicians to another and accepted on faith.

Faith in whom? In the *Treatise on Logic* Maimonides identifies as a distinct source of knowledge what one receives from persons for whose trustworthiness one has proofs. From such people, he says, we may accept knowledge passed on "in tradition," without asking them for a distinct proof for each of their affirmations, and he doubtless has in mind (among others) earlier or contemporary physicians.[65] "I met many people [i.e., physicians] in every town to which I came and they told me that they have found what I just mentioned," Maimonides writes, affording a rare insight into his practice as a physician.[66] Although Maimonides elsewhere warns that one must not accept from anyone claims on faith alone without prior examination,[67] we saw that in point of fact he was fully aware that the accepted medical knowledge largely consisted of recipes handed down within the profession. In his medical writings, Maimonides often teaches the "specific properties" of drugs, which he collected from the medical literature current in his time (notably Galen, who lived exactly

1,000 years earlier). Like his contemporaries, he apparently considered the physicians, past and present, as trustworthy.

Nonetheless, physicians naturally made their own experience with certain remedies that they administered to their patients. They were thus led to consider pieces of traditional knowledge as confirmed or disconfirmed by personal experience. Maimonides thus writes[68]:

> Bezoar has not been mentioned by Galen.... Mineral bezoar is a multicolored stone which is found in Egypt. The latter-day physicians have told marvels about it, but nothing has been confirmed. I have tried all the mineral stones available here in the cases of stings by scorpions, and they do not bring about any improvement. I prescribed them often, but to no avail. By contrast, the reports concerning the bezoar originating in animals have been confirmed and its usefulness has been established by experience.... When you apply it to the wound, the patient will heal and be saved. Among all the drugs, having their origin in mineral, vegetal, or animal substances, the following three kinds [of drugs] have proved their mettle by experience in a way not leaving any place to doubt.

Thus although the notion of experience did not imply a systematic effort to test the efficacy of remedies, physicians learned from the successes and failures of their treatments. They integrated this feedback into the body of knowledge that they passed on as "experience." In this process, Galenic medical theory remained unimpinged. The Galenic pharmacopoeia, too, was considered as established by experience and remained largely intact. Still, physicians occasionally modified their views on the efficacy of this or that drug in the light of their own or their contemporaries' experience.

Maimonides, we see, was caught in a web of contradictory commitments, which he was unable to reconcile. He had to recognize the validity of the "specific properties," although it was negated by the Aristotelian theory of science, which he upheld; he would wish no knowledge claim to be accepted on faith alone, but because it was impossible to try out all purportedly efficacious drugs, he had to draw on allegedly empirical know-how described in centuries-old books and handed down by supposedly trustworthy confreres. This contradiction reappears on another level too: Maimonides believed that the dietary rules of the Law follow scientifically valid goals and stated that the Law forbids one to make use of specific properties (i.e., those that are not "required by natural philosophy"[69]). Yet he had to allow their use, by virtue of their supposed efficiency ("it is allowed to use all remedies... that experience has shown to be valid even if reasoning does not require them"[70]). Maimonides' philosophy of empirical science, in sum, was inadequate to deal with the science of his day, which he could not and did not wish to dismiss.

The stake here was greater than is apparent. Epistemology, for Maimonides, was not of merely theoretical interest. Rather, in his struggle against all forms of idolatry, one of his main arguments was that idolatry proceeds on premises that are all entirely false, with the consequence that its interdiction by the Law is not arbitrary but well founded. The precepts in the *Laws Concerning Idolatry*, Maimonides writes, "all... have in view deliverance from the *errors* of idolatry and from other *incorrect* opinions that may accompany idolatry."[71] This holds specifically of astrology and all the practices based on it – predictions of individual or collective fates, as also astral magic. To buttress his affirmation that astrology is all false, Maimonides argued that it is a nonscience inasmuch as it is not grounded in any of the sources of trustworthy knowledge (see preceding discussion, p. 136). This epistemological argument, we can now realize, rests on shaky ground. The practitioners of astrology or astral magic readily conceded that their doctrines did not qualify as a science in the Aristotelian sense (based on "demonstrations"). But they claimed that their practices are *efficacious*, and are thus on equal footing with the "specific properties" of medicine[72]: Their practice, they argued, is based not on "reasoning," but on "experience" gathered by practitioners during many centuries. Abraham Ibn Ezra (1089–1164), for one, the greatest medieval Jewish astrologer and indirectly the target of Maimonides' criticism in the *Letter on Astrology*, explicitly put forward this argument. Contrary to astronomy, in which one disposes of "apodictic demonstrations," he wrote, the proofs of astrology are based on "experience, *just as in the science of medicine* there are things that run against what is implied by physics."[73] In his writings, Ibn Ezra very often states, apropos of a given astrological postulate, that "this has often been tried out and has succeeded."[74] Now because Maimonides himself recognized that medical "experience" – that is, empirical knowledge that does not follow from Aristotelian theory, but whose validity is certified by tradition – is epistemologically legitimate, he had no cogent argument against the astrologers' claim. In addition, astrologers now and then succeeded in their predictions, just as some patients healed after (although not necessarily as a result of) being treated by physicians. This, to be sure, added credence to their claims. Maimonides himself admitted that expert astrologers often made correct predictions.[75]

As an intellectual tool, Maimonides' philosophy of empirical science was lame. To substantiate the claim that astrology is forbidden because it is erroneous, Maimonides needed an epistemology showing it to be a pseudoscience. The established theory of science readily allowed him to show that it indeed was not a science in the Aristotelian sense, a claim, however, that the astrologers did not dispute. But he had no means to counter the astrologers' claim that their craft was as legitimate, and as grounded in experience, as medicine. He had no epistemology at his disposal with which to differentiate the would-be experience of the physicians from that of the astrologers, except by holding that the former group, but not the latter, is "trustworthy." At bottom, therefore, Maimonides could only state, but not establish by a rational argument, the claim that astrology and its cognates were pseudosciences. This of course is not a criticism of Maimonides: It simply points out the limits of the science of his day.

5.3. MAIMONIDES' PHILOSOPHY OF TEXTUAL INTERPRETATION (HERMENEUTICS)

Medieval philosophers counted revelation among the sources of knowledge. As we saw, Maimonides advised the rabbis of Montpellier that one may give credence to what "a man receives from the prophets [i.e., revelation] or from the righteous [i.e., those who faithfully transmit the contents of revelation]." The reliability of one's knowledge thus hinges on one's ability to identify these sources and transmitters of knowledge. In the introduction to his *Commentary on the Mishnah*, Maimonides goes to considerable length in stating the criteria by which a true prophet can be distinguished from a false one and then describes how the Law, having been revealed to Moses, was handed down from one generation to another in an uninterrupted and trustworthy chain of transmission – called *qabbalah*.[76] Through these historical outlines, Maimonides aimed to establish the infallibility of the Jewish tradition in the face of criticism, notably by the Karaites and the Moslems, who recognized the validity of

Moses' prophecy, but alleged that it was distorted or falsified during its long transmission by the Jews. Against both, the authenticity of revealed knowledge, especially the revealed Law, had to be set on secure foundations by showing that its transmission conformed to the rule stated in the *Treatise on Logic*, according to which trustworthy persons are a legitimate source of knowledge (namely for premises for dialectical arguments).[77]

Granted that the authoritative books of Judaism convey revealed truths, to get at them, one must be able to understand the relevant texts. This is more hazardous than it may seem. As is well known, Maimonides opens the *Guide* with the following statement: "The first purpose of this Treatise is to explain the meanings of certain terms occurring in the books of prophecy," which, he adds, "the ignorant" misunderstand.[78] Maimonides then reviews many terms and expressions occurring in Scripture, explaining why, if taken literally, they suggest a false, that is, corporeal, conception of God. For Maimonides this is the greatest philosophical error and the worst form of idolatry. He goes on to spell out for each term the meaning or meanings that avoid anthropomorphic consequences.

Along with specific textual interpretations, Maimonides also reflects on the conditions of interpretation. Analyses of this kind belong to the philosophical discipline known as "hermeneutics," which is part of the philosophy of science (viz., of the philosophy of human science).[79] A guiding principle of Maimonides' hermeneutics is that, correctly understood, Scripture cannot contradict reason, that is, what has been demonstrated by science. An apparent contradiction between Scripture and science signals that we have misunderstood Scripture, in particular the "parables and secrets" that are "the key to its understanding."[80] Take the verse "Let us make man in our image, after our likeness" (Genesis 1:26). The simple-minded will be prone to understand it as implying that God has man's physical shape; by contrast, the philosophically schooled, knowing that this cannot be the intended meaning, will identify a "secret." They will thereupon set out to discover the true meaning and eventually will recognize that, far from implying the corporeality of God, this verse states a philosophically sound tenet concerning man's intellectual form.[81]

On the level of hermeneutic theory, Maimonides thus holds that *without the succor of demonstrative science one is condemned to misinterpret much of Scripture.* Verses are not "earmarked" as to whether they should be interpreted literally or metaphorically: This has to be decided by the reader, who must draw on his or her scientific and philosophical knowledge. One can easily fall prey to the illusion that one understands Scripture by virtue of being able to read Hebrew. In point of fact, many words and phrases are, as it were, encoded – they have a particular, philosophic, sense, so that understanding them on their ordinary meaning inevitably leads to error, even heresy. For the naive reader, the revealed text is therefore full of pitfalls.

Reason not only provides a yardstick for the identification of secrets but also the key for deciphering them. According to Maimonides, wherever science provides a valid demonstration, the revealed text *must* be interpreted accordingly. He makes this clear in the following impressive statement:

> Know that our shunning the affirmation of the eternity of the world is not due to a text figuring in the Torah according to which the world has been produced in time [i.e., created]. For the texts indicating that the world has been produced in time are not more numerous than those indicating that the deity is a body. Nor are the gates of figurative interpretation shut in our faces or impossible of access to us regarding the subject of the creation of the world in time. For we could interpret them as figurative, as we have done when denying His corporeality. Perhaps this would even be much easier to do: we should be very well able to give a figurative interpretation of those texts and to affirm as true the eternity of the world, just as we have given a figurative interpretation of those other texts and have denied that He, may He be exalted, is a body.[82]

Maimonides here acknowledges that, should Aristotelians come forward with a demonstration of the eternity of the world, he would have no difficulty showing that this is the doctrine stated in the biblical text. As we saw, it is only because no such demonstration has been adduced that he chose to adhere to the traditional interpretation. This approach concedes that, whenever science demonstrates a principle, Scripture must be interpreted in conformity with it. Maimonides' hermeneutics thereby institutes the demonstrated truths of science as a key to the interpretation of Scripture. Moreover, he holds that such an interpretation will always be within reach, for, as we saw, "the gates of figurative interpretation [are not] shut in our faces." This significant statement amounts to an outright rebuttal of the very principle of fundamentalism, which holds that under all circumstances Scripture must be interpreted literally – even if it flies in the face of well-established scientific truths.[83]

But Maimonides' rejection of fundamentalism is purchased at a high price. On his view, in order to understand, say, the verse about man's having been created in "the likeness" of God, we need to know *beforehand*, through independent sources, what his true likeness is, namely that it is intellectual, not physical. Scientific knowledge is the key that allows one to identify the terms or phrases that must not be interpreted literally and to decipher their true meaning. Without prior scientific knowledge, the text of the divine message is either misleading or remains sealed and shut, like an enciphered message whose code has been lost. In the past, the Israelites possessed the necessary scientific and philosophic knowledge,[84] but because this wisdom has been lost in the exile, at present it is the science acquired by Aristotle and his Muslim followers that affords access to the proper understanding of revelation. Only where human reason reaches its limits (e.g., on the issue of creation) can one lend credence to the text's literal meaning. In short, the bare text, without scientific keys to its secrets, tells us nothing, so that, for unaided readers, the true meaning remains beyond reach. For a Jewish theologian, this is a bold position.

5.4. CONCLUSION

Maimonides was drawn into epistemological reflections when he had to defend the choices he made on the level of the body of knowledge against opposite claims. His stance here is dual: Although he views Aristotelian sublunar science as unshakably true, he casts serious doubt on Aristotle's celestial physics. Correspondingly, his epistemology is ambivalent too. On the one hand, he upholds man's cognitive powers, which allow him to transcend the empirically given. Sound knowledge of sublunar nature is therefore attainable, just as Aristotle had taught. This stance sustains Maimonides' appeal to science as the underpinning of metaphysics and his resulting, oft-repeated (and, from a historical point of view, critically important) exhortation for the study of science for religious ends. On the other hand, Maimonides argues that, as a matter of principle, man's cognitive powers are limited: Most notably cosmogony is beyond the ken of man, because it necessarily involves inference from an existing state to a preceding one of which we can have no knowledge. Moreover, Maimonides draws argument from an inner-scientific tenet, namely that there is no regularity in the heavens (they are the handiwork of a Particularizer), to conclude that they are unknowable too. On both counts Maimonides undermines one of the constitutive principles of science, namely the premise that nature is always regular and thus knowable to man.

Maimonides' position on empirical knowledge is contradictory as well, although no theological considerations are involved here. As all his contemporaries do, Maimonides recognizes specific properties as being grounded in experience, although they run against the Aristotelian theory of matter. Experience, for Maimonides, consists mainly of purportedly empirical know-how, transmitted by a trustworthy tradition. This construal leaves Maimonides quite helpless in the face of the claims of astrologers to the effect that their art is as solidly based on experience as medicine is. Maimonides presumably held that the medical professional group was more trustworthy than that of the astrologers, but this is a sociological, not an epistemological, criterion. In fact, astrologers in Maimonides' time were probably no less successful than physicians.

Last, in his hermeneutics, Maimonides contends that, to get at the meaning of the biblical text, the reader must be equipped with prior scientific knowledge. In regard to the bare text of, say, Genesis, one can read into it the theory of creation *ex nihilo* just as well as the theory of the eternity of the world: Thus had the eternity thesis been demonstrated, Maimonides would have interpreted creation accordingly. Because it has not been demonstrated, the literal meaning of Scripture is not contradicted by scientific truth and it must be accepted, in continuity with tradition. Notwithstanding his epistemological pessimism with respect to some domains of physical reality, Maimonides thus sets a high stake on scientific knowledge. Only individuals equipped with science can correctly identify the "riddles" in the text and interpret them rightly; the naive and uneducated reader will necessarily err (unless he or she entrusts himself or herself to a competent master) and, alas, will not enjoy the world to come. Indeed, Maimonides considers physics to be indispensable on the road leading up to the metaphysical knowledge of God (as far as that is within human reach), which is the goal of human existence and, in the Messianic days, will be the "one preoccupation of the whole world."[85] In Maimonides' thought about science – its scope and possible validity – many lines of force were simultaneously active, resulting in an inherently ambivalent stance that was to leave its marks on the multifarious Jewish attitudes to science from the thirteenth century until this very day.

ACKNOWLEDGMENT

I am grateful to Professor Ruth Glasner and particularly to Professor Josef Stern for their helpful observations on a draft of this essay.

NOTES

1. Doubt on its authorship has recently been cast by Professor Herbert A. Davidson. In what follows I assume Maimonides to be the author, but only to illustrate widely agreed-on points.
2. Lerner 1963b, p. 228 (modified).
3. *Treatise on Logic*, Chapter 8. The first two are the "common notions" in Euclid's *Elements*.
4. Maimonides, "Introduction to the Mishnah," in Shailat 5752 (= 1992), pp. 350–1 (Arabic original), 53–4 (Hebrew translation).
5. *GP* 1.73, p. 210. Maimonides refers to Apollonius' *Conics*, written ca. 190 B.C.E. and available to him in its Arabic translation.
6. The epistemological argument is not Maimonides' invention. On its long history, see Freudenthal 1988.
7. *GP* 1.73, p. 210. Note that Maimonides does not distinguish between "existence" proved in mathematics (asymptotes) from "existence" entailed by physical theory (antipodes). He similarly affirms that astronomical statements are true because they follow from the first principles of reason (*Treatise on Logic*, Chapter 8).
8. For Maimonides, imagination was a bodily function, as opposed to that of intellect: It is incumbent on a man who wishes to reinforce his intellectual powers while reducing the hold on him of imagination to follow an appropriate way of life. See, e.g., *GP* 1.32.
9. By contrast, Maimonides was well aware that the impossibility of knowing "the nature" of π or of $\sqrt{2}$ (their numerical values can be given only approximately) is not due to a limitation of man's intellect, but to the intrinsic mathematical natures of π and $\sqrt{2}$ themselves; cf. *CM*, 'Eruvin 1.5, 2.5.

10. *Post. Anal.* 1.2, 71b35 ff.
11. *Post. Anal.* 1.2, 71b17–19.
12. See, e.g., *Physics* 2.3, 2.7; *Metaphysics* 5:2; *Treatise on Logic*, Chapter 9.
13. *Post. An.* 1.13, 78a21ff. There are thus two "roads" to knowledge, at times construed as downward ("analysis") and upward ("synthesis") movements, respectively. In the Latin tradition they were called *demonstratio quia* and *demonstratio propter quid*. The question of how one passes (by a mental process Aristotle calls "induction") from the former to the latter was discussed by Aristotle and his commentators, but need not detain us here.
14. In the treatise *On Sophistical Refutations* Aristotle also discussed sophistic arguments, which, however, are not relevant to the present discussion.
15. See Hyman 1989. For an important qualification see J. Stern 2001, pp. 57–9.
16. *GP*, 2.24, p. 326 and 2.22, p. 319. Maimonides concludes his exposition of the Aristotelian theory of the four elements and four qualities with these words: "All this is correct and clear to whoever treats his own soul equitably and does not deceive it" (*GP*, 2.19, p. 304). In his letter to Samuel Ibn Tibbon, Maimonides says that Aristotle's intellect has attained the utmost of what human intellect is capable of attaining without the aid of prophecy. See Shailat 5748 (= 1988), p. 553.
17. *GP*, "Introduction to the Second Part," p. 235.
18. *GP* 2.19.
19. *GP* 2.19, p. 310.
20. Note that Maimonides bases his argument on "particular," irregular, phenomena, in opposition to arguments from design that proceed from the regularity of nature.
21. *GP* 2.19, p. 310.
22. This point has been emphasized by the late Amos Funkenstein (1977). Funkenstein also pointed out the implications of this philosophy of nature for Maimonides' political doctrines.
23. My view of Maimonides' much-debated stance on creation follows Davidson 1979.
24. *GP* 2.24, p. 326.
25. *GP* 2.11, pp. 273–4.
26. The classic account is Gauthier 1909; for more recent accounts in English, see Sabra 1984, 1998; Saliba 1999.
27. See Langermann 1991a.
28. *GP* 2.24, p. 326. Ptolemy's *Almagest* dates from the first century C.E., i.e., some four centuries after Aristotle. Maimonides similarly notes

that "the science of mathematics [including mathematical astronomy] had not been perfected in his [Aristotle's] time and since the motions of the sphere were not known in his time to the extent to which we know them today" (*GP* 2.19, p. 308).

29. *GP* 2.11, pp. 273–4. Note that the ecliptic's inclination does not conflict with Aristotle's science, whereas eccentric spheres do.
30. *GP* 2.24, p. 326 (slightly modified).
31. This view has been taken primarily by Pierre Duhem (1861–1916), a French scientist, philosopher of science, and historian of science. As a devout Catholic, Duhem sought to promote the instrumentalist view of science in order to "salvage" Catholic dogma from the threats of contemporary science (atomist theory, for instance). To this effect he argued, among other things, that science progressed most when scientists adhered to the instrumentalist philosophy of science. See notably Duhem 1969. Although many of Duhem's historical analyses have been shown to be wrong, his book remains a classic.
32. In his influential essay. "Three Views Concerning Human Knowledge" ([1956]/1963, p. 111), the late Sir Karl R. Popper (1902–94) has aptly defined instrumentalism "as the thesis that scientific theories – the theories of the so-called 'pure' sciences – are nothing but computation rules (or inference rules); of the same character, fundamentally, as the computation rules of the so-called 'applied' sciences." On this view, which has become standard in subsequent philosophy of science, "instrumentalism" is the thesis that "scientific theories are useful and that scientists are justified in using them even if the entities they countenance are fictional" (Morgenbesser 1969, p. 201). Thus it is opposed to the position called "realism," which holds that scientific theories consist of the statements reflecting (more or less precisely) reality, and positing entities that exist. On the entire issue see in more detail Freudenthal 2003.
33. Shailat, 5748 (= 1988), p. 553.
34. *GP* 2.15, pp. 289–90.
35. *GP* 2.14 (in Fine), p. 289. See the detailed analysis in Kraemer 1989, pp. 66–74.
36. *GP* 2.24, p. 327.
37. See Freudenthal 1996.
38. *GP* 2.17, pp. 295–6.
39. *GP* 2.17, p. 295.
40. *GP* 2.17, p. 297ff.
41. Pines 1997, Vol. 5, p. 356.
42. See the classic article, Davidson 1974.
43. *Book of Knowledge* 1.1; see Maimonides 1974a, p. 34a.

44. *GP* 3.51, p. 618–9.
45. Here the following intriguing question suggests itself: Given that the science on which the *Guide* is based is known to be entirely false, and that such concepts as "form," "matter," etc., appear to be vacuous, are not then Maimonides' most basic statements without any truth value? And if so, what benefit can the modern reader draw from Maimonides' *Guide*?
46. *GP*, Introduction to the First Part, p. 6; *Book of Knowledge*, "Laws Concerning the Basic Principles of the Torah," Chapters 1–4.
47. Freudenthal 1995.
48. See Shailat 5748 (= 1988), p. 502.
49. It is on a par with the arguments of creationists, medieval and contemporary, who discard the evidence of fossils by saying God could have created and placed in the soil objects appearing to man as if they were so-and-so many millions of years old.
50. The term "scientism," to be distinguished from "scientific," denotes an attitude of great confidence in science, in its progressive character, and in the benefits it can bestow on humanity; it is the opposite of an "antiscience," or "obscurantist," attitude to science.
51. See Freudenthal 1996.
52. For example, letter dated 10 Marheshvan 5716, in Schneersohn (rabbi of Lubavitch) 5740 (= 1980), pp. 97–8; letter dated 18 Tevet 5722, ibid., pp. 89–96, esp. pp. 92–4. The rabbi of Lubavitch also used the arguments against the evidence from fossils, mentioned in n. 49.
53. See Freudenthal 2001.
54. The bone of contention that opposed the Rationalist and the Empiricist schools in the fierce battle that divided Hellenistic medicine between the third century B.C.E. and the third century C.E. was the question of whether medicine should be based essentially on rational deductions from first principles or on knowledge directly gained from experience. Galen (ca. 129–200 C.E.), the foremost doctor of antiquity, discussed these debates in many of his writings and took a middle position. A great number of his writings were known to Maimonides in their Arabic translations, and Galen is the physician whom Maimonides held in highest esteem, notwithstanding his harsh critique of him as a philosopher.
55. Maimonides, *On Asthma*, 11.3, quoted after Bos 2002, pp. 61–2 (translation slightly modified).
56. The term "occult quality" is also used in this context. In medieval science and philosophy this term simply meant "unintelligible" and "hidden," in the sense that the quality in question could not be explained on rational grounds and, furthermore, could not be perceived by the senses

(unlike manifest qualities such as coldness). After the scientific revolution of the seventeenth century, however, the term "occult quality" has acquired a decidedly negative connotation and I therefore avoid using it. In his *Treatise on Poisons and Their Antidotes*, Maimonides writes, "All these antidotes, when they save from poisons, do not act by way of their qualities. Rather, they act by way of the totality of their substance – i.e. through their [specific] quality, as it is said – [a fact that] is unknown to physicians. This means, as the philosophers have explained, that they act by way of their specific form." Muntner 5702 (= 1942), pp. 104ff.

57. Muntner 1961, pp. 12–14.
58. Muntner 1961, p. 13. This in fact is a classic argument raised by the Empiricists to refute the Rationalists' position, and Maimonides may echo Galen's brief exposition of the argument in "On Medical Experience," Chapter IV, which was available in Arabic; see Walzer 1985, p. 71.
59. *Treatise on Logic*, Chapter 8.
60. Maimonides, *Aphorisms of Moses* 21:54; in Muntner 1957, p. 251. This statement is borrowed from Galen.
61. *GP* 3.37, p. 544.
62. Maimonides, *Aphorisms of Moses* 22.18; in Muntner 1957, p. 270.
63. *Commentary on the Aphorisms of Hippocrates*, in Muntner 1961, p. 13ff.
64. Muntner 1961, p. 14.
65. *Treatise on Logic*, Chapter 8.
66. *Samei ha-mawet we-ha-refu'ot ke-negdam*, in Muntner 5702 (= 1942), p. 146.
67. *Aphorisms of Moses* 25:69, in Muntner 1957, p. 390ff.
68. *Samei ha-mawet we-ha-refu'ot ke-negdam*, in Muntner 5702 (= 1942), pp. 106–7. Elsewhere Maimonides writes, "Of this [drug] I do not myself have any experience, but I felt obliged to mention what I knew [from hearsay], so that eventually someone else may try to use it and perhaps save a person and thus draw benefit" (ibid., p. 147).
69. *GP* 3.37, p. 543.
70. *GP* 3.37, p. 544.
71. *GP* 3.37, p. 540.
72. *GP* 3.37, p 543.
73. Sela 2001a, p. 13 (quoting the Introduction to *Reshit Hokhmah*).
74. Sela 2001, p. 11.
75. Maimonides, "Introduction to the *Mishnah*," in Shailat, 5752 (= 1992), p. 332 (Arabic original), pp. 32–3 (Hebrew translation).
76. A similar account is given also in the introduction to *Mishneh Torah*: see Maimonides 1974, pp. 1b–5a. The term *qabbalah* here of course does not denote the body of esoteric teachings known as the *qabbalah*.

77. See *Treatise on Logic*, Chapter 8, and *supra*, pp. 144–5.
78. *GP* "Introduction to the First Part," p. 5.
79. The best introduction to hermeneutics and the best exposition of its development is still that in Gadamer 1989.
80. *GP* 2.2, p. 254.
81. *GP* 1.1, p. 21.
82. *GP* 2.25, p. 327.
83. In contemporary Judaism, the fundamentalist position has been often and explicitly stated by R. Menachem Mendel Schneersohn, the last rabbi of Lubavitch; see n. 52. The fact that Maimonides' hermeneutics is antifundamentalist does not imply that Maimonides himself was "liberal." He believed that his reading of the Scripture was *the* only correct reading, and he did not countenance the possibility that what he considers to be truth can be overthrown in the future. He held some idolatrous views to be dangerous and argued that their proponents should be executed.
84. *GP* 1.71, p. 175ff. This idea is a recurrent motif among Jewish and non-Jewish scholars, going back to Antiquity; see Roth 1978.
85. *MT* 14, Kings and Wars, 12.5.

DAVID SHATZ

6 Maimonides' Moral Theory

6.1. INTRODUCTION: THE STATUS OF MORALITY IN MAIMONIDEAN THOUGHT

What sort of life constitutes the highest perfection for a human being? For Maimonides, as for Aristotle,[1] the answer is not moral excellence, but rather intellectual perfection, that is, "the conception of the intelligibles [eternal truths], which teach true opinions concerning the divine things" (*GP* 3.54, p. 692). Attaining this perfection leads to immortality.[2] Morality, by contrast, is "a preparation for something else" (viz., the life of contemplation) "and not an end in itself" (*GP* 3.54, p. 635). "To [the] ultimate perfection there do not belong either actions or moral qualities" (*GP* 3.27, p. 511). The subordination of moral perfection to intellectual perfection is already found in Maimonides' early work, the *Commentary on the Mishnah*: "Man needs to subordinate all his soul's powers to thought... and to set his sight on a single goal: the perception of God... I mean, knowledge of Him, in so far as that lies within man's power."[3]

Moral perfection cannot be supreme, Maimonides argues, for the highest perfection cannot involve, as part of its essence, anyone else besides the person who is questing for perfection. The ultimate perfection must be achievable even by a solitary individual with no social connections. Because moral habits are only dispositions to be useful to other people, "it [moral perfection] is an instrument for someone else" (*GP* 3.54, p. 635. See also 1.34). Just as God's perfection does not depend on anything outside Himself, so too the perfected person is a self-sufficient agent and his ultimate perfection does not require others for its attainment.

Maimonides alludes to yet another reason why moral virtues cannot be part of the ultimate perfection. In the course of asserting that the ultimate perfection consists only of intellection, he states that the ultimate perfection "consists only of opinions toward which speculation has led and that investigation has rendered compulsory" (*GP* 3.27, p. 511). Unlike scientific and metaphysical truths, moral claims cannot be supported by a demonstration that renders them "compulsory." At one point Maimonides chastises Jewish thinkers (most likely Saadia Gaon) who accepted the terms of the *mutakallimūn* and referred to Torah laws against stealing, killing, and the like as "rational" laws (*EC*, 6). His objection, one surmises, is that, although these laws serve a purpose and are rational in that sense of being purposive, they are not rational in the way that demonstrated beliefs in geometry, mathematics, science, or metaphysics are.

At least some of morality, in fact, consists only of commonly accepted opinions. Consider Maimonides' reading of the narrative of Adam and Eve in the Garden of Eden (*GP* 1.2). Adam, he says, originally possessed demonstrative knowledge – knowledge of *emet vesheqer*, the true and the false. But by his sin he fell into an inferior state in which he came to be, as the Bible puts it, "a knower of good and evil," that is, one who exercises moral judgment. Such judgments are inferior to judgments of science and metaphysics for two reasons. The first is that they are not demonstrable in the sense that they can be deduced from self-evident premises. Similarly, at *Guide* 2.33, p. 364, the final eight commandments of the Decalogue are characterized thus: "they belong to the class of generally accepted opinions and those adopted in virtue of tradition, not to the class of the intellecta." Although one or two passages suggest that ethics is grasped by the intellect, the predominant Maimonidean view is decidedly otherwise.[4]

The second reason for the inferiority of moral cognition is that the very possibility of moral judgment depends on the shameful fact that human beings are creatures of passion, possessing acquisitive desires and lusts, as a result of being composed of matter as well as of form (intellect). It is no surprise that the fall of humankind occurs when moral judgment is introduced into a world that previously had witnessed only intellection directed at "the true and the false." As a further indication of morality's relatively low status, we should note that whereas Maimonides' philosophic sources saw moral knowledge as a function of "the practical intellect," and whereas he recognizes a practical function of the rational faculty, Maimonides never used the term "practical intellect" nor the term "practical rational faculty." In this way, Howard Kreisel suggests, Maimonides assures that only the theoretical intellect is recognized as intellect and that the only function of the rational faculty that truly matters is the theoretical.[5]

There can be little quarrel then that neither the practice of morality nor moral theorizing could rank as high for Maimonides as pondering science and metaphysics. That having been said, it would be a colossal mistake to ignore what Maimonides does say about ethics. His writings contain extensive discussions of proper *de'ot*, or ethical characteristics, of the processes of ridding oneself of bad ethical traits and acquiring good ones, and of the attempt to "quell the impulses" of matter that distract people from intellectual pursuits and impede cognition of what is not physical. The quelling of such impulses is associated with the attainment of holiness (*GP* 3.8, 3.33). Morality is a preparation for contemplation and constitutes no trivial task; how one conducts that preparation is a topic to which Maimonides devoted considerable attention.

Furthermore, although there is a certain sort of morality that precedes and is prerequisite for the *vita contemplativa*, there is another sort of morality that is a *consequence* of intellectual perfection and represents an "overflow" or "emanation" from intellectual achievement. This morality, we shall see, is quite different from morality as we have considered it so far. Let us call the morality needed for intellectual perfection propadeutic morality and the morality that results from intellectual perfection consequent morality. In what follows we explore the two dimensions of morality, propadeutic and consequent, and compare and contrast them.

The crucial texts for the discussion that follows are Maimonides' introduction to his commentary to the moralistic Tractate *Avot* (Ethics of the Fathers), an introduction widely known as *Eight Chapters*, the section of the *Mishneh Torah* known as *Hilkhot De'ot, Laws of Character Traits*, and *Guide of the Perplexed*, especially 1.54 and 3.54.[6]

6.2. PROPADEUTIC MORALITY IN THE LEGAL WRITINGS

6.2.1. *Virtue Ethics*

Contemporary philosophers distinguish between virtue-centered ethical thories and action-centered ones. In an ethics of virtue the focus is not on the rightness and wrongness of actions, but on the goodness or badness of certain character traits. Virtue ethics examines the psychological characteristics of good and bad people, identifying traits like compassion, humility, gentleness, temperance, and courage, which are regarded as virtues, and traits like callousness, arrogance, meanness, intemperance, and cowardice, which are regarded as vices. Actions are important only insofar as they are conducive or inimical to the production of virtuous or vicious characteristics or insofar as they are the effect of virtuous or vicious traits.

As an adherent of and authority on Jewish law, Maimonides obviously had to devote the lion's share of his attention to questions about how to act. His legal code *Mishneh Torah* accordingly offers myriad rulings about the rightness or wrongness of certain actions as judged by Jewish law. But as a philosopher he also exhibits a conspicuous concern with virtues and vices, psychological dispositions as distinct from the actions they cause or are produced by. Thus, for instance, in his discussion of repentance, he stresses that repentance is not only for sinful deeds but also for bad character traits.[7] On some occasions he interprets a rabbinic statement about a sinful act as referring to vice.[8] Again, as Herbert Davidson points out, in his *Eight Chapters* Maimonides reserves the terms "virtuous" and "vicious" for character traits rather than for actions.[9] With Aristotle, Maimonides distinguishes two kinds of virtues and vices: moral and intellectual. Many actions prescribed by the law are important as instruments or means: They build virtue.

There is some conflict in Maimonides' writings as to whether the instrumental value of ethical action and of virtue is that they conduce to individual development or instead to communal order, in which case they are not necessary for an individual living in isolation. In *Mishneh Torah* 1, Principles of the Torah, 4.12–13, the aim of the law is said to be both that it gives composure to the mind and that it contributes to social order. But in *Guide* 3.27, p. 510, we read that one of the aims of the law, "welfare of the body," refers to "the acquisition by every individual of moral qualities that are useful for life in society so that the affairs of the city may be ordered." Also in this vein is a passage in 2.40, p. 382, which speaks of the ruler's aim of "the well ordering of the community." Other passages, too, such as those quoted earlier from 3.54, suggest that the value served by moral virtue is served only in social contexts – if you suppose an individual is "alone, acting on no one," moral virtues are "in vain and without employment and unheeded" and "do not perfect the individual in anything" (*GP* 3.54, p. 635). Still other passages, however, focus on the role of morality in individual perfection: "it being impossible to achieve true, rational acts – I mean perfect rationality – unless it be by a man thoroughly trained with respect to his morals and endowed with the qualities of tranquility and quiet" (*GP* 1.34, p. 77). In *Eight Chapters* 4, specific commandments are related to the acquisition of virtuous qualities. Just why in some passages but not in others Maimonides sees virtue as serving social order rather than individual development is not clear, but this need not detain us at this point.[10] It is the fact the moral virtues are instruments that is important here.

6.2.2. *Moral Instruction as Therapy for the Soul*

A core idea in *Eight Chapters*, in which Maimonides treats what I have called propadeutic morality, is that "the improvement of moral habits is the same as the cure of the soul and its powers" (*EC* 1). Using an analogy commonplace in Greek thought, he maintains that, just as a doctor who cures bodies needs to know the body he is curing, what the parts of the body are, and what things make the body sick or healthy, so too one who treats the soul – the "wise man" – "needs to know the soul in its entirety and its part, as well as what makes it sick and what makes it healthy." The rabbis, in Maimonides' loose paraphrase of a Talmudic passage (*Avodah Zarah* 22a), stated that "piety serves to bring about the holy spirit." Hence following a proper cure and regimen for defects of the soul makes knowledge of God possible (to the extent humans may know Him) and even brings about prophecy; contrariwise, moral vices are "veils" (*EC* 7) that may prevent prophecy.[11]

The example of medicine supplies more than an analogy to what must be done for the sick soul. Health of the body contributes substantively to health of the soul, and indeed plays a large role with respect to the development of morality. Virtue and vice have a basis in bodily temperament. But the analogy to medicine is more central to Maimonides' discussion than is the substantive connection between somatic medicine and soul-healing. The health of the body involves maintaining an equilibrium. Just so, the mean is the standard for health of the soul: Virtue lies in the mean between two extremes of temperament.

Here we encounter Maimonides' presentation of the well-known Aristotelian doctrine of the mean[12]:

> Good actions are those balanced in the mean between two extremes, both of which are bad; one of them is an excess and the other a deficiency. The virtues are states of the soul and settled dispositions in the mean between two bad states [of the soul], one of which is excessive and the other deficient.[13]

Thus the virtuous state of the soul that produces "moderation" in action is a mean between lust at one extreme and total insensibility to pleasure on the other, both of which are "completely bad." Liberality is the mean between miserliness and extravagance, courage the mean between rashness and cowardice, wit the mean between buffoonery and dullness, humility the mean between haughtiness and abasement, generosity the mean between prodigality and stinginess.[14] In each case, one of the two extremes is worse than the other (miserliness and cowardice being worse than the opposite extremes), whereas the mean is the ideal.

A person does not possess virtue or vice at the beginning of life, and the soul's dispositions cannot be acquired or changed in one swoop. The agent must repeatedly perform actions that will inculcate a specific trait and must do so over a long period of time. Furthermore, the acquisition of a virtuous trait may well require the person to perform acts that deviate from the mean.

Such deviation may be a means of either (1) corrective therapy that moves his or her characteristics on to the mean or (2) preventive therapy that sustains someone on the mean. Suppose a person tends to the extreme of miserliness. He must correct this by going to the other extreme and performing acts of extreme generosity, so that his character will end up in the middle between the extremes, that is, at the mean. Once cured, he can be encouraged to perform actions at the mean between extravagance and miserliness. Looking again at the analogy to medicine, when a body is out of equilibrium, "we look to which side it inclines in becoming unbalanced and then oppose it with its contrary until it returns to equilibrium."[15] This concept was illustrated by Aristotle using an analogy: One can straighten a bent twig by bending it in an opposite direction.[16] A person might also incline away from the mean in one direction as preventive therapy, that is, to prevent his going to the opposite extreme.

Maimonides agrees with Aristotle on another significant point. One extreme, he holds, is more opposed to the mean than the other.[17] Put another way, the virtue is closer to one vice (the less bad one) than to the other. Cowardice is more opposed to bravery than is rashness, intemperance more opposed to temperance than is insensibility. In these cases the extreme to which we are more naturally drawn is more opposed to the intermediate condition (the mean). It is easier to move an extravagant person toward liberality than a miserly person, and easier to move an insensible person toward temperance than a lustful person. But it is not only the need to counteract a natural tendency that accounts for one extreme being worse than the other: One extreme is inherently worse.

The notion of therapy for the soul – corrective or preventive – enables Maimonides to develop in *Eight Chapters* the concept of the *fāḍil*, what his medieval Hebrew translators termed the *ḥasid* and English translators render as "pious man" or "virtuous man."[18] The *ḥasid* intentionally deviates from the mean, inclining in his acts toward the less bad of two extremes, in order to avoid the worse extreme of the pair. People of this type would "incline from moderation a little toward insensibility to pleasure, from courage a little toward rashness, from generosity a little toward prodigality, from humility toward abasement, and likewise with the rest." Some of them would fast, rise at night, abstain from eating meat and drinking wine, keep away from women, wear garments of wool and hair, dwell on mountains, and seclude themselves in desolate places with an eye to medical treatment. Yet only those who suffer from an ailment should behave in extreme ways; people who do not suffer illnesses of the soul will be harmed by extreme behavior. Were it not for the necessity of therapy, ascetic behavior would be reprehensible.

This point is illustrated by Maimonides' treatment of the Nazirite (Numbers 6), someone who vows not to partake of meat and wine.

Acccording to *Mishneh Torah* 1, *Laws of Character Traits* 3:1, and *Eight Chapters* 4, the Nazirite is a sinner, and for this reason the Torah requires that, with the aid of the priest, he must secure atonement for his sin. A person whose soul is not diseased should not go toward any extreme; doing so will make his soul sick, just as a healthy person becomes sick when he takes medicine. Unfortunately, those who observed the pious people did not realize that the modes of conduct practiced by Ḥasidim are not good for all people, and they became sick by emulating their actions.

So much for the broad contours of Maimonides' discussion in *Eight Chapters* and *Laws of Character Traits*. At this point I would like to address several major issues that Maimonides' "propadeutic" moral theory confronts.[19]

6.2.3. The Doctrine of the Mean, Biblical Law, and Rabbinic Tradition

As noted earlier, Maimonides' ethical theory is heavily influenced by Aristotle's *Nicomachean Ethics*. In particular, the theory of the mean, the distinction between intellectual and moral virtue, the five-part nature of the soul, the strategy of therapeutic deviations from the mean, the notion that one extreme is worse than the other – these are all Aristotelian teachings. Herbert Davidson has further called attention to similarities between Maimonides' *Eight Chapters* and the Islamic philosopher Alfarabi's *Fuṣūl al-madanī* [*Aphorisms of the Statesman*]. Maimonides tells us he will cite extensively from other sources without attribution, justifying this practice by indicating that he sees no point in saying "so-and-so said." Alfarabi clearly is prominent among his unnamed sources.[20]

At the same time as he cites philosophers, however, Maimonides seeks to incorporate teachings of the Bible and of the rabbis of the Talmud and *midrash*. What we have in his writings therefore is a reading of biblical law and rabbinic tradition through Aristotelian and Farabian eyes – and a reading of Aristotle and Alfarabi through the prism of biblical and rabbinic tradition. The philosophic tradition itself is modified by Maimonides through teachings of the rabbis and through some ideas that are integral to Maimonides' philosophy.

I focus here on the several instances in which Maimonides prescribes deviation from the mean. This point is best grasped by noting

Aristotle's (and Alfarabi's) distinction between the arithmetic mean, which is always fixed, and the relative mean, which "increases and decreases at different times and with reference of the things to which it is related."[21] To some extent Aristotle allowed for deviations from the mean. With regard to some emotions (spite, shamefulness, envy) and some actions (adultery, theft, murder) it is not the excess of these things that is bad, but the emotions or acts themselves.[22] And we have already discussed therapeutic deviation and the slight deviation away from the worse extreme. But the deviations Maimonides allows go beyond this.

Let us begin with *Laws of Character Traits* 2:3: "in the case of some character traits, a man is forbidden to accustom himself to the mean. Rather, he should move to the other extreme." One such trait is humility, the other is anger.

Humility: "The good way is not that a man be merely humble, but that he have a lowly spirit" (*Laws of Character Traits* 2:3). In support, Maimonides quotes R. Levitas in *Avot* 4:4: "Have a very, very lowly spirit."

The significance of this seeming departure from the mean is best seen by means of a contrast to Aristotle. Aristotle favors the proud man, which he defines as a person who deems himself worthy of great things and indeed is worthy of them. The proud man represents the mean between extremes. At one extreme is the vain man, who deems himself worthy of great things but is not worthy of them; at the other is the humble man, who is worthy of great things but deems himself worthy to a degree less than his true worth. The proud man is both proud of his virtue and worthy of it; thus he expects others to honor him for his virtue. The humble man does not accept the honor to which he is entitled. The humble man, says Aristotle, is ignorant of himself.[23]

For Aristotle pride is "the crown of the virtues"[24] (he refers here to moral as opposed to intellectual virtues) and the "prize" for (moral) virtue.[25] According to Daniel Frank, the fact Maimonides demands not merely humility but extreme humility reflects his belief that "to take an interest in worldly honor is to forget God, to live as if God did not exist. It is to place the mundane above the divine."[26] As Maimonides states in the name of the rabbis, "whoever is haughty is as if he denies God." So whereas Aristotle values honor, Maimonides, with his theocentric perspective, disdains it.

The exceedingly humble Maimonidean man accepts insult to a remarkable degree. Maimonides tells a story (which originates as a *Ṣūfī* tale) about a man who was asked, "On what day of your life did you have the most joy? " The man describes a day on which he was traveling on a ship whose passengers included merchants and wealthy men. He was in the lowest part of the ship, wearing tattered garments, and while lying down was urinated on by one of the men on board: "My soul was not pained at all by his deed, nor was I in the least agitated. Then I greatly rejoiced that I had reached the point where the contempt of that base man did not pain me, and I paid no heed to him."[27]

Is this approach compatible with the approach of the mean? That depends on whether Maimonides' prescription of extreme humility is merely therapeutically useful or instead good in itself. In both *Eight Chapters* 4 and *Laws of Character Traits* 2.2, extreme humility is given as an example of the therapeutic mean; and from the commentary to *Avot* 4.4 we get the same impression. God, furthermore, is called *anav* [humble], not exceedingly humble, so *imitatio Dei* would demand only ordinary humility. At the same time it must be conceded that Maimonides's wording in *Laws of Character Traits* 2.3 is a universal prescription – "a man is forbidden... to accustom himself to the mean," suggesting that ordinary humility is simply unacceptable. The context and flavor of the *Ṣūfī* tale suggest it is not to be explained by therapy but by some real sense that the behavior of the offending individual and the general situation of the victim are not cause for pain; there is no reason to care about others so as to be insulted.[28] The various texts of *Laws of Character Traits* are confusing in that, as Howard Kreisel cleverly puts it, "the person who is extremely humble possesses a trait which is not good (1.1, 1.3), is a righteous person who acts beyond the strict letter of the Law (1.5), while acting in a way mandated by the Law (2.3)."[29] These contradictions demand interpreters' attention, but we can say with some confidence that the extreme humility of *Laws of Character Traits* 2:3 seems related to the requirement of theocentrism.

Anger: This is the second trait with respect to which extreme behavior is counseled. In contrast to Chapter 1, in which he prescribed the mean, in Chapter 2 of *Laws of Character Traits* Maimonides writes, "It is proper for a man to move away from it to the other extreme and to teach himself not to become angry, even over something it is proper to be angry about" (*Laws of Character Traits* 2.3). A person may feign anger in order to admonish others, "but his mind shall be tranquil within himself, like a man who feigns anger but is not angry." In this instance, too, Maimonides cites rabbinic sources, for example, "Anyone who is angry – it is as if he worships idols" (*Shabbat* 115b). Adapting *Yoma* 23a, he continues: "The way of the just men is to be insulted but not to insult; they hear themselves reviled and do not reply; they act out of love and rejoice in afflictions. Scripture says about them: 'And those who love Him are like the sun rising in its power.'"

Here again a contrast to Aristotle is helpful.[30] Aristotle saw irascibility and inirascibility (feeling no anger at all) as the extremes between which lies the mean of good temperedness. So, whereas inirascibility is a vice for Aristotle, it is a virtue for Maimonides. For Aristotle, the virtue is good temperedness, that is, feeling anger as appropriate when insulted and acting on it. Feigning anger is no part of the virtue for Aristotle, as Aristotle's virtuous man exhibits a harmony between inner feeling and outer act.[31] For Maimonides it is otherwise. Notice that the traits of inirascibility and extreme humility are related, in that both reflect a lack of concern for honor. Likewise for Aristotle, good temperedness and pride are related in that both reflect a concern for honor.

It has been argued that for Maimonides the ideal of *imitatio Dei* demands a lack of any emotion whatsoever, as God has no emotional states; and that this is why in *Laws of Character Traits* he favors inirascibility.[32] Against this explanation I note that in *Laws of Character Traits* Maimonides does not counsel passionlessness generally, but only lack of anger. More likely, therefore, his point in *Laws of Character Traits* is only about anger, and he is not saying that other of God's "attributes of action" should be imitated in action only and not in feeling. Still, anger is for Maimonides the paradigm of a bodily based emotion (*GP* 1.54, 3.8).[33] Another important element in Maimonides' condemnation of anger is that, like arrogance, anger reflects failure to make God central in one's life. Caring about honor and insult are antithetical to a God-centered life.[34]

The Law: A larger problem with the claim that Maimonides harmonized Torah and philosophic ethics is that Torah law seems to diverge from philosophic ethics[35] by mandating many actions that are not on the mean. Initially, it may be tempting to think of Torah law as identical with the prescriptions of *phronēsis* [practical wisdom] and to think of divine commandments as a shortcut to the results *phronēsis* would yield if exercised. By observing Torah law, one would think, one obviates the need for *phronēsis* and can move that much more quickly to theoretical pursuits. One achieves virtue by obeying the law, and one incurs vice by disobeying it. However, this seemingly attractive picture does not fit the facts.

To take one example, the law does not prescribe how much to eat. Rather, it produces virtues that with the exercise of *phronēsis* will result in a person's choosing the right amount to eat. Thus practical judgment is still necessary, so that the law is not a full substitute for, that is, not a full functional equivalent of, *phronēsis*.[36]

More importantly, the Torah mandates acts that simple adherence to the mean does not. It proscribes certain foods or food mixtures (meat and milk) and forbids certain specific sexual acts that ordinary ethics does not. The Torah commands leaving a corner in the field for the poor, giving tithes, releasing the poor from their debts in the Sabbatical and Jubilee years, giving charity adequate to providing what someone lacks, returning a stray animal or any lost object to its owner, and other deeds that require action in excess of the mean. Some required acts, such as relieving an enemy's animal of its burden and the prohibition against taking revenge, reflect the curbing of anger already described.

Torah law also requires rising before the elderly and honoring and fearing parents. Based on Talmudic teaching, one's duty to fear parents applies even if parents take their child's purse full of gold and cast it into the sea (*Mishneh Torah* 14, Rebels, 6.7). The biblical duty to rescue someone in danger likewise goes beyond the mean's requirements. In addition, the virtuous man eschews all idle talk (*Avot* 1:16).[37] The duty to rebuke a sinner is quite different from these duties in the trait it promotes – it is mandated to remove shyness – but this conduct too goes to excess (impudence). It is true, as Maimonides notes, that the Torah does not prohibit all food and drink or intercourse and does not mandate giving all one's wealth to the poor or to the Temple. The Laws incline one away from the mean without legislating the extreme. Still, the legislated behaviors are decidedly not at the mean.

Given these Torah-legislated deviations from the mean, must Maimonides give up asserting a convergence between philosophic ethics and Torah? Again we must consider that most people tend toward excess in one direction and Torah law is therefore preventive therapy. One of a pair of extremes is more opposed to the mean than the other; often we have a natural tendency toward one excess rather than another, a tendency that needs correction by the Law, which moves us in the other direction. Although the *behavior* of the observant Jew is not on the mean, the *character trait* is, as Torah law corrects natural tendencies. On this reading, the Torah is in harmony with philosophy even though the philosophers do not themselves adopt the precepts of the Torah.

The previous explanation of why the Torah law deviates from the mean is not wholly satisfactory. Many observers of the Law may have a tendency not toward stinginess but toward generosity. It is not clear why they should obey the Torah's laws, insofar as such obedience will keep them from the mean and only performing actions that are closer to stinginess will put their traits at the mean. Perhaps this is the problem Maimonides has in mind in *Guide* 3.34, when he states that some people may be harmed by the Law, but must nonetheless obey it because, unlike medicine, law is not calibrated and adapted to the individual. By observing Torah law, someone whose natural tendency is toward generosity or humility may go to that pole in a manner that is truly excessive. Nonetheless, he must obey.

Speaking more broadly, vice and virtue are not coextensive with obedience and disobedience relative to the Law.[38] Obedience to the law is conducive to virtue and disobedience is inimical to the development of virtue – but this suggests that obedience has instrumental value only. Furthermore, on rare occasions disobedience of a command may be needed to acquire moral virtue. According to one scholar, Maimonides thinks the rabbis would allow deviations from the Law in such cases, in which one can then better engage in finding philosophic truth (notwithstanding 3.34).[39]

The Nazirite: As noted earlier, in *Laws of Character Traits* and *Eight Chapters* Maimonides portrays the Nazirite as a sinner. But elsewhere in the *Mishneh Torah* 6, Naziriteship 10.14, he restricts his condemnation to those who undertake a Nazirite vow frivolously. Someone who makes the vow in sanctity has acted in a fine and praiseworthy fashion and ranks even above the prophets – this apparently despite the deviation from the mean his vow entails. There is no evidence that this praise is restricted to Nazirite vows that are undertaken as corrective or preventive therapy.[40]

Other extreme behavior: Mortification of the body is required for Torah study[41]; and Maimonides declares that one may abstain from marriage if his soul is so passionately committed to Torah.[42] He says this despite rabbinic condemnation of Ben Azzai for failing to marry. These are definite ascetic strains in Maimonides' legal writings, strains that appear with greater clarity in the *Guide*. They are difficult to reconcile with the mean.[43]

The *Guide* leans strongly in the direction of asceticism. It is true that, even in the *Guide*, Maimonides invokes the theme of balance, suggesting the ideal of the mean. He asserts, for example, as in *Eight Chapters*, that when the Torah states that God has given "just statutes and judgments" (Deuteronomy 4:8), "just" means "equibalanced," and "The Law of the Lord is perfect" (Psalm 19:8) refers to its equibalance and wisdom. In the law "there is no burden and excess – such as monastic life – nor a deficiency necessarily leading to greed and being engrossed in the indulgence of appetites" (2.39, p. 380). This passage refers to acts; *Guide* 3.39 speaks of "moderate moral qualities that form a part of the righteous statutes and judgments" (p. 554).

Yet we are told that a prophet will abolish his desire for "bestial things," which include eating, drinking, sexual intercourse, and in general the sense of touch (*GP* 2.36, p. 371),[44] that people of science and the prophets will renounce and have contempt for bodily pleasures (*GP* 2.40, p. 384), that the sense of touch is "our greatest shame" (*GP* 3.8, p. 433), that "it behooves him who prefers to be a human being, to endeavor to diminish all the impulses of matter" such as eating, drinking, copulation, and anger (*GP* 3.8, p. 434), that one of the law's intentions is "renouncing and avoiding sexual intercourse and causing it to be as infrequent as possible" (*GP* 3.33, p. 533), and that the Nazirite is worthy of praise (*GP* 3:33, 3:48). Clearly the middle way has been rejected except for the ordinary run of individuals, even though a man cannot represent an intelligible if he is hungry or thirsty (*GP* 3.27, p. 511).[45]

We can surmise that the problem with asceticism arises when it is pursued by those who are unprepared for it and still have sensual urges. People who have overcome these urges are at a higher level, and for them asceticism is the proper course. As one scholar has written, "For those who live the life of the intellect, the doctrine of the mean does not provide the path most suitable to follow."[46]

Ḥakham versus *ḥasid*: In *Laws of Character Traits* 1.4–5, after telling us that anyone whose traits all lie on the mean is called "wise" [*ḥakham*] and that "the wise men of old" acted according to the middle way, Maimonides presents a second type, the "pious man," or *ḥasid*:

> Whoever is exceedingly scrupulous with himself and moves toward one side or the other, away from the character trait in the mean, is called a pious man.... The pious men of old used to direct their character traits from the middle way toward [one of the two] extremes; some character traits toward the last extreme, and some toward the first extreme. This is the meaning of "inside the line of the law" [*li-fnim mi-shurat ha-din*]. We are commanded to walk in these middle ways, which are the good and right ways. As it is said, "And you shall walk in His ways."

Recalling Chapter 4 of *Eight Chapters*, we are likely to think that the *ḥasid* of this passage engages in extreme behavior as a means of curing himself from a vice. If so, the *ḥakham* represents the ideal (behavior on the mean) whereas the *ḥasid* represents the ill person in search of a cure, or a person in search of preventive therapy, or one who wishes to prevent himself from going to the worse of two extremes.

If the *ḥasid* engages in therapy – as opposed to being different from the *ḥasid* in *Eight Chapters* – this induces the judgment that *ḥakham* is higher than the *ḥasid*, as the former needs no cure. This judgment is reinforced by the consideration that the *ḥakham* is the one who walks in God's middle ways, and that in Maimonides' citation of a *midrash* on *imitatio Dei* in the paragraph following the one I quoted, he omits the *midrash's* attribution to God of the quality of *ḥesed*, loving-kindness. Why after all would God need therapy? At the same time, the phrase "inside the line of the law," assigned to the *ḥasid*'s behavior, normally signifies an especially positive valuation – supererogation – and it is odd to see it here associated with a lower kind of conduct, namely, piety. In addition, there is no denying that in places Maimonides assigns great value to the *ḥasid*. He quotes a rabbinic statement that *ḥasidut* is a rung below prophecy (*ES*, introduction). In several other places, in sources ranging from the *Guide* to *The Epistle to the Jews of Yemen*, *fāḍil* or *ḥasid* is his favored term for a person of excellence. In the *Guide*, furthermore, God is said to practice *ḥesed*, loving-kindness (3.53, 3.54). In *Mishneh Torah* 14, Laws of Kings, 8.11, *ḥakham* and *ḥasid* appear in a context that suggests a *ḥasid* of the non-Jewish nations is higher than a non-Jewish *ḥakham*. Space does not permit a full evaluation of these conflicting bodies of evidence on the relative values of *ḥakham* and *ḥasid*.[47]

The ḥasid versus the continent man: In Chapter 6 of *Eight Chapters*,[48] Maimonides presents a contrast between two personality types. One is the *ḥasid*, the other the continent man. The *ḥasid* "follows in his action what his desire and the state of his soul arouse him to do; he does good things while craving and strongly desiring them." The continent man "does good things while craving and strongly desiring to perform bad actions. He struggles against his craving and opposes by his action what his [appetitive] power, his desire, and the state of his soul arouse him to do." Maimonides asks which of these types ranks higher. The philosophers along with King Solomon rank the *ḥasid* higher than the continent man, whereas the rabbis appear to rank the continent man higher. For example, Rabban Shimon ben Gamliel says, "Let a man not say 'I do not want to eat meat with milk, I do not want to wear mixed fabric [the prohibited mixture of wool and linen], I do not want to have illicit sexual relations' but [let him say] 'I want to, but what shall I do – my Father in heaven has forbidden me." Likewise the rabbis declare that "Whoever is greater than his friend has a greater [evil] impulse than he" and "The reward is according to the pain."

Seeking to reconcile the respective views of the philosophers and the rabbis, Maimonides writes that the two groups are speaking about different sorts of actions. The philosophers refer to things generally accepted by people as bad: murder, theft, robbery, fraud, harming an innocent man, repaying a benefactor with evil, degrading parents, and the like. A person who desires to do any of these things has a defective soul, according to both the philosophers and the rabbis. But when the rabbis ranked the continent man above the *ḥasid*, they had in mind "the traditional laws . . . because if it were not for the Law, they would not be bad at all. Therefore they said that a man needs to let his soul remain attracted to them and not place any obstacle before them other than the Law." "Traditional laws" include prohibitions against consuming meat and milk, engaging in an illicit union, and wearing wool and linen.

This view of the "traditional laws" invites the question of why those deeds were prohibited in the first place. Maimonides gave us the answer in *Eight Chapters*, Chapter 4. With regard to the prohibition of forbidden foods and a range of laws, "the purpose of all this is that we move very far away from the extreme of lust and go a little from the mean toward insensibility to pleasure so that the state of moderation be firmly established within our souls." The reasoning is exactly the same as applies to tithes, giving of harvest, the law of forgotten sheaves, the Sabbbatical and Jubilee year, and charity sufficient for what the needy lack. These laws move us toward prodigality so we may move far away from stinginess. In all such cases, were it not for the Law, there would not have been anything wrong with doing other than what the Law prescribes. The Torah is interested in inculcating the virtues firmly, and for this it must incline us toward liberality and insensibility. For all that, it is surprising that Maimonides does not say that the goal of such prohibitions is eventually to extirpate the passion. Shouldn't the person eventually lose the desire for the forbidden sexual relations? In the *Guide*, as noted, we find hints of an ascetic morality that eradicates desire.[49]

6.3. ETHICS IN THE GUIDE

When Aristotle assigns supreme value to contemplative activity as distinct from the moral life, the theoretical life is not held to involve any specific practical activity of a moral or political sort. This does not mean that the moral life involves no exercise of reason at all; but the type of reasoning involved in becoming morally virtuous is practical rather than theoretical. Theoretical activity implies no moral or political conduct, even if Aristotle concedes that moral virtue leads to a "secondary" sort of happiness and that some worldly goods are necessary for human life.[50]

One of the reasons Aristotle gives for the supremacy of theoretical activity is that it is godlike. Contemplation is a form of *imitatio Dei*. Aristotle's God is removed from human affairs, and His only "activity" amounts to "thought thinking itself" in a changeless, removed way.[51] In fact Aristotle states that the gods "will appear ridiculous" if they engage in acts of justice.[52]

The idea of *imitatio Dei* is salient in the *Guide*: "The end of the universe is . . . a seeking to be like unto His perfection as far as in its capacity" (1.69, p. 170); *imitatio Dei* characterizes the final perfection of all existent things. Given this principle, Maimonides could have seen intellection on the part of humans as a mode of *imitatio Dei*, just as Aristotle did. But given his "negative theology" that places God beyond human concepts, he could not brook an explicit comparison between human and divine intellection. In 1.1, p. 23, he first makes the comparison, then withdraws it.[53] Although he could not use Aristotle's *imitatio Dei* argument as an explicit comparison between human and divine intellection, however, he did find a different use for *imitatio Dei* in the *Guide*, as we shall now see.

Maimonides differs from Aristotle in at least two respects: (1) For him theoretical activity does result in a particular sort of conduct; (2) this conduct, not the theoretical activity, is what constitutes *imitatio Dei*. Imitation of God's actions is the only sort of imitation open to humans – they cannot know what God is like in himself so as to imitate the divine essence.

Let us approach the issues by means of the *Guide*'s final chapter (3.54). Maimonides canvasses four perfections: perfection of possessions, perfection of body, pefection of moral virtues, and theoretical perfection. As we have seen, the last of these is the true human end because it is self-sufficient, involving no one else. Whatever value moral perfection possesses is instrumental. Given the fact that intellectual perfection has been portrayed as the goal and morality as the means, it is baffling to encounter the passage that concludes the *Guide*:

It is clear that the perfection of man that may truly be gloried in is the one acquired by him who has achieved, in a measure corresponding to his capacity, apprehension of Him, may He be exalted, and who knows His providence extending over His creatures as manifested in the act of bringing them into being and in their governance as is. The way of life of such an individual, after he has achieved this apprehension, will always have in view lovingkindness, righteousness and judgment, through assimilation to His actions. (*GP* 3.54, p. 638)

Maimonides locates this view in a text from Jeremiah 9:22–23, in which the prophet states

Thus saith the Lord: Let not the wise man glory in his wisdom, neither let the mighty man glory in his might, let not the rich man glory in his riches; but let him that glorieth glory in this, that he understandeth and knoweth me. For I am the Lord, who exercises loving-kindness, judgment, and righteousness [*ḥesed*, *mishpaṭ*, and *tsedaqah*] in the earth, for in these things I delight, saith the Lord.

In Maimonides' reading, "the wise man" referred to is a *ḥakham* in the *moral* sense of the term – *ḥokhmah* can refer to moral achievement, even if the word has other senses (3.54, p. 632). Hence the wise man has the third kind of perfection in Maimonides' hierarchy. The mighty man is one possessing perfection of the body (perfection two), the rich man is one having bodily possessions (perfection one). One who "understandeth and knoweth me" has the fourth perfection. But the Lord also performs "loving-kindness, judgment, and righteousness in the earth." So too, must the person who has achieved intellectual perfection. Acts of that kind should come from him. Aristotle's claim that the highest perfection can be seen as *imitatio Dei* now appears, but it seems to support the claim that moral activity is the highest perfection as opposed to contemplation.

Several reactions to this ostensible shift have appeared in the literature.[54] In a 1979 paper, Shlomo Pines took the position that Maimonides does perform an about-face. According to Pines, Maimonides holds that human beings cannot know metaphysics nor even celestial physics. Because of these limits, Maimonides (reminiscent of Immanuel Kant) retracts the claim that intellectual perfection is the highest perfection. Nevertheless, human beings can know the actions of God, and his attributes of action, as is clear from 1.54. Acccording to Pines, "The only positive knowledge of which man is capable is knowledge of the attributes of action, and this leads and ought to lead to a sort of practical activity which is the highest perfection of man. The practical way of life, the *bios praktikos*, is superior to the theoretical."[55]

Pines is right that the activities of the individual who is described at the end of 3.54 are an imitation of God's actions. He is also right that action and virtue that result from scientific knowledge are not the same as action and virtue that result from *phronēsis* and that constitute the third level of perfection.[56] But Pines' allegation of an about-face is highly problematic. After all, Maimonides proclaims clearly that intellectual perfection, not practical activity, is highest, and gives an argument against interpersonal activity being highest (viz., the perfect individual must not be dependent upon others for his perfection). Only a highly esotericist reading of 3.54 would permit us to say that Maimonides maintains the exact opposite of what he says, and although such esotericism may appeal to Pines, we would be wise to seek another explanation of the ostensible shift.

A far more compelling idea is that Maimonides distinguishes between "the perfection of man that may be truly gloried in" and "the way of life of such an individual" who has achieved that perfection. The way of life is not the perfection itself; the way of life is rather a consequence of – an emanation or overflow from – the perfection. By achieving intellectual perfection, the perfect individual engages in a life of *imitatio Dei* with respect to the Deity's actions. This individual acts toward people as God acts toward the world, that is, exercising the same attributes. For this reason Maimonides spells out what loving-kindness, judgment, and righteousness entail (*GP* 3.53); these are what the intellectually perfect individual practices because of the overflow from the intellect.[57] Proof that the actions toward others do not constitute the perfection itself is Maimonides' statement at 2.11, p. 275:

> Know that in the case of every being that causes a certain good thing to overflow from it according to this order of rank, the existence, the purpose, and the end of the being conferring the benefits, do not consist in conferring the benefits on the recipient. For pure absurdity would follow from this assumption. For the end is nobler than the things that subsist for the sake of the end.

There is some question as to whether the effect of the overflow from theoretical perfection is political activity or ethical activity done in a particular way.[58] In the former interpretation, stress is played on the perfect individual *qua* ruler, and the interpretation is that the law given by the perfect lawgiver will manifest *ḥesed*, *mishpaṭ*, and *tsedaqah*.[59] According to the other interpretation, it is not ethical activity of a distinctive kind: Just as God acts without emotion, so the perfect individual acts without emotion. In support of the first reading, note that all references to *imitatio Dei* that are clear as between moral activity and political activity are political (*GP* 1.24, p. 54, 1.38, p. 87, 1.54).[60] The political reading gains support in particular from the correlation Maimonides asserts between *Guide* 3.54 and 1.54. In 1.54, Maimonides describes how Moses came to know God's attributes of action because he needed to know how to govern the people (a practical end). It is worth noting, however, that, either way, practical wisdom is needed for the theoretical knowledge that generates the overflow. As Ehud Benor argues, one has to know what character traits have to be exercised to bring about the particular effects we see in nature. Practical excellence thus precedes theoretical perfection, and it is an overflow from it as well.[61]

On either the political or the ethical interpretation, the "consequent morality" is radically different from the propadeutic morality. It results not from *phronēsis* but from scientific knowledge. In addition, actions now seem more important than the psychological disposition. Recall that propadeutic morality focused on a person's psychological dispositions, traits of personality that involve psychological states like compassion, courage, and so forth. The mean was a particular psychological disposition. So although in *Laws of Character Traits* Maimonides stated that action on the mean, the propadeutic morality, was a type of *imitatio Dei*, there is a clear disanalogy between the virtuous person and the God whom he imitates. The human being has psychological dispositions toward certain states; God has no psychological states at all. He acts in certain ways, but feels nothing. To truly counsel *imitatio Dei*, Maimonides ought to say that the person who engages in *imitatio Dei* has no psychological states at all. In the *Guide* he makes this point explicitly with regard to a ruler–prophet:

> It behooves the governor of a city, if he is a prophet, to acquire similarity to these attributes, so that these actions may proceed from him according to a determined measure and according to the deserts of the people who are affected by them and not merely because of his following a passion. He should not let loose the reins of anger nor let passion gain mastery over him, for all passions are evil; but, on the contrary, he should guard against them as far as this lies within the capacity of man. (*G.P.* 1.54, p. 126)

Thus the ruler should do what is fitting and not administer benefits and adversities out of compassion, anger, and hatred. The process that produces actions of loving-kindness, judgment, and righteousness referred to in the passage is not of the sort undergone by the morally virtuous person. Those actions are not produced by "aptitudes of the soul" or psychological dispositions.

To account for the difference between Maimonides' treatment of psychological dispositions in his legal writings and his account in the *Guide*, Herbert Davidson maintains that Maimonides simply changed his mind and eventually came to demand the extirpation of psychological traits rather than their cultivation.[62] Theoretically one could view the legal writings' account as referring to propadeutic morality and the *Guide*'s as referring to consequent morality, and insist that there is no formal contradiction between the psychological states required by one and the absence of such states in the other. But the lack of reference in the legal writings to anything resembling the "consequent" morality is striking and would suggest that Maimonides came to the idea of emotionless perfection late in his career. At the same time, we must recall that the identification of irascibility as an ideal with respect to anger anticipates the generalized passionlessness of the individual in the *Guide* who imitates God.

Questions remain about the "overflow" from intellectual perfection. Is the end of *imitatio Dei* consciously aimed at by the person who receives the overflow, or unavoidable? Is there an element of the irrational in the desire to return from the cave and lead others?[63] Does God have a "motive" for His overflow? Why does Maimonides imply that political activity is a "descent" when he unpacks the message of Jacob's ladder (1.15)? Questions such as these are stimulated by the reading we have given the closing lines of 3.54.[64]

6.4. CONCLUSION

Despite his stress on intellectual perfection, Maimonides devoted much attention to developing a theory of ethics and a practical regimen of therapy for moral illnesses. Although he champions the doctrine of the mean, he recognizes several important deviations from it. He also developed the notion of a morality that flows from intellectual perfection and that contrasts with the propadeutic morality set out in the legal writings.[65]

NOTES

1. See *Nicomachean Ethics*, Book 10.7.
2. See for example *MT* 1, Repentance, 8, and *Guide* 3.54, p. 635. ("Therefore you ought to desire to achieve this thing, which will remain permanently with you"; "it gives [the individual] permanent perdurance.")

3. The quotation is from Maimonides' introduction to the commentary on *Avot*, known as *Eight Chapters*, Chapter 5, translated in Weiss and Butterworth 1975, p. 75.
4. For a contrary passage, see *Guide* 3.8, p. 432: "The corruption of the intellect and of the body is shunned by the intellect." For a treatment of this passage see Kreisel 1999, pp. 89–91. Presumably the intellect also determines that the mean is the standard of virtue and that intellectual perfection is the highest.
5. See Kreisel 1999, pp. 63–92; Weiss 1990–1, pp. 30–1. On the story of Adam and Eve's sin, see also Berman 1980 and Fox 1990, pp. 152–98.
6. The terms "morality" and "ethics" here are used interchangeably. It is important to realize, however, that morality is more than governing oneself according to right norms of interpersonal conduct. It also, as just indicated, involves the governing of one's impulses.
7. *MT* 1, Repentance, 7.3.
8. See Kaplan 2002.
9. Davidson 1963.
10. See, however, Kreisel 1999, pp. 159–88, who suggests that in contexts where Maimonides wants to express the supremacy of intellectual perfection, he makes the aim of ethics to be (mere) social order.
11. In *Eight Chapters*, Maimonides embeds his discussion in a theory of the soul. The soul has five parts: rational, appetitive, sentient, imaginative, and nutritive. The therapy for the sick soul is directed specifically at two parts, the sentient and the appetitive. It is true that the soul's rational part may bring about good or bad conduct insofar as the agent may hold true or false opinions about what is good and bad. But – and here Maimonides sounds somewhat like David Hume, the eighteenth-century Scottish philosopher – thought does not act. The healthy soul will have correct opinions about what is good conduct and what is bad; but in addition to holding correct opinions, it must govern itself to act in a good rather than bad way. And this is where therapy is required.
12. Recent scholarship on Aristotle suggests that his doctrine of the mean is far more complex than the simplified picture conveyed by my summary of Maimonides. See for example Urmson 1980. However, it is not clear that Maimonides understood the doctrine of the mean as Aristotle did, and for that reason I stick to the simplified formulation.
13. *EC* 4, in Weiss and Butterworth 1975, p. 67.
14. Liberality refers to spending on oneself, generosity to spending for others.
15. *EC* 4.
16. *Nicomachean Ethics* 1109b5–8.
17. See *Nicomachean Ethics* 1109a2–13.

18. See *EC* 4, commentary to *Avot* 5:7, *MT* 1, Character Traits, 1.5–6.
19. At no point in *Eight Chapters* does Maimonides refer to the concept *imitatio Dei* that is found in his later writings, the *Mishneh Torah* and *Guide of the Perplexed*. As we shall see, this concept seems to have undergone an evolution in his various works.
20. See Davidson 1963.
21. *Nicomachean Ethics* 1106a28–b7.
22. *Nicomachean Ethics* 2:6 (1107a8–15)
23. *Nicomachean Ethics* 1125a22.
24. *Nicomachean Ethics* 1124a1–4.
25. *Nicomachean Ethics* 1123b35.
26. See Frank 1989, p. 97.
27. Following the translation in Weiss 1991, pp. 40–1. Weiss notes that this passage appears in the *Commentary to the Mishnah* as a description of the pious person's conduct and in a responsum as the conduct of a philosopher.
28. Certain positions in the community – community leader, judge – require humility rather than extreme humility, a view that poses certain complications in light of Moses, the greatest leader, being described as "very humble." (See Weiss 1991, pp. 108–10.) But the apparent situation is clear enough: There is a departure here from the mean, based on a rabbinic teaching.
29. Kreisel 1999, p. 161.
30. See Frank 1990.
31. Frank 1990.
32. Frank 1990.
33. I thank Josef Stern for this observation.
34. We need to ask again, as we did in the case of extreme humility, how *MT* 1, Character Traits, 2.3, is to be reconciled with texts in Chapter 1. I have no answer to this time-worn question.
35. Philosophic ethics is a term used in the *Letter on Management of Health*, as noted by Weiss 1991.
36. See Kaplan 2002, Weiss 1991, p. 76.
37. See Weiss 1991, pp. 62–81, for further discussion of such examples.
38. See Kaplan 2002. Cf. Marvin Fox's view (1990, pp. 93–123) that the rule of the Torah is the rule of the mean.
39. See Kaplan 2002. Maimonides' reference in *EC* 5 to a "transgression for the sake of heaven" is a piece of the argument.
40. A similar contradiction attends Maimonides' statements about the general issue of making vows to refrain from certain enjoyments; contrast *MT* 1, Character Traits, 3.1 and *MT* 6, Vows, 13.23.

41. *MT* 1, Study of the Torah, 3.12.
42. *MT* 4, Marriage, 15.3.
43. His suggestion in *MT* 1, Character Traits, 1.4, that one should desire only that which one cannot live without is ascetic sounding as well.
44. The prophet does not repudiate what is useful for the body, however.
45. My presentation of the evidence is indebted to Davidson 1987a, pp. 47–50, and Kreisel 1999, pp. 175–82.
46. Kreisel 1999, p. 182.
47. Relevant literature includes Hartman 1976, pp. 88–97; Kogan 1990; Kreisel 1999, pp. 179–80; Lamm 1981; Schwarzschild 1977; Twersky 1980, 459–68.
48. See Weiss and Butterworth 1975, pp. 78–80.
49. More on this in subsequent discussion. Moses was an ascetic – see *MT* 1, Principles of the Torah, 7.6.
50. *Nicomachean Ethics* 10.8. This and the next paragraphs follow Frank's (1985) wording fairly closely.
51. See *Metaphysics* 12.9.
52. *Nicomachean Ethics* 10.8, trans. by Frank 1985 on p. 487.
53. See also Seeskin 2000, Chapter 5.
54. Hermann Cohen took Maimonides as affirming the supremacy of ethical action. See Cohen 1924.
55. Pines 1979, p. 100.
56. See also Altmann 1972.
57. This interpretation is given by Harvey 1980, pp. 211–12; Shatz 1990, p. 100; Kreisel 1999, pp. 125–58.
58. The thesis that people should stay in solitiude (3.51, p. 621) can be relegated to those on the ascent to intellectual perfection.
59. See Goldman 1968.
60. See Kreisel 1999.
61. Benor 1995, pp. 37–61, esp. pp. 56–8.
62. Davidson 1987a, pp. 46–72.
63. See Kreisel 1999, pp. 10 and 134.
64. Once the *Guide*'s final passages are interpreted as standing by the view that intellectual perfection is supreme, there is but one passage I know that seems to support the assertion that ultimate perfection is practical, not theoretical. It comes in Maimonides' discussion of *imitatio Dei* in 1.54 and is cited by Pines as support for his view that the final perfection is practical: "For the utmost virtue of man is to become like unto Him, may He Be Exalted, as far as he is able; which means that we should make our actions like unto His" (1.54, p. 128). However, in this passage "virtue" may refer to ethical virtue, not perfection (Davidson 1992–3,

p. 86). If it were taken to refer to perfection, it would create enormous textual difficulties because of the contrast with 3:54. So, reading "virtue" in a restrictive way seems preferable.

65. I thank Charles Raffel and Kenneth Seeskin for comments on an earlier version.

HAIM KREISEL

7 Maimonides' Political Philosophy

7.1. INTRODUCTION[1]

Human beings are social animals according to Aristotelian philosophy. We form societies because we naturally desire the companionship of other human beings. We are also dependent on others for the fulfillment of our basic human needs. Rare is the solitary individual who is capable of producing all that is minimally required for human existence. Thus the "state of nature" for the Aristotelian philosopher is not a presocial state, even if this state is regarded as only a hypothetical construct; it is the social life.

Human society still poses a type of paradox to the Aristotelian philosopher. Although people tend to possess an inherent need to live together, they are incapable of doing so if left to their own devices. The strong would immediately take advantage of the weak. Cruelty and other evil passions would thrive unchecked, inevitably creating a situation at least analogous to Hobbes' state of nature in which life is nasty, brutish, and short. Yet it is nature itself that provides a remedy to this situation. It confers on some individuals the ability to rule others, to organize them in a manner in which they can function in harmony despite their divergent characteristics.

Medieval Aristotelian philosophy is exceptionally holistic. Political philosophy, a practical science, is intrinsically connected to the theoretical sciences of physics and metaphysics. All entities are characterized by a natural goal, *telos*, to which they strive as members of a given species. The goal that humans share with all other species is that of survival and the perpetuation of the species. This is a collective goal that we can achieve only by means of society. Beyond this is the attainment of the goal that belongs exclusively to us as human beings. The defining characteristic of humans that sets us apart from members of all other species is the intellect. Hence the ultimate *telos* of human beings is the perfection of the intellect, which lies in knowledge of the theoretical sciences culminating in metaphysics. Although we may choose to pursue any number of goals as individuals, this goal belongs to us as human beings. It is a natural one that is not determined by us, but discovered by way of rational investigation. Furthermore, it is one that characterizes the individual as such, and not the collective. One may say that the ultimate goal of humanity is to produce perfect individuals.

Yet even if we are made aware of this goal and seek to attain it, not all are equipped to achieve the perfection of the intellect. Elitism characterizes nature as it does so many of our human institutions. The proper intellectual potential is required, in addition to strenuous learning and a cultural and physical environment conducive to intellectual advancement. The proper ethical traits are also necessary to achieve this goal. One who is a slave to one's physical desires may well progress in knowledge, but is incapable of mustering all the psychic forces necessary to attain its heights. The ethical virtues, in addition to serving as a means to intellectual perfection, also contribute to our existence as social animals. They are more accessible than the intellectual virtues to the members of society at large. The medieval philosophers employ Aristotle's doctrine of the mean as the criterion for determining the character traits that are considered virtues. By many of them, however, one can detect a predilection toward a mild form of asceticism, in order to avoid being enslaved by one's physical desires and prevented from learning to one's full capacity. In short, the initial goal of humanity is a collective one, whereas the ultimate goal belongs to the individual. Society is necessary for both goals. The individual is by nature a social animal who requires society for existence and for enabling that individual to achieve ultimate perfection.

Although society is in a crucial sense a natural entity, the type of political association that governs it is not. Nevertheless, Aristotelian philosophy provides the yardstick by which the governance of a particular society can be judged. All societies share the common task of providing their inhabitants with the basic essentials of life and the conditions for the continuation of the species. The excellence of society is determined not only by the manner in which it accomplishes this task, the level of social harmony and mutual cooperation that it achieves, but also by its devotion to the promotion of the goal of human perfection. Societies whose governance leads to the pursuit of wealth or conquest as ends in their own right are imperfect ones. These are imaginary goods that do not constitute true perfection. Democracy, in which everyone is free to pursue one's own goal without being directed to the true goal of humanity, is also found wanting. Given this approach, the leadership of the philosopher–king as posited by Plato – the person who has attained human perfection and is equipped to guide society at large in the pursuit of this goal – is regarded as the most desirable form of leadership.

Yet even if society becomes convinced that only the true philosopher could provide ideal leadership – certainly no small "if" – why would such an individual take on this role? Perfection after all lies in the cultivation of one's intellect, not in imaginary goods, such as wealth, honor, and power. Why return to the darkness of the cave, as depicted in Plato's myth, and all the personal suffering this move entails, after experiencing the sublime brightness of the sun? Although Plato answers this dilemma by an appeal to the duty owed by the philosopher to the society that nurtured him, the medieval philosophers view the willingness of the philosopher to lead society in terms of the ideal of *imitatio Dei*.[2] Perfect individuals are those who, after having attained ethical and intellectual perfection, extend their perfection to those around them by contributing to their wellbeing. This is analogous to God's extension of divine perfection to all existents by ordering them in the best manner possible. That is, assuming a leadership role in society in order to contribute to others is seen as part and parcel of ultimate perfection for it reflects an imitation of God's actions. This activity does not take the place of intellectual perfection but supplements it. It is not only analogous to God's governance of the world, but in a crucial sense represents an extension of divine governance.

The medieval Aristotelian philosophers do not develop their approaches in a spiritual–cultural vacuum, but in the shadow of their religious traditions, all anchored in the idea of divine revelation. In the case of Judaism and Islam, the revelation that serves as the cornerstone of the religion consists of divine law, in addition to speculative and ethical teachings. The challenge facing the medieval Aristotelian philosophers lay in developing a political philosophy that reconciles the central ideas of Greek political thought with the revelatory idea, and all that is accepted as given in revelation. It was the genius of the tenth-century Islamic philosopher Alfarabi to create a theoretical structure that fuses these diverse elements into a harmonious whole. His most famous treatises on politics, *The Political Regime* and *The Opinions of the Inhabitants of the Virtuous City*, open with a discussion of metaphysics and natural science before turning to the topic of governance. The Plotinian doctrine of emanation that links God with the chain of existence becomes the starting point for the ideal state. Plato's philosopher–king is transformed by Alfarabi into the prophet–legislator, the perfect individual who receives an emanation from the Active Intellect, resulting in the ability to lay down the ideal legislation for a particular society in a given period. We may think of this particular form of emanation as an illumination of the intellect. What we term "revelation" is in essence the same phenomenon. God does not willfully single out individuals to convey to them certain messages or hand down to them specific laws. Revelation is a natural phenomenon – all phenomena being traced to the agency of God as the First Cause – involving the intellectual–psychic powers of the perfect individual. It lies in the individual's attainment of exceptional insights into theoretical matters as well as knowledge how to best govern society. The ideal lawgiver, king, and religious leader fuse in the person of the perfect individual who experiences this illumination. Only one who has attained perfection is capable of directing society by means of teachings and laws, both "civil" and "religious," to the perfection that it is capable of attaining.[3]

Given the inability of most members of society to appreciate metaphysical truths pertaining to God and the world, these truths are presented to society at large by the ideal lawgiver in figurative form. The masses understand the images in a literal manner, in keeping with their limited ability, though this understanding is a false one; the philosophers understand the true meaning of the images; the gifted students are gradually weaned from an imaginative understanding to an intellectual one. Alfarabi envisions a series of ideal legislations, each tailored to the particular circumstances of the society of the lawgiver who experiences revelation. In the absence of such an individual, the rulers would necessarily be of lesser perfection, though they too should possess true philosophic knowledge, in addition to other gifts necessary for leadership. They would maintain the existent ideal legislation, rather than lay down a new one. At the same time they would make the necessary modifications that circumstances demand, and in keeping with the aims of the ideal legislation.

Maimonides is greatly influenced by Alfarabi's theoretical model.[4] It provides him with the Archimedean point for understanding the Law of Moses and subsequent Jewish legal developments, in addition to many other matters that are central to his philosophy. To appreciate Maimonides' political thought one must keep in mind that his interests lay specifically in *Jewish* law and the well-being of Jewish society, rather than in developing a new theoretical philosophic model that is universal in nature. Yet although his concerns may be parochial, the goals he posits for the individual Jew and for Jewish society are the same ones characterizing humanity in general. Human perfection is the same for Jew and non-Jew alike. In his view, the purpose of the divine Law transmitted by Moses, the Torah, is to direct Jews to the universal goal of humanity within the context of their particular circumstances. Moreover, it appears that Maimonides self-consciously acted as the ideal leader, though not lawgiver, in accordance with his understanding and adaptation of Alfarabi's model to the circumstances of Jewish society. This is a society that in Maimonides' time not only lacked an independent state – the widely dispersed Jewish communities were all under non-Jewish dominion – but also any form of effective central Jewish leadership. Jewish law was the main thread that bound together the far-flung Jewish communities.

For all Maimonides' fame as a philosopher, it is the realm of Jewish law to which he devoted most of his efforts. In this manner he was able to exert a profound influence on Jewish society. He became the consummate master of Jewish law, one of the greatest Jewish legal authorities of all time. His pioneering legal works – foremost among them, the first complete code of Jewish law, the *Mishneh Torah* – revolutionized the entire field already in his own time. They continue to exert a vast influence on all Jewish legal authorities to the present day. The overriding concern that characterizes Maimonides as philosopher and Maimonides as legal authority is the desire to guide Jewish society in general, and individuals of gifted intellect in particular, to the highest level of perfection of which they are capable of attaining. This concern required him to adopt positions that are consistent with the Jewish legal tradition and best preserve the commitment to Jewish law on the part of all Jews. At the same time Maimonides interprets Jewish law in a manner that best promotes its goals in accordance with his philosophic understanding of the purpose and strategies of the divine Law as transmitted by Moses.

7.2. THE PURPOSE OF THE DIVINE LAW

Maimonides presents a summary of the purpose of the divine Law in the *Guide of the Perplexed* 3.27. He ascribes to it two main goals: the well-being of the soul and the well-being of the body. The well-being of the soul lies in imparting to society at large true beliefs in fundamental matters, in particular relating to God, in a manner that most of its members are capable of understanding. The rational investigation and philosophical proof of these matters, which individuals possessing the necessary aptitude are required to pursue, constitute human perfection. The well-being of the body, or body politic, lies in laws that enable the members of society to live together and not harm each other. This goal consists also of inculcating the ethical virtues, which promote social harmony. Although the divine Law attains the latter goal in a far more effective manner than human legislations, it is the former goal, with its focus on the state of the soul, or more accurately, intellect of the members of society that is the characteristic that sets the divine Law apart from other legislations. The Torah promotes pursuit of the Truth and not only social harmony.[5]

The most important truth imparted by the Torah in Maimonides' view is the monotheistic idea – the view that a single deity is the root of all existence. A full theoretical understanding of this idea constitutes intellectual perfection. The idea has crucial ethical dimensions as well, and ideally it should infuse the whole of one's being. The dominant popular belief standing in opposition to the monotheistic idea is that of polytheism, particularly the belief that the planets are gods. This belief was reinforced by a vast array of idolatrous rituals and gave rise to a whole set of erroneous beliefs – astrology being one prominent example.[6] To ensure the victory of the monotheistic idea, the first objective of the divine Law is to eliminate polytheism and idolatry. Already the patriarch Abraham, according to Maimonides, sought to achieve this objective by way of public teachings. Yet the lesson of history in his view is that teachings to society at large must be backed by forceful political measures in order to be effective.[7]

In his understanding of the divine commandments transmitted by Moses, Maimonides attempts to show how all of them are designed to promote the dual goal of physical and spiritual–intellectual well-being. Mystical–magical explanations for ritual laws are eschewed by Maimonides in favor of historical–anthropological explanations that treat them in the context of the idolatrous practices they are designed to combat and replace.[8] Instead of a ritual system bolstering the belief in many gods, the divine Law mandates a system that gives constant expression to the belief in one God. The ritual system it mandates is appropriate to the situation of the Jewish people in the time of Moses. The divine Law goes to great lengths in its attempt to keep them from returning to the beliefs and practices of the nations surrounding them.

As for the commandments contributing to the well-being of the body, Maimonides views many of them as inculcating the moral virtues in accordance with the Aristotelian doctrine of the mean. This is the doctrine that is most suitable for society at large. The "mean" itself, however, does not have any intrinsic value for Maimonides. He stresses in a number of treatises that the individual ultimately should gauge all of his actions from the perspective of whether they contribute to his knowledge and love of God.[9] Maimonides does not appear to allude to an antinomian position appropriate for the elite, but rather to the necessity for them to go beyond the demands of the Law in their quest for perfection.

It is important to note that, although the initial rationale for many of the commandments designed to combat idolatry is no longer valid – for example, the prohibition against mingling crops or wearing a garment of wool and linen[10] – because of the success of the Torah in eradicating the idolatrous religions of old, Maimonides insists that all the commandments remain mandatory. The reasons for the commandments and the basis for the obligation of Jews to observe them are two separate, albeit related, issues. Commandments are to be obeyed because of the authority of God, in Maimonides' view, irrespective of the reason for their legislation. They can be abrogated or altered only if the authority to do so can also be traced to God. As we shall see momentarily, Maimonides denies that this possibility exists. He is adamant in maintaining that none of the commandments have ever been annulled, or will be in the future.[11] What changes then is not the practice of the commandments but their rationale, how one should view the commandments while observing them. Maimonides presents different types of explanation of the commandments in his great legal work, the *Mishneh Torah*, which are designed to contribute to the spiritual state of the observer, in keeping with the ultimate human goal.[12]

In interpreting Maimonides' political thought, we must always keep in mind the central focus of his thinking. Maimonides has much to say about issues that concern modern political theorists. Yet one would be doing him a grave injustice if one divorces his positions from their context. He approaches all political issues from the perspective of the traditional Jewish legal system, on the one hand, and his philosophic understanding of the goals of this system, on the other. Insofar as Maimonides sees Mosaic Law as being divine, many issues that concern him are not applicable to strictly human legislations. Perhaps the most significant of these issues is the problem whether the divine Law transmitted by Moses can be abrogated or amended.

7.3. STATIC AND DYNAMIC ASPECTS OF MOSAIC LAW

Whereas Alfarabi envisions a series of ideal lawgivers, Maimonides parts company with his philosophic mentor by positing only one. He depicts Moses as having attained the highest level of human perfection that is possible, and whose revelation alone assumed the form of legislation. According to Maimonides, no prophet before or after Moses has a legislative function. Nor will any prophet arising in the future have legislative authority. The divine Law transmitted by Moses will continue to be the law governing the Jewish people even in the time of the king–messiah.[13] Maimonides insists that not only will this law never be abrogated, it will never be amended or altered in the slightest manner.

The dissonance between this position and his approach to the historical reasons for many of the commandments is evident. Maimonides' stance does not result from a purely supernatural view of Mosaic Law rooted in Jewish tradition – namely, God is the author of the Law and has assured the Jews by way of revelation that this law will never be changed no matter what the circumstances. The considerations involved in Maimonides' position are more varied. Although he formulates his approach in a manner that traces the divine Law received by Moses in its entirety to the immediate agency of God, together with God's assurance that this Law will remain forever the same, a number of his views may be interpreted as suggesting that Moses was not simply a passive recipient in the framing of the commandments. Rather they resulted from the *theoretical* knowledge he attained in the state of revelation, a knowledge that enabled him to lay down a perfect legislation.[14] The treatment of Mosaic Law as divine is due to its perfection,[15] and not to God being its immediate agent. This interpretation, if anything, makes Maimonides' stance all the more problematic.

Even if Maimonides entertains an esoteric view on the issue of the Law of Moses, it is certainly important for him to continue to inculcate the view that God is the author of the Law. Any other teaching would lead the masses to label Mosaic Law as a human product, hence imperfect, less binding, and subject to change. Maimonides has no doubt that the Law of Moses was, is, and will continue to be the one most conducive to the attainment of human perfection, and the only law deserving the label "divine." He is exceptionally critical of both Christianity and Islam, and of the societies they fostered, even if he appreciates the positive aspects of these religions in comparison with the idolatrous religions of the past.[16] The immense political power of these religions, coupled with what he considered their severe ethical and spiritual–intellectual shortcomings, help explain his radical stance regarding the Mosaic Law's inviolability. Although he is able to cite opinions in Jewish tradition in support of his stance, the tradition is hardly unequivocal on this issue. Maimonides' position may best be appreciated from the perspective of the challenges posed to Mosaic Law by the other monotheistic religions laying claim to revelation. Once the possibility for any formal change in Mosaic Law is conceded, the floodgates are opened for its complete abrogation as argued by the proponents of the other religions. To meet this challenge, it is preferable to adopt a radical stance negating the possibility for even the slightest change in Mosaic Law throughout all of history.[17]

Surprisingly, in a remark he makes in passing, Maimonides appears to concede that he can envision as a *theoretical possibility* a divine Law more appropriate to his own period than the Law of Moses. He suggests that this Law would not include sacrifices, which were no longer appropriate as a mode for worshipping God. At the same time he points to the wisdom reflected by the Law of Moses in this matter, for it limits the practice of this historically relative manner of worship to a single place, the Temple in Jerusalem, to be performed only by certain individuals and under fixed circumstances. Thus the Law of Moses lays down conditions for the performance of sacrifice that result in the practical suspension of this manner of worship for much of Jewish history up to the present day. It does not place such limitations on the more appropriate and nonhistorically relative manner of worship – namely, prayer.[18] One may infer from Maimonides' stance that the reinstitution of sacrifices in the messianic period[19] – an inevitability given his view of the inviolability of the Law of Moses and the necessary rebuilding of the Temple – represents for him a type of regression. Yet political theory, just as all other areas, involves the necessity to choose between competing considerations. In attempting to improve the part, one may at times destroy the whole.[20] For Maimonides, it is preferable to maintain that all the commandments transmitted by Moses will be practiced in the messianic period, thereby underscoring the absolute inviolability of the Law, than to adopt a stance regarding the future that would serve to undermine the commitment to the Law in the present.

Although we may appreciate some of the considerations that lead Maimonides to adopt his stance on the permanence of Mosaic Law, at first blush it appears to be an untenable one when viewed from a purely social perspective. Any law that remains so inflexible to changing historical circumstances can hardly hope to survive. A static law may be possible, and even appropriate, to certain areas – for example, the cultic. Yet it can hardly continue to address so many other areas in the life of a nation in light of the rampant economic, technological, cultural, and political changes confronting it. One must keep in mind that, in the Middle Ages, as in Late Antiquity, Jewish communities tended to be autonomous, with Jewish law governing most aspects of the Jews' social–political life.

Maimonides is well aware of this problem, though he eschews Alfarabi's model that posits the desirability of successive ideal legislations. Instead, he chooses to address it in a manner that is both consistent with Jewish tradition and reminiscent of the role assigned by Alfarabi to the "princes of the law" – those individuals who lack the perfection necessary for issuing a new ideal legislation, but have the ability to adapt the existent legislation to the changing circumstances of society.[21] Maimonides treats the Torah as having institutionalized the mechanisms by which worthy individuals can bring about the necessary change. The authority given by the Torah to the high court, the Sanhedrin (the right to interpret the divine Law in applying it to new situations; the right to issue new laws that are completely binding by *divine* authority, though not having the same status as the divine commandments themselves, and that can legally be revoked; the right *temporarily* to suspend most of the divine commandments when the situation demands such radical measures; as well as the responsibility for judging all major court cases), allows for the constant growth and change in Jewish law in response to new challenges. At the same time, all the divine commandments in the Torah remain completely fixed. Maimonides treats the individuals who were ordained by their colleagues to serve as members of the high court in the formative period of rabbinic law as great philosophers as well as legal authorities. They were not popularly elected to this position, but appointed based on their merit by those exceptional individuals who had already attained this position based on theirs. They possessed the knowledge of how to apply Mosaic Law to their period not only in accordance with the legal tradition but also with the ultimate aims of the Law. In short, although the structure of the Torah is completely inflexible, it contains suitable mechanisms within this structure to allow for its adaptation to the circumstances of successive generations.

7.4. THE INSTITUTIONS OF GOVERNMENT

Authority for all aspects of government of the Jewish people was vouchsafed by God on Moses. Moses is the prophet par excellence who functioned as lawgiver, king, judge, and supreme religious authority. Although the first of these functions fell to Moses alone in history, the others became fixed institutions, some already in the time of Moses. The Sanhedrin, for example, was established by divine command, with Moses serving as its first leader. God "ordained" its members by bestowing on them the divine spirit.[22]

Employing a loose analogy, one may view the function of the king as corresponding to the executive branch of government whereas the Sanhedrin combines the legislative and judicial branches. An additional branch of government in the Jewish model is that of the priesthood. This branch is responsible for the cultic functions, primarily the order of sacrifice. The Torah serves as an extended constitution, from which the various branches of government derive their authority. This is not to say that the demarcation of powers is the same in both models, and the manner in which individuals attain their positions is completely different. Insofar as Maimonides is a legal authority basing his views on traditional rabbinic texts, it is not surprising that he treats the members of the Sanhedrin as the most important heirs to Moses' leadership, for they are responsible for the interpretation of the Law and its application. All institutions, including that of kingship, derive their authority solely from the Torah. The rulings of the Sanhedrin are binding on king and high priest alike. The king's responsibility is to adopt the measures appropriate to the preservation of the social order, the promotion of the physical infrastructure and the conduct of foreign affairs. Even in these areas, his acts are considered binding only if the Sanhedrin considers them compatible with the Torah. In certain instances, such as the waging of a war not mandated by the Torah, the king has first to obtain the agreement of the Sanhedrin.[23]

Although this approach to government is reflective of rabbinic thought, not all of Maimonides' positions simply reproduce his rabbinic sources. One of Maimonides' most important contributions to this picture lies in his discussion of the place of revelation and the prophet in the governance of society. Because the prophet must achieve ethical and intellectual perfection, no individual is more capable of leading society. As expected, Maimonides treats the prophet as the ideal leader in a number of discussions.[24] Yet his position on the authority of the prophet is almost paradoxical in nature. The clear predilection in his legal writings is to limit the prophet's authority rather than extend it. He goes to far greater lengths in this direction than many of his predecessors, or successors. Maimonides establishes nearly impossible tests to verify the veracity of a person who lays claim to a prophetic mission. Even if all these tests are passed, the legal authority granted this individual remains fairly narrow.[25] In essence, the prophet is not granted any rights that are not possessed either by the king or the Sanhedrin. Moreover, not only does the prophet have no authority to alter the Torah in any manner, the prophet has no authority even to decide questions of Law by an appeal to revelation. Such an appeal automatically marks the person as a false prophet who is to be immediately executed.[26] It appears that Maimonides deprives the individual most fit to interpret and adapt the divine Law to his period of any authority to do so.

On this issue too it appears that Maimonides' foremost consideration is to preserve the Torah against the most serious challenges facing it. He completely rejects the view that because revelation comes from God the authority of the prophet is independent of and on equal footing with the divine Law. He argues that because the divine Law was transmitted by God through Moses in a unique manner, all authority, including prophetic authority, must be based on the Law. The Law itself indicates that it will never be changed and, moreover, that all legal decisions based on the Law are now solely in human hands.[27] In other words, once God bestows the divine Law, God is, as it were, out of the picture in regard to legal matters. Everything is decided by the human institutions established by the divine Law, and in accordance with the authority vouchsafed on each. Not only do humans have no right to tamper with the divine Law or with the authority of the institutions it establishes, God too has relinquished this right. Hence revelation is powerless to grant the prophet any authority the Law does not acknowledge, including the right to decide legal questions. Maimonides' approach to Judaism leaves no room for prophets or any other form of charismatic leadership that is not completely bound to the Torah and its institutions. Maimonides has noted the lessons of history well on this point. The masses are too willing to transfer their allegiance from the commitment to the Law to commitment to charismatic leaders claiming revelation. Maimonides attempts to safeguard Judaism as best he can from this ongoing dangerous phenomenon.

Significantly, those reaching prophetic perfection have other avenues to express their leadership potential in Maimonides' thought. Although he attempts to eliminate the reappearance of prophets claiming a prophetic mission, he treats some of the great rabbinic authorities of the past as having attained prophetic perfection. This is particularly true of his treatment of Judah the Prince, the head of the Sanhedrin and author of the Mishnah, the first formal systematic attempt to organize the Torah's oral tradition.[28] He even treats the classical prophets as functioning primarily as heads of the Sanhedrin, which is the basis for their involvement in legal matters.[29] In other words, a prophet cannot determine matters of law as a prophet, but can do so as a member of the institution that is responsible for such matters. Decisions by the Sanhedrin are decided by majority vote of its seventy-one members. The vote of the prophet carries the same weight as that of any other member. This individual can make no appeal to revelation in deciding points of law.

In the messianic period this picture remains essentially the same in Maimonides' view.[30] The messiah for Maimonides is both prophet and ideal king. He will free Israel from its enemies, rebuild the Temple, gather the dispersed Jews, and usher in a period of world peace in which all nations acknowledge and worship the one God. All the commandments that until this point could not be performed for technical reasons will once again be performed. Not only will nature not change its course in this period, the king–messiah himself is not characterized by any supernatural traits, leaving aside the near-impossible social–political tasks he succeeds in accomplishing. Even he has no authority, despite his being the ultimate philosopher–(prophet–) king, to legislate a new divine Law or alter the existent one in any way.

7.5. SOCIETY AND THE PERFECT INDIVIDUAL

We have seen that for Maimonides the ideal society is one in which those achieving perfection assume a leadership role within the framework of the existent institutions of governance. Society's ultimate goal is to guide those with the aptitude for perfection to the perfection of which they are capable. The masses are not to be ignored or exploited; the opposite is true. They too are to be guided to truth and virtuous living in accordance with their capacity. Maimonides understands that one cannot legislate virtue, and one certainly cannot require the simple-minded to grasp theoretical scientific truths. One can, however, legislate actions that serve to promote virtue, virtue being in large measure an acquired habit, and one can mandate the necessity of learning and of holding certain official beliefs, even if one does not grasp them properly. The proper intellectual–ethical environment is thereby created for the potentially perfect, while those lacking the proper potential are steered to the highest level that they are capable of attaining.

Maimonides' discussions on society and human perfection are firmly anchored in the Aristotelian approach presented in the introduction to this chapter. Human beings are social animals who require society for their existence and for the survival of the species, whereas the ultimate goal of humanity is achieved by the perfect individual as an individual. Very few are equipped by nature to reach this goal. Maimonides is not oblivious to the inherent tension between the situation and needs of the collective and that of the perfect individual, despite the fact that he paints a symbiotic picture of the relation between them.[31] He addresses different aspects of this issue, two of which I now briefly discuss.

In several passages Maimonides notes the solitary existential condition of the one pursuing perfection. Although they too require society for their needs, he counsels them to live a life of physical solitude as much as possible.[32] Interaction with others tends to serve as an impediment to perfection. This is the case not only in evil or imperfectly governed societies but also in well-governed ones. Maimonides is not very optimistic in how far Jewish law can go in positively transforming its average practitioner. Human nature remains fairly constant. The divine Law can work only with what there is. It is designed to promote perfection in a social context *as much as possible*.[33] Given that it is geared to a society in which most people will remain imperfect, the Law is limited in the amount of good it can accomplish. For all its ultimate aspirations, the first task of divine Law is to ensure social order and address the needs of the community at large. This means that the intellectual elite are likely to find themselves in a difficult and lonely situation, even in a perfect society. Maimonides notes that "the Law does not pay attention to the isolated" (*GP* 3.34, p. 534). As is true of the workings of nature, to which divine Law is likened, at times it may even bring harm to the individual. Although it is not clear that Maimonides has the most gifted individuals in mind, there is little doubt that he feels that the regimen they must pursue should be more strenuous than that mandated by divine Law. He denounces the ascetic life as an ideal to be taught to society at large because of the effect it may have on those who view physical and material deprivation as spiritual goals in their own right. The intellectual elite, however, should live a moderately ascetic life *in the midst of society*.

A related point of tension revolves around the issue of why a person who has attained perfection should become involved in politics. The obvious answer to a contemporary reader would be that, having reached perfection, an individual of this description would now look for new challenges, other mountains to climb, as it were. The problem with this answer is that it assumes perfection is a goal that, once attained, makes the task complete. Maimonides follows the medieval Aristotelian tradition in thinking of perfection and its accompanying spiritual pleasure as an active state. Not only does progress up the ladder of knowledge give one pleasure, but the continued contemplation of things that one has already grasped offers pleasure as well. In fact, no other form of pleasure is greater. Furthermore, perfection is a state that requires constant effort to maintain and enjoy. No one who has seen the light of Truth would willingly leave this state for all the kingdoms in the world.

As I have already indicated, the medieval philosophers view the duty of the philosopher to assume an active leadership role in terms of *imitatio Dei*.[34] The political life thus completes the perfection of the contemplative one even if it is of a lower nature. Maimonides adds a number of important points to this model. First, those achieving perfection assume a political role primarily because of the experience of an internal feeling of compulsion. Nature, as ordered by God, is altruistic on this score. Built into its operations is the desire of those attaining perfection to share it with others, a desire that overcomes their personal preference to be left alone in order to continue to live the contemplative life. Second, Maimonides describes a state in which one can continue to contemplate even while interacting with others and living an active social life. This is the state achieved by Moses and the Patriarchs. It may be likened to one in which the individual descends the mountain in order to lead those below while at the same time remains on the summit. The philosopher–leader thus attempts to realize a state in which one continues to live in one's isolated inner space, beholding the eternal truths, while outwardly guiding others to the perfection of which they are capable.[35]

7.6. ISSUES PERTAINING TO CIVIL SOCIETY

An essay on Maimonides' political thought would be incomplete without a few words about his stance on some of the issues that dominate contemporary discussions. I would like to address three of them that have received considerable attention in the past few years: the rights of the accused versus justice for the victims, the purpose and effectiveness of punishments in general and capital punishment in particular, and what should be society's attitude to foreigners living in its midst.

Maimonides would certainly be characterized in today's circles as a proponent of "law and order." The primary task of civil society, in his view, is to protect its citizens. This is accomplished by ensuring that the law is observed by everyone, from the king and members of the high court down. Although Maimonides feels that people in general should deal mercifully with each other – and those on the lowest rungs of society should be treated with the utmost mercy and concern – he shows little tolerance for willful lawbreakers of any stripe. Mercy is a positive trait so long as it is not misplaced. The following statement nicely captures the essence of his thought on the subject: "The wrongdoer and the worker of injustice should not be protected when he seeks our protection and should not be pitied, nor should his rightful punishment be abolished in any way" (*GP* 3.39, p. 554). After having shown that even those seeking God's protection by fleeing to the divine altar are forcefully removed from there by command of the divine Law and handed over for punishment, Maimonides continues: "All the more if the man in question has sought the protection of a human individual; the latter ought not to protect or to pity him, for pity for wrongdoers and evil men is tantamount to cruelty with regard to all creatures."

Maimonides views the punishments prescribed by the Torah as an important deterrent to crime, not only as a mode of exculpation or atonement.[36] The severity of the crime is the primary criterion for determining the level of punishment. Yet the frequency of the occurrence of a crime, the easier its performance, and the more tempting it is to the perpetrator are also factors taken under consideration by the divine Law in issuing penalties. Hence the Torah often mandates punishments that are heavier than the nature of the crime would seem to warrant. In this manner potential criminals, who weigh the risks and benefits of a wrongful act, are discouraged from performing it. The Torah lays down four different types of capital punishment to be administered by the high court for different levels of the most severe, willfully performed offences (e.g., murder, incest, and idolatry); whipping for lesser categories of offense; and monetary penalties in certain defined cases (incarceration is not included as a form of punishment). Still other categories of offense are subject to heavenly rather than earthly punishment. As is true for most of his contemporaries, Maimonides displays no reservations regarding the appropriateness of capital punishment given the severity of the crimes involved and the great damage, whether *physical or spiritual*, they bring to society.

The issue of punishment, however, is not as straightforward as appears at first glance. The Torah assumes a person to be innocent until proven guilty. In the rabbinic interpretation of the Torah, many legal qualifications are presented to the carrying out of punishments. All transgressions must be deliberate – rather than inadvertent or performed out of compulsion – in order to merit any form of punishment. In capital cases, so many additional conditions have to be met in order to execute the accused that it is highly improbable that any culprit who is caught would not be set free. In short, the Torah as interpreted by the rabbinic authorities is certainly on the side of the rights of the accused.

Maimonides' *Mishneh Torah* accurately presents the legal interpretations of the Torah presented in rabbinic literature that greatly limit the circumstances in which the Sanhedrin can find the defendant guilty and subject to the mandatory punishment decreed by the Torah. Yet given his own personal tendencies in this matter, he makes the most of the exceptions found in his rabbinic sources to the very limiting circumstances in which punishments can be carried out. In this way he seeks to avoid the major harm to society that would occur by allowing so many offenders to escape any form of punishment because of legal technicalities. One significant and broad exception to these limitations is the discretionary right possessed by judges to impose punishments that are not mandated by the Torah to perpetrators of wide ranges of crimes. These punishments include excommunication, incarceration, whipping, monetary fines, and even the death penalty. In other words, perpetrators of crimes may escape the punishment mandated by the Torah for any number of legal reasons, but the judges still have the right to impose on them some form of punishment, including capital punishment, when they decide that the situation warrants it. Although Maimonides' position is anchored in rabbinic sources, he is very liberal in his interpretation of the extent of the prerogative of the court to dispense these punishments. He views this right as an important weapon in the hands of the rabbinic leadership to ensure obedience to the Torah, its interpreters, and to their rulings.[37]

Analogous to the discretionary right of judges to punish is the right of the king to sentence to death those who rebel against his authority. Although rabbinic literature has relatively little to say about this subject from a strictly legal perspective, Maimonides expands some of the statements found in his sources into comprehensive legal rulings. He poignantly extends the right of the king to punish offenders to cover many crimes that do not appear to fall under the category of rebellion. Not only does it include disobedience to any of the king's expressed orders given to an individual when the order does not contradict any law of the Torah, but also any major crime against the social order as guaranteed by the king. Maimonides states in *MT* 14, Kings and Wars, 3.10, "Anyone who kills another without there being adequate evidence of the crime, or without having been forewarned, even if there is only one witness [ordinarily, both conditions must be satisfied by at least two witnesses giving testimony in order to condemn], or in the case of a person who inadvertently kills a person he hates – the king has the right to kill the perpetrator and to 'mend the world' according to the needs of the hour. He may kill many on the same day, hang up their bodies and let them remain hanging for many days in order to instill fear and to crush the evil doers of the world." The king also has the right to issue discretionary punishments of lesser severity, such as flogging and incarceration.[38]

To be effective, any law must in practice be given teeth to punish offenders, not only in theory. Inculcating the right mode of behavior and holding out threats of heavenly punishment are insufficient in deterring many evildoers. Maimonides is well aware, as were some of the sages, that the rabbinic interpretation of the divine Law is problematic from this perspective. By expanding on the scope of discretionary punishment accorded to kings and to the rabbinic courts, he is able to overcome the challenge a strict interpretation of divine Law poses to social stability, or "the welfare of the body" that is necessary for every society, and to the very observance of the divine Law that leads to the "welfare of the soul." To promote these goals he has no qualms in suspending the protection that the divine Law offers the individual in those cases in which the individual exploits this protection to society's physical and spiritual detriment. Maimonides is aware of the dangers that are inherent in the exceptional authority accorded to rabbinic judges and kings in this area, and how easy it is for them to misuse it. He admonishes the judges not to treat this authority lightly and that all the punishments they impose should be "for the sake of heaven." Furthermore, they must keep mind the importance placed by the divine Law on the respect one owes to one's fellow human beings.[39] In summary, the discretionary right to punish should be exercised solely in order to "breach the gaps" in the observance of the divine Law in accordance with what the situation requires, just as the right possessed by the kings should be exercised to "mend the world" – that is to say, to promote a just and harmonious social order.

As for the attitude to resident aliens living in the Jewish state, the basic thrust of Maimonides' political thought is very much in harmony with his rabbinic sources. I am not dealing with the issue of converts who are considered as full-fledged Jews according to Jewish law, but with the issue of those living in Israel as non-Jews in a period in which there is a Jewish state ruled in accordance with the Torah. According to the rabbinic interpretation of the Torah, all resident aliens are required to abide by the seven *Noaḥite* laws incumbent on all non-Jews: the prohibition against idolatry, cursing God, murder, incest, robbery, eating the limb of a living animal, and the injunction to establish courts of justice that will judge according to the provisions governing *Noaḥite* law.[40] There is no requirement to convert, and this appears to be the case even in the messianic period.[41] The non-Jew obeying these laws is accorded eternal felicity in the afterlife.[42] Although most of these laws are important for any social order, the first law is important in keeping with the particular goal of the divine Law as Maimonides' views it. Maimonides goes beyond his rabbinic sources by adding another condition. The non-Jew is required to accept these laws on the basis of a belief in the revelation of the divine Law to Moses, and not on the basis of rational considerations.[43] A shared belief in the Torah from a formal perspective, even on the part of those who are not required to obey the majority of its commandments, further binds ideologically the resident alien with Jewish society and provides a more homogenous spiritual environment, without insisting on complete uniformity.

Maimonides' conclusion of his discussion of the resident alien is particularly worthy of note: "We should deal with as much civility and lovingkindness with resident aliens as we deal with an Israelite, for we are commanded to give them sustenance" (*MT* 14, Kings and Wars, 10.12). Although they are not full-fledged citizens of the state for they have chosen not to convert to Judaism, society is nevertheless obligated to promote their welfare and not treat them as despised "others." Maimonides continues the passage by turning to a more contemporary issue: how Jews living in a non-Jewish ruled state should act toward non-Jews *who do not observe the seven* Noaḥite *laws*: "Regarding gentiles, the sages commanded that we are required to visit their sick, bury their dead as is the case with Jewish dead, and support their poor together with the Jewish poor, because of the ways of peace. It is stated: 'God is good to all and His mercy is upon all His creatures (Psalm 148:9).' It is further stated: 'Its [the Torah's] ways are pleasant ones and all its paths are those of peace (Proverbs 3:17).'" No utilitarian motives for this ruling are presented in this context – namely, if the Jews do not behave well toward gentiles they will be treated poorly in turn. Rather, Maimonides' stress is on displaying the quality of mercy toward all those with whom one is in contact. He maintains that this too is a form of *imitatio Dei*.[44]

One should not conclude from the last passage, however, that the requirement to act mercifully toward humanity outweighs Maimonides' commitment to the monotheistic idea. Idolatry reflects the worst sickness of the soul in his thought. It poses the greatest threat to the spiritual–moral health of society. We have seen that he considers the rooting out of idolatry an integral part of the primary goal of the Torah. Maimonides views war as a justifiable means to accomplish this end, in some cases even mandatory. The Torah commands the king to wage war against the nations of Canaan and also to free Israel from its adversaries. Other wars are optional according to the Torah and may be initiated by the king with the approval of the Sanhedrin.[45] Although the reasons for waging nonmandatory wars may be varied – for example, material gain, the expansion of borders – in effect Maimonides turns every war waged by a Jewish king into a holy war. He maintains that the inhabitants of all the conquered areas, even outside the Land of Israel, are required to accept the *Noaḥite* laws on pain of death. Maimonides subtly suggests that putting an end to idolatry should be the main goal of every war of conquest.[46]

This stance is eerily reminiscent of the religious fanaticism of the Almohads, who emphasized the need for everyone to hold true beliefs and whose conquest of sections of Spain and policy of forced conversion forced Maimonides and his family to flee the country. He may well have been influenced by their ideology despite the fact that he and many other Jews were its victims. Alfarabi's view that nations who set as their main goal conquest and material wealth are ignorant ones for they pursue imaginary ends may also have helped shape Maimonides' approach to this issue.[47] Only a noble goal is a sufficient reason to undertake war. In light of this position, it is understandable why he maintains that Jewish soldiers fighting wars not explicitly commanded by the Torah should regard their activity as sanctifying the name of God.[48] The notion that the primary purpose of the wars explicitly commanded in the Torah is to stamp out idolatry is even more pronounced in Maimonides' treatment of this issue. He maintains that the Israelites were not commanded to wage a war of genocide against the seven Canaanite nations and against the Amalekites. They were commanded to wipe them out only if they refused to surrender and accept the *Noaḥite* laws after being petitioned to do so. Those who did were to be spared.[49]

Maimonides ties these themes together in his depiction of the messianic period:

> The sages and prophets did not long for messianic times in order to rule the world and subjugate all the nations, and not to be exalted by the nations, and not to eat, drink and be merry, but to be free to engage in the divine Law and its wisdom without oppression or interference, in order that they merit the World to Come.... In this period there will be no hunger, war, envy or rivalry, since goods will be found in great abundance and delicacies will be as plentiful as the soil. The entire world will be devoted solely to the attainment of knowledge of God. All Israel will be great sages, knowing the hidden matters and attaining knowledge of their Maker to the extent of human capacity, as it is stated: "The world will be filled with the knowledge of God as the water covers the sea" (Isaiah 11:9) (*MT* 14, Kings and Wars, 12.4–5).

In other words, the messianic period is primarily characterized by the creation of the optimal social conditions the world over for the individual's pursuit of perfection.

7.7. CONCLUSION

Western society is committed to the ideal of liberal democracy – an open society in which its members are free to hold conflicting views and maintain divergent lifestyles as long as they do not interfere with the rights of others to do the same. The ideal polity is one that not only treats all its members as equal in the eyes of the law, but also allows for a marketplace of ideas and choices without government interference or even official preference. Stress is placed on the duty of the government to protect *basic rights* of the *individual*, even when the individual makes use of these rights in a manner that does not find favor with the majority, and may even pose a challenge to the objectives that most members of the society hold dear. At the same time, the majority has the right to determine the general direction in which society moves and can change its direction when it sees fit.

Maimonides' political philosophy is problematic for one who is committed to this ideal. The context of his thought is reminiscent of societies ruled by religious fundamentalists, with all the negative associations evoked by such regimes in the mind of the western reader. Yet it also offers the reader a chance to evaluate better the underlying assumptions on which western society is based, and afford an opportunity to appreciate the rationale for alternative systems. The political philosophy of Maimonides is predicated on the belief that there are absolute truths, and that the highest value in life lies in holding these truths and acting in accordance with them. Furthermore, it is the duty of the government not only to guarantee social order, but to adopt the necessary measures to ensure that the members of society learn and accept these truths as far as it is in its, and their, power to do so. Freedom of choice is an important theological principle for Maimonides. Any law would be meaningless if human actions were predetermined, as it would not be in one's own power to obey or disobey.[50] But, as noted before, although as individuals we are not coerced in our choice of what goals to pursue and actions to perform, we do not determine the goals that *should* be pursued by us *as human beings*. These goals are divinely naturally ordered.

From a political perspective, there is no intrinsic value in upholding the freedom of the individual to believe falsehoods or the right to make bad choices. Nor does it make sense to entrust the direction of society to the majority who are ignorant of the true path and tend to equate the good life with material acquisition.[51] In Maimonides' positive approach to liberty, the task of government is to free the individual precisely from all that prevents the attainment of truth and goodness in accordance with one's ability. Indeed, the government would be doing its members a great disservice if it acted otherwise. It must utilize the instrument of law to guide the masses in the right path, rather than act in accordance with popular views grounded in a lack of understanding.

Maimonides develops his political thought within the context of a traditional society that is, for the most part, a homogenous one governed by sacred texts grounded in revelation. The vast majority of people are committed to the belief that God legislated Mosaic Law and that obedience to it is crucial to one's state in this world and in the next. Maimonides uses philosophy to interpret Mosaic Law in a way that maintains this society and reorients it. His purpose is not to undermine its foundations but to bolster them.[52] As opposed to a more straightforward traditional Jewish model, his model is noteworthy for how it combines a belief in revelation of a divine Law to the Jewish people with the rationalist tradition of his period, for how it balances Jewish particularism with universal ideals, for how it ascribes to the Jewish tradition a critical political role in the education of its subjects and instills in them virtuous thought and deed according to accepted philosophic standards and what the people are prepared to accept. Maimonides is convinced that most polities have failed miserably on this point, but then, most polities are ruled by the ignorant in his view.

He is committed to the belief that Judaism is different on this score, though it too requires adjustments in his own period on the part of the Jewish equivalent of philosopher–kings to enable it to accomplish its objectives. He attempts to create a society whose leaders not only are steeped in and loyal to Jewish tradition, but who also possess a thorough knowledge of non-Jewish cultures and draw into Judaism the best of what these cultures have to offer. Rather than turn Jewish society into an insular one that erects walls in an attempt to ward off outside influences, the ideal leaders attempt to turn

Jewish society into one committed to educational progress while upholding its traditional foundations. Intellectual advances made by non-Jews are viewed as important not just for technological innovation, but in order to understand traditional Judaism better. The ideal leaders serve as filters for separating the positive intellectual developments made by Jews and non-Jews alike from the negative ones.

Ultimately, all progress is measured in terms of a better understanding of the monotheistic idea and in acting in accordance with this understanding. In Maimonides' view, the acceptance of this idea and all that it entails is the foundation for living a life that is truly human. Hence one must be intolerant of views and activities that pollute the thought of people by supporting the belief in false gods or that there is no God, although these views and activities cause people no *physical* harm.

For a person who accepts the right of all individuals to think out loud and act as they choose, Maimonides' political model appears to violate the most basic human rights, as is true of all theocratic models. But even if one rejects the principles on which Maimonides bases his philosophy, there is little reason to regard the existence of basic, or inalienable, human rights as self-evident. They serve as the foundation for a certain type of polity that many regard as ideal because of the value system held by the protagonists of such rights. To argue that history shows the evil results of governments attempting to impose on society views of truth and goodness not in accordance with the liberal model is to beg the question. Liberal societies are hardly immune from the critique that, for all the advantages they offer, there is a price they pay for the great amount of individual freedom enjoyed by their citizens. Part of the price takes the form of a lack of a moral–spiritual cohesiveness binding the segments of society and infusing them with a shared goal that goes beyond the acquisition of wealth and power or the protection of the rights of the individual. For all its grave faults from a liberal perspective, Maimonides' model provides this type of social cohesiveness. His model also has a universal dimension that attempts to bind all of humanity together.

Does this mean that Maimonides can contribute to contemporary western political thought only by providing it with an improved version of a model whose foundations are opposed to those of liberal democracy? In my view Maimonides has much to teach those who are committed to any system of government but dissatisfied with the direction in which their society is moving. He shows us to what extent an individual can work to maintain a system while at the same time instill in it a new dimension and move it in a different direction. He teaches us that even when one is committed to the truths on which one's society is based, one should not necessarily accept the common understanding of these truths. At the same time one always must gauge the consequences of one's teachings and actions and see where compromises are necessary in one's public activity in order not to bring more harm than good to society. Lies may enslave but the truth does not always set one free. Finally, one should never lose sight of one's ultimate goals and values, which should provide the basis for all one's activity. Maimonides' own political activity reflects an outstanding example of ideal leadership in the context of the beliefs and situation of the society to which he belongs. From his example we all can learn much in how to act in our own.

NOTES

1. I am indebted to Leo Strauss for much of the spirit of my reading of Maimonides, if not the letter. For the most important introduction to the reading of medieval political philosophy see Strauss 1952.
2. See *Republic* 514–21. For a discussion of this ideal in medieval philosophy, see Berman 1961; see also the bibliography in Kreisel 1999, p. 302, n.1.
3. For a study of Alfarabi's political philosophy, see Galston 1990.
4. For Maimonides' indebtedness to Alfarabi, see in particular Strauss 1987, pp. 101–33; Berman 1974.
5. For a discussion of these goals see Galston 1978–9.
6. *GP* 3.37; *MT* 1, Idolatry, 11.8.16.
7. *GP* 3.29; *MT* 1, Idolatry, 1.3. See Kreisel 1999, pp. 29–35.
8. *GP* 3.29,32,37.
9. *EC*, Chapter 5; *MT* 1, Character Traits, 3.3. See Kreisel 1999, pp. 175–88.
10. *GP* 3.37; cf. Deuteronomy 22:9, 11.
11. *Introduction to Commentary on the Mishnah*; *MT* 1, Principles of the Torah, 9.1.
12. Compare, for example, Maimonides' approach to ritual purity in *Guide* 3.47 and *MT* 10, Ritual Baths, 11.12. For reasons in the commandments in *MT*, see Twersky 1980, pp. 430ff.

13. *MT* 14, Kings and Wars, 11.1.
14. See Reines 1969; Bland 1982a.
15. *GP* 2.40.
16. For Maimonides' approach to these religions see Novak 1986.
17. Kreisel 1999, pp. 16ff.
18. *GP* 3.32.
19. *MT*, Kings and Wars, 11.1.
20. See Maimonides' remarks in *GP* 3.34.
21. *The Political Regime*, p. 80 (Lerner and Mahdi 1972, p. 37).
22. Numbers 11:16–25; cf. *Sanhedrin*, 2a.
23. *MT* 14, Kings and Wars, 5.2. See also subsequent discussion. Jewish law also accepts the decrees of non-Jewish governments as binding on their Jewish subjects, particularly in civil matters, only so long as they do not come into direct conflict with the Torah according to the judgment of the rabbinic authorities, whether it is the Sanhedrin or its spiritual–legal heirs.
24. See, for example, *GP* 2.36–37.
25. For a discussion of this issue see Blidstein 1999; Kreisel 2001, pp. 158–167, 189–205.
26. *MT* 1, Principles of the Torah, 9.1.
27. See *Introduction to the Commentary on the Mishnah*; *MT* 1, Principles of the Torah, 7.7, 9.1. Mosaic prophecy is distinguished by Maimonides from that of all other prophets by the fact that all of Israel were eyewitnesses to the revelation of the Ten Commandments by God to Moses at Sinai. For a discussion of this issue see Kreisel 2001, pp. 192ff.
28. See *Introduction to the Commentary on the Mishnah*; Kreisel 2001, pp. 167, 311.
29. Kreisel 2001; *MT* 1, Introduction.
30. See *MT* 14, Kings and Wars, 11–12. For a discussion of Maimonides' approach to the king–messiah and the messianic period, see in particular Funkenstein 1977; Ravitzky 1991; Lorberbaum 2001, pp. 77–89.
31. See Levinger 1989, pp. 149–54.
32. *GP* 2.36, 3.51; see Kreisel 1999, pp. 175–82.
33. See Kreisel 1999, pp. 189–223.
34. See n. 2 of this chapter. See also Galston 1978, Harvey 1980.
35. *GP* 2.37; 3.51, 54. See Kreisel 1999, pp. 125–58.
36. *GP* 3.41.
37. See *MT* 14, Sanhedrin, 24.4–10.
38. See Blidstein 2001, pp. 133–49, 196–211; Lorberbaum 2001, pp. 55–61.
39. *MT* 14, Sanhedrin, 24.10.
40. *MT* 14, Kings and Wars, 9.1–14.
41. Blidstein 2001, pp. 245–50; see, however, Kellner 1991a, pp. 33–47.

42. *MT* 14, Kings and Wars, 8.11; *Commentary on Mishnah Sanhedrin*, 10.2.
43. For a discussion of this issue see Schwarzschild 1962; Kasher 1986; Nehorai 1992; Blidstein 2001, pp. 260–1.
44. See Blidstein 2001, p. 243.
45. *MT* 14, Kings and Wars, 5.1–4.
46. *MT* 14, Kings and Wars, 4.10, 8.10. For Maimonides' approach to war see Blidstein 2001, pp. 230–245, 253–263.
47. See Alfarabi, *The Political Regime*, pp. 86–104 (Lerner and Mahdi 1972, pp. 41–53).
48. *MT* 14, Kings and Wars, 7.15; see Lerner 1963a.
49. *MT* 14, Kings and Wars, 6.4.
50. *EC* Chapter 8; *MT* 1, Repentance, 5.1–7.1.
51. See *GP* 3.54.
52. This political model receives its most serious philosophical challenge by Spinoza, who was well acquainted with Maimonides' thought and used many of his ideas to draw diametrically opposed conclusions and destroy such traditionalist society. See Kreisel 2001, pp. 544–86 (particularly the bibliography on p. 546, n.3).

DAVID NOVAK

8 Jurisprudence

8.1. THE RATIONAL STRUCTURE OF THE LAW

To appreciate Maimonides' jurisprudence, it is best to begin by looking at how one can be a jurisprudent or *halakhist* in the normative Jewish tradition. The Talmud notes that "one is not to derive the law from theoretical law [*halakhah*] or from a particular case [*Ma*ʿ*aseh*], but only when they say to him that it is the practical law [*halakhah le-ma*ʿ*aseh*, literally, "the law for a case"]."[1] Thus there is theoretical law from which practical law is not to be deduced because it is too general or only hypothetical.[2] Then there is actual lawmaking from what one might call the political lawmaker, which is specific and to which analogies to other laws can usually be made.[3] Finally, there is case law from the rabbinic respondent, which is too particular for one to make analogies to other laws or to simply induce from it what the specific law is. After all, each case might be exceptional.[4]

Maimonides was a lawmaker in all three respects. That is, he was a general theorist, a codifier of specific law, and a casuist who decided the law in particular cases. Nevertheless, when one is seeking Maimonides the philosopher, it is his theoretical contribution that is of most interest.[5] Indeed, his philosophical treatment of Jewish law needs to be understood within his overall view of practical reason. One must also see the relation of practical reason to contemplative or metaphysical reason, which is the apex of reason for Maimonides.

It is best to begin a consideration of Maimonides' philosophy of law by looking at how he categorizes the various areas of Jewish law. In his first major work, *The Commentary on the Mishnah*, Maimonides divides the law into five categories in terms of their respective means of derivation[6]: (1) The first comprises those laws for which an undisputed tradition assigns a scriptural origin. (2) The second comprises those laws that tradition assumes to be Mosaic in origin ("laws given to Moses at Sinai"), despite the fact that no specific scriptural origin has been assigned to them. (3) The third comprises those laws derived by interpretation, and about which there has been dispute among the rabbis. These disputes are either exegetical, being concerned with the proper hermeneutic of Scripture, or conceptual, being concerned with legal principles. (4) The fourth comprises those laws established by prophets and rabbis to provide a safety net for scriptural commandments ("a fence for the Torah"). A prime example of this is the prohibition of eating fowl with milk (which is scripturally permitted) because fowl looks and tastes so much like meat that ordinary people will confuse what is scripturally prohibited with what is scripturally permitted.[7] Maimonides stipulates that, because there are scholarly disputes about the necessity of many of these specific decrees, the final criterion of their authority is whether or not they have been accepted by the majority of the Jewish people.[8] (5) The fifth comprises those laws that were enacted as the result of rational deliberation for the purpose of properly ordering interhuman relationships, or for the sake of "the improvement of the world in religious matters," namely, to properly order the human relationship with God.

In his later work on the enumeration and categorization of the commandments of the Written Torah, *The Book of the Commandments*, Maimonides designates only the first category of laws as being scriptural per se.[9] Only they comprise the 613 commandments of the Written Torah, a number set forth in a late Talmudic homily, but one that began to be used in the time of the Geonim to more rigidly distinguish between scriptural and rabbinic law.[10] Only these commandments are not subject to dispute, much less to repeal.[11] Yet even the second category of "Mosaic" laws, which is not considered scriptural, is still not subject to repeal. That is because these laws happen not to have been disputed by any of the rabbis. Conversely, if they had been subject to any such dispute, then they would be subject to repeal, although being subject to repeal does not mean there is any necessity to actually do so.[12] But this distinction between the first two categories is more formal than substantial because the indisputable-hence-nonrepealable character of *both* scriptural and traditionally Mosaic laws is taken for granted. Nevertheless, the nonrepealable character of these laws is not because of anything inherent in them but, rather, it is because of subsequent rabbinic consensus about their revealed status, a consensus that happens to have been unanimous.[13]

In this later work on the Mosaic commandments, which is in effect an elaborate prolegomenon to his great compendium of the law, *Mishneh Torah*, Maimonides claims the legal status of the third, fourth, and fifth categories to be identical. All of them are authoritative because of the authority the Torah has given the rabbis to propose laws for popular acceptance (or rejection). All of them are thus rabbi-made laws.[14] However, their authoritative status is tentative inasmuch as it depends on subsequent acceptance by other rabbis and popular acceptance as well. It is thus disputable, and what is disputable is subject to repeal ipso facto.

Despite the fact that Maimonides has made the clearest distinction possible between divinely made scriptural law and humanly made rabbinic law, they still have an essential point in common: Both areas of the law are teleologically determined, thus to be teleologically understood, and consequently to be applied with their ends in mind whenever known.[15] The specific difference between divinely made law and humanly made law is that for divinely made law the reasons or purposes of the law are assumed only after the fact, a posteriori, and therefore only tentative. We can only surmise what was in the mind of the divine lawgiver when he made the law; we cannot know his thoughts a priori. So, even if we cannot connect a divinely made law with what seems to be its reason, or even if we think the law no longer serves what seems to be its original purpose, the law stands anyway. What God has created may not be annulled; hence a scriptural commandment may not be repealed, even if political circumstances prevent the actual practice of the law here and now.[16] Conversely, in humanly made law, the reason exists before the fact because we already know *why* the rabbis made a law in the first place. Indeed, the rabbis could not have made the law unless they had persuaded others of its desirability. Therefore we may repeal the law if we think it no longer serves its original purpose or that purpose no longer pertains, even if we do not have the legal power to actually do so here and now.

We can appreciate the teleological character of Maimonides' thought even about scriptural law by looking at the fourteen criteria for determining what is a scriptural law that he proposes in his introduction to *The Book of Commandments*, which is his most methodological treatment of law. From all fourteen criteria, one might arrive at the following definition of a divinely made commandment: *A divinely made commandment is a specific prescription, having a number of particular details, which is commanded for the sake of a general reason.* Thus the particular details are subsumed under a specific commandment, and the specific commandment is subsumed under a general reason. Neither a reason connected to a specific commandments nor a reason for the commandments as a whole is itself one of the 613 commandments of the Written Torah.[17] Instead, these reasons function as principles that inform us of the nature of the commandments. And because only a few of these reasons are explicitly mentioned in the Torah, whereas many more are derived by speculation, Maimonides does not enumerate them in *The Book of Commandments* or even in *Mishneh Torah*, in which he only mentions them *en passent*. The task of more systematic legal teleology had to wait for his more philosophical discussion of the commandments in the third part of the *Guide*.[18] As for the particular details, even they gain more validity by being seen as parts of larger normative wholes than they would be if they were taken to be only the specific, almost random rules that they appear to be prima facie.

Maimonides consistently asserts that even though Scripture only mentions reasons in connection with a few of the commandments, we must assume that all the commandments have them. To assume otherwise would be an affront to the wisdom of the divine lawgiver.[19] The fact that most of these reasons are only implicit should not, however, prevent us from finding out what they are, even if the task seems endless.[20] Finally, the exclusion of what could be termed "ad hoc directives" (literally, "which do pertain to future generations"), that is, commandments given only for Israel before entering the Promised Land, seems to be because their reasons are no more general than these directives themselves; hence they are lacking according to the criterion of universal perpetuity.[21]

The reasons for the commandments are the purposes for which they were originally formulated by God. Nevertheless, no matter how well we might understand these reasons, we are never able to simply deduce from them all the particular details of the commandments. Thus the irreducible authority of revelation and its tradition in law lies in the irreducibility of these very details. Even if we could explain every "why" about the law, we could never explain every "how." A good example of this is the various numbers of animals the Torah prescribes for various sacrifices. Even though Maimonides is convinced we know the general reason for the sacrificial system (the sublimation of the idolatrous inclination for visible and tangible objects in worship), he sees no point in even pondering these numerical details. In the *Guide* Maimonides addresses this point: "Those who imagine that a cause may be found for suchlike things are as far from the truth as those who imagine that the generalities of a *commandment* are not designed with a view to some real utility."[22] By emphasizing the rationality of the law, even law stemming directly from revelation, without resorting to the totalizing rationalism characteristic of some modern Jewish thinkers, Maimonides saves revelation from being reduced to a facsimile of merely humanly reason and saves the law from being reduced to merely divine caprice. And, seeing the reasons for the commandments [*taʿamei ha-mitsvot*] to be their *purposes*, Maimonides' teleology is built on solid rabbinic precedent, even though, as with all rabbinic precedents he brings into his thought, they were further developed by his thought. Nothing from the past about which he thought ever remained exactly the same.

8.2. PRECEDENTS FOR THE DEVELOPMENT OF MAIMONIDEAN LEGAL TELEOLOGY

We can see how Maimonides builds on rabbinic precedent when we look at the development of the meaning of the Hebrew word *taʿam* and the Aramaic word *taʿama*. In late biblical and rabbinic Hebrew and Aramaic, the word simply means a rule itself as in "Everything that is by a decree [*min taʿam*] of the God of heaven let it be done diligently" (Ezra 7:23). In early rabbinic sources, it usually means either an explicit scriptural source, or a scriptural source determined by simple exegesis or one derived by more complicated hermeneutics.[23] But in later rabbinic sources, it comes to mean the purpose of a law, that is, why the law was formulated to begin with.[24] That purpose can either be one we (more often than not) assume was in the mind of the divine lawgiver when we examine a scriptural law, or one we know was in the mind (and on the tongue) of human lawgivers because a public argument has already been made for it.[25]

In one key passage dealing with rabbinic legislation, the Talmud states "the matter is brought into the discussion because of its reason [*be-torat ta'ama*]."[26] This statement is attributed by the Talmud to the fourth-century Babylonian sage, Rava. In fact, we can readily see him in many ways to be Maimonides' closest rabbinic predecessor. For Rava, more than any of the other sages, seemed to have stressed the rationality of the law, both revealed and rabbinic.[27] He expanded the range of law designated as rabbinic as much as possible, and thereby narrowed the range of scriptural law as much as possible. Indeed, it was Rava who seems to have limited the use of the term "reason" [*ta'ama*] to designate a *telos*. His approach was most effective in the area of rabbinic legislation, in which there are no specific scriptural norms to be interpreted and thus the field is open for human legislation *de novo*.

All rabbinic legislation, as distinct from scriptural laws and Mosaic traditions, requires a reason that is directly evident as its justification. For example, the rabbis were quite concerned with finding the specific Torah justification for writing the Scroll of Esther [*megillah*] and including it in the canon of Scripture. After hearing about earlier discussions in which specific warrants from the Pentateuch were proposed for this inclusion, thus enabling the recitation of the *megillah* to be a reading of Scripture on the festival of Purim and thereby giving this festival status, a predecessor of Rava, Samuel of Nehardea, stated, "Had I been there, I would have given a better argument than all of them. It says, 'they upheld it and accepted it' (Esther 9:27), namely, they upheld in heaven what they had already accepted on earth." Rava then stated that all the other arguments could be refuted except that of Samuel, which is irrefutable.[28] The distinguishing feature of Samuel's argument is that it does not derive the inclusion of the Scroll of Esther *from* a scriptural prescription at all. Instead, it interprets a verse as describing a human enactment, that of the sages during the time of Esther. This human enactment receives *subsequent* divine approval because it was based on a human consideration of the overall purposes of the Torah, one of which is to relate all instances of great deliverance to an awareness of the presence of God and thus to affirm that nothing in nature or history is accidental.[29]

Maimonides' connection to Rava's rationalism comes out when we compare the following two texts:

Rava said that at the time a person is brought into the court of heavenly justice, they say to him, 'Did you conduct your business dealings honestly? Did you set aside time for the study of the Torah? Did you engage in procreation? Did you look forward to salvation? Did you reason wisely? Did you infer one thing from another?[30]

Maimonides paraphrases Rava's words about "inferring one thing from another" as follows:

A person is obligated to divide his time for learning into three parts: one third for Scripture; one third for the Oral Tradition; and one third for understanding and discerning the end of a matter from its beginning. He should derive one thing from another, compare one thing to another, and understand by means of the methods through which the Torah is interpreted until he knows the root of these methods; how he can derive what is forbidden and what is permitted from these things he has learned from revealed tradition. This is what is called *talmud*.[31]

Although Maimonides speaks of "the methods through which the Torah is interpreted," which is a rabbinic term covering the various hermeneutical devices used in scriptural exegesis, it seems that he meant more than this. He is suggesting a methodology sufficient to explain all aspects of the law, which is clearly more than the strictly exegetical devices used by the rabbis. Thus Maimonides' real concern here is to suggest a methodology adequate for the true science of the law. Along these lines he speaks of three types of ratiocination: (1) discerning the end of the matter from the beginning, (2) deriving one thing from another, and (3) comparing one thing with another. I would suggest that these three types of ratiocination can be termed (1) teleological inference, (2) deduction, and (3) analogy. Indeed, teleological inference is distinct from either deduction or analogy. It is distinct from deduction, the kind done in an ordinary syllogism, because in a deduction the premise is a whole and the conclusion is something included as a part therein. As for analogy, which is the comparison of two distinct wholes, teleological inference can supply these two wholes with their implicit commonality, namely, a larger whole in which they *both* participate as means to a similar end. Teleological inference makes an analogy far less arbitrary than when analogy is left at the level of simple comparison, without inclusion in some larger context.

This teleological emphasis comes out even more sharply when we look at Maimonides' later treatment of Rava's dictum in the *Guide* (in which he, quite significantly, presents it as the opinion of "the sages"). There he writes that "a man is required first to obtain knowledge of the Torah, then to obtain wisdom, then to know what is incumbent upon him with regard to the legal science of the Law – I mean the drawing of inferences concerning what one ought to do."[32] Between acquiring the data of Scripture and Tradition and properly applying it, comes "wisdom . . . being the verification of the Torah through correct speculation."[33] Wisdom is the knowledge of ends. As he writes at the very beginning of the *Guide*, "The term wisdom [*ḥokhmah*] is applied in Hebrew . . . to the apprehension of true realities, which have for their end the apprehension of Him, may he be exalted . . . [and] it is applied to acquiring moral virtues."[34] Furthermore, this teleological inference strengthens analogy in a way deduction cannot. In explicating this point, I shall attempt to show that the legal logic of Rava enabled Maimonides to employ the philosophical logic of Aristotle with genuine Jewish integrity. In other words, it is not that someone like Maimonides read Aristotle (and his Islamic followers) and then decided to apply his teleological method to Judaism, or to "synthesize" Judaism and Aristotelianism. That is more like modern historicism than medieval rationalism of someone like Maimonides. Rather, it seems that Maimonides learned from Aristotle how to further develop teleological tendencies *already* present within the normative Jewish tradition. One might say that Aristotle helped Maimonides retrieve wisdom he believed to be originally Jewish.[35]

This point is seen quite well when we compare two texts of Maimonides, both of which deal with the role of medical science in the process of legal decision making.

The first text concerns the question of how one is to determine whether or not an animal had been suffering from a fatal condition [*ṭrefah*] before being slaughtered. Such a determination is the basis of the judgment of whether or not the meat of this animal is fit for Jewish consumption [*kasher*]. Maimonides writes, "One is not to add onto the number [seventy] of these fatal conditions . . . even if it is known to us from medical practice that it will not live . . . You only have [in this matter] that which the sages designated, as it says in Scripture, 'according to the law which they shall instruct you' (Deuteronomy 17:11)."[36]

What we see here is that no comparisons are to be made on the basis of current medical information; nothing is to be added or subtracted irrespective of what we now know through science. Indeed, Maimonides' choice of Deuteronomy 17:11 as his scriptural warrant for this view is significant because the verse ends with the words, "you shall not depart from what they [the sages] will tell you, neither to the right or to the left." These words have two very well-known rabbinic interpretations, with which many of Maimonides' readers would be familiar. The first interpretation is that this is the warrant for the authority of the rabbis to add to the law rules that are not found in Scripture.[37] This is a warrant for rabbinic reason. The second interpretation is that the rulings of the sages are to be obeyed "even if it seems to you [that they are teaching] left is right or right is left."[38] This is a warrant for rabbinic authority. In other words, at least in some areas of the law, specific reasons are not required for the understanding and application of the law, at least not immediately. Here all we need is the traditional authority of the rabbis as conduits of the tradition.

The second text from Maimonides concerns the question of human viability, that is, which wounds in a human being are considered fatal and which are not. Significantly, a human being who is fatally wounded is called a *ṭrefah*, which is the very same term designating an animal suffering from a fatal condition. In the case at hand, determination of whether a murder victim was already a *ṭrefah* would be a prime factor in determining whether his or her murderer would be subject to the death penalty. To be sure, the act of murder is prohibited regardless of the medical condition of the victim.[39] Nevertheless, if it is determined that the victim was indeed a *ṭrefah*, then the murderer would not be executed.[40] That is because there is an insoluble doubt as to whether the victim died as a result of the act of the murderer or from his or her previously fatal wound. In cases of doubt concerning human life (even the life of the murderer), one is to follow the more lenient legal practice.[41] However, the resolution of the doubt concerning the condition of the victim could offer a more certain, a more scientific, criterion for what to do with the murderer. In other words, if we find that the victim's previous wounds are not fatal after all, then we no longer have any doubt about the liability of the murder for the death penalty. Thus Maimonides writes,

> If one was is the very throes of death because of a humanly caused act, for example, one who was beaten until he was on the verge of death: the one who murdered him is not to be executed by the court... Every person is assumed to be in good health... until it is known for sure that he is suffering from a fatal wound [*ṭrefah*] and the physicians say that this wound has no cure in a human being, that he will die from it and from nothing else.[42]

Now in this ruling, unlike the previous one, we do follow the opinion of the physicians, and these opinions are the result of comparing one case with another. Why do we make comparisons when judging who is a human *ṭrefah*, but not when judging what is an animal *ṭrefah*? That comparisons are not to be made in cases of animal *ṭrefah* is already presented in the Talmud, but there no reason is given.[43]

It would seem, though, that for Maimonides there would be an answer to this distinction between a human *ṭrefah* and an animal one. For a human *ṭrefah* is of concern in a murder trial. And the reason for the prohibition of murder is clearly evident. As Maimonides himself put it, "even though there are sins more serious than murder, none of them entails the destruction of civilization."[44] Conversely, in the case of the laws of the slaughter of animals for food, Maimonides cites them in an earlier work as the prime examples of "a traditional commandment for which there is no reason [*ta'am*]."[45] Furthermore, even if we do have some notion of the reason of the commandment in general, as he subsequently asserts in a later work, we still have no notion of how the various specifics of the commandment are correlated with that general reason.[46]

Such, of course, is not the case with the laws dealing with murder. There the teleology, both general and specific, is clearly evident. As such, comparisons of specific points are possible in a way that could not be so in dealing with laws of the slaughter of animals for food. Where a teleological continuum (an *entelechy* in Aristotelian terms) is present, one can draw analogies between the various specifics in a way one cannot do when the specifics are not seen as being in correlation with an overarching end.

Although we have seen that a teleological tendency is already present in Talmudic sources, whose Babylonian authors cannot be assumed to have been influenced in any way by the Aristotelian corpus (or by any Greek philosophical school), by his own admission Maimonides was greatly influenced by Aristotle and the Aristotelians.[47] This influence can be seen, especially, in his philosophy of law. His Aristotelian teleology enabled him to enunciate a legal logic, developing the insights of the rabbis, most particularly Rava.

I purposely selected two examples in which Maimonides discusses medical science not only because Maimonides himself was a distinguished physician and medical theorist, but because Aristotle uses a medical example when presenting a fundamental aspect of his teleology:

> If it has a common significance, it must fall under one science . . . A diagnosis and a scalpel are both called medical, because one proceeds from medical science and the other is useful to it. The same is true of "healthy;" one thing is so called because it is indicative of health, and another because it is productive of health; and the same applies to all other cases.[48]

Elsewhere, using the same medical model, Aristotle says that "what denotes and what produces health are 'commensurately' related to health."[49] Teleology explains how many things are related to one another and can be properly compared. They are so interrelated because they are all related ultimately to one good – one end.[50] Thus in the preceding text, without the common relation to health as an end, a diagnosis and a scalpel would have almost nothing in common. Any analogy between them without this teleological connection would be highly tenuous.

8.3. MAIMONIDES' USE OF LEGAL TELEOLOGY

We saw at the beginning of this essay that Maimonides regarded the essence of positive rabbinic legislation [*taqqanah*] to be (1) "the proper ordering of matters between humans," and (2) "the improvement of the world in religious matters."[51] In the *Guide*, he sees these same two ends, namely, "the improvement [*tiqqun*] of the body" and "the improvement of the soul" to be the two purposes for which the divine law of the Torah was instituted.[52] This correlation between divine lawmaking and human lawmaking is consistent with the *Guide*'s conclusion that the greatest purpose of the law is *imitatio Dei*.[53] In fact, in the area in which revealed law is already completed but human law is still in the making, teleology is more descriptive with respect to the former, more prescriptive with respect to the latter. Human law is as good as its approximation to revealed law because the content of revealed law is immutable.[54] It can only be partially described in teleological categories, and these categories can be only partially used in its application. But with human law, both the content and the application admit (in theory, if not yet in premessianic practice) of a totally teleological interpretation. As such, *imitatio Dei* can be seen at least as much in the making of new human law as in the understanding of the old revealed law. Finally, there is no ultimate conflict between the two types of law because human law is made for what is perceived by the rabbis to be the transcendent end of the revealed law. In essence, then, both are divine law, in their ends if not in their origins.[55]

For Maimonides, the range of rabbinic, humanly made law, is wider than for any other medieval Jewish legal theorist because he believes that this category of law not only covers what is explicitly called a rabbinic "enactment" [*taqqanah*] or "decree" [*gezerah*], but also covers any law the rabbis derived by scriptural exegesis.[56] Thus the vast body of rabbinic exegesis of Scripture is only taken to be an allusion [*asmakhta*] to Scripture. In the majority of cases, rabbinic exegesis of Scripture is only an informal connection to an actual scriptural passage, not something grounded in the power of the rabbis to legislate for the Jewish people. That is why Maimonides (to my knowledge at least) never cites any such scriptural allusions when codifying rabbinic law, but only cites either reasons already given by the rabbis or reasons of his own.

What Maimonides has done is to assign vast importance to the role of practical reason in the divinely created cosmic order. This can best be seen in his treatment of the question of the preparation of rabbinic legislation and its possible repeal. As we shall soon see, the two processes are symmetrical inasmuch as the positive procedures of legislation are paralleled by the negative procedures of repeal.

Maimonides sees two prerequisites for responsible rabbinic legislation: (1) The authorities must deliberate "according to what seems proper in their eyes" and (2) they must discern the likelihood whether the proposed legislation will be accepted by the majority of the law-abiding members of the community.[57]

It would seem that the first prerequisite involves teleological reasoning. That can be seen in the way Maimonides designates the process of repeal. There he invokes the criterion of the *Mishnah* that a later court may not repeal the legislation of an earlier court "unless it is greater in wisdom and in numbers."[58] Because the court he is speaking of is the Sanhedrin of seventy-one members, how can any later court be larger? Maimonides' answer to this question is straightforward: The larger number refers to the larger number of sages (outside the actual seventy-one members of the Sanhedrin) who approve the later legislation to replace earlier legislation. But how does one determine who is wise, let alone whose wisdom is greater than someone else's? Here Maimonides says that the later court has discerned "another reason" [*ta'am aḥer*] for its proposed repeal of the earlier legislation.[59] It seems that they either disagree with the reason for the original legislation on rational–teleological grounds or they see new and better means to the original end. In other words, they consider themselves wiser than their predecessors, at least regarding the specific law under consideration, but without any need to explicitly (and arrogantly) claim their own jurisprudential superiority in general.

More conservative Jewish jurists roughly contemporary with Maimonides saw two areas of rabbinic legislation to be beyond repeal. The first area concerns those decrees that the rabbis made to protect the laws of the Torah itself from violation. The second concerns those decrees that received wide popular support in Jewry when they were first legislated. The first area seems to be so close to the immutable laws of the Torah so as to share their very immutability. The second area seems to protect any legislation that received wide popular acceptance at the time it was legislated against any repeal in the future, even if there is popular rejection of it in the future. In other words, popular will in the past has a veto over popular will in the future. But Maimonides accepts neither of these restrictions. In effect, he seems to assume that practical reason, indeed all reason, is only as good as its contemporary arguments make it.

In the case of decrees made to protect the sanctity of scriptural laws (the best examples of which are rabbinic additions to the Sabbath laws), Maimonides writes that this restriction applies only when the earlier ruling "has spread throughout all Israel."[60] That is, it applies only when its authority is *still* respected by the vast majority of Jews here and now. This would be the case even if the later court were "greater in wisdom," which we have seen means being capable of making more convincing rational arguments. By implication, though, if this is *no longer* the case, then repeal would be justified. This point is further brought out by Maimonides' insistence that if a much later court conducted an investigation and found that a formerly popular decree had now lost its popularity, that later court has the authority to repeal it.[61] It seems that he requires such formal repeal, even though the law itself has already fallen into disuse, because keeping an ineffective law on the books, so to speak, could very likely weaken the effectiveness of the law itself as a whole.[62]

In fact, Maimonides goes so far as to say that, even without these popular grounds for repeal, any law, even a law of the Torah, can be repealed temporarily, even by those having less authority than the earlier sages when they determine that such a temporary measure is needed here and now "to return the masses to lawfulness."[63] That, of course, is a judgment of practical reason functioning above and beyond the specifics of the law. One can thus conclude that, for Maimonides, practical reason governs the lives of the Jewish people except where there is a specific law of the Torah, and even that can be temporarily repealed if that same practical reason determines that there is here and now what we might call a "teleological emergency," which calls for radical action on the part of the authorities without delay.

In the area of adjudication, which unlike legislation does not require the actual institution of the Sanhedrin, the role of practical reason is in one respect more circumscribed, but in another less so. It is less circumscribed because, unlike explicit rabbinic legislation, adjudication does not require any institution like the Sanhedrin. It is the day-to-day business of rabbinical judges [*dayyanim*], requiring nothing more than a normatively constituted Jewish community anywhere for whom these judges can function.[64] Nevertheless, it is more circumscribed because the cases brought before judges are usually quite specific, most often being subsumed under one or another of the norms that make up the whole law.[65] But even here, Maimonides is able to assign a prominent role to practical reason, and to do so with much the same conceptuality he employed in his constitution of the process of legislation.

One can see this best by looking at how Maimonides formulates the range of the authority of rabbinical judges in civil cases:

A judge is to judge in civil matters according to the way his intelligence inclines to ascertain the truth. And when he is certain about the matter, even if there is no clear proof, then he should conclude according to what he knows ... The matter is left to the mind of the judge according to what appears to him to be the truth.[66]

Then Maimonides asks this question:

If that is so, why did the Torah insist upon two witnesses? That is because anytime two witnesses actually do come before the judge, he is to judge according to their testimony, even though he does not really know whether what they testified is true or a lie.[67]

Notice how Maimonides constitutes the judicial function. He has avoided two possible extremes, namely, (1) assuming that the presence of two witnesses is a *conditio sine qua non* of any civil proceeding and without which no judgment can be rendered at all, or (2) assigning a role to practical reason that can simply make up law as it goes along, albeit under the influence of general principles.[68] Maimonides' middle path, as it were, is to state that, when two witnesses are not present, then – and only then – may the judge takes matters into his own judicial hands, guided solely by his own discernment of the truth. To be sure, such ascertainment might miss the mark inasmuch as it is practical reason and not the type of theoretical reason that admits of precise demonstration. But if the judge is morally and intellectually honest, then at least it is not a lie, which could be the case with witnesses who know how to lie effectively and who have not been disqualified in advance because of their being morally disreputable.[69] In other words, practical reason takes over when the superior wisdom of the Torah is specifically silent. The Torah's commandments, then, are only a negative, not a positive, condition, that is, they need not be present in every case; they must only not be directly and permanently contradicted.

Now, of course, all practical reason is not necessarily teleological. Here Maimonides might only be discussing the practical wisdom of a judge to surmise from the character of the litigants and the circumstances at hand who is right and who is wrong. In fact, he actually follows the previously quoted text by cautioning contemporary judges not to take on themselves such broad discretionary powers because they are not as intellectually qualified as earlier generations. Nevertheless, he goes on to say if the judge's opinion inclines in the direction of one of the litigants, then he should "negotiate with the litigants until they agree . . . or submit to arbitration, or he should remove himself from the case."[70] The first option might be to simply convince the litigants of the judge's own insight into the case and its participants. The last option might be based on the law that a judge who is partial to one litigant over another should disqualify himself from adjudication.[71] But the option to submit to arbitration is based on teleological considerations. For arbitration is presented in the Talmud as something that increases peace [*shalom*] as the common good [*bonum commune*] precisely because after arbitration nobody is innocent and nobody is guilty as would be the case after a formal trial.[72] As such, the common good as the goal of all society is enhanced by a person's not exercising his personal right to full justice for himself [*bonum sibi*].

At the end of this chapter, Maimonides writes the following about the teleology of practical reason as adjudication:

> All of these matters are to be according to the way the judge judges them to be right for the occasion and what the time requires. And in all of them, let his deeds be for the sake of God, and let not human dignity ever be light in his eyes.[73]

And then at the very end of the chapter, Maimonides speaks about the additional dignity due those of the Jewish people who "uphold the Torah of truth." For him, that is the honor of the Torah itself [*kevod ha-torah*]. He concludes by saying, "the honour of the Torah is nothing but acting according to its laws and its ordinances." At first glance, this phrase is a bit odd because it would seem to contradict the beginning of the chapter, in which he has just assigned to judges a very wide range of authority for the use of their extralegal powers of practical reason. Now he seems to say they must judge only according to the strict letter of the law and remain silent when it is silent. Perhaps what Maimonides is hinting at here is that the true content of the Torah is not only its literal laws but, even more, the truths it teaches, truths to which humans are to aspire in their attraction to God. Thus it is only by constantly seeking these truths that a judge can truly judge here on earth, even though he can never be demonstrably certain that he has achieved true justice in any particular case. All particular judgment is tentative, especially when it applies to only one case at a time. And this is precisely why the ends of the law must, in effect, create rulings when the specifics of the law are not at hand.

8.4. REASON: PRACTICAL AND THEORETICAL

One cannot fully understand Maimonides' approach to practical reason unless one understands how he relates it to theoretical reason. The following passage is the key to that understanding:

> Accordingly, if you find a law the whole end of which and the whole purpose of the chief thereof, who determined the actions required by it, are directed toward the ordering of the city ... and if in that Law attention is not at all directed toward speculative matters ... you must know that that Law is a nomos and that the man who laid it down belongs ... to those who are perfect only in their imaginative faculty. If, on the other hand, you find a Law all of whose ordinances are due to attention being paid ... to the body and also to the soundness of belief ... with regard to God ... and that desires to make men wise ... you must know that this guidance comes from Him, may He be exalted, and that this Law is divine.[74]

That this statement not only applies to the Jews and their law, but just as much to the gentiles and their law, hence to law per se, is brought out earlier by the discussion of the *Noaḥite* laws in the *Mishneh Torah*. There he writes that, if one follows the *Noaḥite* laws because he regards them as divine law, he is assured of the bliss of the eternal, transcendent realm [*ha-ʿolam ha-ba*]. However, even if he only follows them because they are rationally evident solely on political–moral grounds, he is then still considered one of the wise.[75]

It would seem that Maimonides recognizes three types of practical reason in the following ascending order: (1) the practical reason of ordinary jurists, who simply accept the laws of their particular society as given and make deductions from them in the process of ordinary adjudication. All law, for them, is positive statute. (2) The practical reason of philosophically inclined jurists and statesmen, who attempt to base legal and political reality on rationally evident principles about human sociality by a process of ordinary ratiocination [*qiyās*].[76] (3) Finally, the practical reason of true metaphysicians, those who correlate practical reason and theoretical reason in one continuum.[77] Thus Maimonides has made the teaching of the law part of the larger area of practical reason concerned with the virtues, and he has made practical reason the precondition and the consequence of theoretical reason. At the end of the *Guide*, he writes thus:

> It is clear that the perfection of man that may be glorified in is one acquired by him who has achieved, in a measure corresponding to his capacity, apprehension of Him, may He be exalted, and who knows His providence extending over all His creatures as manifested in the act of bringing them into being and in their governance as it is. The way of life of such an individual, after he has achieved his apprehension, will always have in view loving-kindness [*ḥesed*], righteousness [*tsedaqah*] and judgment [*mishpaṭ*], through assimilation to His actions, may He be exalted.[78]

So I do not think it too bold to say that Maimonides would regard a metaphysically grounded jurist, one who truly understands and correlates the twofold teleology of the Torah, to be engaged in this beneficial *imitatio Dei*. Subsequent Jewish jurisprudents and students of the law, who have so benefited from this teleological jurisprudence, especially as developed by Maimonides, might very well agree.

8.5. CONCLUSION

Like all of his intellectual endeavors, Maimonides' jurisprudence should be seen as a chapter in his overall philosophical project, which is the intellectual knowledge of God. That knowledge is the end of all cosmic striving, especially that of the heavenly intelligences, followed by that of intelligent human beings.[79] Moreover, because God is an active creator, the highest knowledge of God is not so much *what* God *is* as *why* God created what he *did*. Knowledge of God, then, is to discover as much of cosmic teleology as is humanly possible.

For Maimonides, the law of the Written Torah is a divine creation.[80] The law is not divine; it is a datum from God. God is therefore not directly present in the law he has already given. Like other created data, the law itself does not usually proclaim its own ends in specific matters. Rather, it is the task of the interpreter of created data to discover those implicit ends through patient research, using the scientific methods developed by human reason as its discursive language.[81] This enables the philosopher as jurisprudent of divinely given law to better know it and apply it. Maimonides' whole approach to the law is teleological, which is the transcendent thrust of the law.[82] That is why a science of the law is both a possibility and a desideratum for him.[83] That is why metaphysics, whose main concern is with transcendence, is the epitome of Torah study as science.[84] And, even though this approach is heavily influenced by Aristotle and the Aristotelians, it has enough precedent in the Jewish tradition to be defended against the perennial charge that it is a covert attempt to make Greek philosophy determine the truth of Judaism.

One should see Maimonides' great attempt to distinguish between scriptural and rabbinic law, and the respective methods for their analysis and adjudication, to be motivated by his commitment to teleology. Scriptural law is totally purposeful in all its specifics, but because neither we nor our ancestors are its author, we along with our ancestors can only surmise some of those purposes. We can only try to read the mind of God, as it were, and never succeed in reading all of it, even all of it that created the finite Torah. Rabbinic law, conversely, is explicitly purposeful. The rabbis have told us why they legislated as they did. In fact, without having persuaded first themselves and the Jewish people thereafter of these purposes and what must be done for their sake, the rabbis would never have been the effective legislators they were.

Because teleology is more accessible to our practical intellects when dealing with rabbinic law than with scriptural law, we can see why Maimonides wanted to constrain the amount of scriptural law and why, conversely, he did not want to constrain the amount of rabbinic law. With scriptural law we are engaged in the more theoretical and more restrained pursuit of discerning God's purposes.[85] But with rabbinic law we are engaged in the more practical and less restrained pursuit of imitating God's purposes. Theory influences practice and practice transcends theory, that is, when we take the purposes we have discerned from the Torah – and the rest of created nature (especially from the heavenly spheres) – and apply them to the task of lawmaking for a society committed to the divine, purposeful law that is epitomized by the Torah.[86] But I think Maimonides would agree that only for such a divinely oriented society is a truly philosophical jurisprudence possible and desirable.[87]

NOTES

1. B. *Baba Batra* 130b.
2. Sometimes a legal opinion is considered to be correct in principle yet too general to be practically effective, hence it is not publicly advocated (see B. *Shabbat* 12b and *Betsah* 28b). Sometimes the opinions of a particular authority are considered to be too hypothetical to be practically conclusive, hence his opinions are usually not publicly advocated (see B. *Eruvin* 13b and 53a).
3. See B. *Berakhot* 33b, B. *Ketubot* 56a.
4. See B. *Berakhot* 9a, B. *Yevamot* 77a, B. *Ketubot* 82a, and Y. *Ḥagigah* 1.8/77d.
5. Indeed, for subsequent generations, Maimonides' theoretical law superceded his practical in influence. It was the more practically applicable code of R. Joseph Karo, *Shulḥan Arukh*, that became the final authority for practical, i.e., codified, Halakhah rather than *Mishneh Torah* (see Twersky 1980, pp. 531–5). As for Maimonides' work as a casuist, most of his responsa were written in Arabic and had little influence on European authorities. Furthermore, many of his responsa, especially those written in Hebrew, often dealt with more conceptual points already developed in the *Mishneh Torah.*
6. *CM*, Introduction, 1:11–13.
7. See *MT* 14, Rebels, 2.8.
8. *MT* 14, Rebels, 2.7.
9. *The Book of Commandments*, Introduction, 1.
10. *Makkot* 23b–24a; also *Shabbat* 87a, *Yevamot 47b*, *Nedarim* 25a, *Shevuot* 29a, Exodus Rabbah 32.1.
11. *CM*, Sanhedrin 10 (*Ḥeleq*): Thirteen Foundations, no. 9.
12. See *CM*, Introduction, 1:11–13.
13. Thus the rabbis themselves determined just which scriptural norms are to be permanent and which are ad hoc directives in and for a certain period in the past only. See M. *Pesaḥim* 9.5, B. *Sanhedrin* 15b, and Maimonides, *The Book of Commandments*, Introduction, Section 3.
14. *MT* 14, Rebels, 1.1.
15. See, e.g., *MT* 1, Repentance, 3.4.
16. For the created status of the Torah, see *GP* 1.65. Even at the time of the Messiah, Maimonides insists all the commandments are to be kept

because the new political circumstances of the messianic regime will enable all of them to be kept (see *MT* 14, Kings and Wars, 11.3–12.1). And that is because the natural order of the world, the world into which the Torah was given (see *GP* 2.40), will remain the same because the Messiah is not supernatural but only politically superlative.

17. *The Book of Commandments*, Introduction, Section 5.
18. See *GP* 3.35ff. Nevertheless, Maimonides in *The Book of the Commandments*, negative commandments, no. 365, followed the view of R. Isaac on B. Sanhedrin 21a that cautions against too much public speculation on the reasons of the commandments for fear many people will use these reasons not to bolster their observance of the commandments but, rather, to avoid them by thinking they can accomplish the end a commandment intends by a means different from the one prescribed by the Torah.
19. *GP* 3.26.
20. See *GP*, 3.31.
21. *The Book of Commandments*, Introduction, sec. 3.
22. *GP* 3.26, p. 509.
23. See, e.g., T. *Menaḥot* 6.19, Y. *Ḥagigah* 2.1/77c–d, ibid. 2.3/78a.
24. See, e.g., B. *Rosh Hashanah* 29b, B. *Sukkah* 42b, B. *Megillah* 4b, also B. *Sanhedrin* 21a.
25. See B. *Avodah Zarah* 36a–b. Cf. ibid. 35a.
26. B. *Berakhot* 23b.
27. See, e.g., B. *Qiddushin* 32a–b re Ps. 1:2, B. *Eruvin* 21b and 68b, B. *Taanit* 8a, B. *Makkot* 23b.
28. B. *Megillah* 7a.
29. For rabbinic speculation about divine approval of human reasoning, see B. *Baba Metsia* 59b.
30. B. *Shabbat* 31a.
31. *MT* 1, Study of the Torah, 1.11, based on B. *Qiddushin* 30a. See also B. *Sotah* 20a, 22a.
32. *GP* 3.54, p. 634. See ibid., Introduction, 5. For the origin of the phrase "the end of a matter from its beginning," see Y. *Sotah* 8.10/23a re Ecclesiastes 2:14.
33. *GP* 3.54, p. 632.
34. *GP* p. 632. See, also, Novak 1983, p. 185ff.
35. Cf. *MT* 2, Sanctification of the New Moon, 17.24; *GP* 1.71.
36. *MT* 5, Slaughtering Meat, 10.12–13. For a problematic self-contradiction on this point by Maimonides, however, see *Teshuvot ha-Rambam* 2, no. 309 re *Shehitah*, 8.23.
37. B. *Shabbat* 23a.
38. *Sifre Devarim*, no. 154, p. 207.

39. See M. *Niddah* 5.3; B. *Shabbat* 151b.
40. B. *Sanhedrin* 79a, ibid. 37b, *Makkot* 7a.
41. See B. *Yoma* 83a.
42. *MT* 11, Murder, 2.7–8. For Maimonides' general acceptance of medical–scientific consensus for halakhic purposes, see *CM*, *Yoma* 8.4.
43. B. *Baba Batra* 130b. See T. *Sanhedrin* 7.7, *Niddah* 7b, Y. *Ḥagigah* 1.8/76d.
44. *MT* 11, Murder, 4.9.
45. *CM*, *Berakhot* 5.2, ed. *Qāfiḥ*, 1:42. See Y. *Berakhot* 5.3/9c. For other laws that are considered noncomparible because the reasons for their exceptional characteristics are unknown, see B. *Shabbat* 132a, B. *Moʿed Qatan* 7b, B. *Sanhedrin* 27a.
46. See *GP* 3.26.
47. See *GP* 1.71, in which Maimonides says that he agrees with Aristotle "with great regard to any point he has demonstrated" (Pines 1963, p. 182). That covers a good deal.
48. *Metaphysics*, 1060b36–1061a7, pp. 64–65.
49. *Topics*, 107b6–10, pp. 318–319.
50. See *Nicomachean Ethics*, 1096b26–32; *Posterior Analytics*, 95a1–5; also, Owens 1978, p. 119ff.
51. *CM*, Introduction, 1:11–12.
52. *GP* 3.27. By "the body," Maimonides means what we would call "the body politic."
53. See *GP* 3.54 (end) re Jeremiah 9:23.
54. See *CM*, *Sanhedrin* 10, 2:143–144 (prin. 8); *MT* 14, Kings and Wars, 12.2.
55. See *GP* 2.40; also, Novak 1983, p. 290ff.
56. See *The Book of Commandments*, Introduction, Section 2.
57. See *MT* 14, Rebels, 2.5.
58. *MT* 14, Rebels, 2.2 re M. *Eduyot* 1.5.
59. *MT* 14, Rebels, 2.1.
60. *MT* 14, Rebels, 2.3.
61. *MT* 14, Rebels, 2.7. Even when the power of formal repeal was no longer in effect because of the absence of the Sanhedrin, Maimonides still used the criterion of contemporary acceptance to justify departure from earlier (even talmudically established) rules and procedures. See, e.g., *MT* 4, Marriage, 16.7.
62. Along these lines, see *Avodah Zarah* 35a, *Baba Batra* 31b–32a.
63. *MT* 14, Rebels, 2.4. See B. *Sanhedrin* 46a.
64. See B. *Gittin* 88b, Maimonides, *MT* 14, *Sanhedrin*, 5.8–9.
65. Cf. B. *Eruvin* 63b, *GP* 3.34.
66. *MT* 14, Sanhedrin, 24.1, based on B. *Sanhedrin* 6b re II Chronicles 19:6.

67. *MT* 14, Sanhedrin, 24.1.
68. Cf. Plato, *Statesman*, 294A–C; Aristotle, *Politics*, 1286a8ff.
69. For the limitations of the institution of legal testimony, see *MT* 1, Principles of the Torah, 8.2.
70. *MT* 14, Sanhedrin, 24.2.
71. See B. *Ketubot* 105b re Exodus 23:8; B. *Shevuot* 30a re Leviticus 19:15; *MT*, Sanhedrin, 21.1ff.
72. See B. *Sanhedrin* 6b; *MT* 14, Sanhedrin, 22.4.
73. *MT* 14, Sanhedrin, 24.9. For similar language regarding the royal function, see *MT* 14, Kings and Wars 4.10; also, Novak 1992, p. 193ff.
74. *GP* 2.40, 383–384.
75. *MT* 14, Kings and Wars, 8.11. See Novak 1983, p. 276ff for the conceptual implications of the disputed text of Maimonides here.
76. Re *qiyās*, see Wegner 1982, p. 44ff.
77. For the distinction between a metaphysically inclined jurist and one not so inclined, see *CM*, Introduction, 1:20–21; *Guide*, 3.31 and 54.
78. *GP* 3.54, p. 638.
79. See *GP* 2.4–6, 3.13.
80. *GP* 1.65.
81. Maimonides regards human language as "conventional and not natural" (*GP* 2.30, p. 358). Even though human linguistic ability is natural, not conventional (i.e., humanly created), the content of human language itself is devised by human beings in order to understand nature (see ibid., p. 357). That is why "the Torah speaketh in the language of the sons of men" (ibid. 1.26, p. 56), for if it did not speak a language humans have used and understood, how could it be intelligible to them? Hence the same linguistically developed methods for understanding nature can be applied to the study of the Torah as a science.
82. See, e.g., *MT* 7, Sabbatical and Jubilee Years, 13.13.
83. See *GP* Introduction, p. 3.
84. See *MT* 1, Principles of the Torah, 1.1–6; 4.13.
85. For Maimonides, such teleological insight, whether in nature or in law, implies that these ends are transcendent because they are intended by the transcendent creator. Contra the Aristotelians, cosmic teleology not only does not deny *creatio ex nihilo*, it ultimately affirms it (although not by scientific demonstration), i.e., when better understood than even Aristotle understood it (see *GP* 2.18–19). That is why a divinely given law's origin can only be appreciated after one has discerned the purpose of the law as a whole (ibid. 2.40). That is exactly how one can appreciate the divine source of the universe, viz., by discerning the universe's full purpose (ibid. 2.18–19). Therefore, although the law does not come *from*

nature (let alone from human convention), it is *like* nature in both its source and its end, who are one.

86. Maimonides did not, however, confine divine law to the Torah. See *MT* 14, Kings and Wars.
87. Parts of this chapter are adapted from Novak 1990, pp. 99–134 and Novak 1998, pp. 92–121.

SARA KLEIN-BRASLAVY

9 Bible Commentary

Although Maimonides did not write a running commentary on any book of the Bible, biblical exegesis occupies a central place in his writings, especially in the *Guide of the Perplexed*.[1] In the Introduction to the *Guide*, Maimonides explains that the book is addressed to a believing Jew who observes the commandments and accepts the Bible as authoritative but has read Aristotelian philosophy and accepts it too. When such people discover contradictions between a literal understanding of the Bible and the principles of philosophy, they become perplexed. Maimonides' exegesis is intended to resolve their perplexity by showing that biblical truth is identical with the truths of philosophy so that one can be a Jew and a philosopher at the same time.

Two assumptions determine the character of Maimonides' exegesis. First he accepts Alfarabi's political theory according to which the ideal state is one whose beliefs are based on philosophy. Religion comes after philosophy and offers educational myths that imitate philosophical truths by images that can be understood by the masses. Second, he considers the Bible an esoteric work that conceals philosophical truth from the masses, allowing them to retain their faith, but reveals it to those who have the requisite degree of knowledge and the capacity to comprehend it. In addition to allowing Maimonides to resolve contradictions between the literal meaning of the biblical text and philosophic truth, these assumptions allow him to explore the philosophic meaning conveyed by educational myths or concealed from the masses by parables and other devices that occur in the Jewish literary tradition.

The second assumption plays a more important role in Maimonides' biblical exegesis. Maimonides identifies the Account of the Chariot with metaphysics and the Account of the Beginning with physics.

According to the Talmud,[2] the Account of the Chariot may be conveyed only to a person who is "wise and understands by himself" and only in "chapter headings,"[3] which Maimonides takes to mean by allusions. The Account of the Beginning should be transmitted to one student only. He therefore believes that philosophic esotericism is mandated by the Talmud. It follows that, when discussing these subjects in his biblical exegesis, he must also write in an esoteric fashion, hiding the true meaning from the masses and revealing it to those of discernment. That is why he often fails to provide a full and clear treatment of the words or passages he takes up and alludes to their meaning with hints or clues that only certain readers will understand. In addition, his treatment of certain topics is scattered through various portions of the *Guide*, making it difficult for unsophisticated readers to grasp his meaning. Intelligent readers, however, can assemble an interpretation on their own. This makes Maimonides' biblical exegesis an intellectual challenge that appeals to people who have long since given up their attachment to Aristotelian philosophy.

The two main components of biblical texts that require interpretation according to Maimonides are individual terms, on the one hand, and passages consisting of one or more consecutive verses, what he calls "parables," on the other.

9.1. INDIVIDUAL WORDS

With respect to individual terms, the key issue is equivocation, a phenomenon that comes in two forms. The first form involves equivocal terms dealt with by Aristotelian logic (which he knew through Alfarabi's writings).[4] Such equivocal terms appear in ordinary as well as prophetic language. Maimonides does not offer a theory of equivocation because he assumes that his reader is already familiar with it. Instead he enumerates equivocal terms commonly found in the Bible and explains why their misunderstanding can lead to error. The second type of equivocation is characteristic of prophetic discourse and can be resolved only by looking at the etymology of the words in question. Maimonides provides the theory of this type of equivocation in *Guide* 2.29, in which he introduces his interpretation of the Creation and the Garden of Eden, and *Guide* 2.43, in which he discusses the visions of prophets other than Moses.

9.1.1. Equivocal Terms of the First Type

There is no question that the first type of equivocation receives the most attention. In the Introduction, Maimonides states that one of the purposes of his work is to interpret terms of this type – completely equivocal terms, derivative terms, conventional terms, and amphibolous terms.[5] He then devotes forty-two chapters to assembling a lexicon of equivocal terms.

Maimonides establishes the meaning of these terms by a philological method, generally deriving and illustrating their several senses from the Bible. Later, when he comes to interpret verses that contain these terms, he relies on his lexicon.[6] This is in line with his tendency to ground his biblical interpretation as far as possible on Jewish literary tradition, the Bible, and, as we shall see later, the *midrash*.

His typical procedure is to state the term in question, show the various meanings it can have, and cite a text from the Bible that reflects each of those meanings. Let us consider two examples:

At *Guide* 1.15 Maimonides discusses the synonyms *natsov* and *yatsov*, whose root meaning is "to stand" or "to stand erect." He then lists their different meanings, beginning, as usual, with the physical sense and progressing toward more abstract senses. Drawing on three verses, the first meaning he cites is "standing erect" in the physical sense: "And his sister stood at a distance" (Exodus 2:4[7]); "kings of the earth take their stand" (Psalm 2:2); and Dathan and Abiram "came out and stood" (Numbers 16:27). Here the meaning is obvious from the context. The second meaning, "to be stable and permanent," he finds in the verse: "Your word stands firm [or erect] in heaven" (Psalm 119:89). Because God's word is not a physical substance, in this context "stand" must have an abstract meaning such as "be stable and permanent."[8]

Guide 1.4 deals with the three synonymous verbs *ra'oh*, *habet*, and *ḥazoh*, all of which refer to perception. The first meaning involves the sight of the eye. As an example of this meaning of *ra'oh*, he offers this: "As he [Jacob] looked, he saw a well in the field" (Genesis 29:2). Its second meaning involves intellectual apprehension, as in this:

"my heart has had great experience of [literally: has seen much] wisdom and knowledge" (Ecclesiastes 1:16). Because the heart cannot see in a physical sense, it is obvious that the kind of sight involved here is abstract – intellectual apprehension.[9]

Sometimes the meaning that can be derived from biblical verses is only what we might call "a structure of meaning." In this case the reader must fill in the content in each biblical verse by looking at its semantic axis and taking account of its context. This is particularly true of *ishah* [woman], as explained in *Guide* 1. 6 and 3.8, as well as *ish* [man], whose derived meaning is alluded to in *Guide* 1.6 and 3.8 as well.[10]

The first meaning of *ishah*, "a human female," is so obvious that Maimonides does not illustrate it by a biblical verse. Its first derivative meaning is "a female among the other species of living beings" (*GP* 1.6, p. 31). Maimonides learns this from the verse "take with you seven pairs of all clean animals, the man and his woman (Genesis 7:2). A second derivative meaning is "any object apt for, and fashioned with a view to being in conjunction with some other object" (ibid.), as in: "Five curtains shall be coupled together, a woman to her sister" (Exodus 26:3). This last is "a structure of meaning," in that it defines woman as a subject related to another subject but does not indicate what this subject is. Maimonides has no way to derive from the biblical text "the content" of the term, and hence what the noun "woman" actually means in concrete biblical verses and passages.

At *Guide* 3.8 (a nonlexicographic chapter) Maimonides interprets *eshet ish zonah* [a married harlot], an image of his own creation, based on the book of Proverbs.[11] He does not explain the word "woman," but it is evident that he implicitly uses the second derivative meaning of the noun in *Guide* 1.6 and fills the structure of meaning with a philosophical content. He identifies the "object apt for, and fashioned with a view to being in conjunction with some other object" with matter or, more precisely, the matter of the sublunar world. *Eshet ish zonah* denotes the nature of matter according to Aristotelian philosophy:

How extraordinary is what *Solomon* said in his wisdom when likening matter to *a married harlot*, for matter is in no way found without form and is consequently always like *a married woman* who is never separated from a *man* and is never *free*. However, notwithstanding her being *a married woman*, she never ceases to seek for another man to substitute for her husband.... This is the state of matter. For whatever form is found in it, does but prepare it to receive another form. (*GP* 3.8, p. 431)[12]

The lexicon serves, first and foremost, to eliminate any tendency to think of God in corporeal terms. This is consistent with Maimonides' view (*GP* 2.25, p. 328) that it has been demonstrated that God is not a body. Thus a reader who comes across terms that seem to treat God as corporeal must select another meaning.

As always, Maimonides tries to remain within the scope of Jewish literary tradition. To justify his interpretation of terms that relate to God, he cites the rabbinic dictum that "the Torah speaks in the language of human beings."[13] As he understands it, this dictum means that the Torah uses language suited to the masses' understanding and mode of apprehension. Because the masses apprehend only those things that can be grasped by the senses or by the imagination, and not of those that can be apprehended by the intellect, the only things whose existence they accept are corporeal. What is more, the masses understand God by comparison to themselves; hence they think that God possesses the same perfections as they do. Because it is addressed to a wide audience, the Bible describes God as having a body and exemplifying human perfections. Nonetheless, Maimonides thinks that by his day even the masses "should be made to accept on traditional authority the belief that God is not a body; and that there is absolutely no likeness in any respect whatever between Him and the things created by Him" (*GP* 1.35, p. 80) so that no one should interpret terms that relate to God in their physical sense.

Consequently after presenting the various meanings of an equivocal term, along with its proof texts, Maimonides often explains which may be applied to God. Then he offers examples of such uses, thereby interpreting concrete biblical verses. For example, after explaining the second meaning of *natsov* and *yatsov* at *Guide* 1.15 – "to be stable and permanent" – Maimonides notes that "in all cases where this term occurs with reference to the Creator, it has this meaning." Then he gives an example of such a verse, from Jacob's dream: "And behold, the Lord stood upon it" (Genesis 28:13). That is, he explains, the Lord was "stably and constantly upon it – I mean upon the ladder." At *Guide* 1.4, he remarks that "every *mention of seeing*, when referring to God, may He be exalted, has this figurative meaning" and cites several examples. One of them comes from Micaiah's description of his vision of God: "I saw the Lord" (1 Kings 22:19). In this verse God is the object of seeing. If the sight in question is that of the eye, the verse would imply that God is a physical object. Because God is not corporeal, we must apply the second meaning of the verb and understand that Micaiah had an intellectual apprehension of God. Maimonides also cites a verse in which God is the subject: "And God saw that it was good" (Genesis 1:10). In this case, attributing eyesight to God would mean that he has a physical organ. Because God is not physical, we must interpret sight in this verse too as intellectual apprehension.

Maimonides' lexicon is not limited to the interpretation of biblical verses that risk presenting God in an anthropomorphic fashion. Nor do all the lexicographic chapters deal with terms applied to God in the Bible.[14] Some deal with verses that address other subjects, such as the Account of the Beginning, the Account of the Chariot, and prophecy. Thus the lexicon also assists in the interpretation of esoteric passages. Needless to say, Maimonides expects his reader to be active, using the lexicon while reading the Bible and taking "every equivocal term in that one from among its various senses that is suitable in that particular passage" (*GP* 1.8, p. 34). Thus biblical exegesis is not limited to the interpretations actually made or alluded to in the *Guide*; it is a process to be continued by its reader.

9.1.2. Equivocal Terms of the Second Type

Equivocal terms of the second type are those whose meanings are determined by their etymology. Maimonides applies here an exegetical method already used in the Bible and *midrash*, but claims that he is relying on prophetic language:

> The prophets use in their speeches equivocal words and words that are not intended to mean what they indicate according to their first signification, the word being mentioned because of its derivation. (*GP* 2.29, p. 347)[15]

He proves this claim from two prophetic visions in which the central image is explained, in the very same vision, according to the etymological meaning: *maqqel shaqed* [a branch of an almond tree] (Jeremiah 1:11–12)[16] and *kluv qayits* [a basket of summer fruit] (Amos 8:1–2). *Shaqed* is derived from the verb *shaqod* [to hasten].

Maimonides explains that "Scripture accordingly proceeds to say *ki shoqed ani* and so on (Jeremiah 1:12). Thus the intention of the parable did not concern the notion of rod or that of almond" (*GP* 2.43, p. 392).[17] Amos saw *kluv qayits. Qayits* is derived from *kets* [end] and, as the prophecy itself explains, *ba ha-qets* [the end has come] (Amos 8:2). These visions do not have an esoteric content, but forecast the future. Nevertheless, Maimonides claims that in their visions the prophets saw "things whose purpose it is to point to what is called to the attention by the term designating the thing seen because of that term's derivation or because of equivocality of terms" (ibid.). He also applies the etymological method of interpretation to prophetic visions whose content is esoteric: Ezekiel's and Zechariah's visions of the chariot. Hence, even though etymological interpretations are not based directly on the biblical vocabulary, they are still based on biblical language.

Although the interpretation of equivocal terms describing God or a human being's apprehension of God is also intended for the masses,[18] etymological interpretations are addressed only to the intellectual elite. Because the visions of the chariot are esoteric, Maimonides does not explain them fully, as he does with equivocal terms of the first type. He merely hints at their meaning and leaves it for the reader who is "wise and understands by himself" to grasp them.

Maimonides mentions the following words: *ḥashmal* (Ezekiel 1:4), *regel ʿegel* (Ezekiel 1:7), *neḥoshet kalal* (ibid.) (II.29, II.43), and *neḥoshet* (Zechariah 6:1) (2.29). In *Guide* 3.1 he refers also to *pene shor* [the face of an ox] (Ezekiel 1:10).[19] He offers only hints about the first two words (*GP* 3.2 and 7). For example, "the feet were round, 'like the sole of a calf's [*egel*] foot' (Ezekiel 1:7)" (*GP* 3.2, p. 418), thus alluding to the interpretation that *egel* is derived from *agol* [round]. But the reader is left to identify the round substance Maimonides has in mind within the context in which it appears.[20]

Maimonides applies the same method of interpretation to esoteric biblical texts that do not relate prophetic visions but employ terms that should be interpreted etymologically as literary devices: the story of the Garden of Eden, which he takes to be written by Moses, who prophesized without the help of the imaginative faculty; the scenes in heaven in the first two chapters of Job, written by someone who prophesized through the Holy Spirit and apprehended the content of his prophecy by the intellect alone; and a *midrash* dealing with the Garden of Eden, written by rabbinic Sages rather than prophets.

In all of these cases the terms interpreted etymologically are names of supernatural creatures: *Naḥash* [serpent] in Genesis 3; "Satan" in Job 1–2; and the demon *Samma'el* in *Chapters of Rabbi Eliezer* (13). Because in Maimonides' opinion supernatural creatures do not fit "the true realities of existence" (*GP* 1.70, p. 174), they should be interpreted figuratively in a way that fits Aristotelian philosophy. The story of the Garden of Eden is an esoteric text. Hence Maimonides only alludes to the interpretation of *naḥash* [serpent] (in the Bible) and *Samma'el* (in the *midrash*) claiming that their significance is indicated by their etymology. Here again the reader has to understand the allusion by himself and interpret the names within their context using the principles of Aristotelian philosophy. Because Maimonides only hints at their meanings, there could be different interpretations and hence different identifications of the serpent and *Samma'el.*

Maimonides gives a more ample hint about the meaning of "Satan":

> Know that [the word] *satan* derives from *steh* [turn away] from him and pass on" (Proverbs 4:15). I mean to say that it derives from the notion of turning-away and going-away. For it is he who indubitably turns people away from the ways of truth and makes them perish in the ways of error. (*GP* 3.22, p. 489)[21]

Even this hint needs further exegesis by readers who are acquainted with Aristotelian psychology and with other chapters of the *Guide* in which Maimonides provides additional hints about the identification of "Satan."[22]

9.2. DIVINE REVELATION

The lexicon also makes it possible to interpret descriptions of revelations that involve anthropomorphic terms. The most important passages that can be interpreted this way are God's revelation to Micaiah (1 Kings 22:19) and God's promise to reveal himself to Moses in the cleft of the rock (Exodus 33–34).

Micaiah describes his vision by saying: "I saw the Lord sitting on his throne, and all the host of heaven standing beside him" (1 Kings 22:19). As we have seen, Maimonides interprets part of this description in *Guide* 1.4, in which he says that Micaiah did not perceive God with his eyes but had an intellectual apprehension. It follows that the rest of his vision, too, should not be interpreted anthropomorphically. Elsewhere Maimonides explains two more equivocal terms that appear in Micaiah's vision: *kisse* [throne] (*GP* 1.9) and *yeshivah* [sitting] (*GP* 1.11). Although Maimonides does not cite Micaiah's vision as an example of terms used in their derivative sense, the reader is invited to interpret it with the help of the lexicon. One sense of "throne" is "heaven," another is "His greatness and sublimity." The figurative meaning of "sitting" is "steady stable and changeless states." When applied to God it means that He is stable and undergoes no manner of change. In this way, the reader can interpret Micaiah's vision as the recognition that God, who is immutable, is permanent in heaven, that is, is the prime mover of the heavenly spheres[23]; or, alternatively, that God's sublimity and greatness are stable and immutable.

Maimonides explains eight terms that appear in God's revelation in the cleft of the rock: *maqom* [place] (*GP* 1.8), *natsov* or *yatsov* [to stand or stand erect] (*GP* 1.15), *tsur* [rock] (*GP* 1. 16), *avor* [to pass] (*GP* 1.21), *kavod* Y.H.V.H [the glory of Y.H.V.H] (*GP* 1.64), *ra'oh* [to see] (*GP* 1. 4), *panim* [face] (*GP* 1.37), and *aḥor* [back] (*GP* 1. 38). In all of these chapters, except *Guide* 1. 64, he cites fragments of verses from Exodus 33:21–23 as examples of the meaning of the term in question.[24]

The way in which the reader should understand the revelation in the cleft of the rock can be illustrated by Maimonides' interpretation of Exodus 33:21: "Behold, there is a place by me where you shall stand upon the rock." The verse contains three terms that must be understood in a figurative sense: "place," "stand," and "rock." In *Guide* 1.8, Maimonides explains that the figurative meaning of *maqom* [place] is "rank," it denotes "an individual's rank and situation . . . with reference to his perfection in some matter" (*GP* 1.8, p. 33). At the end of the chapter, he adds that "in this verse [Exodus 33:21] the term *maqom* signifies a rank in theoretical speculation, and the contemplation of the intellect – not that of the eye" (*GP* 1.8, p. 34). Clearly the meaning of "place" is determined from its context and from the interpretation of other terms in these verses.

In verse 23, God tells Moses that "you shall see My back." Because God is not corporeal we must again interpret "sight" as intellectual apprehension. By the same token, "place" must refer to the rank of this apprehension. According to *Guide* 1.16, the figurative meaning of "rock" is "the root and principle of every thing" (*GP* 1.16, p. 42). When applied to God it designates that "He is the principle and the efficient cause of all things other than himself" (ibid.). Maimonides' illustration of this sense of the term is precisely our verse – "you shall stand upon the rock." As he explains,

> Rely upon, and be firm in considering, God, may He be exalted, as the first principle. This is the entryway through which you shall come to Him, as we have made clear when speaking of His saying [to Moses], "Behold, there is a place by Me." (ibid.)

Because the derivative meaning of "to stand" is "to be stable and permanent" the import of the verse is that God is telling Moses to have a stable and permanent intellectual apprehension of Him as the first principle.[25]

9.3. PARABLES

According to the Introduction, the second purpose of the *Guide* is the interpretation of "obscure parables occurring in the books of the prophets" (*GP* Introduction, p. 6). By "parables" Maimonides means verses and passages that have two meanings: an external meaning and an internal or hidden meaning. The external meaning is apprehended by a reading of the text in a conventional way, the internal meaning by a reading of it in a philosophic way. The internal meaning contains "wisdom that is useful for beliefs concerned with the truth as it is" (*GP* Introduction, p. 12), that is, with philosophical truths. Nevertheless, the external meaning of the well-constructed parable contains wisdom that is useful for practical life, especially for "the welfare of human societies" (ibid.).

In Maimonides' view, the Bible was written by three kinds of prophets: Moses, the prophet par excellence; the majority of other prophets in the Bible; and the authors of the *Hagiographa*, who wrote with the Holy Spirit. The common denominator is that their prophecies are based on intellectual apprehension of theoretical truths and that all of them used imagination to convey these truths.[26] Thus all the prophets communicated their visions in images and parables rather than in scientific or philosophical language. Maimonides' theory of prophecy justifies the assertion that the inner meaning of the biblical parables reflects the truths of Aristotelian philosophy and at the same time explains their literary form.

Maimonides devotes several chapters or portions of chapters in the *Guide* to the interpretation of biblical texts he takes to be parables. The most important are these:

Guide 2.30, which deals with the creation of the universe. According to Maimonides, this account is cosmology – a description of the structure of the physical world according to Aristotelian physics[27] – and not cosmogony. At *Guide* 1.1–2 and 2.30 he interprets the stories of the creation of man and of the Garden of Eden (Genesis 1–3). At *Guide* 1.7 he treats the story of Adam's sons (Genesis 4–5). In Maimonides' opinion, all three of these stories convey philosophic anthropology rather than historical narrative.

Guide 1.54, which addresses God's revelation to Moses in the cleft of the rock (Exodus 33–34). According to Maimonides these biblical chapters are concerned with the doctrine of the divine attributes, Moses' prophecy, the prophet as political leader, providence, and the knowledge of God possible for man.[28]

Guide 1.15 and 2.10, which offer two different interpretations of Jacob's dream.[29] According to the first, the dream represents the structure of the physical world, its discovery by man, the apprehension of God as the prime mover of the spheres, and the imitation of God by the prophet (who is also a political leader). According to the second, it has only one subject: a vision of the sublunar word.[30]

Guide 3.1–7, which focuses on Ezekiel's chariot vision. Maimonides interprets it as an apprehension of the structure of the celestial world, primary matter, the four elements of the lower world, and of the separate intellect.

Guide 3.8 and part of the Introduction to the *Guide*, which interpret parables about "woman." According to Maimonides, these parables deal with the physics of the sublunar world and anthropology.

Guide 2.22–23, which addresses the Book of Job. Maimonides concludes that it deals with theories of providence, the source of evil, human misery and happiness, as well as theodicy.

9.3.1. *Two Types of Parables*

Although he sometimes devotes parts of chapters, entire chapters, or series of chapters to the interpretation of a single parable, in many cases we can grasp the full meaning of the parable only by reading other portions of the *Guide*. In the Introduction, he distinguishes two types of parables. The first type consists of parables that employ equivocal terms or expressions. To understand their hidden meaning we must interpret these terms. From the listed meanings of each term, the reader must choose the one that best fits the context and combine the appropriate meanings of each term to comprehend the parable. Determining which meanings are appropriate presupposes a general understanding of the subject of the parable.

The second type consists of parables in which "the parable as a whole indicates the whole of the intended meaning" (*GP* Introduction, p. 12). In such cases, not all the words contribute to the hidden meaning. Some simply adorn the parable, whereas others create a deliberate obscurity and conceal the true meaning from unqualified readers. To understand these parables, we need only interpret the parts that convey its meaning and can ignore the rest.

9.3.1.1. THE FIRST INTERPRETATION OF JACOB'S DREAM. Maimonides' example of a parable of the first kind is Jacob's dream (Genesis 28:12–13). In the Introduction, he divides the parable into seven units of meaning, thereby demonstrating that it is a parable of the first type, but does not explain them. We saw that, at *Guide* 1.15, he deals with the meaning of "to stand" and cites Genesis 28:13: "And behold, the Lord stood upon it" to illustrate the use of the verb with reference to God. He follows this up with an interpretation of the whole dream. To understand it fully, however, we must complete the interpretation from other parts of the *Guide*. The parable contains seven units of meaning as indicated by the following expressions: (1) "ladder," (2) "set up on the earth," (3) "and the top of it reached to heaven," (4) "and behold the angels of God," (5) "ascending," (6) "and descending," (7) "and behold the Lord stood above it." Units (1), (2), (3), and (7) describe the ladder[31]; units (4), (5), and (6) compose a dynamic description of the movement of the angels on the ladder: "angels of God ascending and descending."

According to Maimonides' interpretation, the parable turns on three issues: cosmology, epistemology, and politics. The description of the ladder refers to the first two issues. The words *shamayim* [heaven] and *erets* [earth] are not explained in this chapter, nor do they figure in his lexicon. They are, however, explicated in two nonlexicographic chapters of the *Guide*: 1.70 and 2.30. According to 1.70, "heaven" is the highest heaven, the sphere that encompasses the universe. According to 2.30, "earth" is an equivocal term, used in a general and particular sense. In the first, it denotes the four elements that compose all the substances of the sublunar world; in the second, the specific element of earth. Maimonides does not explain the term "ladder." On the basis of his interpretations of "heaven" and "earth," though, we may infer that "ladder" refers to the hierarchy of the physical substances. At *Guide* 1.15, he mentions the upper sphere first, reflecting the fact that Jacob saw the world descending from heaven to earth. Maimonides provides just such a description of the world in philosophic language at *Guide* 2.4, p. 28: "just as bodies begin similarly with the highest sphere and come to an end with the elements and what is composed of them."

There is an epistemological side to this part of the parable as well. Maimonides explains that the ladder Jacob saw also reflects scientific progress; the ladder is also "the ladder of sciences" because "upon it climbs and ascends everyone who ascends, so that he necessarily apprehends Him who is upon it" (*GP* 1.15, p. 41). The philosopher proceeds gradually from knowledge of the lower sublunar substances to knowledge of the upper sphere and of God. Hence Jacob's dream describes the path by which the philosopher attains the highest knowledge possible for human beings – knowledge of the existence of God, the prime mover of the spheres.

By contrast, the dynamic description has practical significance. It presents the prophets as political leaders, a central idea in Maimonides' philosophy. This part of the dream is composed of three equivocal terms: *mal'akhim* [angels], *olim* [ascending], and *yordim* [descending]. At 2.15 Maimonides does not say that "angel" is an equivocal term with several meanings, as he does later at *Guide* 2.6; he merely explains the meaning of the term in Jacob's dream by citing two verses in which the context makes it clear that "angel" denotes a prophet: "He sent an angel and brought us forth out of Egypt" (Numbers 20:16), and "an angel of the Lord came up from Gilgal to Bochim" (Judges 2:1).

The terms "ascending" and "descending" are also equivocal. Maimonides explains them at *Guide* 1.10 as follows:

> Similarly the term [to descend] is also used to denote a lower state of speculation; when man directs his thought toward a very mean object, he is said to *have descended,* and similarly when he directs his thought toward an exalted and sublime object, he is said to *have ascended.* (*GP,* 1:10, p. 36)

When prophets ascend they apprehend certain rungs of the ladder, which is to say certain physical truths. When they descend they are focusing on practical issues that are lower objects of thought; namely, the government of the people and their instruction. Maimonides draws the reader's attention to the fact that the Bible speaks first of ascending and then of descending. The prophet, we might say, is like Plato's Philosopher–King, the ideal political leader who governs the people by imitating God's actions in the world. Hence he must first ascend and apprehend the physical world, and only then descend to rule the people on the basis of this apprehension. Here the ladder is no longer conceived as simply the physical world but as God's attributes of action, knowledge of which serves as a model for the government of society.

9.3.1.2. THE "MARRIED HARLOT." To illustrate the second type of parable, Maimonides cites Proverbs 7:6–21 in the Introduction. According to his interpretation the inner meaning of the parable is anchored in the image of *eshet ish zonah* [a married harlot] and the ban on following her. None of the other details in the parable contribute to its meaning. As we have seen, Maimonides also invokes the image of the married harlot at *Guide* 3.8. There the married harlot is a metaphor for sublunar matter. Because privation always accompanies matter, matter is the cause of corruption. According to Maimonides, the same image is used in Proverbs to refer to a specific kind of matter: that of the substance "man."[32] Although Maimonides does not say so explicitly, here he interprets "a married harlot" in a different way than in *Guide* 3.8. The harlot is still a married woman, matter connected to form, but in the Introduction she is a harlot not because she puts off one form and puts on another but, because, instead of helping her husband (*ish* = form = intellect), she is the cause of bodily desires, the pursuit of which prevents the intellect from attaining its perfection.

Maimonides speaks of the role of man's matter in *Guide* 3.8 too, but there he presents it as a philosophic doctrine, not an interpretation of the image, a married harlot. In the Introduction he interprets the parable on the basis of the same doctrine and explains that it is concerned with a practical issue: instruction about proper conduct. Because matter is the cause of bodily desire, the warning against the pursuit of a married harlot is a warning against the pursuit of bodily desires and the pleasures that result from their fulfillment. In neither place does Maimonides explain how matter is the cause of desire. Elsewhere he provides two explanations for it. According to 3.12, p. 445, the cause is the temperment of the body;[33] according to the interpretation of the story of the Garden of Eden as discussed at 2.30, it is the human imagination.

9.3.2. *Interpretation of Parables by Means of Midrash*

As we have seen, Maimonides tries to ground his interpretation of the Bible in Jewish tradition and establishes his lexicon on the basis of biblical language. Another way of interpreting the Bible within Jewish tradition is to use rabbinic *midrash*. The assumption underlying this approach is that the Sages, the authors of the *midrashim*, were philosophers in their own right as well as authoritative exegetes of the Bible.

Maimonides does not think that every interpretation offered by the Sages should be accepted. He often emphasizes that the interpretation he relies on is found in all the *midrashim*, which is tantamount to claiming that the Sages reached a consensus. He rarely cites the name of the specific Sage on whose opinion he is drawing and speaks instead of *a* Sage or *the* Sages. The use of *midrash* to interpret biblical parables is found particularly in his interpretations of Jacob's dream, the Creation story, the account of the Garden of Eden, and the first two chapters of Job.

Maimonides applies *midrash* to biblical exegesis in several ways. The most common is based on aggadic expansion, in which the Sages added elements not found in the original text. These elements are taken by Maimonides in various ways.

9.3.2.1. THE SECOND INTERPRETATION OF JACOB'S DREAM. According to the interpretation of Jacob's dream given at *Guide* 2.10,

Jacob had a vision of the sublunar world. This interpretation is based on the equivocal term "angel" that Maimonides explains at *Guide* 2.6, but not at *Guide* 2.10. At *Guide* 2.10 he assumes that the hints he offers in this chapter to the meaning of the parable enable the reader to apply the correct meaning of "angel" in Jacob's vision and to complete the interpretation without further assistance.[34]

At *Guide* 2.6 he derives some of the meanings of "angel" by his customary method, relying on biblical verses in which the sense is evident from the context. However, he also presents the first meaning of the term as a "structure of meaning" to be filled with a specific content: "the meaning of *mal'akh* [angel] is messenger" (*GP* 2.6, p. 262). Hence whatever plays the role of a messenger or someone who carries out an order can fill this structure of meaning and be considered an angel. Maimonides fills in the structure of meaning with philosophic content that satisfies the requirement of the structure of meaning established on the basis of the biblical text, thus giving that content its legitimacy. In this way, he considers the four earthly elements to be such messengers. In the philosophical part of *Guide* 2.10, he mentions the elements as one of the physical phenomena that are four in number. In this way, the reader has to understand the meaning of "angels" in the interpretation of Jacob's dream, which follows the philosophical discourse, on the basis of the two chapters and conclude that the angels are the four elements.

The biblical passage does not say how many angels Jacob saw. Maimonides does not interpret it directly but alludes to *midrashim* that explain it. To extract the number four, corresponding to the four elements, Maimonides turns to the *midrash*:

> All the manuscripts and all the midrashim agree that *the angels of God*, whom [Jacob] saw *ascending and descending* were only four and not any other number – *two ascending and two descending*. (*GP* 2.10, p. 272)[35]

Then he indicates that, according to the *midrash*, "the four [angels] gathered together upon one step of the ladder, all four being in one row – namely, the two who ascend and the two who descend" (ibid.).[36] Although the *midrash* does not explain who the angels were, Maimonides supposes that it, too, understands "angels" as the elements. The meaning then is that the four elements Jacob saw in his dream – the two that ascend (fire and air according to Aristotelian philosophy) and the two that descend (water and earth) – compose the substances of the sublunar world; that is why they are described as occupying one step of the ladder.

9.3.2.2. THE CREATION OF MAN. As we have seen, Maimonides holds that the Bible contains esoteric doctrines. Because the esoteric meaning should not be divulged, the Sages who interpreted the parables did so with parables of their own rather than explain the original text in plain language. Consequently their exegesis is itself esoteric and must be interpreted. Maimonides, too, may not diffuse the "mysteries of the Torah," and does not fully explain such biblical passages and the *midrashim* that interpret them so that his interpretations are also esoteric. But instead of adding yet another layer of parable, he employs hints to draw the reader's attention to the points that can serve as keys for understanding the *midrashim* and the biblical texts they interpret. Maimonides attributes this method of interpretation to the Sages,[37] implicitly claiming that he is using a method already applied in Jewish exegetical tradition. As he explicitly says at *Guide* 2.30, his interpretation consists of selecting *midrashim* that hint at the meaning of the biblical text, commenting on them briefly, adding his own hints for understanding, and arranging this material so that it yields the logical sequence of ideas that constitute the inner meaning of the text.

Maimonides leaves it for readers of the *Guide* to understand the hints and comments. Ultimately they must construe the biblical texts and the *midrashim* that explain them. The reader must know Aristotelian philosophy and be acquainted with the entire *Guide* in order to apply Maimonides' instruction in the Introduction: "You must connect its chapters one with another" (*GP* 1 Introduction, p. 15). Because comprehension of the biblical texts is based on hints, different understandings of Maimonides' interpretations are possible.

Let us consider the interpretation of the creation of man at *Guide* 2.30. Maimonides centers his interpretation on Genesis 1:27, "male and female created He them." He hints that the verse does not recount a historical event – the creation of the first man and woman – but expounds philosophic anthropology by explaining the composition of the substance "man." Man is composed of matter (female, *ishah*, Eve) and form (male, *ish*, Adam), which always exist together and are physically inseparable. Similarly, "He took one of his ribs and closed up its place with flesh" (Genesis 2:21) does not describe the creation of the first woman from Adam's rib, but tells us about the relationship between matter and form, namely matter opposes form.

Maimonides hints at the meaning of the story by alluding to its interpretation in *Genesis Rabbah* 8:1. Instead of quoting the *midrash* verbatim, he paraphrases it in Arabic, thereby emphasizing what he considers to be the Sages' hints to the interpretation of the biblical text. Then he adds some remarks that elucidate the hints and buttress the interpretation from two other biblical verses:

> One of these dicta is their saying that *Adam and Eve* were created together, having their backs joined, and that this being was divided and one half of it, namely *Eve*, taken and brought up to [Adam]. The expression "one of his ribs" (Gen. 2:21), means according to them one of his sides. They quote as proof the expression, a "rib of the tabernacle" (Exod. 26:20), which [the Aramaic version] translates: *a side of the tabernacle*. In accordance with this, they say that [of his ribs] means: of his sides. Understand [you, the reader] in what way it has been explained that they were two in a certain respect and that they were also one; as it says: "bone of my bones, and flesh of my flesh" (Gen. 2:23). This has received additional confirmation through the fact that it says that both of them have the same name: for she is called *ishah* [woman] "because she was taken out of *ish* [man]." It also confirms their union by saying: "And shall cleave unto his wife, and they shall be one flesh" (Gen. 2:24). How great is the ignorance of him who does not understand that all this is necessary with a view to a certain notion. (*GP* 2.30, pp. 355–56)

9.3.2.3. THE GARDEN OF EDEN AT *GUIDE* 2.30. Maimonides uses this method to explain two other parables: sin in the Garden of Eden (*GP* 2.30) and the first two chapters of Job (*GP* 3.22). Here I briefly consider the first of these.

The hints about the interpretation of the story of the Garden of Eden in *Guide* 2.30 come after those about the creation of man and woman and focus on the protagonists and their relationships. According to Maimonides the story explains Eve's "seduction" – that is, why matter is carried away by desire. He bases his understanding mainly on an aggadic expansion in *Chapters of Rabbi Eliezer* (13), which introduces another player to the story: Samma'el. Maimonides does not recount the entire *midrash* but calls his reader's attention to the points that he considers to be hints to the meaning of the story.

As we have seen, Maimonides understands Adam to be man's form. On the basis of Genesis 1:26 ("Let us make man in our image, after our likeness"), he creates the formula: "the image of God and His likeness" (*GP* 1.1, p. 23; 1.2, p. 24; 3.8, p. 431). The terms "image" and "likeness" are explained in *Guide* 1.1, from which we learn that "the image of God and His likeness" denote man's intellectual perfection. As the form of man, Adam is the actual intellect. Eve is man's matter. Because the relation of matter to form defines matter in every substance, it is plausible that Maimonides understands Eve as man's body (and the bodily powers, the inferior parts of the soul: the vegetative and the animal).

With regard to the other two characters in the story, the serpent and Samma'el, Maimonides says they should be interpreted etymologically, but does not provide an explanation. Instead, he provides another hint: According to the Sages, Samma'el is Satan. Thus we can use Maimonides' treatment of Satan in his interpretation of the Book of Job (*GP* 2.22) to explain Samma'el in this *midrash*.

As we have seen, Maimonides invokes the etymology of "Satan" at *Guide* 3.22, saying that Satan "turns people away from the ways of truth and makes them perish in the ways of error." He adds several other hints, of which the most important is the saying by Rabbi Simeon ben Laqish, whom he cites by name: "Satan, the evil inclination, and the angel of death are one and the same."[38] At *Guide* 2.12, p. 280, Maimonides identifies "the evil inclination" with imagination, explaining that "every deficiency of reason or character is due to the action of the imagination or consequent upon its action." Thus Satan in Job 2 and Samma'el in the Garden of Eden both refer to the imagination.

Chapters of Rabbi Eliezer adds yet another hint: Samma'el "rode" on the serpent. At *Guide* 1.70, p. 171, Maimonides explains the verb "to ride," noting that its derivative meaning is "domination over a thing." Hence Samma'el is imagination, which dominates the serpent. The serpent does not act on its own but is only a medium used by Samma'el, who is the real seducer. From an Aristotelian standpoint, the serpent is human desire, and the serpent ridden by Samma'el irrational desire. Because Maimonides claims that "serpent" should be understood etymologically, we may infer that the noun *naḥash* [serpent] is derived from *ḥash* [agile in carrying out a task]. The sin of the Garden of Eden consisted in following irrational desires for objects given by imagination.[39] Imagination induces man's body (Eve, matter) to pursue physical desires and thus keeps Adam, the intellect, from contemplating the intelligibles and being a perfect actual intellect.

9.3.3. The Garden of Eden in Guide *1.2*

Guide 1.2 does not provide a comprehensive interpretation of the story of the Garden of Eden. Instead, Maimonides is concerned with one issue: the human condition before and after Adam's transgression. He also offers an allusive answer to the question: What was Adam's sin? Because the sin explains the reversal in his condition, the answer is also the answer to the question: Why did Adam's condition change?

The topic is not presented as a direct interpretation of the biblical story but in a peculiar literary form: Maimonides tells us an autobiographical story of a discussion he had years ago with "a learned man," most likely a free thinker, who proposed "a curious objection." He argued that the Bible tells an absurd story; namely that God intended man to be just like the other animals, without intellect. When man disobeyed, it was his disobedience that endowed him with the capacity to distinguish between good and evil. Assuming that it is the intellect that distinguishes between good and evil, Maimonides' interlocutor inferred that man received intellect, his form, as a result of disobedience and was thus rewarded rather than punished for his sin.

Maimonides' interpretation of the story is both a discussion of the correct exegesis of the biblical text and of the philosophical issues that it raises. He replies that this man had not read the biblical text carefully, on the one hand, and does not know philosophy, on the other. The biblical text tells us that man was created "in the image of God and His likeness." Thus he already had a perfect theoretical intellect before he sinned. According to Maimonides, the intellect distinguishes between truth and falsehood, not between good and evil. It follows that the claim that man acquired his intellect as a consequence of sin is a mistake from the philosophical point of view as well.

Maimonides understands "good" and "evil" in Genesis 3:5 as "fine" and "bad," which demarcate relative moral judgments as opposed to metaphysical truths. Thus, after his transgression, man was endowed with the capacity to make decisions on the basis of what Maimonides, following Aristotle, calls "generally accepted opinions." Maimonides suggests that there is also absolute good and evil, which follow and are determined by intellectual perfection. Because intellectual perfection is good, everything that contributes to its attainment is good, whereas everything that prevents it is bad. The commandment not to eat from the tree of knowledge is prescribed by the perfect intellect. It is a ban on the pursuit of sensual and imaginative ends and hence on relative moral judgments.

Man's sin was that he pursued his desires. His punishment was the loss of the power of intellectual apprehension and hence of intellectual perfection. In its place, he acquired the power to apprehend generally accepted opinions and became absorbed in "judging things to be bad or fine" (*GP* 1.2, p. 25o) instead of contemplating intelligibles.

At the end of the chapter, Maimonides provides a second interpretation of the story, using another method of interpretation – interpretation by hints. He hints at the meaning of the story by focusing on food and what man was permitted to eat and not permitted to eat. He transgressed the divine commandment by eating, and his punishment was that he was "deprived of everything he ate before and had to eat the meanest kinds of food which he had not used as aliment before" (*GP* 1.2, p. 26).[40] Maimonides thus calls attention to the central place of eating in the story and hence also of the objects of eating, but he does not explain what "eating" means. The reader is supposed to follow the hint and complete the interpretation by drawing on Maimonides' answer to his interlocutor and on *Guide* 1.30 – a lexicographic chapter that explains the equivocal term *akhol* [to eat].

The reader may interpret the hints in several ways. I believe, however, that none of them provides a coherent interpretation of the story. A plausible view is that "eating" means apprehension and refers to the apprehension of intelligibles as well as generally accepted opinions. Before he sinned, man apprehended the intelligibles – every tree of the garden – and had a perfect intellect. He sinned by pursuing sensual and imaginative desires and seeking to apprehend the generally accepted opinions, the tree of the knowledge of good and evil. His punishment was deprivation of intellectual perfection, the exile from Eden. Instead, he was forced to satisfy his material needs – sent "to till the ground" – and to occupy himself with judging things as fine or bad, worthy or unworthy of pursuit – to "eat the grass of the field."[41]

9.3.4. *The Book of Job*

Job is the only biblical book that Maimonides explains in full. He considers it a parable of the second type: a story that contains details that have only an aesthetic function or that are intended to conceal the true meaning from unqualified readers. He therefore devotes only two chapters of the *Guide* (3.22–23) to its exegesis and claims that he has "summed up all its notions, nothing being left aside" (*GP* 3.23, p. 497). Although from one perspective, Job is a parable of the second type, replete with details that add nothing to an understanding of its meaning, according to Maimonides, most of the book does not have a hidden meaning. Maimonides explains "literally" many parts of it. To grasp the meaning one must focus on important verses, extract the main ideas, and ignore the rest. Nevertheless, there are some esoteric portions that require interpretation, for example, the scenes in heaven, parts of Elihu's speech (Job 33:23 and 29), and the image of Leviathan in God's revelation.

Although concise, Maimonides' interpretation is full of insights. It provides several solutions to the problems of evil, theodicy, and divine providence. Here I can offer only a brief discussion of one aspect of the interpretation. As Maimonides reads it, the Prologue of Job presents a theological perplexity in biographical form:

> A righteous and perfect man, who was just in his actions and is most careful to avoid sins, was stricken – without his having committed a sin entailing this – by great and consecutive calamities with respect to his fortune, his children and his body. (*GP* 3.22, p. 486)

Maimonides derives this statement from three things: (1) the description of Job as "a man [who] was blameless and upright, one who feared God, and turned away from evil" (Job 1:1; cf. 1:8 and 2:3), (2) the calamities that befell him (1:13–19 and 2:7), and (3) the inferences than an observer may draw from these verses. The perplexity arises from the contradiction between the implicit presupposition that God is just and the facts described in the story. It is important to note that Maimonides interprets "upright" in the biblical text as "just in his actions," understanding that Job exemplified moral virtue and performed good deeds. Hence he does not need to interpret the long descriptions of Job's behavior. Apparently he regards them as aesthetic devices related to the literal aspect of the story. Because a man is allotted reward and punishment according to his actions, Job deserved reward. The notion we take away from the story about Job's misfortunes is that it tells us about three types of calamity: loss of fortune, loss of children, and loss of bodily health. Everything else we read about these misfortunes pertains solely to the aesthetic aspect of the story.

The perplexity evoked by Job's life leads to the main issue of the book: divine providence. The opinions of Job and his friends are different solutions to this issue. Maimonides summarizes the lesson of Job's speeches and says that Job tried to solve the problem by denying God's providence over the sublunar world. Although God knows what occurs to individual people, according to Job, he abandons them because of his contempt for them. Maimonides cites ten verses as proof, of which the most important is this: "It is all one; therefore I say, he destroys both the blameless and the wicked. When disaster brings sudden death, he mocks at the calamity of the innocent" (Job 9:22–23).

God's appearance from the whirlwind – which returns the narrative to Job's life story – causes Job to recant and acknowledge that his original conception of providence was mistaken.[42] Here again, Maimonides summarizes the biblical account and then explains the purpose of the revelation:

> The purpose of all these things is to show that our intellects do not reach the point of apprehending how these natural things that exist in the world of generation and corruption are produced in time and of conceiving how the existence of the natural force within them has originated them. They are not things that resemble what we make. (*GP* 3.23, p. 496)

God's revelation provides the main lesson of the book: On the one hand it teaches the foundation for the belief that God exercises providence over the sublunar world. This belief is manifested in the descriptions of natural objects and especially of the Leviathan, which stands for all the animals of the sublunar world. On the other hand, it teaches that God's governance of the world is different from ours and that we are not in a position to understand it. In Maimonides' view,

"The two notions are not comprised in one definition. . . and there is nothing in common between the two except the name alone" (ibid.).

The answer to the initial perplexity presented by the story of Job is that it derives from an incorrect assumption: an anthropomorphic model of God according to which God governs the world in the same way man governs the state and that God is subject to the same moral rules as man. Rejecting this assumption eliminates the perplexity. Cases like Job's do not contradict the claim that God is just and exercises providence over the world because God's justice and providence are not to be understood in human terms. Nor can the story lead to Job's initial conclusion that God abandons individual members of the human species because of his contempt for them. The revelation does not, however, provide an alternative theory of providence to replace the one it refutes.

9.4. CONCLUSION

Maimonides' biblical exegesis was addressed principally to the intellectual elite of his age. It sought to reconcile the authoritative Jewish text, the Bible, with Aristotelian philosophy and demonstrate that the Bible professes the ideas that were prevalent in his cultural milieu. Thus it paved the way for philosophical interpretations of the Bible in the later Middle Ages. Subsequent generations continued his endeavor and wrote philosophical commentaries on the Bible, inspired by the exegesis included in the *Guide*. It should be noted, however, that Maimonides' biblical interpretations are idiosyncratic and very different from those of other exegetes, earlier and later.

First, he was not interested in commenting on entire books to help readers understand them; hence he did not write running commentaries on the text. Instead, he focused on two types of passages: those that seemed to corporealize God and those he considered to have an inner philosophical meaning.

Second, he had his own particular way of interpreting biblical words. Rather than explain words in their context, as other biblical commentators did, he built a lexicon of equivocal words for use in biblical exegesis. Although he also provided sample verses to illustrate the different meanings of the words he explained, thus interpreting the verses, the importance of the lexicon is as a tool for further biblical exegesis rather than as an interpretation of concrete verses. His interpretation of words is an "open" exegesis; the lexicon is a manual that his readers can use for their own interpretations rather then an authoritative exegesis of verses.

Third, his biblical exegesis is not a systematic and clear explanation of biblical passages. The main role of his lexicon is to eliminate the tendency to think of God in corporeal terms. Because he chose to assemble a lexicon of equivocal terms, he did not provide a running commentary on the Divine revelations in the Bible, leaving it to readers to explain them with the help of the lexicon. Because of his assumption that the Bible is an esoteric work and some of its content should not be divulged in public, he only hinted at the meaning of what he considered to be esoteric passages. Here too the readers had to complete the understanding of the passages by their own efforts.

For modern readers, Maimonides' biblical exegesis is an example of how a great Jewish medieval philosopher coped with the challenge of the science and philosophy of his age and rendered the biblical text significant and relevant for his contemporaries. From his biblical exegesis, modern scholars who are interested in Maimonides' thought can learn which philosophical ideas he knew and which he actually endorsed. More significantly, they can learn some of his own doctrines. The interpretations of the story of the creation of man, the Garden of Eden, Adam's sons, and the parable of the married harlot in the introduction to the *Guide* present Maimonides' philosophic anthropology. His interpretation of the Book of Job presents some of his views on Divine providence and theodicy and complement what he wrote on these subjects in other chapters of the *Guide*. In this way the study of Maimonides' biblical exegesis contributes to a deeper understanding of his thought.

NOTES

1. Words in italics denote the Hebrew words in the original Arabic text (except for biblical verses and verse fragments, which have been romanized to facilitate reading).
2. M. *Ḥagigah* 2:1
3. B. *Ḥagigah* 13a
4. *Categories* 1a 1–6.
5. At *Guide* 2.30 he mentions another type of equivocal term, those used in both a general and particular sense.

6. In *Guide* 1.8, however, he bases the meanings of *maqom* on midrashic and talmudic language. Sometimes, too, Maimonides understands biblical terms on the basis of a philosophical–semantic axis and gives them a philosophical meaning.
7. Translations of biblical passages are based on the Revised Standard Version or the New JPS translation (depending on which is closer to Maimonides' understanding of the verse), modified as necessary to make the point clear.
8. As in the Revised Standard Version rendering, "Thy word is firmly fixed in the heavens."
9. *Lev* is also an equivocal term. In addition to "heart," the physical organ, it also can mean "mind" (as the translations render it here) or "intellect" (cf. *GP* 1.39).
10. Some meanings of the terms "place" (1.8), "ladder" (alluded to in 1.15), "rock" (1.16), and "angel" (2.6) are of this type, too.
11. Maimonides does not cite the verse or chapter from which he derives this image. As we shall see, in the Introduction to the *Guide*, he interprets Proverbs 7:6–21 as a parable centered on this image. The expressions "a married woman," cited here and at *Guide* 3.8 in Hebrew, and *eshet ish zonah* [harlot], cited in the Introduction to the *Guide* in Hebrew as well, do not appear in Proverbs 7:8–21, but in Proverbs 6:26. As in the Introduction to the *Guide* (p. 13), Maimonides claims that Solomon's "entire book is based on this allegory," which can be found in other chapters of Proverbs as well, it seems to me very plausible that Maimonides derives this image from the biblical parallelism in this verse. The parallelism enables him to identify the married woman mentioned in the first term of the parallelism with the harlot in its second term.
12. In *Guide* 1.6, Maimonides does not explain the second derivative meaning of "woman." *Guide* 3.8 completes the interpretation. In his interpretation of "woman" he also alludes to the meaning of "man" as form, the essence of a substance. But Maimonides does not refer here to the "structure of meaning" of the term, but only to its "content," its meaning in Proverbs.
13. B. *Berakhot* 31b.
14. Cf. *GP* 1.6, 7, 14, 30.
15. At *Guide* 3.43, he explains the same phenomenon slightly differently. He says that the prophets describe what they see in their visions. Language renders the images they see.
16. This example occurs also in 2.29.
17. Cf. also 2.29, p. 347–48.
18. Cf. *GP* 1.35.

19. Maimonides is aware of the fact that there are other terms of this kind in the Bible; at *Guide* 2.29, p. 348, he makes this remark: "the same applies to other words."
20. Basing himself on Aristotelian philosophy, Crescas, a fourteenth-century commentator on the *Guide*, suggests that "the sole of a calf's foot" is "the [celestial] sphere, which is round" (commentary on *Guide* 2.29).
21. For these interpretations, see Klein-Braslavy 1986c and the bibliography cited there.
22. See the interpretation of the story of the Garden of Eden in Subsection 9.3.2.3.
23. Thus this vision is analogous to Jacob's vision of God in the dream according to Maimonides' interpretation in *Guide* 1.15.
24. At *GP* 1.64 he cites another verse that describes this revelation – Exodus 33:18.
25. Cf. also H. Kasher 1995.
26. But the explanation for the use of imagination by the members of each group is different.
27. See Klein-Braslavy 1978.
28. As we have seen, the terms in God's promise to reveal himself in the cleft of the rock are interpreted in other chapters of the *Guide*.
29. At *MT* 1, Principles of the Torah, 3.7, Maimonides offers a third interpretation for this parable.
30. See Klein-Braslavy 1987.
31. Maimonides includes the seventh unit in this group because he takes *nitsav alav* to mean standing on or above *it* – the ladder – and not "next to *him*" – i.e., Jacob, as some commentators understand the text.
32. Maimonides refers here to the interpretation of the image at 3.8 and says that "we shall explain in various chapters of this Treatise his wisdom in likening matter to a *married harlot*. . . " (*GP*, Introduction, p. 13).
33. Cf. also *Guide* 2, premise 26, p. 240.
34. For Maimonides' method of using hints in biblical interpretations, see Subsection 9.3.2.2 on his interpretation of the creation of man.
35. Cf., for example, *Chapters of Rabbi Eliezer* 4, *Numbers Rabbah* 2a.
36. Maimonides alludes to *Genesis Rabbah* 68:12, which he paraphrases immediately after this claim, by way of grounding his interpretation. He may also have in mind *Ḥullin* 91b, in which the idea seems to be even clearer.
37. *GP* 2.29.
38. B. *Baba Batra* 16a.
39. According to this interpretation, the serpent and Samma᾿el seem to be parts of Eve, as Eve is a part of "man."

40. In fact, here Maimonides uses the method of the "books of the Prophets" and sets forth his interpretation of the story using the equivocal term *akala* (in Arabic).
41. Maimonides embeds "to till the ground" and "eat the grass of the field" into his text in Hebrew.
42. Maimonides provides also another interpretation to God's appearance from the whirlwind.

MENACHEM KELLNER

10 Spiritual Life

"Spirituality" is a word for which there is no counterpart in classical Hebrew. *Ruḥaniut*, the word in modern Hebrew, is itself a translation of the English term. *Ruḥaniut* is derived from *ruaḥ*, which means breath or wind, and, derivately, spirit. Its first occurrence is at the very beginning of the Torah:

> When God began to create heaven and earth – the earth being unformed and void, with darkness over the surface of the deep and a wind from God sweeping over the water – God said, "Let there be light"; and there was light.[1]

By Maimonides' time *ruaḥ* had developed a wide range of uses, including, very importantly, *ruaḥ ha-qodesh*, the spirit of holiness (or, as more usually translated, "the holy spirit"), and, very differently, *ruaḥ ṭum'ah*, the spirit of ritual impurity (often used to mean demons). The one meaning the word does not have in classical or even medieval Hebrew is "spiritual" in the sense of "spiritual life." The closest one can come to this expression, I think, in classical Judaism is "holy life."

Maimonides might not know how to answer us if we asked him whether he thought a Jew ought to lead a spiritual life, but if asked how a Jew ought to lead a holy life, he would have an answer, an answer I elucidate in this chapter. Furthermore, the holy life, he would say, both makes possible and is itself made possible by true love of God. We shall, therefore, examine what Maimonides teaches on the interrelated questions of how to live the holy life and how to love God.

At the outset it will be useful to distinguish three different views of holiness.[2] On one view, holiness is an essential feature of certain places, people, objects, or times; on this view, holiness is "hard-wired" into parts of the universe. Judah Halevi (d. 1141) held this view, at least with respect to the holiness of the Land of Israel, the holiness of the commandments, and with respect to the special character of the Jewish people, the "holy nation."

In addition to certain things being holy from the very moment of creation, Halevi also held that holiness can be conferred from without, but not on every person, place, thing, or time. This appears to be the brunt of the following passage from Halevi's *Kuzari* (3.53): "Actions [prescribed] by the religious Law," Halevi maintains, when properly performed, have actual, not "only" statuatory or institutional consequences[3]:

> when it has been completed in the proper way, and you see the heavenly fire, or discover another spirit within yourself, which you did not know [beforehand], or [you witness] veridical dreams and miracles, you know that they are the result of all you did before and of the mighty order with which you have come into contact and which you have [now actually] attained.[4]

Halevi holds that proper fulfillment of the commandments of the Torah thus brings about real change in the universe. On his view, holiness can inhere in certain things, not in others; just as non-Jews cannot prophesy, so not everything can be or become holy. The substrate makes a difference.

On a second view, the universe, as it were, starts out all of a piece, at least with respect to holiness. At various times God renders times, places, or objects holy. This is certainly one way of reading verses such as "And God blessed the seventh day and declared it holy, because on it God ceased from all the work of creation that He had done" (Genesis 2:3). A reasonable way of understanding this and similar verses is that God took a day like every other day (the seventh) and rendered it sacred, changing its nature from that time on.

An example of the second view, it appears to me, may be found in the kabbalistic commentary of Rabbi Ḥayyim ben Moses Attar (1696–1743) to the Torah, *Or ha-ḥayyim* (on Numbers 19:2). According to Rabbi Ḥayyim, before receiving the Torah the Jews were like any other people; on accepting the Torah they became ontologically distinct (my language, not his!) from all other nations. Rabbi Ḥayyim writes, "The distinction by virtue of which the Jewish People were elevated above the other nations is the acceptance of the

Torah, for without it, the House of Israel would be like all the other nations." In the sentences that follow Rabbi Ḥayyim makes it very clear that the Jews are distinguished from non-Jews on a very basic, spiritually fundamental level. After Sinai, the Jews are ontologically distinct from Gentiles, even if before Sinai they were not.[5]

Both these views share in common the idea that however it becomes holy, a holy place, person, time, or object is, once holy, objectively different from profane places, persons, times, and objects. On both these views, holiness is real, it inheres in sacred places, and so forth, it is intrinsic to them; it is, one might say, part of their metaphysical makeup. I characterize them both therefore as "ontological" or "essentialist" views of the nature of holiness. Holy places, persons, times, and objects are ontologically distinct from (and religiously superior to) profane places, persons, times, and objects. This distinction is part of the universe.

Let me try to make this point clearer with an analogy. Radioactivity existed before Geiger discovered a way to measure it. Similarly, holiness exists in holy places, persons, times, and objects, even though there is no way for us (currently) to measure it. It is "out there," a feature of the objectively real world, even if not part of the world susceptible to laboratory examination.

I find a third view of holiness in the thought of Moses Maimonides. On this view holiness cannot be characterized as ontological or essentialist because holy places, persons, times, and objects are in no objective way distinct from profane places, persons, times, and objects; holiness is a status, not a quality of existence. It is a challenge, not a given; normative, not descriptive. It is institutional (in the sense of being part of a system of laws) and hence contingent. This sort of holiness does not reflect objective reality, it helps constitute social reality. On this view, holy places, persons, times, and objects are indubitably holy, and must be treated with all due respect, but they are, in and of themselves, like all other places, persons, times, and objects. What is different about them is the way in which the Torah commands that they be treated.

It is useful to begin our analysis of Maimonides' views on holy living by glancing at the biblical and rabbinic evidence. What is called holy in the Torah? First and foremost, obviously, God. In a text that was to have profound influence on Jewish liturgy, the prophet Isaiah wrote (6:1–3),

In the year that King Uzziah died, I beheld my Lord seated on a high and lofty throne; and the skirts of His robe filled the Temple. Seraphs stood in attendance on Him. Each of them had six wings: with two he covered his face, with two he covered his legs, and with two he would fly. And one would call to the other, "Holy, holy, holy! The Lord of Hosts! His glory fills all the earth!"

God is also called "the Holy One of Israel" some fifteen times in the Bible. God's being the Holy One *of* Israel has direct consequences:

For I the Lord am your God: you shall sanctify yourselves and be holy, for I am holy. You shall not make yourselves unclean through any swarming thing that moves upon the earth. For I the Lord am He who brought you up from the land of Egypt to be your God: you shall be holy, for I am holy. (Leviticus 11:44–45)

Verses such as this, and others, such as "Speak to the whole Israelite community and say to them: You shall be holy, for I, the Lord your God, am holy" (Leviticus 19:2), admit, it seems to me, of very different interpretations. One of way of looking at them is to see them as teaching that God is holy and through the process of election Israel also becomes holy. Just as God's holiness is essentialist, so also is Israel's.

But these verses also admit of a different interpretation, the one held by Maimonides. On this interpretation, Israel is holy when it behaves in certain ways. Holiness on this view is a challenge, and not a gift.[6] I am not making any claims about the way in which the authors of the biblical books actually understood holiness; rather, I am pointing out that their words are ambiguous and not only can be but have been interpreted in very different ways.

The same ambiguity may be found in the language of the opening formula of blessings ordinarily recited before the fulfillment of any positive commandment (as established by the Talmudic rabbis): "Blessed are You, Lord our God, Who has sanctified us with His commandments and commanded us to." Following Rabbi Ḥayyim ben Moses Aṭṭar, one can understand this language as affirming that the imposition of the commandments has made Israel intrinsically holy, or, on the other hand, as affirming that holiness is a consequence of fulfilling the commandments and that it means nothing more than that. Again, I am making no claims about what the Talmudic Sages intended when they instituted this formula (assuming they all intended the same thing by it, which I consider unlikely); rather, I want to show how Maimonides understood it.

Maimonides' position appears to follows from his consistent nominalism and from his insistence on the absolute transcendence of God. With respect to the first, he writes,

> After what I have stated about providence singling out the human species alone among all the species of animals, I say that it is known that no species exists outside the mind, but that the species and the other universals are, as you know, mental notions and that every existent outside the mind is an individual or group of individuals.[7]

The implications of this position for our purposes here are far-reaching. Holiness cannot inhere in the people of Israel, for example, in any essential fashion because there is no such *thing* as the people of Israel, there are only individual Jews.[8] There can furthermore be no such thing as holiness as such; at most there can be sacred objects, places, times, and perhaps individuals. Nor can there be ritual purity as such; only ritually pure or impure objects, places, and individuals.[9]

This must be emphasized: Maimonides' philosophical nominalism does not amount to conventionalism. He may think that the difference between a holy object and a profane object is to be found, not "out there" in the world, but "only" in legal [*halakhic*] institutions, but that does not mean that he holds the difference to be a matter of social convention and nothing more. For Maimonides, *halakhic* institutions are grounded in the Torah, revealed by God to Moses at Sinai, as opposed to reflecting some objective aspect of reality itself.

This must be further emphasized: Maimonides was convinced that the Torah reflects the wisdom of a beneficent God. Thus, to take a simple example, eating kosher food is a *halakhic* requirement; but it is *also* good for you. One should keep kosher because of the command, not because of the benefit, but that does not mean that the benefit will not accrue. The Land of Israel is holy *and* it is a pleasant land, flowing with milk and honey.

It is crucial to emphasize this also: Holiness may exist "only" at the level of *halakhic* institutions, but that does not mean that a person who holds this view must be insensitive to the numinous experience of encountering a place or thing or person that she or he holds sacred. There is no reason to think that Maimonides did not prize such experiences. In short, a nominalist can also have religious experiences!

With respect to my claim about God's transcendence: The Torah obligates Jews to be holy, because God is holy (Leviticus 19:2). Were that interpreted to mean that Jews (or sacred objects, times, and places) are or can be essentially holy, we would be saying that God and certain created entities share a characteristic, namely, the characteristic of holiness. This is something that Maimonides repeatedly disallows.[10] Holiness, it follows, must be *institutional*, a matter of *halakhic* definition, not ontological, somehow actually in the universe.

So much for theoretical considerations. What does Maimonides himself actually say on the topic of holiness generally?[11] There are a small number of texts in which he explicitly addresses the definition of holiness. The most important of these, I think, is found in *Guide of the Perplexed* 3.47:

> As for His dictum, may He be exalted, *Sanctify yourselves therefore and be ye holy, for I am holy* (Leviticus 11:44), it does not apply at all to ritual impurity and purity. Sifra states literally: This concerns sanctification by the commandments. For this reason, transgression of the commandments is also called ritual impurity.... The term ritual impurity is used equivocally in three different senses: It is used of disobedience and of transgression of commandments concerning action or opinion; it is used of dirt and filth... and it is used according to these fancied notions, I refer to touching or carrying certain things or being under the same roof with certain things.[12] With reference to this last sense, we say: "The words of the Torah are not subject to becoming impure."[13] Similarly, the term holiness is used equivocally in three senses opposed to those three senses.[14]

"Holiness," therefore, can mean one of three things:

1. obedience to the commandments concerning action or opinion
2. physical cleanliness
3. ritual purity

With respect to the first and second, it is readily apparent that there is nothing "essentialist" or "ontological" at stake here. When one obeys the Torah, when one holds true views, one has achieved a state of holiness. When one is physically clean, one may be called holy. With respect to the third, Maimonides explicitly teaches that matters of ritual purity and impurity are institutional, not ontological:

> It is plain and manifest that the laws about ritual impurity and purity are decrees laid down by Scripture[15] and not matters about which human understanding is capable of forming a judgment; for behold, they are included among the divine statutes [*ḥuqqim*].[16] So, too, immersion as a means of freeing oneself from ritual impurity is included among the divine statutes. *Now "ritual impurity" is not mud or filth which water can remove, but is a matter of scriptural decree and dependent upon intention of the heart.* Therefore the Sages have said, If a man immerses himself, but without special intention, it is as though he has not immersed himself at all. Nevertheless we may find some indication of all this: just as one who sets his heart on becoming ritually pure becomes so as soon as he has immersed himself, *although nothing new has befallen his body*, so, too, one who sets his heart on purifying himself from the impurity that besets men's souls – namely, evil thoughts and wicked moral qualities[17] – becomes pure as soon as he consents in his heart to shun those counsels and brings his soul into the waters of pure reason. Behold, Scripture says, *I will sprinkle pure water upon you, and you shall be pure: I will purify you from all your ritual impurity and from all your fetishes* (Ezekiel 36:25). May God, in His great mercy, purify us from every sin, iniquity, and guilt. Amen.[18]

Could we ask for a clearer statement? Matters of ritual purity and impurity are decrees of the Torah, having no objective correlation in the "real" world. These laws reflect no objective reality, on any level or in any dimension; rather, they create social/*halakhic* reality.

Thus, if we take Maimonides at his word in *Guide of the Perplexed* 3.47, "holiness" is the term used by the Torah to characterize obedience, cleanliness, or ritual purity. It refers to nothing that can actually and objectively inhere in entities, persons, places, or times. Now that we understand the nature of holiness in general, we may finally get to the point of our discussion and characterize the holy life as understood by Maimonides.

The fifth of the fourteen volumes of the *Mishneh Torah* is *Sefer Qedushah*, the *Book of Holiness*. This volume contains three sections: "Forbidden Intercourse," "Forbidden Foods," and "[Kosher] Slaughtering." What do these three issues have in common?

Maimonides explains in *Guide of the Perplexed* 3.35: The purpose of the laws concerning forbidden foods, he tells us there,

as we have explained in the Commentary on the *Mishnah* in the Introduction to *Avot*,[19] is to put an end to the lusts and licentiousness manifested in seeking what is most pleasurable and to taking the desire for food and drink as an end.

The laws concerning forbidden intercourse, he also explains there, are designed

to bring about a decrease of sexual intercourse and to diminish the desire for mating as far as possible, so that it should not be taken as an end, as is done by the ignorant, according to what we have explained in the Commentary on *Tractate Avot*.[20]

Maimonides does not explicitly explain the purpose of the laws concerning ritual slaughter here (indeed, he does not mention them at all in this passage in the *Guide of the Perplexed*), but it is not hard to see how they would fit into the rubric of forbidden foods.

Indeed, Maimonides makes this tolerably clear in his introduction to the *Mishneh Torah*, in which he describes *The Book of Holiness* as follows:

The Fifth Book. It includes in it precepts having reference to illicit sexual unions, and those that relate to forbidden foods; because in these two regards, the Omnipresent sanctified us and separated us from the nations, and of both classes of precepts it is said, *And I have set you apart from the peoples* (Leviticus 20:26), . . . , *Who have set you apart from the peoples* (Leviticus 20:24). I have called this book: The Book of Holiness.[21]

One achieves holiness by refraining from forbidden food and from forbidden sex.[22] That is why the laws concerning forbidden foods and the laws concerning ritual slaughtering (which turn certain classes of edibles from forbidden to permitted) are classed together in the *Book of Holiness*.

Maimonides derives this connection between holiness and refraining from forbidden activities from a midrashic passage cited in the fourth introductory principle to his *Book of Commandments*:

We are not to include charges which cover the whole body of the commandments of the Torah. There are injunctions and prohibitions in the Torah which do not pertain to any specific duty, but include all commandments . . . With respect to this principle other scholars have erred, counting *You shall be holy* (Leviticus 19:2) as one of the positive commandments – not knowing that the verses, *You shall be holy* (Leviticus 19:2) [and] *Sanctify yourselves, and be you holy* (Leviticus 11:44) are charges to fulfill the whole Torah, as if He were saying: "Be holy by doing all that I have commanded you to do, and guard against all things I have enjoined you from doing." The Sifra says: "*You shall be holy*, keep apart;" that is to say, hold aloof from all the abominations against which I have admonished you. In the Mekhilta the Sages say: "*And you shall be holy men unto Me* (Exodus 22:30) – Issi the son of Yehudah says: with every new commandment the Holy One, blessed be He, issues to Israel He adds holiness to them." That is to say, this charge is not an independent one, but is connected with the commandments wherein they have been enjoined there, since whoever fulfills that charge is called holy. Now this being so, there is then no difference between His saying, *You shall be holy*, and, "Obey My commandments." . . . The Sifre says: "*And you be holy* (Numbers 15:40), this refers to the holiness of the commandments."[23]

Maimonides explains here that the biblical statement, "You shall be holy," is not to be counted as one of the 613 commandments of the Torah because it encompasses the whole Torah. While doing so, Maimonides lets slip, as it were, a point crucial to our purposes: Jews are not made holy by having been given the commandments, rather, they become holy when they fulfill them. That does not mean that as one fulfills commandments one's ontological status changes from profane to holy; rather, it means that "holiness" is the way in which the Torah characterizes obedience to the commandments. As Maimonides says at the end of the passage, holiness refers to the holiness of [fulfilling] the commandments.

Returning to the exposition of this passage, Maimonides cites the explanation of *Midrash Sifra* to "You shall be holy": keep yourself apart or separate yourself from illicit enjoyments (*perishut* [renunciation]). From what in particular must one refrain in order to achieve holiness? In the *Mishneh Torah* Maimonides explains: forbidden foods and forbidden sex.

Maimonides connects the *perishut* spoken of here with the *Perushim*, or Pharisees, in "Ritual Impurity of Foods," 16.12:

Although it is permissible to eat ritually impure foodstuffs and to drink ritually impure liquids, the pious of former times used to eat their common food in conditions of ritual purity, and all their days they were wary of every ritual impurity. And it is they who were called Pharisees, "separated ones," and this is a higher holiness. It is the way of piety that a man keep himself separate and go apart from the rest of the people and neither touch them nor eat and drink with them. For separation leads to the purification of the body from evil deeds, and the purification of the body leads to the hallowing of the soul from evil thoughts, and the hallowing of the soul leads to striving for imitation of the Shekhinah [divine presence]; for it is said, *Sanctify yourselves therefore and be ye holy* (Leviticus 11:44), *for I the Lord Who sanctify you am holy* (Leviticus 21:8).[24]

Acting like the Pharisees is a form of "higher holiness." It involves separating oneself from all forms of ritual impurity and from all people who are in a state of ritual impurity. This is not because there is anything intrinsically wrong with being ritually impure.[25] It is because such separation "leads to the purification of the body from evil deeds," which, in turn, "leads to the hallowing of the soul from evil thoughts," which itself "leads to striving for imitation of the Shekhinah."

I understand Maimonides to be saying here that the aim of holiness is moral behavior (separation from evil deeds), which in turn makes possible intellectual perfection (separation from evil thoughts); that, in turn, brings one to strive for *imitatio Dei.*[26] This is to translate Maimonides' rabbinic vocabulary into the language of medieval Aristotelianism.[27] But one need not agree with this translation to see that on the evidence of the text here presented, holiness for Maimonides means the outcome of a kind of behavior. It is nothing that can be said to exist in and of itself, it is not some sort of superadded essence, it is nothing ontological. It is simply a name given to certain types of (extremely important, highly valued) behavior, and, by extension, to persons, places, times, and objects. It is, and this is a point which must be emphasized, something which is not given, but must be earned. Holiness is not an inheritable status.[28]

It is important to note that for Maimonides holiness in this sense is not restricted to Jews. Although I am not a devotee of the sort of Maimonidean numerology indulged in by Leo Strauss, sometimes it is simply too striking to be ignored. The *Mishneh Torah* comprises fourteen volumes. The precise midpoint, then, is the end of volume seven. Volume seven, devoted to laws relating to agricultural matters, ends with a section called "Sabbatical Year and Jubilee."[29] This section is divided into thirteen chapters. The thirteenth chapter is divided into thirteen paragraphs.[30] The last of these paragraphs reads as follows:

Not only the Tribe of Levi, but each and every individual human being,[31] whose spirit moves him and whose knowledge gives him understanding to set himself apart[32] in order to stand before the Lord, to serve Him, to worship Him, and to know Him, who walks upright as God created him to do, and releases himself from the yoke of the many foolish considerations which trouble people – such an individual is as sanctified as the Holy of Holies, and his portion and inheritance shall be in the Lord forever and ever. The Lord grant him adequate sustenance in this world, the same as He had granted to the priests and to the Levites. Thus indeed did David, peace upon him, say, *O Lord, the portion of mine inheritance and of my cup, Thou maintainest my lot.* (Psalm 16:5)[33]

Any human beings (Jews or non-Jews) who set themselves apart from the foolishness of ordinary pursuits, behave properly, worship God, and come to know God[34] are as sanctified as the Holy of Holies in the Temple in Jerusalem. Again, we see that holiness is a function of a kind of behavior; it is not an essentialist quality having ontological status. It is a *name*, not something really "out there" in the universe.

The universal character of holiness comes out in a second passage in the *Mishneh Torah*:

It is among the foundations of religion to know that God causes human beings to prophesy, and that prophecy does not rest upon anyone but a sage great in wisdom, powerful with respect to his [moral] qualities – [i.e.] one whose passions do not overpower him with respect to anything in the world, but, rather, through his intellect he always subdues his passions – and who has a very broad and well-established intellect. A person filled with all these qualities, sound of body, upon entering "pardes" and continuously dwelling upon those great and remote matters, and having an intellect prepared to understand and conceive them, and who continues to *sanctify* himself, by separating himself from the ways of most people who walk in the darkness of the times, and who zealously trains himself and teaches his mind not to have any thoughts concerning vain things, the nonsense of the time and its snares, but his mind is always directed above, bound under the throne in order to understand those sacred and pure forms, and who examines the entire wisdom of God from the first form till the navel of the world, learning from this God's greatness; the holy spirit immediately rests upon him, and at the time the spirit rests upon him, his soul mingles with the degree of the angels known as Ishim and he becomes another man, and understands through his intellect that he is not as he was, but has risen above the degree of other wise humans, as it says of Saul: "You will prophesy and become another man." (1 Samuel 10:6)[35]

The sanctification spoken of here relates to the process of becoming a prophet. As is well known, Maimonides teaches that prophecy is a natural, human quality.[36] All humans (Jew and Gentile) can, in principle, aspire to prophecy. One sanctifies oneself by separating oneself "from the ways of most people who walk in the darkness of the times." Becoming holy is a status open to all and is achieved through certain kinds of elevated behavior. If anyone can aspire to holiness, and if achieving it is consequent on behavior, holiness can hardly be ontological in any of the senses previously discussed.

We may now return to our argument. In the *Mishneh Torah* Maimonides makes holiness mean refraining from forbidden foods and forbidden sex. In his *Book of Commandments* he in effect explains that by connecting holiness to renunciation. After explaining (again in the *Mishneh Torah*) that the Pharisees were called such because they strove for a higher level of holiness through separation from improper behavior and thoughts, Maimonides connects two distinct verses to make a single argument: "Sanctify yourselves therefore and be ye holy" (Leviticus 11:44), "for I the Lord Who sanctify you am holy" (Leviticus 21:8). Holiness, as defined here, leads to *imitatio Dei.*

The notion of *imitatio Dei*, in turn, is connected by Maimonides to holiness in a variety of interesting ways. To see this, we must look at the first text in which Maimonides discusses the imitation of God, *Book of Commandments*, positive commandment eight:

Walking in God's ways. By this injunction we are commanded to be like God (praised be He) as far as it is in our power. This injunction is contained in His words, *And you shall walk in His ways* (Deuteronomy 28:9), and also in an earlier verse in His words, *[What does the Lord require of you, but to fear the Lord your God,] to walk in all His ways?* (Deuteronomy 10:2). On this latter verse the Sages comment as follows: "Just as the Holy One, blessed be He, is called merciful [*raḥum*], so should you be merciful; just as He is called gracious [*ḥanun*], so should you be gracious; just as he is called righteous [*Tsaddik*], so should you be righteous; just as He is called saintly [*ḥasid*], so should you be saintly."[37] This injunction has already appeared in another form in His words, *After the Lord Your God shall you walk* (Deuteronomy 13:5) which the Sages explain as meaning that we are to imitate the good deeds and lofty attributes by which the Lord (exalted be He) is described in a figurative way – He being immeasurably exalted above all such description.[38]

One imitates God through merciful, gracious, righteous, and saintly behavior. The point is reiterated in the second text in which Maimonides deals with the imitation of God, *Mishneh Torah* 1, Character Traits, 1.5–6:

The ancient saints trained their dispositions away from the exact mean towards the extremes; in regard to one disposition in one direction, in regard to another in the opposite direction. This was supererogation. We are bidden to walk in the middle paths which are the right and proper ways, as it is said, *and you shall walk in His ways* (Deuteronomy 28:9). In explanation of the text just quoted, the sages taught, "Even as He is called gracious, so be you gracious; even as He is called merciful, so be you merciful; even as He is called holy, so be you holy." Thus too the the prophets described God by all the various attributes, "long suffering and abounding in kindness, rightous and upright, perfect, mighty, and powerful," and so forth, to teach us that these qualities are good and right and that a human being should cultivate them, and thus imitate God, as far as he can.[39]

Maimonides changes his source here in interesting ways. The midrashic compilation *Sifrei*, followed by Maimonides in the *Book of Commandments*, spoke of mercy, graciousness, righteousness, and saintliness. The text here speaks of graciousness, mercy, and holiness. I subsequently discuss the possible significance of this, but here let it be noted that there is no known source for Maimonides' formulation. I have not examined all the known manuscripts of the *Sifrei*, but in printed texts the first time that "holiness" is introduced into this discussion is here in "Character Traits."[40]

In the third text in which Maimonides discusses *imitatio Dei*, *Guide of the Perplexed* 1.54, p. 128, he reverts to the original formulation of the *Sifrei*, or at least quotes part of it without the addition of holiness:

For the utmost virtue of man is to become like unto Him, may He be exalted, as far as he is able; which means that we should make our actions like unto His, as the Sages made clear when interpreting the verse, *Ye shall be holy* (Leviticus 19:2). They said: *He is gracious, so be you also gracious; He is merciful, so be you also merciful* (*Sifre* Deuteronomy 10:12). The purpose of all this is to show that the attributes ascribed to Him are attributes of His actions and that they do not mean that He possesses qualities.

Becoming Godlike, Maimonides makes very clear here, means behaving in a particular fashion. To achieve holiness, and thus to imitate God, one must act graciously and mercifully. Maimonides is not even willing to attribute holiness to God in any sort of essential or ontological fashion. "Holy, holy, holy! The Lord of Hosts! His glory fills all the earth!" said the prophet Isaiah, and what the prophet had to have meant, according to Maimonides, is that God's actions are gracious and merciful. If Maimonides is thus unwilling to attribute holiness to God in any sort of essential or ontological fashion, how much less so can he be willing to attribute it to any other entities, persons, places, and times.

It is very difficult to know what the addition of holiness to the passage from the *Sifrei* in "Character Traits" signifies. It is possible that Maimonides had a different text in front of him, but I consider that highly unlikely, and that for a number of reasons. He quotes the received text in the *Book of Commandments* and repeats at least part of it in the *Guide of the Perplexed*. Second, it seems odd that only Maimonides should have had access to a version including holiness, one that is quoted in no other source. It seems more likely to me (as has been suggested by most of Maimonides' commentators) that he purposefully introduced into the passage from the *Sifrei* a portion of another midrashic text, *Sifra* to Leviticus 19:2. That verse reads, "You shall be holy, for I, the Lord your God, am holy" and on it the *Sifra* says, "As I am holy, so you be holy."[41]

Is there any significance to this? In the context of our present discussion the following suggestion makes sense to me, but I must offer it tentatively, as there is no way to know if it is true. By introducing "holiness" into a passage talking of mercy and graciousness, Maimonides emphasizes the nonontological character of holiness. Just as mercy and graciousness are matters of action and character, so also is holiness. It is just possible, in other words, that Maimonides alters the text of the *Sifrei* in a way not likely to arouse comment in order to hint at his nonontological understanding of the holiness of persons.

To this point, I focused on how a person achieves holiness for Maimonides. I have argued that for Maimonides holiness is not some sort of superadded essence; it is the way in which Judaism characterizes what we might call (in a very non-Maimonidean idiom) "God-liked" behavior. One achieves holiness, not by becoming like God (hardly a possibility for any creature), but by imitating God's attributes of action; by acting, as it were, like God.[42] This being so, it should not surprise us to discover that it is behavior also which brings about the opposite of holiness, profanation:

There are other things that are a profanation of the Name of God. When a man, great in the knowledge of Torah and reputed for his piety does things which cause people to talk about him, even if the acts are not express violations, he profanes the Name of God. As, for example, if such a person makes a purchase and does not pay promptly, provided that he has means and the creditors ask for payment and he puts them off; or if he indulges immoderately in jesting, eating or drinking, when he is staying with ignorant people or living among them; or if his mode of addressing people is not gentle, or he does not receive people affably, but is quarrelsome and irascible. The greater a man is the more scrupulous he should be in all such things, and do more than the strict letter of the law requires. And if a man has been scrupulous in his conduct, gentle in his conversation, pleasant towards his fellow-creatures, affable in manner when receiving them, not retorting, even when affronted, but showing courtesy to all, even to those who treat him with disdain, conducting his commercial affairs with integrity, not readily accepting the hospitality of the ignorant nor frequenting their company, not seen at all times, but devoting himself to the study of Torah, wrapped in a prayer shawl and crowned with phylacteries, and doing more than his duty in all things, avoiding, however, extremes and exaggerations – such a man has sanctfied God, and concerning him, Scripture saith, *And He said unto me, 'Thou art My servant Israel, in whom I will be glorified.'* (Isaiah 49:3)[43]

God's name can be sanctified or profaned: It depends entirely on how one behaves.

It is not just individuals who are expected to lead holy lives; the people of Israel as a whole is also expected to be holy. In what sense is Israel a holy nation? In a series of studies[44] I have sought to defend the view that according to Maimonides Jews *as such* are in no way distinct from non-Jews. By this I mean that Maimonides rejected any understanding of the election of Israel that presented Jews as ontologically distinct from Gentiles and superior to them. That being the case, in whatever sense Israel may be called holy, it cannot be in ontological or essentialist terms. There must be something about the way in which the nation lives that makes it holy.

Maimonides held Jews to be distinct from Gentiles only to the extent that the former adhered to the Torah. In that he never doubted the divinity of the Torah, Maimonides also never doubted that true adherents of the Torah were, with very few exceptions, better people than those who did not adhere to it. I am not trying to say that Maimonides denied the idea of the election of Israel; that would be ridiculous. He held the idea, but in an unusual fashion.

Maimonides' conception of the election of Israel reflects other ideas of his. One of these is his adoption of the Aristotelian notions that human beings are rational animals[45] and that, when born, humans are only potentially rational. Adopting on a useful analogy suggested to me by Professor Daniel J. Lasker, all humans are born with the same hardware. What we do with that hardware (i.e., the software we run) determines the kind of people we become. Torah on this account is a challenge, not a gift, a demand, not an endowment.

Connected to all this is Maimonides' uncompromising and unprecedented insistence on strict doctrinal orthodoxy.[46] In effect, for Maimonides, in the final analysis, it is what we affirm (after we have learned to behave properly) that makes us what we are.

All this being so, it should come as no surprise that Maimonides does not count belief in the election of Israel as one of the dogmas of Judaism; indeed, to the best of my knowledge, he mentions the doctrine explicitly only once in all of his writings.[47] In fact, Maimonides' nominalism makes it impossible for him to attach any special qualities to the people of Israel as such (as opposed to individual Jews). "Israel" as a Platonic idea, so to speak, cannot exist. The term can be no more than a name, a convenient shorthand expression.

What, then, can we make of the holiness of the Jewish people? After all, the Torah itself teaches that the nation of Israel is holy:

> Now then, if you will obey Me faithfully and keep My covenant, you shall be My treasured possession among all the peoples. Indeed, all the earth is Mine, but you shall be to Me a kingdom of priests and a holy nation. These are the words that you shall speak to the children of Israel. (Exodus 19:5–6)

and

> For you are a people consecrated to the Lord your God: of all the peoples on earth the Lord your God chose you to be His treasured people. (Deuteronomy 7:6)

It seems clear to me that Maimonides must interpret passages such as these as normative and not descriptive. Indeed, this is precisely what he does with the first of them (he nowhere mentions the second[48]) in his *Book of Commandments*, as we previously saw.[49]

I have found two places in his writings, however, in which Maimonides might be thought to be attributing holiness to the people of Israel in a descriptive, as opposed to a prescriptive, fashion. The first of these is *Mishneh Torah* 5, Forbidden Intercourse, 19.17:

All families are presumed to be of valid descent and it is permitted to intermarry with them in the first instance. Nevertheless, should you see two families continually striving with one another, or a family which is constantly engaged in quarrels and altercations, or an individual who is exceedingly contentious with everyone, and is excessively impudent, apprehension should be felt concerning them, and it is advisable to keep one's distance from them, for these traits are indicative of invalid descent.... Similarly, if a person exhibits impudence, cruelty, or misanthropy, and never performs an act of kindness, one should strongly suspect that he is of Gibeonite descent, since the distinctive traits of Israel, the holy nation [*ha-ummah ha-kedoshah*], are modesty, mercy, and loving kindness, while of the Gibeonites it is said, *Now the Gibeonites were not of the children of Israel* (2 Samuel 21:2), because they hardened their faces and refused to relent, showing no mercy to the sons of Saul, nor would they do a kindness unto the children of Israel, by forgiving the sons of their king, notwithstanding that Israel showed them grace at the beginning and spared their lives.[50]

I think that it is fair to read Maimonides in this passage as writing persuasively. He wants to convince Jews to act with "modesty, mercy, and lovingkindness" *so as to be* a holy nation.[51] This is certainly consistent with the way in which Maimonides reads texts attributing holiness to (or, actually, demanding it of) individuals, as we previously saw.

The second passage is from *Mishneh Torah* 14, Sanhedrin, 25.1–2:

It is forbidden to lead the community in a domineering and arrogant manner. One should exercise one's authority in a spirit of humility and reverence. The man at the head of the congregation who arouses excessive fear in the hearts of the members thereof for any but a religious purpose will be punished. It will not be given to him have a son who is a scholar, as it is written: *Men do therefore fear him; he will not see any [sons] that are wise of heart* (Job 37:24). He is also forbidden to treat the people with disrespect, even if they are ignorant. He should not force his way through the holy people [*ʿam ha-qodesh*][52] [to get to his seat].[53] For even if they be simple and lowly, they are the children of Abraham, Isaac, and Jacob, the hosts of God, brought forth out of Egypt with great power and with a mighty hand.[54]

In this passage Maimonides calls the Jewish people "the holy people." The source of this expression is instructive: The prophet promises that the Jews will be called by a new name after the future redemption, "The Holy People, the Redeemed of the Lord."[55] The prophet is not characterizing the Jews as a holy people in the present, he is prophesying that they will be so called after the redemption. The appelation is predictive, not descriptive. Further, given the point Maimonides is driving home in this passage, that leaders should be meek in their demeanor (like Moses, as he explains in the continuation), it makes excellent sense for him to emphasize the special character of those led. Isaiah's expression works well for him in that fashion. It would be a mistake, it appears to me, to read out of this isolated expression a retreat from Maimonides' repeated position that holiness in people is a matter of their behavior, not of their essence.

Maimonides may be understood in all this as teaching that the Torah engages in what might be called the construction of social reality. Religious reality is not a given, not something found in the universe. Torah, for Maimonides, seeks to inject religious meaning into human life, as opposed to finding it already present in reality. A life thus lived is "spiritual." This has important consequences for our understanding of Maimonides. He is ordinarily understood as holding that only a life of philosophical examination of God is worth living. From our discussion here it is apparent that one can achieve a significant level of holiness, of spirituality, without philosophical perfection. Such a life is surely worthwhile, a life of meaning (even if it has no continuation in the world to come).[56]

Perishut, separation from moral impurity, may thus lead to a life of holiness, but it surely does not by itself lead to the best kind of spiritual life. To achieve that, one must go beyond separation from moral impurity to a life lived in the light of the love of God.

All Jews are commanded to love God: "You shall love the Lord your God with all your heart and with all your soul and with all your might" (Deuteronomy 6:5). Pious Jews recite this verse every morning and evening of every day of their lives. What is the nature of this love? Maimonides is often depicted as if he held love of God and knowledge of God to be identical.[57] This is not quite true.

Let us look at the texts in which Maimonides speaks of knowledge and love of God. He raises the issue explicitly first in "Principles of the Torah," 2.1:

And what is the way that will lead to the love of Him and the fear of Him? When a person contemplates his great and wondrous works and creatures and from them obtains a glimpse of His wisdom which is incomparable and infinite, he will *immediately* love Him, praise Him, glorify Him, and long with an exceeding longing to know His great name.[58]

Maimonides tells us here that love of God is an immediate consequence of knowing God; he does not reduce one to the other.

But there are other texts in which he seems more or less to equate the two: "One only loves God with the knowledge with which one knows him. According to the knowledge will be the love: if the former be little or much, so will the latter be little or much."[59] What Maimonides actually says here is that the more one knows God, the more one loves God. He does not say that love of God is nothing more than knowledge of God.

A passage in the *Guide of the Perplexed* seems to support both interpretations:

As for the dictum of Scripture: *And thou shalt love the Lord with all thy heart* (Deuteronomy 6:5) – in my opinion its interpretation is: with all the forces of your heart; I mean to say, with all the forces of the body, for the principle of all of them derives from the heart. Accordingly the intended meaning is... that you should make His apprehension the end of all your actions.[60]

On the one hand, we are told here that, in order to fulfill the Scriptural command to love the Lord, one must use all the forces of one's body. On the other hand, we are further told here that the goal of using all the forces of one's body to love the Lord is make knowledge of God the end of all one's actions. Everything we do should serve the end of furthering our knowledge of God.[61] The points made here are expressed again toward the end of the *Guide* (3.28, pp. 512–13):

...*with all thy heart, and with all thy soul, and with all thy might* (Deuteronomy 6:5). We have already explained[62] ... that this love becomes valid only through the apprehension of the whole of being as it is and through the consideration of His wisdom as it is manifested in it.

In this passage, Maimonides seems to present love of God as a consequence of knowledge of God, and not as the same thing. This makes excellent sense: Love of God means not just the intellection of truths about God, but the direction of all one's actions and of all one's body toward that love.

Near the end of the *Guide* (3.51, p. 621), Maimonides reiterates the relationship of dependence between love and knowledge: "Now we have made it clear several times that love is proportionate to apprehension." The more we know God, the more we love God.

What is the nature of this love we are commanded to have for God? Maimonides tells us in *Mishneh Torah* 1, Repentance, 10.5:

What is the love of God that is befitting? It is to love God with a great and exceeding love, so strong that one's soul shall be knit up with the love of God such that it is continually enraptured by it, like love-sick individuals whose minds are at no time free from passion for a particular woman, and are enraptured by her at all times ... even intenser should be the love of God in the hearts of those who love Him; they should be enraptured by this love at all times.[63]

Maimonides reiterates the point again in 10.6: "It is known and certain that the love of God does not become closely knit in a man's heart till he is continuously and thoroughly possessed by it and gives up everything else in the world for it" and makes much the same claim in some passages in the *Guide*, defining the passionate love of God as "an excess of love, so that no thought remains that is directed toward a thing other than the Beloved."[64]

Let us now look at the last passage in the *Guide* (3.52, p. 630) in which the issue comes up explicitly:

You know to what extent the Torah lays stress upon love: *With all thy heart, and with all thy soul, and with all thy might* (Deuteronomy 6:5). For these two ends, namely love and fear, are achieved through two things: love, through the opinions taught by the Law, which include the apprehension of His Being as He, may He be exalted, is in truth; while fear is achieved by means of all actions prescribed by the Law, as we have explained.

Maimonides' position here is tolerably clear: We achieve love of God through the apprehension of God's being to the greatest extent possible for humans. This does not mean that loving and apprehending God are the same.[65] Love of God means more than knowing God. True love of God involves knowledge of God, to be sure, but it also involves the direction of all one's heart, all one's soul, and all one's body to a life lived in the light of the love of God. The spiritual life for Maimonides thus has at least two crucial components: separation from moral impurity and love of God.

Maimonides' conception of the nature of holy living is a valuable key for understanding the complicated interplay of religious and philosophical issues in his thought and an invaluable key for unlocking his perception of the truly perfected (religious) life. As we have seen, philosophical ideas like nominalism and the transcendence of God led Maimonides to reject any notion of ontological holiness. This is connected in his thinking to two important and interrelated religious messages. The first has to do with a point emphasized by an important group of Maimonidean interpreters, in particular Hermann Cohen, Steven Schwarzschild, and Kenneth Seeskin: Holiness is an ethical ideal.[66] Holiness is not out there, waiting to be found, rather, it is made.

This has important implications: Holiness is not the sort of notion that can be restricted to any particular person, nation, object, place, or time. In principle, any person, any nation, and object, any place, any time can be holy. Holiness as an ethical challenge is thus addressed to all people, not to Jews alone. This, I think, sums up Maimonides' conception of the messianic era.

The second religious message that grows out of Maimonides' conception of the holy life relates to his understanding that human beings are given nothing on a silver platter. We are given tools and a challenge, and it is then up to us to the earn what we receive. God plays more than fair: The tools with which we are endowed are all that we need to achieve our perfection: parents, health, ability to seek what is good for us, and intellectual abilities. It is then up to us to take advantage of all these and make something of our lives. In particular, it is up to us to make of our lives something holy, not something wasted. All this fits in well with Maimonides' overall approach: humanity, Judaism, divine providence, prophecy, immortality; none of these are given us as presents, rather, we can achieve them if we apply ourselves diligently. Maimonides' conception of holy living both contributes to and follows from his conception of Judaism as a religion of challenges, not of endowments.

Ultimately, and this perhaps explains why Maimonides' vision of Judaism has attracted so few adherents over the generations, his is a religion addressed to emotionally and spiritually mature human beings (not Jews specifically, human beings generally): It is a religion of challenges, not endowments; of demands, not bequests. It is, admittedly, the religion of an elite, but it is open to all willing to make the effort to join that elite, and it aims toward a (messianic) future when all will have joined that elite.

NOTES

1. Genesis 1:1–3. I cite from *Tanakh*, 1985; the relevant phrase ("a wind from God sweeping over the waters") is more traditionally translated as "And the spirit of the Lord hovered over the face of the waters."
2. I am deeply grateful to Professor Joshua Golding for helping me to think through this issue; he is no way responsible for the use to which I put his insights here!
3. I put the word "only" in scare quotes to emphasize that, on the view I find in Maimonides, holiness is indeed "only" institutional, but still extremely important; but as Halevi would understand him, Maimonides' view makes holiness *only* institutional, i.e., relatively unimportant.
4. I cite the translation of Barry Kogan, forthcoming in the Yale Judaica Series. I wish to thank Professor Kogan for his collegial generosity in sharing the translation with me before publication.
5. For a discussion of different views on the nature of the distinction between Jew and Gentile, see Kellner 1991a.
6. Even 2 Samuel 6 and 1 Chronicles 13, often understood as teaching that the ark of the covenant had some sort of inherent and dangerous holiness, do not teach that. Uzzah's death was not an automatic consequence of his having touched the holy ark, but was a *punishment* by God for having done so. Similarly, with the account in 1 Samuel 5, the sufferings of the Philistines were *inflicted* by God as punishment and warning. There is nothing of Indiana Jones in the biblical text itself.
7. *GP* 3.18, p. 474. Maimonides repeats the point at the end of the same chapter (p. 476): "It would not be proper for us to say that providence watches over the species and not the individuals, as is the well-known opinion of some philosophic schools. For outside the mind nothing exists except the individuals; it is to these individuals that the divine intellect is united. Consequently providence watches only over these individuals." Maimonides immediately continues thus: "Consider this chapter as it ought to be considered; for through it all the fundamental principles of the Law will become safe for you and conformable for you to speculative philosophic opinions; disgraceful views will be abolished. . . . " Elisheva Oberman and Josef Stern first drew my

attention to these passages. Alfred Ivry makes this perceptive comment: "Maimonides, as a good Aristotelian and would-be nominalist, would like to 'save the phenomena' and not add to them immaterial entities of a conjectural and ultimately redundant sort." See Ivry 1992, p. 116. Maimonides' nominalism affects other aspects of his thought. See Silman 1986.

8. In Kellner 1991a, I argue that Maimonides maintained that Jews as such were in no way intrinsically different from any other people. I did not connect that issue to his nominalism, as I do here. I hope to issue a revised and greatly expanded Hebrew translation of my book, in which the point made here will be taken up at much greater length. In the meantime, see Kellner 1993b, 1996, 2001a, 2001b.
9. I defend many of these assertions in Kellner forthcoming.
10. See the second and third of Maimonides' "Thirteen Principles," *MT* 1, Principles of the Torah, 1.8, and *GP* 1.54.
11. My thinking on the question of holiness in Maimonides was greatly helped by W. Harvey 1977; Seeskin 1996, 2000, pp. 93–109, 115–23, and 134; Kreisel 1999, pp. 50–3 and 151–6; and Silman 1993.
12. That is, matters of ritual purity and impurity are "fancied notions," having no objective correlates in the "real" world.
13. Babylonian Talmud, Tractate *Berakhot* 22a.
14. *GP* 3.47, pp. 595–6.
15. *Gezerat ha-katuv*. On this expression see the discussion in Stern 1998, pp. 49–66.
16. This statement is interesting in light of the claim made by Maimonides in *GP* that the divine statutes [*ḥukkim*] can be understood. On the whole issue see Stern 1998.
17. *Deʿot raʿot*. For many reasons I would prefer to follow Herbert Danby and translate this as "false convictions" but I fear that would be incorrect. On the expression *deʿah* as "moral quality" in Maimonides, see *GP* 3.35, p. 535. For discussion, see Septimus 2001.
18. Immersion Pools, 11.12. I cite from Danby 1954, p. 535, with emendations and emphases added. For an extended discussion of this passage see Kellner forthcoming.
19. Maimonides prefaced his commentary to the mishnaic tractate *Avot* with an introduction consisting of eight chapters. This text is generally known as *The Eight Chapters of Maimonides*; the reference here is to the fourth of them.
20. *GP* 3.35, p. 537.
21. I cite the translation of Hyamson 1974, p. 18b.
22. Further on this connection, see Character Traits, 5.4 and *GP* 3.33 (p. 533). Relevant also is Forbidden Intercourse, 22.20.

23. See Chavel 1967, Vol. 2, pp. 380–1 (emended).
24. Danby 1954, p. 393. Compare *GP* 3.33, p. 533, and, on the connection between holiness and *perishut*, *MT* 1, Principles of the Torah, 7.1 (quoted at n. 36 of this chapter) and 7.7. See further *CM*, Sotah 3.3.
25. Maimonides writes in paragraph 9,

 > Just as it is permissible to eat and drink common food that is ritually impure, so it is permissible to allow ritual impurity to befall common food in the Land of Israel; and ritual impurity may be imparted to common food that is at the outset in fit and proper condition. Similarly, it is permissible to touch any things that are ritually impure, and to incur ritual impurity from them, for Scripture warns none but the sons of Aaron and the Nazirite against incurring ritual impurity from a corpse, thereby implying that for all other people it is permissible, and that it is permissible even for priests and Nazirites to incur ritual impurity from other ritually impure things, except only the ritual impurity of corpses.

26. The point made here is well stated by Kreisel 1999, p. 156: "The dominant motif characterizing Maimonides' discussions of God is the negation of corporeality. His view of holiness as lying in the ethical virtues in general, and restraint of corporeal desires in particular, connects this notion with the negation of one's own corporeality. One must particularly negate that which is associated with the most corporeal of our senses." The literature on Maimonides' conception of human perfection is vast. Much of it is summarized and analyzed in Kellner 1990. Later studies include: Benor 1995; Bruckstein 1997; W. Harvey 1994; Kasher 1998; Kreisel 1991; Rosenberg 1983; Seeskin 2000, pp. 97–106; Shatz 1990; and Lorberbaum 1999.
27. For a defense of this approach, see Kellner 1999, pp. 127–141.
28. In general, I agree with Avraham Nuriel's criticism of Yeshayahu Leibowitz's interpretation of Maimonides, to the effect that there is relatively little actually of Maimonides in Leibowitz's exposition of his thought; but on at least one important issue, I believe that Leibowitz was absolutely correct. As Leibowitz used to like to say in his many public lectures on Maimonides, the latter insisted that humans are given nothing on a silver platter; everything must be earned. It can be shown that for Maimonides this "everything" includes one's humanity, one's status as a Jew, providence, prophecy, a share in the world to come, and, as I am arguing here, holiness. See Nuriel 2000.
29. For Maimonides, the reinstitution of the Jubilee is intimately connected to the messianic era. See *MT* 14, Kings and Wars, 11.1. It not likely to be simply coincidental that the passage cited immediately below ends the first half of the *MT* and a discussion of messianism ends the second half.

30. The significance of the number thirteen in Judaism and for Maimonides (the author, it must be recalled of "Thirteen Principles" of Judaism) is addressed by R. Isaac Abravanel (1437–1508) in *Rosh Amanah*, Chapter 10. See Kellner 1993a, p. 79, and Kellner 1982, p. 98. Abravanel missed an important Maimonidean source in this connection: *MT* 2, Circumcision, 3.9.
31. *Kol ish va-ish me-kol ba'ei 'olam*. That Maimonides understands the expression to mean all human beings is made clear in Sanhedrin, 12.3 and Kings, 8.10.
32. *Le-hibbadel*. It would have been helpful for the argument being made here had Maimonides used some variant of *p-r-sh* (from which the word "Pharisee" is derived) in this passage, as he could have, but one must deal with texts as written, not as one would like them to have been written.
33. I quote (with emendations) from Klein 1979, p. 403.
34. By which I take Maimonides to mean that one can achieve intellectual perfection only after having achieved moral perfection (through performance of the commandments, at least where Jews are concerned). I need not insist on this interpretation, however, in order to advance the argument being made here.
35. *MT* 1, Principles of the Torah, 7.1, emphasis added. On this passage, see Kellner 2001b, pp. 36–42.
36. *GP* 2.32.
37. Maimonides quotes here (in the original Hebrew, even though the *Book of Commandments* was written in Arabic) from *Sifrei* Deuteronomy, *piska* 49, without the prooftexts found in the *Sifrei*.
38. Quoted with emendations from Chavel 1967, Vol. 1, pp. 12–13.
39. Quoted, with emendations, from Hyamson 1974a, pp. 47b–48a.
40. The *Sifrei* passage is found, in various forms, in half a dozen places in rabbinic literature. Although some of the traditionalist commentaries on the *MT* take note of the textual discrepancy, none seem to think it worthy of particular attention.
41. This passage from the *Sifra* is quoted by Maimonides in the text from *GP* 3.47, cited at n. 16 of this chapter.
42. In *GP* 1.54 Maimonides explains that God may be known through His actions only, and not as He is, in and of Himself. For further details, see Kenneth Seeskin's chapter in this volume.
43. *MT* 1, Principles of the Torah, 5.11; Hyamson 1974a, pp. 41a–41b.
44. Note 9 of this chapter.
45. In his earliest work, *Logical Terms*, Maimonides wrote, "Rationality we call man's difference, because it divides and differentiates the human

species from others; and this rationality, i.e., the faculty by which ideas are formed, constitutes the essence of man" (*Logical Terms*, 10). See the translation of Israel Efros 1938, pp. 51–2. Herbert Davidson has recently raised questions about the attribution of this text to Maimonides. See Davidson 2001. But even if we accept Davidson's conclusions about this text, there can be no doubt that Maimonides held the view here attributed to him. For texts and discussion, see Kellner 2002.

46. For discussion, see Kellner 1999.
47. *MT* 1, Idolatry, 1.3: "After Moses had begun prophesying and God chose Israel as an inheritance, He crowned them with commandments and taught them how to worship Him." God sent Moses to save the Jews in Egypt from a total relapse into idolatry. This, Maimonides says, God did, "out of His love for us and in order to keep His oath to Abraham." God loves the Jews, not because they are ontologically unlike other nations, but because of the love Abraham showed God and the oath He in consequence made to him. My thanks to Professor Warren Zev Harvey for drawing this text to my attention. It is worth noting in this context that Maimonides rarely speaks of God's love for human beings. The passage quoted here is one of the rare exceptions to that generalization. This passage, I might further note, appears to be based on Deuteronomy 4:37, a verse nowhere cited explicitly by Maimonides.
48. I rely here on Qāfīḥ 1972.
49. In *GP* 2.35 (p. 368) Maimonides cites Exodus 19:6 to emphasize the greatness of Moses; he cites the verse in a clearly normative and prescriptive fashion in 3.8 (p. 435) and so also in 3.32 (p. 526).
50. Rabinowitz and Grossman 1965a, p. 125.
51. In Kellner 2001, I analyze this passage and show that it makes little sense to read it as if Maimonides is actually attributing particular moral qualities to Jews and to Gibeonites.
52. See Isaiah, 62:12: And they shall be called 'The Holy People, the Redeemed of the Lord.'
53. Literally: "march over the heads of the holy people."
54. Cited, with emendations, from Hershman 1949, p. 75.
55. Malbim's commentary on this verse is exquisitely Maimonidean: The Jews will be *called* a holy nation thanks to the holiness of their actions and their righteousness.
56. For Maimonides, if there is any afterlife at all, it is only for those who have perfected their intellects. For details, see Kellner 1999, pp. 127–41.
57. For recent studies of Maimonides on the love of God, see Lamm, 1992–3; Kreisel 1999, chapter 7; and Seeskin 2000, pp. 158–65.
58. Hyamson 1974a, p. 35b.
59. *MT* 1, Repentance, 10.6; Hyamson 1974a, p. 92b.

60. 1. 39, p. 89.
61. There are some passages in which Maimonides makes this explicit. See *MT* 1, Character Traits, 3.2: "A man should direct all his thoughts and activities to the knowledge of God, alone." All one's activities, even cohabitation, should have thus ultimate end in view (Hyamson 1974a, p. 49b).
62. In *MT* 1, Principles of the Torah, 2.1–2 and the fifth of the *Eight Chapters*, among other places.
63. Hyamson 1974a, p. 92b.
64. See S. Harvey 1997.
65. Compare further, Benor 1995, pp. 56–8. For a very useful discussion of love and knowledge in Maimonides see Kaplan 1995.
66. See Seeskin 1996.

AVIEZER RAVITZKY

11 Maimonides

Esotericism and Educational Philosophy

> Understand his way: affirmation replaces negation and tranquility replaces turmoil the reverse is reversed all in order to conceal the forbidden.
>
> Samuel of Lunel on Maimonides[1]

11.1. A DIVISION OF OPINIONS

At the beginning of the thirteenth century, just a few years after Maimonides' death, his Hebrew translator Samuel Ibn Tibbon sketched a critical and incisive picture of his contemporaries and their response to Maimonides' philosophic teaching. None of the readers or interpreters of the *Guide* were omitted. On the one hand, he wrote, "Many of our generation revile his words and called his light darkness." They vilified Maimonides' writings and found them religiously defective. On the other hand, there are people who support Maimonides, but they too betray his original intention. They accept his teaching only because they have not understood its full import: "Had they however fully understood the profound intention of the Master, they would have undoubtedly acted just as their [anti-Maimonidean] colleagues, and only a very few would remain [Maimonidean]."[2] The community was thus divided between critics, who attacked Maimonides for his audacity, and supporters, many of whom ignored it. Only a precious few succeeded in plumbing the depths of his doctrine, and only these were worthy of being called his true followers.

Clearly the author of these words was unmoved by public opinion. On the contrary, he emphasized the deep chasm between

Maimonides' beliefs and the traditional beliefs of his contemporary coreligionists. In his view Maimonides' religious doctrines were far more radical than many of his readers imagined, perhaps even more radical than his opponents imagined. Beneath Maimonides' overt statements lurked obscure and far more controversial views. Ibn Tibbon was keenly aware that disclosure of this covert dimension could exact a high price, but he was not deterred; in his view, the secrets of the *Guide* are identical to the secrets of the Torah.

Although Ibn Tibbon's views reflect the ideological schism of his own time, they anticipated the two central controversies that have characterized Maimonides scholarship over the centuries. The first dealt with the legitimacy of the overt doctrines of the *Guide*. It subjected them to a critical assessment focusing on Maimonides' explicit beliefs and the intellectual trends from which they emerged. The second concerned interpretation of the *Guide* rather than assessment. It asked, What is the correct method for its study? and it tried to "fully understand the profound intention of the master" and discover his hidden secrets. Unlike the former controversy, this one focused on the issue of esotericism.

The first controversy began during Maimonides' lifetime and climaxed during the thirteenth century, deeply dividing the Jewish communities of Spain and Provence. As Maimonides' legal authority grew, the tone and impact of the critique became more restrained. The target was no longer Maimonides himself but rather his philosophy, his students, or his interpreters – in the modern period, against "the forgers" who had supposedly falsified his writings.[3] Generally speaking, Maimonides' personality was elevated far above the tumult of the discussion. In this way, the author of the *Mishneh Torah* protected the author of the *Guide* and conferred him with legitimacy.

A different fate awaited the controversy over the secrets of the *Guide*. Here the tone became more intensive, perhaps because of Maimonides' growing stature among rabbinic authorities. It was to be expected that many scholars felt compelled to ascertain the philosophical views of the most eminent legal [*halakhic*] authority since the sealing of the Talmud. It was an issue that did not lend itself to dispassionate discussion. In fact, the controversy over the esoteric Maimonides spilled over to the modern period and reappeared with renewed energy in the twentieth century.

These developments contain an element of irony, perhaps even paradox. In his legal writings, Maimonides attempted to resolve disputes that had arisen over the meaning and implication of the commandments. There is every reason to think he wanted to do something similar for philosophy. Given the exigencies of life in exile, and what he considered the loss of a whole tradition of Jewish learning, the need to formulate an acceptable theology was imperative. Nonetheless the response evoked by Maimonides' philosophical writings had a divisive effect, giving rise to a multidimensional polemic: theological, interpretative, and evaluative.

The dispute regarding the "authentic" Maimonides rapidly became a debate over the essence of Judaism and its identity. What is Torah and what is reason? What are the foundations of faith? What is the difference between "internal" and "external" sources of meaning? What exactly did Maimonides mean by "the true science of the Law?" These issues became an integral part of the controversy. The proliferation of disputes led to a proliferation of interpretive options and to new paths of understanding. Even if Maimonides intended to establish foundations and fix the borders of the religion, the floodgates were opened and the borders expanded.

The debate was fueled by the juxtaposition of exoteric and esoteric teachings in the *Guide*. Maimonides himself asked his enlightened readers to pore over its hidden meanings. The fact that these meanings were not apparent made it inevitable that people would come up with different accounts of what was said: some conservative, some radical, some harmonious, some dichotomous, some agnostic, some dialectic. Thus it was the search for hidden meanings that led to a widening of the borders, providing intellectual breadth for those who were unable to find it within the constraints of traditional doctrines.[4] With each interpreter coming up with a different view of what was concealed, Maimonides' writing created any number of problems. With new problems came yet more controversy and growing areas of discussion and exploration.

This chapter attempts to clarify Maimonides' esotericism and its place in Jewish intellectual history. I have addressed the question in two other places and will not recapitulate what has already been said.[5] Because over the past few years a series of new studies has appeared, I attempt to take a bird's-eye view of the topic and offer a critical response. Rather than destroy and reconstruct, my intention is to reflect and clarify.

11.2. PEACE AND TRUTH

According to Maimonides, the ideal law has two goals: social welfare and intellectual development. The first aims to establish order, guarantee personal security, and prevent violence. The second aims to inculcate correct opinions within the community and guide its members toward intellectual and spiritual perfection. It thereby directs people along the path of truth. The fulfillment of both functions rather than the first alone is what distinguishes divine law from human.[6]

The question is whether the two functions are compatible or promote one another. Maimonides had no doubt about influence in one direction: from social harmony to the pursuit of truth. Without the former, the latter would be all but impossible. But what about the reverse? Is truth a precondition for a peaceful society? Or, to put it another way: Is a society that has been exposed to critical thinking more secure than one that has not?

Like several of his predecessors, Maimonides did not believe that society could rest on a purely intellectual foundation. In fact he warned that truth should not be disseminated indiscriminately, without consideration for the capacity of people to accommodate it. Critical reflection may undermine commonly accepted beliefs and wreak havoc on social and ethical norms. Worse, it does not necessarily provide a reliable alternative. Although the pursuit of truth has the power to construct, it also has the power to destroy. Thus people who have not been trained for this sort of reflection may find themselves with no convictions at all and jeopardize the social order as a result.[7]

We can illustrate this by a parable. Had Maimonides attended Socrates' trial, he would have understood part of the prosecutors' motive. Presumably he would not have demanded Socrates execution, but he would have attempted to silence him – precisely because he knew Socrates' questions were valid. Socrates was unflinching in his quest for truth. In his own words, "All day long I never cease to settle here, there and everywhere rousing, persuading, reproving every one of them."[8] Important as it is, in Maimonides' opinion, this kind of intellectual "persuasion" does not belong in the public realm for not only does it endanger the philosopher, it endangers society as well. Maimonides was concerned with the preservation of the social order and, in the terminology of our parable, placed the welfare of the Athenians above that of Socrates.[9]

In other words, Maimonides was well aware that social order relies on myths, conventions, and preconceived notions, and this it is. For practical purposes cherished memories and noble human models can be more important than physics or metaphysics. By the same token, scriptural narrative can be more important than philosophical argument and images of the divine will more important than knowledge of a first cause. Moreover, there is no escaping the influence of social order on primal fears. In his words,[10]

> The Law also makes a call to adopt certain beliefs, belief in which it is necessary for the sake of political welfare, such, for instance, is our belief that He, may He be exalted, is violently angry with those who disobey Him and that it is therefore necessary to fear Him and to dread Him.... In some cases a commandment communicates a correct belief, which is the one and only thing aimed at.... In other cases the belief is necessary for the abolition of reciprocal wrongdoing or for the acquisition of a noble moral quality – as, for instance, the belief that He, may He be exalted, has a violent anger against those who do injustice.

The enlightened student will not be misled. His God is above emotions such as wrath and fury and any other characteristics that imply corporeality. His God is independent of man and unaffected by their acts. The divine "anger" of Scripture is nothing but a human projection on the divine.[11] In other words the wise student will distinguish between a functional belief, whose goal is social welfare, and a belief that is true regardless of its utility. But this is a matter for personal reflection or discussion with a close circle of students. In public even the enlightened person must put utility first.

The majority of Maimonides' medieval commentators were aware of this problem, and some even made it the crux of their interpretation of the *Guide*. Twentieth-century scholars too have taken a renewed interest in it. The credit for this is primarily due to Leo Strauss' contribution to the study of esotericism in philosophy in general and in Maimonides' writings in particular.[12] Relying on the methodological guidelines laid down by Maimonides himself, Strauss and his followers emphasize that the *Guide* addresses its reader by way of revealing and concealing at the same time. It is replete with hints and doublespeak, its central teachings are conveyed piecemeal, with diversions and dispersions. It repeatedly uses covert phrases or repeats previous comments with slight alterations, thus hiding critical messages.

Nor does Maimonides hesitate to contradict himself on the most sensitive subjects, assuming that only the most perceptive reader will notice and that only he will be able to distinguish between the author's secrets and the smokescreen enveloping them from all sides. In other words, a superior philosophic work must confer to its readers the "necessary" opinions together with the "correct" opinions. These are given respectively to the public at large (addressing its imagination) and to the select individuals (addressing its intellect) capable of understanding the true meaning. This was the method adopted by Scripture on cosmological and theological issues, and Maimonides follows in kind. Although he altered the method of obfuscation, he was a firm believer in the principle.

One would be hard pressed to overstate the importance of Strauss' contribution to understanding the *Guide*. But in my view, his interpretation triggers two questions. The first has two parts: Who may enter the sanctum of secrecy? What is the optimal relationship between the enlightened individual and the community? According to Strauss, Maimonides erected a rigid division between them. He created a clear dichotomy between the wise and the masses, designating clear and fixed spheres of interest for each. This division between truth and society is a given that defines the fundamental structure of society and is unaffected by any progress in education.[13] Truth and society are locked in a permanent struggle unless truth hides its face and requests intellectual asylum. This intuition left an indelible imprint on the study of Maimonides in the twentieth century. In the past I too tended toward this view, but according to my present understanding, it requires revision.

The second question is this: What is Maimonides secret? Where does he see the clash between intellect and imagination, or knowledge and preconception? According to Strauss, Pines[14] (at least until their later writings),[15] and their followers, it is the contradiction between faith and reason, religion and philosophy, or Jerusalem and

Athens. Any attempt to harmonize these different worlds is an illusion, remote from the mind of Maimonides the philosopher though close to the heart of Maimonides the religious leader. In its external dimension, the *Guide* presents religious beliefs; in its internal dimension, it conceals philosophic truth. Not surprisingly this method triggered a sharp controversy, with interpretations of Maimonides echoing the personal convictions of his interpreters. The last generation has witnessed a series of alternative interpretations, each with its own characterization of Maimonides' esotericism. This trend too is reviewed in the next section.

II.3. EDUCATIONAL PHILOSOPHY

I begin with the chasm separating the enlightened few from the masses. The picture that emerges from Strauss and Pines is one of dichotomy: Beliefs are true in themselves or necessary for their utility; people pursue knowledge or rely on imagination; communities are enlightened or ignorant. The division between them is rigid and can be breached only by a select few who have mastered philosophy under the tutelage of a fully conversant teacher.[16] From the standpoint of society as a whole, such development is of no interest.

Such a depiction fails to do justice to the full scope of Maimonides' doctrine. No doubt, he emphasized the disparity between the two extremes of the society: the educated and the ignorant. However, he did not understand it as a rigid barrier and certainly did not perceive it as an exhaustive description of society as a whole. He regarded humanity as a broad spectrum, with a permanent flow between the two extremes. Accordingly Maimonides conceded that necessary opinions are a pragmatic imperative, but he rejected the option of letting society wallow in its inferior understanding.

The proper society should provide its members with a cautious transition from socially necessary beliefs to true ones. It must ensure their spiritual advancement, continually providing them with the ladder of intellectual ascent, each person according to his own capacity. The person for whom the secret was concealed yesterday may yet merit its unveiling tomorrow. Moreover the movement is not limited to the individual realm; it spills to the collective as well. Maimonides considered the possibility of improvement in the spiritual condition of an entire society and assigned importance to the intellectual ebb and flow of their progress. In this way, he took up the question of how many of the Torah's secrets ought to be revealed.

In brief, a person is not fated to be either enlightened or vulgar. People are allowed to grow, improve themselves or their society, and aspire the ideal of a society in which everyone is devoted to the pursuit of truth. As we will see, such a vision has interesting implications for Maimonides' understanding of the messianic vision. Although on one level society's welfare is founded on necessary beliefs, on another Maimonides turns the tables and suggests that it may be founded on true beliefs.

In illustrating this point I proceed from the individual to the collective. It will be recalled that Maimonides' emphasized that the Law was not concerned exclusively with social governance and improvement of character; it was also concerned with the pursuit of knowledge. Thus the humanity with whom the Law attempts to achieve its mission is not organized into a static dichotomy but a spectrum in which progress can and in many instances has occurred. According to Maimonides, the Law "desires to make man wise, to give him understanding, and to awaken his attention, so that he should know the whole of that which exists in its true form."[17] In other words, the Torah itself placed the ladder of intellectual growth on earth, enabling every person to ascend and reach for heaven.

Looking over Maimonides' own career, philosophic knowledge was not reserved for the ideal readers of the *Guide*. It is also entrenched in the *Mishneh Torah*, which was intended for everyone.[18] In fact the first book of the *Mishneh Torah* is titled "Basic Principles of the Torah." It is possible that a reader lacking philosophic training might fail to grasp its full import. Nonetheless these foundations provide the reader his first encounter with cosmology and metaphysics and might even raise him to the level of the "perplexed," the philosophic seeker of truth.

By the same token, Scriptures address the reader by way of parables and metaphors. On the one hand, this literary form was designed to serve an esoteric need: It presents the secrets of the Torah in a suppressed and obscure manner, concealing them from the unqualified reader. On the other hand, it fulfills a didactic need: It concretizes abstract ideas, making them more intelligible to the attentive reader.[19] So our concern is not with truth versus necessity or intellect versus imagination. An image is not a sham; it concretizes truth and makes it acccessible. Furthermore it is possible that in certain cases not only does teaching by parable satisfy a didactic imperative, it also answers a philosophic need: Symbols and metaphors are used for imparting metaphysical ideas not given to verbal expression through normal means. It reflects the limitations of language and the elusive nature of truth.[20] Either way, the parable does not divide the society into two groups; it may simultaneously address all of its members at the particular level of every person.

We should also recognize that, according to Maimonides, prophets were philosophers who, in addition to their ability to think, had the ability to organize society and communicate with the average person. Although the meaning of this claim is disputed, many scholars agree that it conferred philosophers with religious legitimacy.[21] Is this legitimacy conferred to the philoso*pher* only or to philoso*phy* as well? In other words, did it grant legitimacy to Maimonides alone or to intellectual achievement in general? In my view, only the second is tenable. The claim that the prophet is also a philosopher was intended not only to protect the enlightened person but also to bring the people closer to the level of the enlightened. It was not intended to sharpen the dichotomy but to soften and, wherever possible, to overcome it.

Interestingly, in the generations after Maimonides, many of his disciples were engaged in the philosophic exegesis of Scripture, book after book, even verse by verse.[22] This literary enterprise exemplified the Maimonidean identification of Torah with wisdom, the prophet with the philosopher. Naturally it also contributed to the legitimization of scientific studies and their entry into Jewish scholarship. It was not by chance that during subsequent generations the same circle of authors, disciples of Maimonides, prepared Hebrew translations of general philosophic literature. Their goals were identical: to make philosophy accessible to the Jewish community. All those involved in this undertaking believed that their actions gave concrete expression to Maimonides' objective.

I have no intention of belittling the importance ascribed by Maimonides to the concealment of radical views and to the distinction between necessary and true beliefs. In discussing the need to hide certain beliefs behind deliberate contradictions, he makes this claim:

> Sometimes in the case of certain dicta this necessity requires that the discussion proceed on the basis of a certain premise, whereas in another place

necessity requires that the discussion proceed on the basis of another premise contradicting the first one. In such cases the vulgar must in no way be aware of the contradiction; the author accordingly uses some device to conceal it by all means."[23]

Numerous commentators in the Middle Ages regarded such contradictions as the crux of the *Guide* and key to understanding issues like creation, prophecy, providence, and divine commandments. As stated by Yom Tov Eshbili (Ritba), a prominent fourteenth-century legal authority: "A cardinal rule for the diviner of secrets is that one should be aware of the frequent appearances of contradictions both in the Scriptures and in the words of the Rabbis. [Moreover], as the secret becomes more profound so does the necessity of its concealment, therefore, only a few words [in such texts] represent the truth and most of them represent its opposite."[24]

Still some interesting facts bear mention. First, other medieval authors of renown wrote equally esoteric works so that Maimonides' uniqueness is attributable to one factor: He prefaced his work with an explicit caveat, saying that he would intersperse his exposition with assertions premised on conflicting assumptions in order to disguise his real intent.[25] Such a public declaration is paradoxical because it almost forces the secret on the reader: Why would a philosopher begin his work by admitting he intended to hide his meaning and by explicitly explaining his methodology of concealment? Was he addressing only the enlightened reader or was he also promoting the textual sensitivity and intellectual curiosity of the student taking his first hesitant steps?

Second, Maimonides dropped a broad hint that contradictions of this kind could be found in the Scriptures themselves: "Whether contradictions due to the seventh cause [intentional concealment] are to be found in the books of the prophets is a matter for speculative study and investigation."[26] So this lesson in esotericism is not limited to the interpretation of Maimonides but can also be used in the interpretation of the sacred literature of Judaism. Third, Maimonides declared that, in addition to politically motivated contradictions, the *Guide* would also incorporate contradictions necessitated by pedagogic considerations. The latter would not obfuscate and conceal but divulge and explain, enabling the student's progression from the crude to the complex. In this case, the contradiction was a lifeline cast to the worthy student, gradually elevating him from the lower (fallacious) stratum of political contradiction to the peaks of intellectual cognition.[27]

To repeat: Maimonides' assessment of the human condition was dynamic. He believed in the possibility of philosophic education. He unequivocally affirmed this belief by giving it normative expression in the *Mishneh Torah*. He distinguished there between the inferior level, manifested in the "fear of God," from the superior level, manifested in the "love of God," which is attained by scholars and prophets. But he added another factor, the path leading from fear to love, from ignorance to illumination[28]:

> When instructing the young, women, or the illiterate generally, we teach them to serve God out of fear or for the sake of reward, till their knowledge increases and they have attained a large measure of wisdom. Then we reveal to them this secret truth, little by little, and train them by easy stages till they have grasped and comprehended it, and serve God out of love."

Maimonides chose his words carefully and left no doubt about the intellectual content of the worship of God. In my understanding, the truth of this claim is not limited to the exoteric level but permeates the esoteric level as well.[29]

That raises the question of whether Maimonides was concerned exclusively with the growth of the individual or whether he also considered the growth of society as a whole. I opt for the second. According to Maimonides, from the time of Scripture to his own day, there has been steady development in the intellectual capacity of the public at large. In ancient times, one could speak of God only in corporeal terms. Any attempt to move toward belief in a God without corporeal qualities was destined to fail: "Hence attributes indicating corporeality have been predicated of Him in order to indicate that He, may He be exalted, exists, inasmuch as the multitude cannot at first conceive of any existence save that of a body alone."[30] But in later periods, when idolatry had all but disappeared, the war was primarily waged against the pagan *consciousness*, manifested in the idea that God had human attributes.[31] Accordingly Maimonides exhorted his contemporaries to reach for a level of spirituality beyond that which is assumed for the original audience of the Torah.

This constitutes recognition of society's ability to improve its level of abstraction and conceptualization. By contrast, Averroes was skeptical of this, maintaining that the multitude ought to be left with its belief in a corporeal god. His view was that challenging even such a false belief at this might undermine the social order. By contrast, Maimonides tried to erase any hint of corporeality in God from the hearts of his people.

There were many followers who broadened Maimonides' notion of collective advancement by incorporating it within a conception of historical progress on the intellectual level. For them the gradual dissemination of knowledge to humanity and the refinement of Jewish religious sensibilities over time was a real possibility. This view legitimated the process of divulging of secret teachings suppressed in earlier generations for fear of disrupting the social order. I cite two examples:

> Moses gave the Torah at a time when the whole world was populated by the idolatrous, and people only believed in objects perceived by the senses . . . but by the time of Solomon, belief in divinity and angels, the relation [of the angels] to other existents and their relation to God became widely known. There was thus no further need of concealment. (Samuel Ibn Tibbon, beginning of thirteenth century) [32]

> Times naturally change, and so do people, and so we can now widen the small openings of perception for more truths than was previously possible, for accepted convention is no longer at logger-heads with intellectual truth as much as it was in the past. (Moses Narboni, middle of the fourteenth century)[33]

According to this view there was a gradual narrowing of the chasm separating popular belief from philosophic knowledge. Subjects that had once been the legacy of the few had become public, and the masses could now be exposed to at least a smattering of the esoteric knowledge from which they had once been protected. The truth was the same but humanity had changed.

As noted, this interpretation developed during the generations immediately following Maimonides, but contemporary scholars are even more audacious. They ascribe to Maimonides belief in the ascent of reason into new spheres of knowledge. Progress means that all of humanity, including the enlightened few, can make progress their predecessors could not have imagined.[34] For my purposes, such interpretations are unnecessary. Suffice it to say that Maimonides acknowledged the possibility of an intellectual flow within the society (in both directions) and of lowering the division between the philosopher and the masses.

The inner logic of this demand to purify the concept of God from all anthropomorphic imagery compels a reassessment of concepts like the divine will, justice, and providence and eventually leads to a reexamination of the human ability to form a coherent theological understanding.

Nor did Maimonides recoil from the idea of an entire society devoted to philosophic reflection. I refer here to the Hebrew nation before its descent into slavery in Egypt. Maimonides depicted Abraham as the paradigm of a philosophic monotheist who created a philosophically educated community:

> Having attained this knowledge, he began to refute the inhabitants of Ur of the Chaldees, arguing with them. . . . He then began to proclaim to the whole world with great power and to instruct the people that the entire universe had but one Creator. . . . He would instruct each one according to his capacity till he had brought him to the way of truth, and thus thousands and tens of thousands joined him to establish the house of Abraham . . . and so it went on with ever increasing figure among Jacob's children and their adherents until they became a people that knew God.[35]

One should pay close attention to this reconstruction. According to Maimonides, Abraham addressed each individual "according to his [intellectual] capacity," and this heralded the establishment of a community of wise believers (the house of Abraham). By so doing he began a new philosophic tradition, which in time evolved into an entire nation (*umma* in its Arabic sense) predicated on intellect, not myth, one in which true beliefs replaced necessary ones. Maimonides was aware that philosophy alone could not sustain such a community; in the long term it was destined to be a cultural failure, as indeed was its fate under Egyptian captivity.[36] Still Maimonides envisaged the possibility of spiritual ascent and historical transformation embracing "thousands and tens of thousands" and eventually becoming a nation. This certainly precludes the static, dichotomous conception of the relation between the enlightened and the masses.

Finally, Maimonides' conception of a messianic utopia is based on the hope that the pursuit of knowledge will become its constitutive and sustaining force. Philosophic esotericism assumes that exposing society to indiscriminate "attacks" by philosophy will compromise its stability. Although this may be true in the short run, it did not prevent Maimonides from putting forward a different view, one in which the philosophic secret emerges from its cave not to threaten the social order but to guarantee it. That is, Maimonides believed that the pursuit of knowledge can engulf the human personality, overcoming the desire for illusory goods, earthly power, and material possessions. In so doing, it also overcomes the destructive urges that engender jealousy, enmity, and violence.[37] To the degree that folly and ignorance give way to contemplation and knowledge of God, one may expect a parallel decrease in the irrational force of evil: "Just as a blind man, because of absence of sight, does not cease stumbling, being wounded, and also wounding others . . . the very sects of men – every individual according to the extent of his ignorance – does to himself and to others great evils." In this way, peace emerges out of knowledge: "For through cognition of truth, enmity and hatred are removed and the inflicting of harm by people on one another is abolished."[38]

Obviously, this should not be understood as the vision of the real, historical community. The conciliation between truth and peace takes place in the utopian community, beyond the world of *realpolitik*. During actual history, the harmonization is possible only in the cognition of individuals who have reached the peak of the human capacity. But Maimonides' utopia is not completely divorced from reality. His vision has normative import insofar as it points in a direction and presents a challenge for real people. If the story of the Garden of Eden teaches that we come from a primordial state of spiritual perfection, Maimonides' messianic vision shows us where we should be going if only as an infinite goal: to ultimate spiritual fulfillment.[39] Because human history takes place between these two poles, it involves the combination of the two for the construction of the good society: myth and knowledge, the revealed and the concealed, the necessary and the true.

11.4. IDENTIFYING SECRETS

What is Maimonides' essential secret? What is that esoteric content that has the power to uproot society or restore the world? Did his interpreters succeed in divulging his real intention? Can we, 800 years after his death, become privy to his secrets?

Medieval commentators tended to search for his covert intentions in classical philosophy, in particular the proximity between him and the Aristotelian or Neoplatonic traditions in their Arabic formulations. Not surprisingly, the range of opinions on this issue extends from a radical interpretation that located the secrets of the *Guide* in the truths of physics and metaphysics and a conservative one that put them within the realm of traditional belief.

For example, it is undisputed that Maimonides viewed the laws of nature as the embodiment of divine wisdom and that this was the basis of his naturalistic approach to reality. In the words of Nachmanides, "We were therefore surprised by Maimonides, who detracts from the miraculous, and accentuates naturalism."[40] The question is this: How far did he go? Did he intend to reinterpret all biblical miracles so that they would agree with the laws of nature?[41] Perhaps he adopted this method only in connection with those stories that describe more than a temporary aberration from the normal course of events but dictate the collapse of the entire cosmos.[42] In a parallel sense Maimonides explicitly identified the "Account of Creation" with physics.[43] Did he mean that there was a total identity between them, rendering the creation story nothing more than a metaphor for the natural order or was his only intention to highlight a thematic parallel between two cosmological descriptions?[44]

The radical interpreter might further ask: If wisdom is a divine attribute, is there any room for the actions of a personal creator – "one that wishes at one time and does not wish at another time"[45] – who brings a world into existence following its nonexistence? The essence of wisdom is that its truths remain valid and unchanged over time. If so, might not Maimonides' esoteric view be the belief in an eternal world with no beginning and no end? Moderate commentators such as Hillel of Verona (thirteenth century) or Isaac Abrabanel (fifteenth century) would be horrified; but audacious interpreters, such as Josef Caspi, Moses Narboni, and Samuel of Lunel (all fourteenth century) would regard this as the inevitable consequence of identifying the "Account of Creation" with Aristotelian physics.

The controversy therefore focused on the question of how far Maimonides' secrets go. Are they confined to purely local issues and their consequences or do they penetrate the roots of faith and the fundamentals of the Torah? Did Maimonides believe in miraculous divine providence that extended to each individual or was it limited to universal laws of nature? Was there an element of divine will in prophecy or is it nothing but a natural state reached by gifted individuals? Is the apprehension of truth the supreme human achievement, and how is it related to commandments dealing with prayer, dietary laws, and the celebration of holidays? How far did he go in the intellectualistic interpretation of traditional religious ideas such as love of God, cleaving to God, the world to come? To what extent was he prepared to allegorize the literal meaning of Scripture? Hundreds of commentators debated these questions. As one would expect, the disputes were not just the product of methodological differences; they were also, and perhaps primarily, the result of personal beliefs and convictions. The issues touched on the most sensitive nerves of their existence and religious identity.

Maimonides' esotericism is a familiar theme among contemporary scholars as well. Its focus is similar, and, although it sometimes ignores its medieval predecedents, it raises many of the same questions. At first blush it might seem that the radical interpretation remained unchanged for it attributes to Maimonides the same philosophical themes and relies on the same methods to identify them. In my opinion, however, there is a major difference between the picture of Maimonides that each paints.[46]

Maimonides' early commentators approached the *Guide* primarily as a philosophic text, whereas their modern counterparts approach it primarily as a political one. According to the former, Maimonides concealed teaching was ensconced in the identity between the true science of the Law and the best of Aristotelian philosophy. What Scripture conceals, philosophy reveals. Hence there is no need for a new system of thought; rather, there is conformity between the two existing systems. On this reading, the hidden message is not revolutionary, but evolutionary. Accordingly, philosophic exegesis of Scripture is imperative, for it substantiates the contention that the prophets were bearers of the truths of physics and metaphysics.

This was not the view of the radical latter-day scholars such as Strauss and Pines. For them Maimonides erected a smokescreen to camouflage his belief in the abyss between the two worlds. Synthesis is impossible; there can be only dichotomy. Although Maimonides' heart was in Jerusalem, his head was in Athens. Therefore the identification of prophets with philosophers should not be read as a true statement but a necessary one. According to Pines, "In view of the fact that it is not supported by any evidence whatsoever, [it should] be legitimately qualified as a 'noble fiction' in the Platonic sense of the word."[47] Maimonides' esoteric efforts were not intended as a philosophic bridge between two worlds, but rather as a political dissemblance of the abyss between them.

These differences raise the question of the relationship between the community and its intellectuals. If, as I believe, the medieval exegetes were correct, it is relevant to speak of a broad spectrum spread between the two groups and a gradual ascent from one to the other.[48] There is room for continuous advancement from an anthropomorphic approach to God to a philosophic one, from emphasizing the miraculous to emphasizing the natural, from a crude reading of Scripture to an allegorical interpretation. There is no need for a quantum leap over the chasm separating the foolish from the wise.

If, on the other hand, the modern scholars are right, then the polarization is unavoidable. The transition from faith in prophetic revelation to acknowledgement of a socially motivated myth (however noble) is revolutionary, not evolutionary. It does not leave room for intermediate positions or for gradual philosophic education. According to the Strauss–Pines conception, the dichotomy exists on multiple fronts: Jerusalem and Athens, the masses and the philosophers, and perhaps Maimonides' heart and his head.

Needless to say, this division does not exhaust the interpretative options proposed over the ages. Many a reader rejected both of the radical interpretations. Their image of Maimonides was more conservative, with little attention paid to the esoteric dimension of his thought.[49] Other commentators severed the connection between Maimonides' secrets and traditional philosophy, looking for their illumination in mystical sources ranging from *Ṣūfī* mysticism to "prophetic" *Qabbalah* to various traditions of philosophic mysticism.[50] Some have tried to show that Maimonides' esotericism rejects all dogmatic positions, alerting the intelligent reader to the anomalies and contradictions that pervade both traditional religion and Aristotelian philosophy.[51]

Over the past few years a new trend has emerged. First introduced in the later writings of Shlomo Pines, it claims that Maimonides' concealed teaching lies neither in Athens nor in Jerusalem. It is expressed in the limitations of knowledge and the cloud of uncertainty that hangs over the human condition. In other words, Maimonides' view of all theological and metaphysical questions was fundamentally agnostic. His positive claims regarding these subjects were no more than a mask, hiding the face of a philosophic skeptic, one who rejected the possibility of human cognition of the noncorporeal world and, as a result, the possibility of immortality as well.[52]

It should be noted, however, that Maimonides' senior disciple, Samuel Ibn Tibbon, had already confronted such an agnostic doctrine (formulated by Alfarabi), and summarily rejected it. So commentators were aware of this option but none ascribed it to Maimonides himself. Although this does not refute Pines' claim, it leads to a sobering conclusion. If Pines is correct, Maimonides' whole undertaking was a failure because for more than 800 years he did not succeed in imparting his true philosophic message to anyone. Rather it was only in our generation, remote from the author's world and divorced from the culture he addressed, that a few individuals have finally deciphered his secret. This is questionable both historically and philosophically. Furthermore it fails to acknowledge the possibility that Maimonides did believe in humanity's ability to free itself from falsity but regarded it as an infinite process and was therefore skeptical of the human ability to complete the process and attain full metaphysical clarity. The secret therefore lies in how we characterize falsity, which beliefs should be discarded, and which are necessary but not true, not in the impossibility of achieving an ultimate positive knowledge.

Very recently, more complex models have been proposed, also tending in the same direction.[53] They paint the following picture: Maimonides presented his teachings in a fragmented, intermittent manner, occasionally even relying on contradictory premises, but rather than deny the possibility of knowledge, his goal was to emphasize its dialectical character. Human investigation of celestial physics and metaphysics may lead to probable but never certain results. Although we may perceive partial truths, appearing and disappearing like flashes of lighting, that is all we are ever going to get. Symbolic and intuitive understanding like that found in the sayings of the prophets can assist this kind of cognition.

Accordingly a responsible author of a philosophic text must provide his reader with the greatest number of heuristic possibilities, relying on different and sometimes contradictory premises. Philosophic claims must be presented intermittently, as flashes of illumination, and sometimes in figurative formulations. In other words, the literary character of the *Guide* does not reflect the political needs of society but the limitations inherent in human cognition. In this way, it is not an agnostic position but a dialectic one.

Although this approach represents "the last word" in Maimonides scholarship, like its precursors, it presents difficulties. First, if reliable philosophy must of necessity be taught in a dialectical manner, as probable but not certain, why did Maimonides adopt a different path in the *Mishneh Torah*, which begins with a summary of the main principles of physics and metaphysics and presents them as conclusive truths? Was it because the multitude requires stable, dogmatic results? If so, then a false (dogmatic) image of Athens has penetrated the heart of Jerusalem. This demands a sharp dichotomy comparable with that presented by Strauss. For what emerges is a deep split between true philosophy, which is dialectic, and the authentic Jerusalem, as presented in the *Mishneh Torah*.

Second, is the assertion of the fragmented and uncertain nature of knowledge an esoteric assertion or an exoteric one? Is the principal of uncertainty, premised on conflicting axioms, something to be concealed or divulged? In other words, if these are obfuscated claims,[54] why is it that, in the decisive question of creation, Maimonides proclaims the intellect's inability to resolve the matter?[55] Why did he divulge his opinion that not only the Mosaic teaching, but also the view ascribed by him to Plato, could be acceptable in certain contexts?[56] We might alternatively argue that the claims concerning uncertainty are overt and for common consumption.[57] This, however, would call into question Maimonides' method of contradiction. For instead of the reader's being explicitly presented with alternative options, the reader must make an effort to expose the presence of any particular contradiction. In addition, why don't the contradictions deal directly with the conflicting philosophical propositions,[58] being limited to the particular (sometimes remote) implications deriving from them?

Third, this approach exposes itself to the same critique as its predecessor for it too must assume that, in the long run, Maimonides was unsuccessful in imparting his principal teaching – all the more so if his audience included ordinary people. Still, the validity and productivity of this approach should be assessed primarily in terms of its ability to explain specific contradictions in the *Guide* in keeping with Maimonides' own admission that he intends to use them.[59]

11.5. EPILOGUE

In the middle of the thirteenth century, Rabbi Yosef ha-Levi Abulafia depicted the esoteric character of Maimonides' philosophical treatise, concluding with the following play on words: "If our master called it the the *Guide of the Perplexed*, because all of its contents are supposedly well arranged, then we sinners, observing it in our blindness, should indeed call it the *Perplexity of the Guides*."[60] These comments were written in a polemical context, but, as previously emphasized, the confusion and the controversy that erupted in its wake were a catalyst for Jewish thought over the generations and for Jewish scholarship in recent times. They also created surprising encounters between Maimonides' text and general philosophic culture.

On the one hand, it cannot be denied that the radical interpretation of Maimonides in the Middle Ages was influenced by the writings of Averroes, the most consistently Aristotelian of the Moslem philosophers. On the other hand, the moderate interpretations attempted to place Maimonides within the mainstream of traditional Judaism. By the same token, there is a clear connection between Strauss' interpretation and his personal critique of the connection between philosophy and theology. Nor can one ignore the probable connection between Pines' later views on Maimonides and the epistemology of Immanuel Kant; nor the possible connection between the dialectical view of philosophy attributed to Maimonides and the skeptical tenor of our times.

Regardless of whether Maimonides chose harmony, dichotomy, or dialectic, his treatise continues to switch identities and mediate between cultures. By way of paraphrase, not only is the truth elusive, so too is the text, and one wonders whether this was not in fact the author's initial intention. At all events, there is one position that does not stand up to critical scrutiny: the position that erects a rigid barrier between the possessors of truth and the ignorant. For not only did the exoteric Maimonides believe in the possibility of education in philosophy, the esoteric one did as well.

NOTES

1. Samuel of Lunel (end of fourteenth century), commentary on the *Guide*, MS Vatikan Neopiti 17, p. 40b.
2. Samuel Ibn Tibbon, *Commentary on Qoheleth*, MS Parma 272, p. 8b.
3. Jacov Emden 1970, p. 56 (cf. *Iggeret Purim*, in Schachter 1988, p. 445); Chaim Elazar Shapira of Munkacz 1943, pp. 92–3.
4. Halbertal 2001, pp. 40–2.
5. Ravitzky 1996, pp. 205–45, 246–303.
6. *GP* 2.40, 3.27. See W. Z. Harvey 1980, pp. 198–203; W. Z. Harvey 2000, pp. 10–13; Kreisel 1999, pp. 166–9.
7. Strauss 1952, Klein-Braslavy 1996.
8. Plato, Apol. 39e.
9. However, see Strauss 1952.
10. *GP* 3.28, pp. 512–514. Cf. 3.36.
11. *GP* 1:54.
12. Strauss 1935, 1952, 1963.
13. Strauss 1952. This was Strauss's view of most of the "premodern philosophers" but Maimonides was his prime example of the phenomenon.
14. Pines 1960, 1963.
15. In Strauss' later articles one detects a certain development in this context (see Strauss 1967, 1983; W. Z. Harvey 2001). In Pines' later studies there was a fundamental change in this respect.
16. See Strauss 1963, p. xix; Cohen (on Strauss) 1997, p. 264.
17. *GP* 2.40, p. 384.
18. Hartman 1976, pp. 28–65; Twersky 1967, pp. 95–118; Twersky 1980, pp. 356–74; Hyman 1976, pp. 46–59; Kellner 1990, pp. 56–9.
19. For other insights regarding this subject, see Stern 1998, pp. 72–3, 103: compare Talmage 1986.
20. Klein-Braslavy 1996, pp. 21, 64; Halbertal 2001, p. 45; Lorberbaum 2001, 2002.
21. Pines 1963, p. cxx; Pines 1968, pp. 9, 45; Halbertal 2001, p. 53.
22. I am referring to Samuel Ibn Tibbon, Jacob Antoli, Moses Ibn Tibbon, Zerahyah ben She'altiel Ḥen, Judah Romano, Emanuel of Rome, and others. See Ravitzky 1981b, pp. 726–9.
23. *GP* Introduction.
24. Yom Tov Eshbili 1983, p. 68.
25. Schwartz 2002, p. 17.
26. *GP* Introduction, p. 19.
27. See Seeskin and Loberbaum in n. 53 of this chapter.
28. *MT* 1, Repentance, 10.5. For an English translation, see Maimonides 1972, p. 85. Note: the ignorance of women was not conceived as a given,

inherent fact but as a sociological phenomenom that can be overcome by education.

29. Regarding the role of the secrets in the legal exposition, see Ravitzky 1990a, pp. 197–204.
30. *GP* 1.26, cf. ibid., p. 46.
31. Halbertal and Margalit 1992, pp. 108–136.
32. Samuel Ibn Tibbon, Commentary on Qohelet, Ms Parma 272, p. 70a (Ravitzky 1981a, pp. 111–114; reprinted 1996, pp. 207–8). Cf. *Perush Tehilim*, ed. Y. Cohen, 1974, Jerusalem, p. 47 (Halbertal 2001, pp. 103–8); Isaac Albalag 1973, *Sefer Tiqqun ha-De*ʿ*ot*, Jerusalem: The Israeli Academy of Sciences and Humanities, p. 51 (Albalag attributed to Maimonides the esoteric belief in the eternity of the world. He allowed himself to divulge this because of the social progress since Maimonides' generation, and until his own generation, at the end of the thirteenth century!); Yehuda Romeno, *Be*ʾ*ur Ma*ʿ*aseh Bereshit*, critical edition, by Caterina Rigo (in preparation), Jerusalem: The World Association of Jewish Studies, lines 1132–3; Samuel of Lunel, MS Vatikan Neopiti 17, p. 47a ("as long as the world continues, the generations will become wiser"), and many others like them.
33. Moses Narboni 1852, *Commentary on the Guide*, 2.19, p. 71a.
34. See Funkenstein 1977, pp. 91–6; Funkenstein 1983, pp. 49–58; Strauss 1963, pp. xxxiii–xxxvii. Strauss also noted the adaptation of Scriptures to the corporeal attributes of God, in the light of ancient culture, as opposed to the spreading of the recognition in an incorporeal God over the generations. I am not sure whether this emphasis concerning the collective intellectual progress signifies a change from his original view.
35. *MT* 1, Idolatry, 1.3.
36. Kaplan 1985, pp. 29–33; Hartman 1988, pp. 319–33; Kreisel 1999, pp. 29–33; Ravitzky 2002, pp. 16–17.
37. For an additional insight regarding the transformation created by human knowledge, see Kellner 2000, pp. 31–33.
38. *GP* 3.11, pp. 440–1. Cf. *MT* 14, Kings and Wars, 12.5; *CM*, Eduyot 7.7; Essay on Resurrection (Maimonides, 1985b), p. 222. See Ravitzky 1991, pp. 224–31 (reprinted 1996, pp. 76– 86).
39. Note: This utopian foundation, making peace contingent on truth, is the only foundation in Maimonides' messianic vision that was substantially developed, not only in his legal work, but also in his philosophic.
40. Nachmanides, *Torath Hashem Temimah: Kitvei Rabbeinu Moshe Ben Naḥman*, C. D. Shewall 1963, p. 154.
41. *GP* 2.29; *CM*, Introduction to Tractate *Avot* (*EC*), Chapter 8.
42. For example: "Sun stand still upon Givon" (Joshua 10:12), in other words, the cessation of the celestial spheres, which means the collapse of the Aristotelian cosmos (*GP* 2.36, 2.29; Schwartz 1999, pp. 38–54),

or the account of the appearance of an "angel" in physical form, which when literally read involves a logical or ontological contradiction ("angel" by definition is an intellect separated from matter. See *GP* 2.49, pp. 41–2).

43. *CM*, Tractate *Ḥagigah*, 2:1; *GP*, Introduction.
44. Ravitzky 1990b, pp. 225–50.
45. *GP* 2.18.
46. I have already dealt with this question in another context (Ravitzky 1990a, p. 180). Here, however, I connect it to my current claim regarding the dynamic continuum between the masses and the enlightened. In addition, because my comments were misunderstood in some essays, I am taking this opportunity to clarify them.
47. Pines 1963, pp. cxx.
48. See also Rosenberg 1981, pp. 92–3.
49. For the historical sources see Ravitzky 1990a, pp. 168–9. For a contemporary view, see Ravitzky 1996.
50. For the connection to *Ṣūfī* mysticism, see Fenton 1981, pp. 1–23; Blumenthal 1982, pp. 55–72. Regarding the connection to prophetic *Qabbalah*, see Idel 1991, pp. 31–81, and several other writings by Idel dealing with Abraham Abulafia. The connection to the different trends in intellectual mysticism is dealt with by Blumenthal 1981, pp. 55–72, Blumenthal 1984, pp. 27–52; Fenton 1987. Another direction was taken by Pines 1986a, pp. 1–14. Apart from all of these, according to a legendry tradition among the kabbalists, Maimonides, before his death, recanted on his philosophical views and adopted the *Kabbalah*. See Scholem 1935; Shmidman 1984.
51. See Harvey 2001, pp. 391–395; Schwartz 2002, pp. 104–80. Schwartz proposed two contradictory esoteric readings: one that undermines the religious authority (of Moses) and the other that undermines the philosophic consistency (of Aristotle), and purposely avoids deciding between them. Schwartz also considered a hypothetical proposal, which views Maimonides' philosophic views as a mask, hiding a conservative religious philosopher. Other researchers have attempted to present the esoteric Maimonidean theory of creation as an intermediate position, between the Aristotelian view and the accepted religious view (a position which Maimonides ascribed to Plato). See Davidson 1979; Seeskin 1991, pp. 55–8.
52. Pines 1979, pp. 82–109, 211–25; Pines 1997, Part 5, pp. 404–62. For an application of this view to the question of creation, see Klein-Braslavy 1986b.
53. The first buds of this conception were presented by Sarah Klein-Braslavy, who focused exclusively on the pedagogical aspect of dispersed,

intermittent writing (Klein-Braslavy 1978, pp. 62–76). Moshe Halbertal developed this idea further when dealing with the esoteric nature of language and the elusive nature of truth (Halbertal 2001, p. 45). However, both of them located the issue at the periphery of political esotericism. This was not the case with the comprehensive development offered by Seeskin (2000, pp. 11–19, 177–88) and Loberbaum (2000, 2001, 2002), who attempted to apply it similarly to the method of contradictions in the *Guide*. I presently combine their comments, even though each of them may have reservations about particular sentences. See also Hyman 1989; Fox 1990, pp. 67–90; Ivry 1991b.

54. As would appear from the comments of Loberbaum, supra.
55. *GP* 1. 71, 2.15.
56. *GP* 2.25.
57. As would appear from the comments of Seeskin, supra.
58. This was Maimonides' method, when presenting the different views on the questions of creation, prophecy, and providence (*GP* 2.13, 2.32, 3.17)
59. *GP* Introduction, p. 18, "the seventh reason."
60. Abulafia's words were printed in *Ginzei Nistarot*, Vol. D (1878), p. 12.

SEYMOUR FELDMAN

12 Maimonides – A Guide for Posterity

My respect for this man [Maimonides] was so great that I considered him to have been the ideal man and his teachings to have been inspired by the Divine wisdom itself.

Salomon Maimon (*Lebensgeschichte*, 1965, Volume 1, p. 307)

12.1. MAIMONIDES, THE PURVEYOR OF PERPLEXITIES

It would not be an exaggeration to say that Maimonides' *Guide of the Perplexed* (henceforth *Guide*) shaped the course of subsequent Jewish religious philosophy, especially during the later Middle Ages. Maimonides had considerable impact also on some Christian medieval thinkers, such as Thomas Aquinas, and was studied by several early modern philosophers, such as Spinoza and Leibniz. The reception of the *Guide* in the medieval Jewish philosophical tradition was quite varied: Many reacted to it so enthusiastically that it became for them a virtual canonical text; others treated it sympathetically but critically; and some rejected it completely or in large part. But even in the latter case, the critique of Maimonides was presented in the language and conceptual framework of the *Guide*. This diverse and pervasive impact of the *Guide*[1] can be in part attributed to the paradoxical result that instead of removing perplexities it raises them and leaves some of them unresolved. This is due to both the form and the content of the work. Maimonides explicitly tells the reader that from a stylistic point of view his book is not a philosophical work that begins by laying out the fundamental principles and then draws the appropriate conclusions from them. Rather, it will present his ideas in a fragmentary way, often by way of hints, scattered throughout the treatise according to no apparent order. Occasionally, Maimonides admits, he will have recourse to parables, as a more direct or explicit mode of discourse is either not available or inappropriate. Moreover, the book is written in the form of a letter to his former pupil, who has moved away but still remains loyal to his teacher, so much so that he appeals to him to resolve certain religious problems that perplex him. Now a letter is a personal form of written discourse and often is intended to be private.

Aware that others may eventually read this rather extended letter, Maimonides specifies the qualifications of those future interlopers. They will have to be exactly like the addressee of the letter: intelligent, well-educated not only in Jewish religious literature but in philosophy and the sciences, and last but not least faithful to Judaism. To those who do not satisfy these requirements the *Guide*, Maimonides warns, will be harmful. Finally, at the conclusion of his Preface Maimonides tells his pupil that he needs to be aware that this very long letter will contain several types of intended contradictions. This is a most curious prefatory comment. Most authors hope and pray that their book is free from contradictions. Before he even begins Chapter 1 of the treatise the reader has been rendered almost paralyzed: How can he make sense of a book written like this?

His situation is compounded and aggravated by the fact that many of the various issues and conclusions that constitute the bulk of the book are formulated in very radical ways (e.g., divine attributes), not easily reconcilable with religious tradition, or are presented in equivocal language that leads to diverse interpretations (e.g., creation of the universe). And having been forewarned that the book contains contradictions, the reader is baffled as to which of the alleged contradictory theses found therein is Maimonides' real view. Thus it is not easy, despite all that has been written on Maimonides, to say what he believed on some of the more controversial issues in medieval religious philosophy. It is no wonder that many of his philosophically qualified readers wrote commentaries or philosophical books of their own dealing with the unresolved perplexities of the *Guide*. Among these philosophical conundrums the following topics were especially vexing: (1) the appropriate language in speaking of God, (2) creation of the universe, (3) the nature of prophecy, (4) divine omniscience and providence, and (5) man's ultimate felicity.

With respect to religious language, Maimonides concluded that the best way to speak about God is really not to speak at all; if we need to say something, we should say it negatively, for example, "God is not ignorant" instead of "God is wise."[2] But of course we do say things about and to God, especially in prayer. So what is Maimonides proposing that we do? Should we dispense with prayer and religious discourse altogether?

On creation Maimonides appears to be a vigorous defender of what he says is the teaching of the Torah: creation *ex nihilo*.[3] Neither Aristotle nor Plato is to be followed. Not Aristotle, for his theory of eternity of the universe entails the impossibility of miracles and thus undermines the very existence of the Torah. Plato's doctrine of creation from matter fares a little better, because it does not rule out miracles; but because this theory has not been proved, there is no need to believe in it. If someone does prove it, Maimonides claims that exegetical liberty will allow us to interpret Scripture accordingly.[4] As we shall see, some of the later Jewish thinkers believed that the debate had by no means been resolved in favor of creation *ex nihilo*. Moreover, some even maintained that Maimonides was a secret Aristotelian on this issue, a position widely held by modern interpreters.

Is prophecy a natural phenomenon, as Maimonides had maintained, or is it wholly supranatural, as most traditional authorities had believed? Not only in the *Guide* but in his legal code the *Mishneh Torah* Maimonides argued for a naturalistic theory of prophetic illumination based upon Aristotelian ideas as interpreted by Alfarabi.[5] But was Amos a philosopher who had reached a very high level of intellectual perfection that he warranted prophetic inspiration?

Maimonides' views on the problems of divine omniscience and providence, which he treats together, are also perplexing. Ostensibly he defends Rabbi Akiva's dictum that, although God knows everything, man has free will. He does so by appealing to his doctrine of negative theology: God's epistemic apparatus is so different from ours that we not only do not understand how it works but ordinary logic cannot make sense of it.[6] Much the same is true of God's providence, which seems to be the conclusion of the Book of Job, as Maimonides interprets it.[7] But there is something in Maimonides' theory that is even more baffling than its agnosticism: He claims that the perfect man is so protected by God that he experiences no evil whatsoever.[8] This is quite counterintuitive.

Finally, when we ask what is man's ultimate goal, in particular is it possible to achieve immortality, the *Guide* is elusive, perhaps even evasive. Although Maimonides does discuss human perfection in the concluding chapters of the treatise, he does not say much about immortality; indeed there are just a few passing references to it in the entire book. Because he did discuss this latter topic in detail in his *Commentary on the Mishnah* and in the *Mishneh Torah*, why was he so reluctant to treat this important issue in his more philosophical *Guide*? Moreover, what he does say about it would suggest that even if he believed in it, immortality for him was not personal, or individual.[9] Was he then a hidden Muslim *faylasūf*, who either denied immortality altogether (e.g., Alfarabi) or allowed it in the impersonal form of complete conjunction or union with the Agent Intellect (e.g., Ibn Bājja or Averroes)?

12.2. MAIMONIDES ACCORDING TO AVERROES: THE RADICAL MAIMONIDEANS

No sooner than the *Guide* had been translated into Hebrew in the early thirteenth century by Samuel Ibn Tibbon (1150–1230, southern France) than questions arose as to what exactly the "Master of the *Guide*" had taught and whether these teachings were philosophically sound and religiously acceptable. Samuel Ibn Tibbon himself, even before completing his translation, sent Maimonides a long letter in which he raises several philosophical questions, especially about an apparent contradiction in the *Guide* pertaining to divine providence.[10] Once the translation was completed, it soon became the standard Hebrew translation and text of the *Guide*, virtually supplanting the Arabic original. Moreover, Ibn Tibbon's Hebrew terminology became the language of Jewish philosophy not only throughout later medieval Jewish philosophy but even in early modern Jewish thought; indeed, it was also used by some of the mystical writers. For our purposes, however, it is Ibn Tibbon the commentator and philosopher who is more relevant. Although he did not write an explicit commentary on the *Guide*, Ibn Tibbon's letter and other writings are replete with discussions of various passages and themes from the treatise. In these discussions Ibn Tibbon advances an exegetical program that was adopted by other commentators, both medieval and modern. According to this exegetical agenda the *Guide* is an esoteric book, just as Maimonides had claimed for the Torah itself.[11] Moreover, one of the important, indeed necessary keys to the correct understanding of the *Guide* is the philosophy of Averroes, just as for Maimonides one of the requisite tools for the true understanding of the Torah is Aristotle's philosophy. Because we shall shortly contrast this program with another approach that adopted a more conservative reading of the text, we shall for convenience refer to the former as the "radical Maimonidean school."

Because Maimonides himself alerted his readers to the fact that his treatise contained contradictions and used parables to express ideas that are not amenable to plain language in a book one of whose main purposes is to explain biblical parables, the careful reader has to be on guard. If a contradiction is detected, which of the two contradictories is to be taken as Maimonides' real view? Ibn Tibbon himself detected an apparent contradiction between two doctrines on divine providence present in the *Guide*. In 3.17 Maimonides (as Ibn Tibbon reads him) advances the theses (1) that divine providence is a function of intellectual perfection, (2) that only the intellectually perfect warrant individual providence, and (3) that this providence consists precisely in the attachment to, or conjunction with, the intellectual domain, the main consequent of which is detachment from the material world and its ensnarements. According to Ibn Tibbon this doctrine is one that virtually all good philosophers accept; in this sense it can be considered "natural": insofar as intellectual perfection is the full realization of what it is to be human, and not a worm, it is the mature expression of human nature. However, in 3.51 of the *Guide*, in what seems to be a digression, Maimonides puts forth the claim that the intellectually perfect person warrants a special kind of providence: Such an individual is divinely protected from all material evils, such as illness or mugging. Now, if divine providence involves the realization that material evils are really not evils, then why does the intellectually perfect person need some kind of supranatural intervention to prevent his being the victim of a mugging? The intellectually perfect are already enjoying divine providence! Samuel reaches the conclusion that Maimonides' real view is the former, especially because that is the true doctrine of divine providence, and that the latter position is a "politically useful, perhaps necessary, doctrine" that is directed toward the masses. After all, Maimonides himself taught us that some of the ideas and commandments of the Torah have this political and pedagogical purpose. But for the intellectually adept the true doctrine of divine providence is found in the *Guide* 3.17.[12]

Important at this juncture in our story is the profound and pervasive influence of the great Muslim contemporary Cordoban philosopher Averroes (1126–98). Second only to Maimonides in his impact upon later medieval Jewish philosophy, Averroes was the key by means of which the true meaning of the *Guide* was to be discovered. In some cases, the explicit teachings of the *Guide* will have to be not only interpreted but modified or even rejected in the light of the true philosophy of Aristotle as interpreted by Averroes. For example, one of Maimonides' more radical teachings was his rejection of affirmative attributes of God and advocacy of negative theology. Samuel Ibn Tibbon, on the other hand, favors the approach of Averroes, who, following Aristotle's theory of analogical predication, maintained that one could attribute positive properties of God as long as the property in question was predicated on God in the prior sense and applied to the creature in the posterior sense.[13]

Perhaps the influence of Averroes is most evident and far-reaching in the discussions of creation of the universe among the "radical Maimonideans," who accepted the doctrine of eternal creation, a theory that Maimonides had explicitly claimed to be incoherent. Eternal creation is the doctrine that although the universe is caused by God it has infinite duration, a *parte ante* as well as a *parte post*. It was advanced by most of the Muslim *falāsīfa*, such as Alfarabi and Averroes, but derives from the Neoplatonists and their commentaries on Aristotle.[14] Moreover, the leading radical Maimonideans maintained that this theory is the authentic teaching of the *Guide*. Samuel Ibn Tibbon assumes this as a given in his philosophical–exegetical work *Let the Waters Be Gathered*.[15] It is discussed and defended vigorously by two radical Maimonideans, Isaac Albalag (late thirteenth century, northern Spain) and Moses Narboni (d. ca. 1362, southern France).

The popularity of this cosmological theory in later medieval Jewish philosophy is not only due to the authority of Averroes. In part it has to do with the ambiguity in Maimonides' treatment of this subject in the *Guide*. Probably more literature has been written on Maimonides' views on creation than on any other topic in his philosophy.[16] For our purposes, it is not necessary to explore or rehearse these ambiguities; it is sufficient to note that even the medieval commentators on the *Guide* were aware of certain equivocations and lacunae in Maimonides' discussions of this issue. First, although he explicitly says that creation is a "pillar of the Torah," does it matter that he says this several times? Is an author's real view always to be found by counting texts?[17] Second, why does Maimonides declare that the Torah view is creation *ex nihilo*, especially when he never cites a text that clearly teaches this doctrine and says explicitly that the Platonic theory of creation from matter is theologically acceptable, as it is compatible with the belief in miracles?[18] Finally, several remarks made by Maimonides suggest that the eternity of the universe under certain interpretations can be made consistent with the Torah. For example, he makes it quite clear in 2.30 of the *Guide* that the "story of creation" as narrated in the Torah is in truth not a temporal, or chronological, account of the creative act. Is this a hint that the creation of the universe is really a constant causal, emanative, relation between God and the world? However these remarks are to be construed, exegetes, medieval and modern, have attempted to read Maimonides as a "secret" Aristotelian or Platonist.[19]

Convinced that eternal creation is true, Samuel Ibn Tibbon, Isaac Albalag, and Moses Narboni attempted to show that this theory is what Maimonides really believed and that this is the view of the Torah, although for pedagogical and political purposes it teaches creation *ex nihilo*. According to Ibn Tibbon the "account of creation" described in Genesis 1 is really a summary description of the process of natural generation in the sublunar world; it is not a declaration of the absolute creation of the heavens and the earth, because they are eternal. For Isaac Albalag, the important prayer "Every day God renews his creation" reveals the truth: Creation is eternally occurring. It never began; it never will cease. Following the lead of Averroes, Albalag maintains that an eternal producer entails an eternal product. For any noneternal act of such a cause would imply a change, but God is immutable.[20] And for Narboni, the eternity of motion is a truth taught by Aristotle and Averroes, and this implies an eternal world. Like Albalag, Narboni maintains that the creative act is really a continuous and continual process of emanation from God, resulting in the existence of the universe. In short, creation is causation, and causation can be atemporal.[21]

Narboni too contributes something new in his doctrine of creation, which may even be a more radical reading of Maimonides. In *Guide* 1.68 Maimonides reiterates the Aristotelian epistemological principle that in perfect cognition the knower, the act of knowing, and the object of knowledge are numerically identical.[22] He follows up this dictum in the next chapter with the thesis that God is the ultimate form of the universe, indeed "the form of forms." In his commentary on the latter passage and in his essay *Epistle on Shiʿur Qoma*, Narboni suggests that these two passages imply the ontological identity of God with the universe. God is not then the transcendent cause or creator of the world, but its immanent ground, or essence. As he puts it in his commentary on *Guide* 1.69, God's being the form of the world implies not only that He is not its remote cause, but that He is "with" the world in an essential and intimate way. For, as the rabbis themselves intimated, if God is the "soul of the world," then He cannot be really separate from it.[23] Spinoza's pantheism is not too far away.[24]

Many of the radical Maimonideans were attracted toward the psychological theory of Averroes, which in turn was derived from Aristotle and his later commentators, according to which the human intellect is capable of attaining immortality by means of intellectual conjunction with the Agent Intellect. Samuel Ibn Tibbon himself construed immortality in this way, and he attributed the doctrine to Maimonides. Narboni in particular was very interested in this question and wrote a separate work on this topic titled *Treatise on the Perfection of the Soul*, as well as a commentary on Averroes' treatise *The Epistle on Conjunction with the Active Intellect*.[25] Although this doctrine is interpreted differently by different thinkers, underlying it is the idea that immortality is a state attained through intellectual activity and achievement, resulting in some kind of unification with the Agent Intellect, which in the medieval Aristotelian theory is one of the causes of human intellection. Narboni accepted Averroes' version of this theory, according to which the immortality achieved is nonindividual. In this theory, immortality consists in the knowledge that is actually attained – remember that, in knowing, the knower and the object of knowledge are identical. Because the knowledge itself is one (e.g., the theorems of Euclid are the same for everyone), there is no real difference between the intellects of Euclid and Gersonides as far as their respective knowledge of classical geometry. Therefore, in Paradise all geometers become and are one and the same entity.[26]

Now, many of the medieval commentators of the *Guide* took this to be at least in part Maimonides' own theory of immortality, although Maimonides offers no explicit and extended discussion of this general topic in the *Guide*. It is in fact a good example of his claim that some of his ideas have to be pieced together from hints scattered throughout the book. In *Guide* 1.70 Maimonides attributes to the philosophers a theory of this kind, and he explicitly says that this theory implies non-individuated immortality. Narboni and others, including some who were not sympathetic to this doctrine at all, also attributed to Maimonides the theory that the human intellect is just a psychological disposition to acquire knowledge, not a subsistent entity, and thus liable to perish, unless it is actualized by the accumulation of cognitions. Again, it is difficult to see how on this account of the intellect immortality can be individuated, especially if we keep in mind Aristotle's theory of the triunity of intellection. Nevertheless, the late Alexander Altmann attempted to find in Maimonides enough material to justify an individuated theory of immortality.[27] However, the question remains open.

12.3. MAIMONIDES, THE JEWISH "SCHOLASTIC"

The radical interpretation of Maimonides did not go unchallenged. Almost simultaneously with it there arose an alternative reading of the *Guide* that saw Maimonides not as a secret Aristotelian or Averroist, but as a faithful disciple of Moses, son of Amram. To be sure, the medieval Moses read philosophy and believed that true philosophy was not only compatible with the Torah but can, indeed must, be used in understanding the Torah. But this does not imply that the Torah and the *Guide* are esoteric books in the sense that the exoteric meaning, addressed *ad captum vulgi*, may in some instances be false, whereas the esoteric meaning, addressed to the *cognoscenti*, is true, even though the latter may contravene the tradition as it is ordinarily understood. Moreover, some of the more radical ideas attributed to Maimonides by his Averroist interpreters, such as eternal creation and nonindividuated immortality, are incorrect readings of the *Guide*. What is especially interesting in this group of more "conservative" interpreters and followers of Maimonides is that they appealed to Christian sources to support their reading of the *Guide*. Their utilization of such Scholastic giants as Albert the Great and Thomas Aquinas has led the late Joseph Sermoneta to label their approach "Jewish Thomism."[28] Two Italian Jewish Maimonideans, Hillel of Verona (ca. 1220–ca. 1295) and Judah Romano (ca. 1280–ca. 1325), were prominent examples of this infusion of Scholastic literature and thought into Maimonidean philosophy.

In his main work, *The Recompenses of the Soul* [*Tagmulei ha-nefesh*], Hillel of Verona is primarily concerned to present in Part 1 the correct theory of the soul and in Part 2 to defend a Maimonidean account of immortality. His psychology is based heavily on Aquinas' interpretation of Aristotle's *De Anima*, which leads him to reject Averroes' doctrine of the unicity of the human intellect, especially its implication of loss of individuality when conjunction with Agent Intellect is achieved. On the other hand, his "Thomism" also results in his deviation from Maimonides' account of the human intellect as a pure disposition, because for Aquinas and Hillel the human intellect is a "formal substance," essentially immaterial and inherently immortal, and thus "separable."[29] Yet he is not a slavish follower of Aquinas either. On the nature of the Agent Intellect, for example, he is faithful to the tradition of Alfarabi and Maimonides, according to which the Agent Intellect is a transcendent separable intellect.[30] But, unlike Maimonides, Hillel insists that in conjunction not only the human intellect survives, but the imagination as well, and thus individuation is possible.[31]

Hillel is most Maimonidean in his discussion of the exact nature of human immortality. He vigorously rejects the traditional popular view that in the afterlife the rewards of the righteous and the punishments of the wicked will be in any way corporeal. Because the soul is an immaterial formal substance, its reward or punishment must be incorporeal. The popular conceptions of the reward in the afterlife as the Garden of Eden, or "Paradise," and punishment as *Gehinnom*, or the burning fire, are just metaphorical depictions addressed to the masses in order to encourage them to follow the right path. In truth, however, the ultimate reward of the righteous is a divine illumination, by virtue of which they are able to "see" God. It is the intellect that is the primary subject and recipient of immortality, and hence its reward is intellectual insight that was not attainable in this life.[32] As Sermoneta notes, here Hillel follows Maimonides' account as presented in his *Commentary on the Mishnah*.[33] However, Hillel departs from Maimonides in several respects: (1) in maintaining the survival of the imagination after death, as we have seen; (2) in granting the perfect sage the power of performing miracles in this life; and (3) in advancing the Platonic idea of the soul's preexistence. Nevertheless, Hillel does not accept the idea of the soul's descent as some kind of punishment or decline, a doctrine found in some later Platonists.[34]

When we come to Judah Romano in the next generation we find a similar concern to transmit the contemporary Scholastic philosophical literature to the Hebrew reading philosophical orbit and to incorporate some of the former's approach and doctrines into his own philosophical system. However, Judah was more independent and original than Hillel of Verona. Although he was respectful and indebted to the Scholastics, he differed from them on several important issues and often sided with Maimonides where the latter and Aquinas disagreed. For example, instead of Aquinas he followed Alfarabi and Maimonides in adopting the transcendent conception of the Agent Intellect. On the other hand, he deviates from Maimonides in maintaining that the human intellect, or "the rational soul," is a substance, not a mere disposition. Here the influence of Aquinas is evident.[35] However, with the radical Maimonideans, and even Hillel of Verona, but contrary to Aquinas, Judah was committed to the conjunction theory of immortality; indeed, he advances it in strong terms, allowing for conjunction with the Agent Intellect in this life, as well as after the separation of the intellect from the body at death. In language redolent with Maimonidean overtones Judah outlines a mode of worship for the attainment of conjunction that stresses not only study but isolation from worldly pursuits and social intercourse.[36] In some passages Judah formulates conjunction as "unification," suggesting complete identity with the Agent Intellect, such that the human intellect becomes universal, as is the Agent Intellect. Whether or not any individuality is preserved at this point is not altogether clear.[37]

One of the more striking features of Judah's philosophy is his theory of hermeneutics. Following Maimonides' dictum in *Guide* 2.25 that "the gates of interpretation are not locked before us," Judah pushes this principle to the extreme. In language that is suggestive of contemporary hermeneutics, he sees the text as "open," or porous, capable of many, indeed numerous, interpretations, virtually without limit. Confronting the biblical text, for example, the interpreter is free to find there whatever "springs" to his exegetical imagination. A given text or passage is susceptible not only to many interpretations, but these diverse readings may even be contrary to each other. Yet they are all legitimate, because the interpreter is at each moment in his reading a different reader, bringing to the text all that he knows and has read throughout the hermeneutical process. In his informative essay on Judah's hermeneutics, Sermoneta shows how Judah derives ten different readings from one verse from Song of Songs – "Thine ointments have a goodly fragrance" (1:3). Each of these interpretations expresses different philosophical theses pertaining to God. Indeed, as Sermoneta has showed, these interpretations are heavily influenced by the Scholastic theologian Gilles of Rome, as well as by Maimonides. Following Maimonides' lead, he accepts the doctrine of negative theology against Aquinas' critique of it.[38]

Yet Judah's reverence for Maimonides was not absolute. This is most evident in his theory of prophecy. According to *Guide* 2.32, prophecy is a natural human capacity, which can be actualized through the proper moral and intellectual disciplines; it is not some miraculous gift supervening ad hoc on the prophet regardless of his or her qualifications. Aquinas, however, maintained that there was another type of prophecy that was superior to natural prophecy, and this former type was completely supranatural in cause and character. Indeed, divine revelation as manifested in the giving of the Ten Commandments, for example, is completely supranatural.[39] On this issue Judah sides with Thomas. The prophecies that really matter are supranatural and constitute a "sacred science," as Thomas taught. In these supranatural revelations truths may be revealed that are inaccessible to human reason, such as creation of the universe *de novo* and commandments that defy our understanding.[40]

12.4. NEITHER MAIMONIDES NOR AVERROES: GERSONIDES

The battle between the radical and the conservative readings of Maimonides continued throughout the fourteenth century. But in the most important Jewish philosopher of the first half of the century the interpretation of Maimonides gave way to the more important undertaking of developing a philosophical approach to Judaism that was independent of both Maimonides and Averroes, indeed of the master philosopher himself – Aristotle. This new approach was forged by Levi ben Gershom, or Gersonides (1288–1344) of the Provence. Besides his achievements in philosophy, Gersonides was an important astronomer, mathematician, and biblical exegete. In philosophy Gersonides continued the tradition of writing commentaries on Averroes' commentaries of Aristotle and contributed several independent philosophical treatises of his own, the most important of which was *The Wars of the Lord* [*Milḥamot ha-shem*; henceforth *The Wars*]. The latter work purports to be a study of six major philosophical problems that Gersonides believes had not been properly treated by his predecessors, most notably Maimonides and Averroes. In effect, however, the work is so comprehensive that it constitutes a veritable philosophical system covering most of the important issues in medieval metaphysics, psychology, and natural philosophy.[41]

In the Introduction to *The Wars* Gersonides clearly evinces both the influence of Maimonides and his deviations from him. He makes it quite evident that his treatise is not written in the style of the *Guide*. No hidden messages, no enigmatic sayings, no parables. These do not belong in a philosophical book. Philosophy is analysis and argument, and that is exactly what the reader of *The Wars* gets, indeed with a vengeance. With the exception of an occasional citation from rabbinic literature and two brief allusions to his own experiences, *The Wars* is replete with philosophical arguments against Aristotle, Averroes, and Maimonides in defense of an alternative philosophical approach that is consistent with Judaism. The work is organized around the following six topics: (1) immortality of the soul, (2) prophecy, (3) divine cognition, (4) divine providence, (5) the heavenly domain, especially the existence and nature of the separate intellects, and (6) creation of the universe. To these purely philosophical issues Gersonides appends two "theological" topics: miracles and testing of the prophet.

Gersonides' discussion of immortality is curious at least for one reason: Although he discusses in detail the views of the late Greek commentators Alexander and Themistius as well as the Muslim philosophers, especially Averroes, he makes no mention of Maimonides at all. True, as we have pointed out, Maimonides does not say much about this topic in the *Guide*; yet this fact did not prevent the earlier commentators on the *Guide* from offering their suggestions as to what they believed was Maimonides' position on this controversial issue. Perhaps Gersonides thought that silence is the best approach when the author in question is virtually silent. At any rate, Gersonides tells us lot about the subject as it was treated by the Greek and Muslim philosophers. His main concern here is the widespread doctrine of immortality of the intellect through conjunction, or unification, with the Agent Intellect. Although Gersonides definitely believes in immortality of the intellect, he rejects the doctrine of conjunction, especially in its strong form as found in Averroes. His arguments against conjunction in general are epistemological and metaphysical. If conjunction requires complete knowledge of what is knowable to man, hardly anyone would attain this state; so the goal is futile. And God does not set goals for us that are in vain. If immortality consists in unification with the Agent Intellect, then we would be the Agent Intellect and the latter would be identical with us. But our intellect and the Agent Intellect are totally different things![42] So we better forget about conjunction or unification as the desired state. Instead, Gersonides offers us a goal that is attainable for many of us. The truths that we do discover and understand are themselves eternal (e.g., the theorems of geometry are always true). Insofar as we accumulate knowledge of these truths, our intellect is constituted by these eternal truths, and hence becomes itself everlasting. This is the acquired intellect, the mature and actualized human intellect at the height of its cognitive power. Accordingly, it is the acquired intellect of each person that is capable of immortality. Because each of us acquires different truths and in different ways, immortality is individual, contrary to the position of Averroes and his followers.[43]

Gersonides' views on prophecy and divine providence are within the general Maimonidean framework, so we shall not discuss them here, except for some minor differences. In his discussion of prophecy, Gersonides pays more attention to what we call today "extrasensory phenomena," such as dreams and precognition, than did Maimonides. Moreover, in these discussions Gersonides employs astrology as an explanatory tool, a subject that Maimonides was highly critical of. Another difference is Gersonides' silence about a problem in Maimonides' theory of natural prophecy, wherein divine intervention occurs only as an impediment to prophecy, not as its supervening cause.[44] This point was to vex later commentators, both medieval and modern, on Maimonides; yet, it does not seem to have bothered Gersonides. On providence, Gersonides accepted Maimonides' general account of divine guidance for those who merit it by virtue of their intellectual perfection. However, the bulk of his discussion of this topic is devoted to the problem of theodicy, a subject that Maimonides treats only secondarily.[45]

Gersonides' most detailed treatment of a Maimonidean theme is in his discussion of the problem of divine cognition. Maimonides, as we have seen, attempted to reconcile the apparently opposing theses of maximal divine omniscience and human freedom by appealing to his doctrine of negative attributes. Because "God knows *x*" has a completely different epistemic logic from "Abraham knows *x*," we cannot understand how it is that God knows what Abraham will do to Isaac and yet at the same time Abraham remains free in his act. Gersonides rejects Maimonides' position on the issue of omniscience and the latter's theory of negative attributes. The latter is not only inconsistent with religious discourse and practice, it suffers from a fundamental logical flaw. If in "God is not evil," the term "evil" is radically equivocal, as Maimonides maintains, then in negating this attribute of God, we are literally ignorant of what we are doing, because we no longer know what this term means. For all we know, with reference to God, the term "evil" means *good*. It is a basic principle in logic that, in the affirmation and negation of a term of a subject, the term must not be equivocal. Instead of the theory of negative attributes, Gersonides proposes that we understand the divine attributes as predications of priority and posteriority. For example, in "God is good" the term "good" applies to God primarily, that is, paradigmatically, whereas in "Abraham is good" the term "good" applies to Abraham secondarily, or derivatively. There is something about God and Abraham that warrants the term "good" to be predicated on them, but they are not good in exactly the same way.[46]

With Maimonides' doctrine of negative attributes disposed of, Gersonides then turns to the original question: What does God know? It is quite clear from his exposition of the arguments of the philosophers against the thesis that God knows particulars, especially future contingents, that Gersonides is in their camp. Of special relevance and significance is his affirmation of the validity of the Aristotelian dilemma: Foreknowledge implies determination and necessity.[47] If God knew that Abraham would sacrifice Isaac, then Abraham had no choice in doing it, as his lifting up the axe was necessitated by God's knowledge. Defending the doctrine of human freedom in the strong sense – that is, the agent could have done other than what anyone would have predicted, even God – Gersonides concludes that God knows only how humans ordinarily behave given the laws of psychology. But it is within the power of anyone to subvert these laws on any given occasion, and God is in no better position than anyone of us to know that this will be the case. After all, the Torah describes God as "testing Abraham." What is the point of a test if the outcome is a sure thing known by the tester? According to several modern interpreters, Gersonides has then a "limited," or "weak," theory of divine omniscience.[48]

The problem that receives the most attention by Gersonides is the venerable issue of creation of the universe. Here too Gersonides finds Maimonides lacking. In the first place, he does not appreciate Maimonides' skeptical position on the question of provability. Just because Maimonides failed to find a proof either for eternity or for creation does not mean that someone else will not find one. Unless Maimonides provides a metaproof of the undecidability of this issue, the debate is still open.[49] Second, and more important, Gersonides rejects the standard position, defended by Maimonides as the Torah view, that God created the world *ex nihilo*. To be sure, Gersonides will argue, God created the universe, but not out of nothing; He created it from some eternal, shapeless body, part of which He fashioned into an orderly system, a cosmos. *Ex nihilo nihil fit*. In short, Gersonides defends a modified version of Plato's doctrine, as outlined in the *Timaeus*.[50] Most of the sixth book of the treatise is devoted to a formal demonstration of the temporal beginning of the universe and a rigorous critique of Aristotle's arguments against creation and for eternity. Gersonides sincerely believes that he has succeeded in providing a proof of the world's beginning. Finally, Maimonides' worry that the doctrine of miracles is possible only on the theory of creation is satisfied by the theory of creation from matter. Because the latter is also a theory of voluntary creation, miracles have a place within this theory, as they do on the doctrine of creation *ex nihilo*.[51]

The positive influence of Maimonides is quite evident in Gersonides' *Commentary on the Torah*, especially in his interpretation of biblical law. Like Maimonides, he firmly affirms the rationality of the commandments, even those that seem to have no reason or purpose. Indeed, Gersonides goes even further in his discussion of the commandments, providing detailed explanations of every commandment, whereas Maimonides was often content to offer a general explanation of a class of commandments. On occasion he departs from Maimonides' account. For example, in *Guide* 3.32 Maimonides explained the sacrificial cult as a concession to the ignorance of the ancient Israelites when they left Egypt. Gersonides is not inclined to accept this pedagogical–sociological explanation of sacrifices. According to him, sacrifices are vehicles of divine revelation, of prophecy. The latter requires isolation of the intellect from the other more material faculties. In offering or performing the sacrifice the person focuses all his attention on the act of devotion to God. This entails complete intellectual attention to the act and its purpose. In destroying the animal, the devotee is showing his disdain for matter and his commitment to that which is superior, God, Who is pure Form. His earthly and material desires symbolized by the animal are abandoned in favor of something higher.[52]

12.5. MAIMONIDES SUBVERTED: ḤASDAI CRESCAS' CRITIQUE OF MAIMONIDEAN ARISTOTELIANISM

Maimonides continued to set the Jewish philosophical agenda throughout the fourteenth and fifteenth centuries; his influence even returned to Spain after its peregrinations to Italy and southern France. Some of Spanish Maimonideans adopted a conservative stance in their interpretation of the *Guide* and were also interested in Scholastic thought (e.g., Abraham Bibago and Abraham Shalom); others pursued a more subversive approach toward Maimonides, one that differed considerably from the radical perspective of the Jewish Averroists. Ḥasdai Crescas and Isaac Abravanel were the outstanding representatives of what we may label a "negative Maimonidean" philosophical program. This is most evident in Ḥasdai Crescas, whose major work *The Light of the Lord [Or Adonai]* begins with and is structured around a radical critique of the Maimonidean conception of Jewish thought.

Written at the beginning of the decline of Spanish Jewry in Christian Spain, when the Jews suffered from forced conversions, riots, and violence, Crescas' treatise proposes a new agenda for Jewish thought, in particular a reconstruction of its theology on a basis quite different from the Aristotelian foundation established and employed by Maimonides. In executing this reconstruction Crescas is not introducing a substitute philosophical system to replace Aristotle, say, for example, with Plato. Rather, he is claiming that Judaism should renounce philosophy altogether. But unlike the vulgar fideist who retreats to the "asylum of ignorance" Crescas uses philosophy to undermine philosophy, especially in its application to theology. However, as often is the case with thinkers who oppose philosophy, Crescas ultimately offers us a *philosophical* interpretation and defense of Judaism *malgré-lui.*

Although Crescas originally intended to write a complete refutation of the Maimonidean enterprise, including a critique of Maimonides' legal code, the *Light of the Lord*, the philosophical part of this deconstruction, alone survives.[53] In the Introduction Crescas makes his intentions quite clear: He opposes Aristotelian philosophy and its application to Jewish theology, especially in Maimonides' use of it to establish the dogmatic foundations of Judaism. Indeed, Crescas is particularly vexed by Maimonides' attempt to formulate a creed and his defense of some of the articles of this creed by means of Aristotelian arguments. In undermining Maimonides' edifice Crescas begins with a demolition of the basic principles of Aristotle's physics and metaphysics, on which Maimonides uncritically relied. Quite rightly, some of the leading Crescas specialists have focused on his radical critique of Aristotle's physics as one of the more original features of Crescas' treatise. Nevertheless, it would be a mistake to construe this aspect of his thought as a piece of science. Crescas was no scientist, had no interest in pure or even practical science, such as medicine, and, unlike many of the Scholastic critics of Aristotle of the thirteenth–fifteenth centuries, wrote no independent treatise on a scientific topic. His sole concern in his critique of Aristotle's physics was to destroy Maimonides' employment of it in laying the foundations of Jewish philosophical theology. It is nevertheless important to note and appreciate Crescas' acute and profound criticisms of some of the basic ideas in Aristotle's natural philosophy, such as his rejection of Aristotle's arguments against the possibility of a vacuum, of the Aristotelian horror of the actual infinite, and of his openness to the possibility of plural worlds, both concurrent and successive, notions repugnant to most medieval philosophers faithful to Aristotle's physics.[54]

But it was not only Maimonides' use of Aristotle that disturbed Crescas. He found Maimonides' creed to be illogical. In his eyes all Maimonides had done was to list thirteen propositions as fundamental to Judaism without, however, indicating why these and not others were so important. Moreover, the list exhibits no internal logic; it suggests that all of the propositions are of equal importance and have the same theological significance. Instead, Crescas formulates a new creed wherein the various dogmas are ranked according to a specific theological logic. Some beliefs are essential to any religion that is worthy of consideration; for example, the unity of God. Other beliefs are essential to the concept of a revealed religion; for example, divine cognition of particulars. On the other hand, some dogmas are essential only within a specific religion; for example, creation of the universe, the coming of a Messiah. Finally, there are doctrines that are found in religious traditions but are not essential to them: The believer has the option to adhere to them or not; for example, plural worlds. In this regard, it is interesting and important to note that, for Crescas, belief in creation of the world is not essential to a revealed religion, even though it is taught by Judaism.[55]

Crescas' treatise is structured around this theological logic of a four-tiered stratification of dogmas. Of special interest are his discussions of divine omniscience and of human choice – second-level beliefs – and creation of the universe, a third-level doctrine. On these topics he reaches conclusions that are in some respects novel to Jewish medieval thought and that in some instances are quite critical of his more "classical" predecessors, Maimonides and Gersonides. For example, although he appears to defend, as did Maimonides, Rabbi Akiva's dictum that "everything is seen but freedom is given," and hence he rejects completely Gersonides' deviation from this reconciliationist position, it turns out that he ultimately opts for a deterministic solution of the dilemma, which found hardly any favor among his successors. According to Crescas, Gersonides' arguments against the traditional doctrine of strong omniscience are invalid and Scripture clearly assumes and states that God knows everything, including the outcomes of future contingents. God is able to know them because his cognitive apparatus is timeless and intuitive, such that He "sees" everything in his eternal present. For us, whose cognitive tools are temporal and discursive, the future is indeterminate if it is contingent, so we do not know the winner of the woman's 200-meter dash in the 3000 Olympic Games. But God knows it, and He knows it now, because for Him there is no real future or past. For God, proposition A, "Ms. Anna F. is the winner of the 200-meter dash in the 3000 Olympic Games," is determinately true, and as such necessary. But the negation of this proposition is logically possible; after all, there is no absolute necessity that this person will win the race or that she will even exist. Accordingly, proposition A is logically contingent, even though it is epistemically and metaphysically necessary, given the facts that God eternally knows it and what is eternally true is necessarily true. The inherent logical contigency of proposition A is enough for Crescas to justify Rabbi Akiva's dictum.[56]

The same inclination toward determinism is even more evident in his analysis of human choice. After canvassing and criticizing the various arguments for and against the existence of the contingent in human choice, Crescas ultimately defends a position that in modern philosophy has been labeled "soft determinism." He clearly and strongly accepts the thesis that every event has a cause, including human actions and choices. Otherwise, the act or decision would be inexplicable and hence capricious, and we could not be held responsible for such actions. But this does not mean that we are not free in what we do or choose to do. As long as the agent is not externally compelled to do what he or she does, the agent is free. What is especially crucial here for Crescas is the mental state of the agent: As long as the agent *feels* no compulsion *ab extra*, he or she is free. Again, Crescas appeals to his previous distinction between what is absolutely, or logically, necessary, and what is logically contingent, albeit causally or epistemically necessary. That I chose to watch the football game on TV instead of washing the dishes is a free act, a genuine instance of choice, even though I am by nature lazy and habituated from childhood to watch football, and hence determined to watch instead of wash. After all, I could have been conditioned by my mother to wash the dishes.[57]

Crescas' discussion of creation is remarkable not only because of his demotion of this dogma to a belief that is not necessary for a revealed religion, but for its openness to the legitimacy of the doctrine of the eternity of the world. And this from a zealous opponent of Aristotle! Crescas' tolerance for the infinite duration of the universe arises out of his sharp and detailed critique of the arguments against Aristotle leveled by both Maimonides and Gersonides. Even if the Torah view is creation of the world, it does not gain any advantage by being supported by bad arguments. In the course of his debate with his Jewish predecessors, Crescas ostensibly commits himself to the traditional doctrine of creation *ex nihilo*, but he interprets this idea in such a way that he finds it easy to render it compatible with the Neoplatonic cosmological theory of eternal creation, which had become one way of reading Aristotle's theory, as we have seen in Isaac Albalag and Moses Narboni.

According to Crescas, to be created is to be caused; to be created *ex nihilo* is to be caused from no antecedent matter. This definition is time neutral: Something could be created *ex nihilo* and have either infinite or finite duration. Thus the world is created *ex nihilo* insofar as it is caused by, or emanates from, God and requires no antecedent matter as necessary condition for its production. After all, God is omnipotent. Moreover, Gersonides' arguments against *ex nihilo* creation are invalid. The crucial point here, however, is Crescas' insistence that the existence of an infinitely enduring world is not only logically possible but even plausible. Now if this is the case, it still would not impair the traditional view that the world was created *ex nihilo*, because an infinitely enduring universe still depends upon God and nothing else. Even Aristotle admits as much.[58] On the other hand, if we prefer to adhere to the more prevalent view among the faithful that the world had a definite temporal beginning, that is, it had a "birthday," which appears to be Maimonides' "exoteric" position, we can still reconcile this with the doctrine of God's omnipotence extending throughout infinite time by appealing to the rabbinic dictum that God has created many worlds successively, each having finite duration. Either way creation *ex nihilo* has been preserved, interpreted as causal dependence on nothing except God.[59]

Immortality of the soul is also a doctrine that is not presupposed by a revealed religion but is taught by the Torah, and hence is a belief having dogmatic status for all Jews. Maimonides was then correct in including this belief in his list of articles of faith, but he was wrong in his understanding of it. In the first place, the soul is not just a mere disposition that will perish with the death of the body, except for the intellect that will survive, as Maimonides seems to have believed. Rather, the soul as a whole is a substance, something that is per se imperishable, although created.[60] Because the soul as such is capable of immortality, it is not just through perfection of the intellect that it achieves this state, as Maimonides and his followers had maintained. And certainly immortality does not require a lifetime study of philosophy. Immortality is earned by the deep and continuous love of God and the performance of the divine commandments. This is attainable by the milkman as well as by the Talmudist; it is questionable whether the philosophers will succeed in achieving it, as they are always subject to doubt. Thus the whole doctrine of conjunction of the intellect with the Agent Intellect is otiose, especially because there is no convincing reason why we should believe in the existence of the Agent Intellect in the first place.[61]

12.6. A CONSERVATIVE COMMENTATOR AND CRITIC OF MAIMONIDES: ISAAC ABRAVANEL

Despite his acuity and originality, or perhaps because of them, Crescas did not succeed in uprooting the philosophical tradition among Spanish Jews or in diminishing the impact of Maimonides. Even those thinkers who had some sympathy with Crescas' strictures against both philosophy and Maimonides continued to study the *Guide*. This is quite evident in Isaac Abravanel, the last representative of the Spanish medieval philosophical and Maimonidean tradition, who left Spain in 1492 as a faithful Jew instead of remaining as a "New Christian."[62] Abravanel has been labeled as an "anti-rationalist" by some scholars.[63] Nevertheless, there is an interesting and revealing confession made by Abravanel in one of his last works that is perhaps a better expression of his attitude toward philosophy and Maimonides in particular. In his response to a letter from rabbi from Crete, Saul ha-Kohen, in which the latter had requested answers to a number of philosophical questions pertaining to Aristotelian philosophy, Abravanel, old and almost blind, answers these complicated and controversial questions in detail. Moreover, about Maimonides he confesses that along with the Torah the *Guide* has been the pivotal point of his thought and writings throughout his whole life.[64] Besides writing a commentary on the *Guide*, which he failed to complete, Abravanel discusses Maimonides in virtually all his philosophical treatises and biblical commentaries. Critical he was of the Master of the *Guide*, but he was also completely involved with him.

Abravanel is perhaps most critical of Maimonides in his religious epistemology, especially in the theory of prophecy. Prophecy and philosophy represent for him two radically different modes of cognition, whose results may and indeed do come into conflict with each other. Nevertheless, we do not have here a "double-truth doctrine," which appeared among a group of Christian philosophers who have been labeled "Christian Averroists." Rather, for Abravanel philosophy often teaches something quite persuasively, yet it turns out that this doctrine is wrong, because it controverts a teaching of prophecy. When this occurs, philosophy yields the floor to prophecy. Why? Because prophets receive their information in a way totally different from and superior to the methods of philosophy. Here Abravanel appeals to philosophical language to express and formulate the crucial difference: Whereas philosophers and scientists arrive at their conclusions discursively by means of a posteriori reasoning from effects to causes, prophets acquire their insights intuitively, a priori from causes to effects. For example, a philosopher or scientist may reach the conclusion that the universe has a beginning by an inference from empirical data. This is in substance the nature of Maimonides' argument for creation. The inference may or may not be warranted, depending on the reliability and strength of the evidence. Not so the prophet: He learns about creation directly through prophecy. The cause of his knowledge that the world has been created is simply God's telling him. Here there is no possibility of error or uncertainty, whereas in philosophy or science there is always room for doubt or revision. One consequence of this epistemological distinction is that the prophet does not need to have any philosophical training. Were Moses and Amos philosophers? This does not imply that we should abandon philosophy altogether; it just means that we should realize what it can and cannot accomplish. After all, didn't Maimonides himself warn us of the limitations of human reason in the *Guide*, Part 1, Chapters 31–4?[65]

Nor does the prophet have to possess a highly developed power of imagination. Indeed, there is a type of prophecy that involves neither intellect nor imagination, wherein the individual just sees, hears, or in general senses something that is very much like what ordinary sense–perception yields but in this case is supranaturally caused. Abravanel adduces the famous story of Jacob's wrestling match with the angel. According to Maimonides, in reality Jacob did not see or grapple with an angel; the whole episode took place in his imagination, in a prophetic dream.[66] Abravanel demurs. Jacob actually experienced a set of sensations that corresponds exactly to that which wrestlers experience while wrestling; only in Jacob's match there was no angel. Instead, God produced in him these sensations, even though there was no real sense object. Abravanel calls this type of prophecy "perceptual prophecy." The Israelites at Mt. Sinai too experienced this kind of prophecy while they heard all of the Ten Commandments, not just the first two, as Maimonides had argued.[67]

Abravanel was virtually obsessed with the issue of creation. Besides commenting extensively on the biblical account in his *Commentary on the Torah*, he wrote several philosophical treatises on the subject. Like Maimonides, he reads the Torah as teaching creation *ex nihilo*, meaning temporal creation from no antecedent matter. He rejects both Gersonides' attempt to insinuate Plato's doctrine of eternal matter into Judaism and Crescas' reinterpretation of creation *ex nihilo* as compatible with the theory of eternal creation. He explicitly excoriates the Jewish Averroists by name for having defended the latter theory and for trying to foist it upon Maimonides.[68] Yet he expresses some dissatisfaction with Maimonides' defense of the traditional doctrine. In the first place, Maimonides did not provide a philosophical argument in favor of *ex nihilo* creation as against creation from eternal matter. Second, Maimonides' dismissal of the *kalām* arguments for creation was not entirely justified. In fact, Maimonides' own use of one of the *kalām* arguments – the Particularization Argument – suggests that creation is provable, and not just a more plausible hypothesis than eternity of the world.[69] Third, there is at our disposal a very powerful argument for creation that was initially formulated by John Philoponus (fl. sixth century C.E.), from whom the *kalām* borrowed much. This argument starts with the premise that the physical world is essentially perishable because matter is entropic; then it concludes that the universe had a temporal beginning, for, as Aristotle proved, whatever has an end has a beginning.[70]

Finally, Abravanel rejects Maimonides' advocacy for the universe's everlastingness. Siding with rabbinic tradition and Crescas, Abravanel is sympathetic to the view that our universe is one of several worlds that God has created and destroyed successively.[71]

12.7. MAIMONIDES IN THE ITALIAN RENAISSANCE: JUDAH ABRAVANEL

Although the catastrophe of 1492 destroyed Iberian Jewry, it did not spell the end of Jewish philosophy. In Italy, where some of the Spanish Jews found refuge, the Maimonidean impulse and impact were still felt; indeed, Isaac Abravanel wrote most of his works while in Italian exile. The influence of Maimonides is also evident in his son Judah (in Italian "Leone Ebreo"), whose *Dialoghi D'Amore* was a best-seller throughout the Renaissance. Although Judah was acutely attuned to the new Platonic trends in Italian Renaissance philosophy, remnants of medieval philosophy, and in particular Maimonides' teachings are present in his book.

This is clearly seen in his discussion of immortality. In the First Dialogue, Judah rehearses the various interpretations of Aristotle's theory of intellect and formulates his own version of immortality of the intellect in terms of this conceptual framework. Like Maimonides he subscribes to the view of Alexander of Aphrodisias that the human intellect is a cognitive disposition, not an immaterial substance, which comes to full actuality as the result of accumulating knowledge throughout one's lifetime. A fully mature intellect is fit to be conjoined, or unified, with the Agent Intellect.[72] But it should be noted that in this context, Judah appears to adopt Alexander's doctrine, perhaps unique to him, that the Agent Intellect is identical with God.[73] This is, however, certainly not the view of Maimonides, for whom the Agent Intellect is one of the subordinate separate intellects.[74] But in the third dialogue, Judah seems to have forgotten this idea and with Maimonides now insists upon a sharp distinction between God and any subordinate and intermediary intellect.[75] Moreover, he injects into his theory a Maimonidean theme. In *Guide* 3.51 Maimonides describes the perfect worship of God as an activity of *intellectual love*, culminating in conjunction with God, and hence immortality. Although it is the intellect that "remains," the contemplative life that Maimonides is exalting is replete with a special kind of passion that is redolent with Platonic love. This is how Judah too conceives intellectual conjunction, combining the language of Plato's *Symposium* with Maimonides' *Guide*. In pursuing this Maimonidean trope, Judah interprets King Solomon's Song of Songs as a parable describing the amorous relationship between man and God in intellectual terms. True love of God is attained and expressed through intellectual perfection, whose culmination comprises knowledge of the separate intellects and God to the extent that this is possible for man.[76]

12.8. MAIMONIDES AND SPINOZA: FATHER OF APOSTASY?

Maimonides' voice was still heard in the seventeenth century. This is most apparent in the works of the apostate Jew Baruch Spinoza (1632–77).[77] The relationship between Maimonides and Spinoza has been studied ever since the middle of the nineteenth century.[78] That there is an important Maimonidean element in Spinoza's thought is not in question, but what needs to be clarified is the precise nature of his influence. At the outset one needs to distinguish between a general medieval imprint in Spinoza from a more specific Maimonidean influence.[79] Those who maximize the Maimonidean imprint offer us a portrait of Spinoza as "a Maimonidean," deeply under the influence of his medieval mentor, perhaps beginning his philosophical education with the *Guide* and never emancipating himself completely from its seductiveness.[80] On the other hand, there are those who find this approach to be a "bias" or even an "obsession" that results in a failure to appreciate Spinoza's originality and modernity.[81] And some minimize the Maimonidean imprint altogether.[82]

Before we attempt to assess the significance of Maimonides for Spinoza, several facts need to be recognized. First, although it may be conceded that a Maimonidean imprint can be detected in several of Spinoza's purely philosophical writings, he refers explicitly to Maimonides in only one of his works, *The Theological–Political Treatise* (1670), and in only one of his letters, Letter 43. It is most likely that there is also an anonymous reference to him in *Ethics* 2.7, which we shall discuss shortly. Second, the only book that Spinoza published under his own name was his *Principles of Cartesian Philosophy* (1663). A study of this work, Spinoza's early letters, and the early monographs – the *Treatise on the Improvement of the Understanding* and the *Short Treatise* – reveals a pervasive and strong Cartesian influence, so much so that some of Spinoza's earliest critics, as well as modern commentators, have seen him as a "great Cartesian."[83] Indeed, the basic metaphysical conceptual framework of the *Ethics* presupposes and develops out of the Cartesian definitions of substance, attribute, mode, and God, as laid out in Descartes' *Principles of Philosophy* 1.51–56. Third, we must not forget that Spinoza lived in the Netherlands and that in the Dutch universities both neo-Scholastic and Cartesian philosophy were taught. We do know that Spinoza studied Latin with the ex-Jesuit Franciscus van den Enden, although it is not certain whether his studies in the latter's school preceded or were immediately begun after his excommunication. And it is not unlikely that from van den Enden Spinoza learned Cartesian philosophy. Recent scholarship on the ex-Jesuit has shown significant similarities between van den Enden and Spinoza on variety of philosophical and political topics.[84] Finally, and perhaps most importantly, in the *Theological–Political Treatise* Spinoza explicitly and forcefully rejects the whole thrust of medieval Jewish, especially Maimonidean, philosophical exegesis of the Bible. Instead, he proposes a new hermeneutics based upon a purely philological and historical analysis of the text that resists any importation of philosophical ideas and interpretations.[85]

The story of Spinoza's break with Judaism and his subsequent excommunication in 1656 still fascinates us.[86] Although we do not know exactly what Spinoza believed or said at the time of his excommunication that warranted this extreme punishment, it is quite clear from his subsequent writings that *he deserved* this penalty, even if he held only some of his later ideas at that earlier time. Even in his earliest writings Spinoza is fully aware of his intellectual break with both his religious and philosophical predecessors. As he says in Letter 2 (1661), he understands God to be a substance consisting of infinite attributes, each one of which is infinite in itself, and one of these attributes, Spinoza insists, is extension; hence God is infinitely extended. Although he does not mention Maimonides, restricting his criticisms only to Descartes and Francis Bacon, it is clear that Spinoza has made a radical and sharp break with the whole medieval philosophical tradition, as well as with Descartes and Bacon, by attributing extension to God. Moreover, in Letter 6, which is a critique of some chemical theories of the famous English chemist Robert Boyle, Spinoza concludes his criticisms of these ideas with the general philosophical claim: "I do not differentiate between God and Nature in the way all those known to me have done." Quite early in his philosophical career Spinoza had reached his monistic and pantheistic theses that there is only one Substance, God, and that this Substance is identical with nature; or, as he states in *Ethics* 4, Preface: "God, or Nature." Cosmological dualism, with its attendant doctrine of creation of the world, eternal or temporal, was even in this early period of Spinoza's philosophical development a medieval myth.

In Letter 2 Spinoza also criticizes Descartes and Bacon for an erroneous theory of the mind, especially concerning its relationship to the body. As he sees it, they still adhered to the Platonic and medieval view that the soul, or mind, is somehow united with the body, albeit their very different natures, the former being immaterial and incorruptible, the latter corporeal and perishable. This, Spinoza again insists, is an error. Although in this early rejection of psychological dualism Spinoza does not state his own view, he eventually develops a theory of psychological monism, according to which the mind and the body are really just one thing, conceived in two different ways.[87] Although Maimonides' psychology is not altogether free from perplexities, as we have seen, his almost obsessive revulsion of the body as the source of sin and error would not make him sympathetic to Spinoza's psychological monism. Some modern scholars have even attributed to Spinoza a "hidden" materialism, which can be found in a number of passages in the *Ethics*.[88]

If then Spinoza's philosophy in its earliest expressions manifests a clear break with the medieval philosophical framework, how is Maimonides relevant to an understanding of Spinoza? For some commentators we should picture the young Spinoza reading the *Guide* and deciding that (1) Maimonides had failed to solve the questions therein, (2) that the *Guide* itself was a source of perplexities, and (3) that the later Jewish medieval philosophers, such as Gersonides and Crescas, were no more successful in resolving these issues.[89] Those who stress the specific Maimonidean imprint on Spinoza are not content with this "table-setting" approach. They also want to highlight the importance of some specific and positive aspects of Maimonides' philosophy for Spinoza.[90] Consider, for example, his claim in *Ethics* 2.7, Scholium, that the mind and the body are one and the same thing, expressed in two different ways. In support of this thesis, he refers to a doctrine of the "Hebrews" that he sees as anticipating, even if "through a cloud," his own view. According to Harry

Wolfson, Spinoza is referring to Maimonides' doctrine in *Guide* 1.68 that God, God's intellect, and the objects of His intellection are one and the same.[91] Assuming the likelihood of this attribution, we still have to pay attention to Spinoza's own editorial comment: Maimonides did not fully understand this point. If he had, he would have realized that if God and the objects of His knowledge are one, and if He knows the world of extended nature, which presumably He does, then one of God's attributes is extension and that God and nature are one and the same thing. Moreover, from this principle, which Maimonides allegedly apprehended through a cloud, a similar argument can be constructed concerning the mind: If the mind and the objects of its thought are also one and the same thing, then if the mind knows the body as an extended thing, which it does, then the mind and the body are one and the same thing. Here Spinoza begins with Maimonides but ends by rejecting him.

An analogous Spinozistic "deconstruction" of a Maimonidean thesis can be seen in *The Theological–Political Treatise*, whose initial chapters deal with prophecy. Spinoza begins his analysis by assuming Maimonides' distinction between imagination and intellect and his contention that prophets use imagination. But he vigorously denies that they have access to intellectual apprehensions of the truth. For if they had, they would not have uttered falsehoods, as when Joshua commanded God to stop the sun from moving.[92] Indeed, the prophets differed among themselves, and this is also an indication that prophetic discourse is not the product of an intellectual act. And this is true also of Moses, whose apprehension of God was just as imaginative as was Joshua's or Isaiah's. In fact, Spinoza transfers Moses' alleged superiority to Jesus: Whereas Moses "saw" God "face to face," that is, imaginatively, Jesus intellectually apprehended God "mind-to-mind."[93] It is quite clear that Spinoza rejected the philosophical role of the prophet, even and especially of Moses.

Nevertheless, there are places in which Spinoza and Maimonides are in accord. They both stressed the subjective character of moral concepts and judgements. Moral beliefs for both thinkers fall short of the epistemic status enjoyed by the truths of mathematics and physics.[94] Following the common practice in medieval Muslim philosophy to subsume moral philosophy under political philosophy, Maimonides sees moral norms primarily within the context of establishing a peaceful and just society. But because human moral and political principles are just commonly accepted beliefs (*mefursamot*, *endoxa*), not genuine knowledge, a purely secular polity and law would be imperfect. A perfect society requires then a divine law.[95] Although Spinoza too highlights the subjective dimension in moral and political beliefs, nevertheless he was not oblivious to the need for moral standards. Indeed, in the *Ethics* there are seeds of an "objectivist" ethic that rises above mere individual preferences. Certain moral precepts are based on reason, for example, the principle of self-preservation, and reason, unlike imagination, is always true. This principle derives from a basic fact of human nature: Every living thing strives to preserve itself. This is Spinoza's theory of *conatus*.[96] In setting forth his doctrine of the "precepts of reason" Spinoza too was attempting to overcome moral subjectivism, but unlike Maimonides he does not appeal to a heteronomically imposed legislation. The divine laws for Spinoza are the laws of nature (e.g., the laws of gravity and the psychological law of association), not the prohibition of wearing a garment made of wool and linen.[97]

Perhaps the most Maimonidean theme in Spinoza is the concluding idea in the *Ethics*, in which Spinoza describes the ultimate stage in the journey to blessedness. At this point this individual has reached the highest form of cognition, "intuitive science," and this cognition is just that "intellectual love of God" that both Maimonides and Judah Abravanel had specified as man's real perfection. Maimonides and Spinoza agree that this state is quite difficult to achieve, but Spinoza is a bit more inclusive in his portrayal of the possibility of blessedness. Whereas Maimonides was most restrictive, virtually denying its realization for most of us, Spinoza was more optimistic, envisioning a society, perhaps small in numbers, governed by reason. These are the truly "free men."[98] Among these liberated individuals there will be some who have even gone beyond this stage and have attained the intellectual love of God. At this juncture the life of the body, our ordinary life rooted in temporality, has been transcended. Whether or not we survive the death of our bodies as individuals, the question that had vexed the medievals, is now no longer relevant. In achieving the intellectual love of God we have already experienced a form of eternity. And this is sufficient.[99]

Philosophers do not philosophize *ex nihilo*: They live and work within a specific historical context that defines to some extent their own outlook and endeavors. In this general sense Maimonides was certainly a factor in Spinoza's intellectual formation. But what makes Spinoza philosophically interesting and important is not his debt to Maimonides or to other medieval thinkers, but his rupture with this tradition, even with Descartes insofar as the latter embodied several medieval traits. Underlying Spinoza's modernity are two fundamental and pervasive themes: (1) the firm belief in the adequacy of human reason, its capacity to obtain true and significant knowledge of God[100]; and (2) his goal to emancipate philosophy from theology and the state from religion.[101] Maimonides did not share Spinoza's "epistemological optimism," as his theory of negative attributes illustrates. Nor would he have accepted Spinoza's vision of a purely secular state based on democratic principles. Whatever Maimonides believed in his heart about the creation or eternity of the universe or any other metaphysical perplexity, his commitment to the supranaturally imposed divine law, the Torah, was unequivocal. And it is this law that should and will govern the perfect society. Spinoza rejected this commitment, and in so doing he no longer regarded Maimonides as a mentor but as a foil on which he whetted his philosophical and political critique.

12.9. CONCLUSION

Maimonides' influence on subsequent Jewish thought has continued until this day. But this chapter in the career of Maimonides requires separate treatment. It is interesting to note, however, that several early modern Jewish thinkers recognized the monumental impact, positive and negative, of Maimonides on themselves and the history of Jewish thought. Moses Mendelssohn (1729–86), usually regarded as the first modern Jewish philosopher, began his philosophical studies with Maimonides and wrote a commentary on Maimonides' *Treatise on Logic*.[102] His younger contemporary Solomon, the son of Joshua (1754–1800), who, like Spinoza, had liberated himself from the shackles of "superstition and prejudice," also began to philosophize with Maimonides and wrote a commentary on Part 1 of the *Guide* and a critical exposition of Maimonides' philosophy in his own autobiography. Quite significantly he assumed as his surname the name "Maimon," and has been known ever since as "Salomon Maimon." He also noted the Maimonides–Spinoza connection, although he mentioned Jewish mysticism too as a formative influence on Spinoza.[103] Perhaps the most favorable attitude toward Maimonides by a Jewish philosopher before World War II was expressed by the great German–Jewish neo-Kantian philosopher Hermann Cohen (1842–1918), who stressed the practical, or moral, dimension in Maimonides.[104] In addition, he defended Maimonides against the criticisms of Spinoza and severely castigated the latter for his disparaging remarks about Judaism and Jews.[105] To be sure, there was a philosophical literature among the Jews before Maimonides; but it pales in significance compared with that of "the master of the *Guide*." It is simply impossible to discuss any Jewish thinker, major or minor, after Maimonides without referring to him. To many he has been the model of what it is to philosophize within the limits of a religious tradition; to others he has been a stimulus to break out of those limits and to forge a new philosophy free from the confines of religion. In either case Maimonides has been a *Guide* for posterity.

NOTES

1. For the most part I limit my discussion to Maimonides' *Guide of the Perplexed*.
2. *GP* 1.51–56.
3. *GP* 2.13, pp. 281–2.
4. *GP* 2.25, pp. 327–8.
5. *GP* 2.32 and 36; *MT* 1, Book of Knowledge, Principles of the Torah, Chapter 7.
6. *GP* 3.16, pp. 19–21.
7. *GP* 3.23, p. 496.
8. *GP* 3.51, pp. 624–6.
9. *GP*, 1.74, the seventh method, p. 221. For a good recent study of this thorny issue see Steven Nadler 2001, Chapter 4.
10. Diesendruck 1936, pp. 341–65.
11. Ravitzky 1990a, pp. 159–207; Ravitzky 1996, pp. 205–45.
12. Diesendruck, 1936, p. 347. Eisen 1999, pp. 263–300.
13. Averroes 1969, pp. 222–5. On Samuel Ibn Tibbon see Ravitzky 1978–9, pp. 80–81.
14. Feldman 1980, pp. 289–320.
15. Vajda 1960, pp. 137–49.
16. Because the literature on this topic is voluminous, I refer here only to Alfred Ivry 1990, pp. 115–38. Ivry supplies an ample bibliography.

17. Ravitzky 1996, p. 239.
18. *GP* 2.25, pp. 328–9.
19. Davidson 1979, pp. 16–40; Harvey 1981a, pp. 287–301.
20. Albalag 1973, Chapter 30; Vajda 1960, Part 1, Chapter 6; Feldman 2000, pp. 15–30.
21. For Narboni, see Sirat 1990, pp. 336–7. Hayoun 1989, Part 3.
22. Aristotle, *Metaphysics* 12.7, 1072b 19–22; 12.9, 1075a1–4.
23. Moses Narboni 1852, ad locum; Narboni 1967, pp. 225–88.
24. Touati 1954, pp. 193–205.
25. Ivry 1977; Bland 1982b.
26. Ivry 1967, pp. 271–97; Davidson 1992.
27. Altmann 1987, pp. 60–129.
28. Sermoneta 1976, pp. 130–5; Sermoneta 1980, pp. 235–62.
29. Hillel of Verona 1981, Part 1, Chapters 2, 4–5.
30. Hillel of Verona 1981, Part 1, Chapter 5.
31. Hillel of Verona 1981, Part 1, Chapters 4, 5, and 7. Hillel's use of Aquinas as a "corrective" to Maimonides is especially interesting because Maimonides was quite influential among several of the Christian Scholastics, including Aquinas, who quotes him by name as "Rabbi Moses." The literature on the relationship between Maimonides and Aquinas is extensive. Jacob Dienstag has compiled a very useful annotated bibliography in his 1975 anthology, pp. 334–45. More recently see Dobbs-Weinstein 1995.
32. Hillel of Verona 1981, Part 2, Chapters 1–3.
33. Hillel of Verona 1981, Part 2, Chapter 2, p. 168, note. Maimonides, *CM*, *Neziqin*, *Sanhedrin* 10.
34. Hillel of Verona 1981, Part 2, Chapter 2, p. 173.
35. Sermoneta 1965, pp. 3–78; Rigo 1998, pp. 181–222.
36. *GP*, 3.51–54. Sermoneta 1965, pp. 16–18.
37. Sermoneta 1965, pp. 33–4, 46–7; Rigo 1998, p. 216. Rigo believes that the influence of Albert the Great on Judah Romano was greater than that of Aquinas (private communication).
38. Sermoneta 1990, pp. 77–114; Aquinas, *Summa Theologiae* I, q. 13, a.2.
39. Aquinas, *Summa Theologiae* 2.2, q. 172, a.1; Altmann 1978, 1–19.
40. Sermoneta 1984, pp. 337–74.
41. C. Touati 1973 is the best comprehensive study of Gersonides' philosophy.
42. Gersonides 1984, Book 1, Chapters 4 and 18.
43. Gersonides 1984, Book 1, Chapters 11 and 13.
44. *GP* 2.32, pp. 361–2.

45. Gersonides 1988, Book 4.
46. Gersonides 1988, Book 3, Chapter 3.
47. Gersonides 1988, Book, Chapters 2 and 4.
48. Gersonides 1988, Book 3, Chapter 5; S. Feldman 1985, pp. 105–33; C. Manekin 1998, pp. 135–70.
49. Gersonides 1984, Book 1, Introduction, pp. 94–7.
50. Gersonides 1999, Book 6, Part 1, Chapters 17–18.
51. Gersonides 1999, Book 6, Part 2, Chapter 1.
52. Gersonides, *Commentary on the Torah* (Venice, 1574), Genesis, Parashat Noaḥ, 21a; Gersonides 1988, Appendix, pp. 245–6.
53. Crescas 1990, Introduction.
54. H. Wolfson 1929; W. Z. Harvey 1998b.
55. Crescas 1990, Introduction; Third Treatise, Introduction.
56. Crescas 1990, Second Treatise, First Principle, Chapter 4; Feldman 1982, pp. 2–28.
57. Crescas 1990, Second Treatise, Fifth Principle, Chapter 3; Touati 1974, pp. 573–8; Feldman 1984, 15–54. Pines and Altmann have argued that Maimonides too was a determinist (Pines 1960, pp. 195–8; Altmann 1974, pp. 25–52). This reading of Maimonides has been challenged by Gellman 1989, pp. 139–50; Hyman 1997, pp. 133–52; Stern 1998, pp. 217–66.
58. Crescas 1990, Third Treatise, First Principle, Chapter 5; Aristotle, *Physics* 7.1, 8.5–6; *Metaphysics*, 12. 6–7.
59. Feldman 1980, pp. 304–16.
60. Crescas 1990, Third Treatise, Second Principle.
61. Crescas 1990, Second Treatise, Sixth Principle; Harvey 1973.
62. Netanyahu 1972.
63. Barzilay 1967.
64. Isaac Abravanel 1574, 7b.
65. Abravanel 1954, First Kings, Chapter 3, pp. 467–78; Abravanel 1959, Genesis, Parashat Yitro, 78b–79a. Abravanel's commentary on Maimonides' treatment of prophecy has been translated into English by A. Reines 1970.
66. *GP* 2.42, p. 389.
67. Abravanel, 1959, Genesis, Parashat va-Yishlaḥ, 153c–154c; Exodus, Parashat Yitro, 79–80; *GP* 2.33; Feldman 1998, pp. 223–36.
68. Abravanel, on Crescas, 1863, 1.3 and 1828, 2b; on Narboni 1828, 2a,3a,10b and 49b.
69. Feldman 1990, 5–25.
70. Aristotle, *On the Heavens*, 1.12; John Philoponus 1899, Books 6, 9 and 17; R. Sorabji 1983, Chapters 13 and 15.

71. *GP* 2.27–29; Abravanel 1863, Book 8; Crescas 1990, Fourth Treatise, First Question; Feldman 1986, pp. 53–77; R. Weiss 1992–3, pp. 195–218.
72. Judah Abravanel (henceforth "Leone") 1937, pp. 38–41, 44–6; 1929, pp. 36–37, 40–3.
73. Leone 1937, p. 45; 1929, pp. 41–2. Alexander of Aphrodisias 1887, p. 89.
74. *GP* 2.4.
75. Leone 1937, pp. 415–23; 1929, pp. 348–55.
76. Leone 1937, pp. 424–7, 444–61; 1929, pp. 356–8, 372–86.
77. Leibniz also read the *Guide* and briefly annotated it. See L. Goodman 1980, pp. 214–36
78. Dienstag 1986, pp. 375–415.
79. Wolfson 1969.
80. Pines 1968, pp. 3–54; 1983, pp. 147–59; Harvey 1981b, pp. 151–72.
81. M. Gueroult 1968, p. 445.
82. J. Freudenthal 1887, pp. 102–3.
83. Bayle 1965, p. 332.
84. Klever 1989, pp. 311–27; 1996, pp. 17–21, 24–6.
85. Spinoza 2001, *Theological–Political Treatise* (henceforth "*TTP*"), Preface; L. Strauss 1982, Chapters 5 and 6.
86. I. S. Revah 1959; S. Nadler 2001.
87. Spinoza 1992, *Ethics*, 2.7, *Scholium*, 2.11–13.
88. S. Hampshire 1971, pp. 210–31; E. Curley 1988, pp. 61–70, 74–8, 139, n. 10.
89. Wolfson 1969, Vol. 1, especially Chapter 1.
90. Harvey 1981b, pp. 151–71.
91. Wolfson 1969, Vol. 2, pp. 24–7.
92. Spinoza, *TTP*, Chapter 2.
93. Spinoza, *TTP*, Chapter 1.
94. *GP* 1.2; Spinoza, *Ethics* 1, Appendix; *Ethics* 4, Preface, Definitions 1–2, Proposition 68; Harvey 1981b, pp. 158–61; 1979, pp. 167–85.
95. *GP* 3.27.
96. Spinoza, *Ethics* 3.6–9; 4.18–22.
97. Spinoza, *TTP*, Chapters 4–5.
98. Spinoza, *Ethics*, 4.67, 71–73.
99. Spinoza, *Ethics*, 5.25–42; Nadler 2001, Chapters 5–6.
100. Spinoza, *Ethics*, 2.47.
101. Spinoza, *TTP*, Preface, Chapters 19–20.
102. Altmann 1973, pp. 10–12, 21–2.
103. S. Maimon 1965a, p. 307; 1965b, pp. 161–3. In his comments on *GP* 1.68 in his autobiography (1965a, p. 366) Maimon remarks that Maimonides' acceptance of the Aristotelian principle of the identity of the knower,

the act of knowing and the object of knowledge leads to a result that ". . . it is not too difficult for the reader to follow" (my translation). His Hebrew translator glosses over this cryptic comment as referring to pantheism (*Toldot Shelomoh,* Maimon 1898, Part 2, 30); S. Atlas 1950–51, pp. 517–47.

104. H. Cohen 1972, pp. 39, 61–4, 94–5, 354–6; 2004, especially Sections 32–52, 120–137.

105. H. Cohen 1924, pp. 290–372, especially pp. 346–53.

Bibliography

SACRED LITERATURE

Babylonian Talmud 1898. 20 vols. Vilna, Poland: Romm.
Midrash Rabbah 2000. 16 vols. Jerusalem: H. Wagshal.
Palestinian Talmud 1948. New York: Shulsinger (reprint).
Sifre Devarim 1969. Ed. L. Finkelstein. New York: Jewish Theological Seminary of America.
Tanakh 1985. *Tanakh, The Holy Scriptures: The New JPS Translation According to the Traditional Hebrew Text.* Philadelphia: Jewish Publication Society.
Midrash Tanḥuma 1884. 2 vols., ed. S. Buber. Vilna, Poland: Romm.
Vayikra Rabbah 1953. 4 vols., ed. S. Margulies. Jerusalem: Ministry of Education and Culture.

EDITIONS OF THE *GUIDE OF THE PERPLEXED*

1929. *Dalālat al-ḥā'irīn*, ed. S. Munk and I. Joel. Jersualem: Janovitch.
1960. *Le Guide des Egarés*, 3 vols., trans. Solomon Munk. Paris: Editions G.-P. Maisonneuve Nouvelle edition (Original edition: Paris, 1856–66).
1963. *The Guide of the Perplexed*, trans. S. Pines. Chicago: University of Chicago Press.
1972. *Moreh Nevukhim*, trans. Y. Qāfiḥ. Jerusalem: Mosad ha-Rav Kook.
2002. *Moreh Nevukhim*, 2 vols., trans. Michael Schwarz. Tel Aviv: Tel Aviv University Press.

OTHER WORKS OF MAIMONIDES

1859. *Qovets Teshuvot ha-Rambam we-Iggerotaw*, ed. A. Lichtenberg. Leipzig, Germany: H. L. Shnoys.
1902. *Ma'amar ha-'ibbur*, trans. L. Dünner. *Die aelteste astronomische Schrift des Maimonides*. Würzburg, Germany: C. J. Becker.

1938. *Maimonides' Treatise on Logic*, ed. and trans. Israel Efros. New York: American Academy for Jewish Research.

1939. *Maimonides' Treatise on Resurrection*, ed. J. Finkel. New York: American Academy for Jewish Research.

1946. *Sefer ha-Mitsvot*, trans. S. Ibn Tibbon, ed. C. Heller. Jerusalem: Mosad ha-Rav Kook.

1947. *Hilkhot ha-Yerushalmi*, ed. S. Lieberman. New York: Jewish Theological Seminary.

1949. *The Code of Maimonides, Book Fourteen: The Book of Judges*, trans. Abraham M. Hershman. New Haven, CT: Yale University Press.

1952. *Iggeret Teman*, trans. B. Cohen, ed. S. Halkin. New York: Jewish Theological Seminary of America.

1954. *The Code of Maimonides, Book Ten: The Book of Cleanness*, trans. Herbert Danby. New Haven, CT: Yale University Press.

1956a. *Sanctification of the New Moon*, trans. S. Gandz, with commentary by J. Obermann and O. Neugebauer. New Haven, CT: Yale University Press.

1956b. *Commentarius in Mischnam*, ed. S. D. Sassoon, in *Corpus Codicum Hebraicorum Medii Aevi*. Par. 1. Copenhagen: E. Munksgaard.

1960. *Teshuvot ha-Rambam*, 3 vols., ed. and trans. J. Blau. Jerusalem: Meqitsei Nirdamim.

1963–1967. *Mishnah ʿim perush Rabbenu Mosheh ben Maimon: maqor we-targum*, 6 vols., ed. and trans. Y. Qāfiḥ/Kafaḥ. Jerusalem: Mosad ha-Rav Kuk.

1964. *Regimen of Health*, trans. A. Bar-Sela, H. E. Hebbel, and E. Faris, in *Transactions of the American Philosophical Society*, New Series, 54, Part 4.

1965a. *The Code of Maimonides, Book Five: The Book of Holiness*, trans. Louis I. Rabinowitz and Philip Grossman. New Haven, CT: Yale University Press.

1965b. *Millot ha-Higayon*, trans. S. Ibn Tibbon, ed. L. Roth. Jerusalem: Magnes Press.

1966. *Commentarius in Mischnam*, ed. S. D. Sassoon. *Corpus Codicum Hebraicorum Medii Aevi.* Pars. I. Copenhagen: E. Munksgaard.

1967. *Maimonides: The Commandments*, trans. Charles B. Chavel. London: Soncino Press.

1974a. *Maimonides, The Book of Knowledge*, trans. Moses Hyamson. Jerusalem: Feldheim.

1974b. *On the Causes of Symptoms*, ed. and trans. J. O. Leibowitz and S. Marcus. Berkeley, CA: University of California Press.

1975. *The Ethical Writings of Maimonides*, trans. Raymond Weiss and Charles Butterworth. New York: Dover.

1976. *Commentary on the Mishnah*, 3 vols., trans. Y. Qāfiḥ. Jerusalem: Mosad ha-Rav Kook.
1979. *The Code of Maimonides, Book Seven: The Book of Agriculture*, trans. Isaac Klein. New Haven, CT: Yale University Press.
1981. *Sefer ha-Mitsvot im Hasagot ha-Ramban*, ed. C. B. Chavel. Jerusalem: Mosad ha-Rav Kook.
1985a. *Iggerot ha-Rambam* [*Maimonides' Letters*]. Jerusalem 1946, ed. D. H. Baneth, 2nd enlarged ed. with supplement by A. H. Halkin. Jerusalem: The Magnes Press.
1985b. *Crisis and Leadership: Epistles of Maimonides*, ed. Abraham Halkin and David Hartman. New York: Jewish Publication Society.
1986. *Teshuvot ha-Rambam [Maimonides' Responsa]*, 4 vols., ed. J. Blau, editio secunda emendata. Jerusalem: R. Mass.
1988–9. *Letters and Essays of Maimonides*, ed. and trans. I. Shailat. Ma'aleh Adumim, Israel: Shailat Publishing.
1996. *Traité de logique*, ed. and trans. R. Brague. Paris: Desclée de Brouwer.
2000a. *Mishneh Torah*, 12 vols., ed. S. Frankel. Jerusalem: Hotzaat Shabse Frankel.
2000b. *Epistle to Yemen*, trans. J. L. Kraemer, in Lerner 2000.
2000c. *Treatise on Resurrection*, trans. H. Fradkin, in Lerner 2000.
2002. *On Asthma: A Parallel Arabic-English Text*, ed. and trans. G. Bos. Provo, UT: Brigham Young University Press.

OTHER PRIMARY SOURCES

Abravanel, Yizhak (Isaac) 1574. *Questions and Answers to Rabbi Saul Ha-Kohen*. Venice: n.p.
1828. *New Heavens [Shamayyim Ḥadashim]*. Roedelheim, Germany: W. Heidenheim.
1863. *Deeds of God (Mifla'ot Elohim)*. Lvov, Ukraine: S. Back.
1954. *Commentary on the Former Prophets*. Jerusalem: Hotsaat Sefarim Torah v' Da'at.
1959. *Commentary on the Torah*. New York: Saphrograph.
1982. *Principles of Faith*, trans. Menachem Kellner. London: Littman Library of Jewish Civilization.
Abravanel, Judah (Leone Ebreo) 1929. *Dialoghi D'Amore*, ed. S. Caramella. Bari, Italy: Laterza & Figli.
1937. *The Philosophy of Love [Daloghi d'Amore]*, trans. F. Friedeberg and J. H. Barnes. London: Soncino Press.
Al-Ghazālī, Abū Ḥāmid. *Al-Iqtiṣād fī-l-i'tiqād*. Cairo: Matba'at as-Sa'āda, 1327 A.H./1909.
al-Maqqarī, Aḥmad ibn Muḥammad 1988. *Nafḥ aṭ-ṭib.*, ed. I. 'Abbās. Beirut: Dar Ṣādir.

Albalag, Isaac 1973. *Sefer Tiqqun De'ot*, ed. Georges Vajda. Jerusalem: Israel Academy of Sciences and Humanities.

Albo, Joseph 1929–30. *Sefer ha Iqqarim*, 5 vols., trans. I. Husik. Philadelphia: Jewish Publication Society of America.

Alexander of Aphrodisias 1887. *De Anima* in Scripta Minora 2.1, ed. I. Brunn. Berlin: G. Reimer.

1989. *On Aristotle's Metaphysics* 1, trans. W. E. Dooley. Ithaca, NY: Cornell University Press.

Alfarabi 1964. *The Political Regime*, ed. Fauzi Najjar. Beirut: al-maṭba'ah al-kāthūlīkīyah. (An English translation of part of this treatise has been prepared by Fauzi Najjar and appears in R. Lerner and M. Mahdi 1972, *Medieval Political Philosophy: A Sourcebook*. Ithaca, NY: Cornell University Press.)

1973. "Letter on the Intellect," in *Philosophy in the Middle Ages*, trans. A. Hyman, ed. A. Hyman and J. J. Walsh. Indianapolis, IN: Hackett, pp. 215–21.

Averroes 1969. *Tahafut Al-Tahafut* [*The Incoherence of the Incoherence*], trans. S. Van Den Bergh. London: Luzac.

Avicenna 1960. *Ash-Shifā'. Al-Ilāhiyyāt [La Métaphysique]*, 2 vols., ed. and trans. Georges C. Anawati. Cairo: Organisation Génerale des Imprimeries Gouvernementales.

1972. *'Uyūn al-masā'il*, ed. M. Cruz Hernandez, trans. George Hourani, "Ibn Sina on Necessary and Possible Existence," *Philosophical Forum* 4.1: 74–86.

1985. *La Métaphysique du Shifā', Livres de VI, à X*, trans. Georges C. Anawati. Paris: Librairie Philosophique J. Vrin.

Ben Gershom, Levi (Gersonides) 1866. *Milḥamot Ha-Shem*. Leipzig, Germany: Carl von Lorck.

1984, 1988, 1999. *The Wars of the Lord [Milḥamot Ha-Shem]*, trans. S. Feldman. Philadelphia: Jewish Publication Society.

Ben Joseph, Maimon 1890. "The Letter of Consolation of Maimon Ben Joseph," ed. and trans. L. M. Simmons. *Jewish Quarterly Review* 2: 62–101.

Cohen, Hermann 1924. *Jüdische Schriften*, Vol. 3, ed. B. Strauss. Berlin: Schwetschke und Sohn.

1972. *The Religion of Reason Out of the Sources of Judaism*, trans. S. Kaplan. New York: Ungar.

2004. *The Ethics of Maimonides*, translated with commentary by Almut Bruckstein. Madison, WI: University of Wisconsin Press.

Crescas, Ḥasdai 1990. *The Light of the Lord [Or Ha-Shem]*, ed. S. Fisher. Jerusalem: Ramot.

Hillel of Verona 1981. *The Book of Rewards and Punishments [Sefer Tagmulei Ha-Nefesh]*, ed. J. Sermoneta. Jerusalem: Israel Academy of Sciences and Humanities.

Ibn Abī Uṣaybi'a, Aḥmad ibn al-Qāsim 1965.*'Uyūn al-anbā' fī ṭabaqāt al-aṭibbā'*. Beirut: Dār Maktabat al-Ḥayah.

Ibn al-'Adīm, 'Umar b. Ahmad 1988–9. *Bughyat aṭ-ṭalab fī tārīkh Ḥalab*, ed. S. Zakkar. Damascus: S. Zakkar.

Ibn al-Qifṭī, 'Ali ibn Yūsuf 1903. *Tārīkh al-ḥukamā'*, ed. J. Lippert. Leipzig, Germany: Dieterich'sche Verlagsbuchhandlung.

Ibn Daud, Abraham 1967. *The Book of Tradition [Sefer ha-qabbalah]*, ed. and trans. G. D. Cohen. Philadelphia: Jewish Publication Society.

Ibn Shaddād, Bahā' ad-Dīn 2001. *The Rare and Excellent History of Saladin*, trans. D. S. Richards. Hampshire, UK/Burlington, VT: Ashgate.

Ibn Tibbon, Samuel 1837. *Yiqqavu Ha-Mayyim [Let the Waters be Gathered]*. Bratislava, Slovakia: M. L. Bisliches.

Ibn Tibbon, Samuel 1987. *Perush Ha-Millot Hazerot*, ed. Even-Shemuel, *Sefer Moreh HaNeukhim*. Jerusalem: n.p.

Lerner, R., trans. 1974. *Averroes' Commentary on Plato's Republic*. Ithaca, NY: Cornell University Press.

Maimon, Salomon 1898. *Toledot Shelomoh Maimon*, ed. I. H. Tabiov. Warsaw, Poland: Tushiyah.

1965a. *Lebensgeschichte [Autobiography]*. Hildesheim, Germany: G. Olms.

1965b. *Giv'at Ha-Moreh [Commentary on the Guide of the Perplexed]*, ed. S. H. Bergamann. Jerusalem: Israel Academy of Sciences and Humanities.

Maimonides, Abraham 1952. *Wars of the Lord [Milḥamot ha-Shem]*, ed. R. Margaliyot. Jerusalem: Mosad ha-Rav Kook.

Narboni, Moses 1852. *Commentary on The Guide of the Perplexed*, ed. J. Goldenthal. Vienna: n.p.

Philoponus, John 1899. *De aeternitate mundi contra proclum*, ed. H. Rabe. Leipzig, Germany: B. G. Teubner; reprinted 1963, Hildesheim, Germany: G. Olms.

Proclus 1955. *De aeternitate mundi*, ed. A. Badawi, *Neoplatonici apud Arabes*. Cairo: Dirāsāt Islāmīya, Chap. 19, pp. 34–42.

Qāfiḥ, Yoseph 1972. *Ha-Miqra be-Rambam*. Jerusalem: Mossad ha-Rav Kook.

Rashi 1982. *Commentary on the Torah*, ed. C. B. Chavel. Jerusalem: Mosad ha-Rav Kook.

Rosenthal, E. I. J. ed. and trans. 1956. *Commentary on Plato's Republic*. Cambridge: Cambridge University Press.

Scheiber, Alexander and Joshua Blau, ed. 1981. *An Artegraph, F. Maimonides From the Adler Collection and the Leningrad Library*. Jerusalem: Israel Academy of Sciences and Humanities.

Spinoza, Baruch 1992. *Ethics*, trans. S. Shirley. Indianapolis, IN: Hackett.

2001. *Theological-Political Treatise*, trans. S. Shirley. Indianapolis, IN: Hackett.

SECONDARY SOURCES AND OTHER TRANSLATIONS AND EDITIONS

Abramson, S. 1972. "Arbaʿa peraqim be-ʿinyan ha-Rambam," *Sinai* 70: 24–33.

Abumalham, M. 1985. "La conversión segun formularious notariales andalusíes: Valoración de la legalidad de la conversión de Maimónides," *Miscelanea de estudios arabes y hebraicos* 34: 71–83.

Altmann, Alexander 1953. "Essence and Existence in Maimonides," *Bulletin of the John Rylands Library* 35: 294–315; reprinted in *Studies in Religious Philosophy and Mysticism*. Ithaca, NY: Cornell University Press, 1969, pp. 108–27.

1972. "Maimonides' Four Perfections," *Israel Oriental Society* 2: 15–24.

1973. *Moses Mendelssohn: A Biography*. Philadelphia: Jewish Publication Society.

1974. "Free Will and Predestination in Saadia, Bahya, and Maimonides," in *Religion in a Religious Age*, ed. S. D. Goitein. New York: Ktav.

1978. "Maimonides and Thomas Aquinas: Natural or Divine Prophecy," *Association for Jewish Studies Review* 3: 1–20.

1987. "Maimonides on the Intellect and the Scope of Metaphysics," in *Von der mittelalterlichen zur modernen Aufklärung*. Tübingen: J. C. Mohr, pp. 60–129.

Ashtor, E. 1973–9. *The Jews of Moslem Spain*, 2 vols., trans. A. Klein and J. M. Klein. Philadelphia: Jewish Publication Society.

Atlas, Samuel 1950–1. "Maimon and Maimonides," *Hebrew Union College Annual*, Part 1: 517–47.

Avishur, Y. 1998. *In Praise of Maimonides: Folktales in Judaeo-Arabic and Hebrew from the Near East and North Africa* [in Hebrew]. Jerusalem: Magnes Press.

Badawi, A., ed. 1947. *Arisṭū ʿinda-l-ʿarab*. Cairo: Dirāsāt Islāmīya. Vol. 5, pp. 253–77.

Baneth, D. H. 1964. "Maimonides' Disciple Yosef ben Shimeon and Yosef ben Aqnin," *Otsar Yehudei Sefarad* 7: 11–20.

Baneth, E. 1908–14. "Maimonides als Chonologe und Astronom," in *Moses ben Maimon, Sein Leben, seine Werke, sein Einfluss*. Leipzig: G. Fock, Vol. 2, pp. 243–79.

Barzilay, Isaac 1967. *Between Reason and Faith: Anti-Rationalism in Italian Jewish Thought 1250–1650*. The Hague/Paris: Mouton.

Bayle, Pierre 1965. *Historical and Critical Dictionary: Selections*, ed. R. Popkin. Indianapolis, IN: Library of Liberal Arts.

Ben-Sasson, M. 1991. "Maimonides in Egypt: The First Stage." *Maimonidean Studies* 2: 3–30.

Benjamin of Tudela 1907. *The Itinerary of Benjamin of Tudela*, ed. and trans. M. N. Adler. London: H. Frowde.

Benor, Ehud 1995. *Worship of the Heart*. Albany, NY: State University of New York Press.

Berman, Lawrence V. 1961. "The Political Interpretation of the Maxim: The Purpose of Philosophy Is the Imitation of God," *Studia Islamica* 15: 53–61.

1974. "Maimonides, the Disciple of Alfarabi," *Israel Oriental Studies* 4: 154–78.

1980. "Maimonides on the Fall of Man," *Association for Jewish Studies Review* 5: 1–16.

Bland, Kalman 1982a. "Moses and the Law According to Maimonides," in *Mystics, Philosophers and Politicians*, J. Reinharz and D. Swetschinski, eds. Durham, NC: Duke University Press.

1982b. *The Epistle on the Possibility of Conjunction with the Active Intellect by ibn Rushd with the Commentary of Moses Narboni*. New York: Jewish Theological Seminary Press.

Blaustein, M. 1986. "Aspects of Ibn Bājja's Theory of Apprehension," in Pines 1986b, pp. 202–12.

Blidstein, Gerald 1999. "On the Institutionalization of Prophecy in Maimonidean Halakha" [in Hebrew], *Da'at* 43: 25–42.

2001. *Political Concepts in Maimonidean Halakha* [in Hebrew]. Ramat Gan, Israel: Bar-Ilan University Press.

Blumenthal, David 1981. *The Philosophic Questions and Answers of Hoter ben Shelomo*. Leiden, The Netherlands: Brill.

1982. *Understanding Jewish Mysticism*. New York: Ktav, Vol. 2.

1984. *Approaches to the Study of Judaism in Medieval Times*. Chicago: Scholars Press.

Bos, Gerrit 2002. *Maimonides, On Asthma*. Provo, UT: Brigham Young University Press.

Brague, Rémi, trans. 1996. *Maïmonide: Traité de logique*. Paris, Desclée de Brouwer.

Brann, R. 2002. *Power in the Portrayal: Representations of Jews and Muslims in Eleventh- and Twelfth-Century Islamic Spain*. Princeton, NJ: Princeton University Press.

Bruckstein, Almut Sh. 1997. "How Can Ethics Be Taught: 'Socratic' and 'Post-Socratic' Methods in Maimonides' Theory of Emulation," *Jewish Studies Quarterly* 4: 268–84.

Buijs, Joseph A., ed. 1988. *Maimonides: A Collection of Critical Essays*. Notre Dame, IN: University of Notre Dame Press.

Burnyeat, M. 1981. "Aristotle on Understanding Knowledge," in *Aristotle on Science*, ed. E. Berti. Padua, Italy: Antenore, pp. 97–139.

Butterworth, Charles E., trans. 2001. *Averröes: Decisive Treatise & Epistle Dedicatory*. Provo, UT: Brigham Young University Press.

Carruthers, M. 1992. *The Book of Memory: A Study of Memory in Medieval Culture*. Cambridge: Cambridge University Press.

Castro, A. 1971. *The Spaniards: An Introduction to Their History*, trans. W. F. King and S. Margaretten. Berkeley, CA: University of California Press.

Chamberlain, M. 1998. "The Crusader Era and the Ayyūbid Dynasty," in Petry 1998, pp. 211–41.

Cohen, Jonathan 1997. *Reason and Change* [in Hebrew]. Jerusalem: The Bialik Institute.

Cohen, M. 1989. "Maimonides' Egypt," in Ormsby 1989, pp. 21–33.

Corbin, H. 1986. "Rituel sabéen et exégèse ismaélienne du rituel," *Eranos-Jahrbuch*. Zürich, 1951, pp. 181–246. Translated as "Sabian Temple and Ismailism," in *Temple and Contemplation*. London: Islamic Publications, pp. 132–82.

Corcos-Abulafia, D. 1967. "The Attitude of the Almohadic Rulers Toward the Jews," *Zion* 32: 137–60.

Cornford, F. M. 1966. *Plato's Cosmology*. London: Routledge & Kegan Paul.

Curley, Edwin 1988. *Behind the Geometrical Method*. Princeton, NJ: Princeton University Press.

Dajani-Shakeel, H. 1993. *Al-Qāḍī al-Fāḍil: His Role in Planning Saladin's State and Conquests* [in Arabic]. Beirut: Mu'assasāt ad-Dirāsāt al-Filasṭīnīya.

Davidson, Herbert 1963. "Maimonides' *Shemonah Perakim* and Alfarabi's *Fusul al-Madani*," *Proceedings of the American Academy for Jewish Research* 31: 33–50.

1974. "The Study of Philosophy as a Religious Obligation," in *Religion in a Religious Age*, ed. S. D. Goitein. Cambridge, MA: Association for Jewish Studies, pp. 53–68.

1979. "Maimonides Secret Position on Creation," in Twersky 1979–2000, Vol. 1, pp. 16–40.

1987a. "The Middle Way in Maimonides' Ethics," *Proceedings of the American Academy for Jewish Research* 54: 31–72.

1987b. *Proofs for Eternity, Creation, and the Existence of God in Medieval Islamic and Jewish Philosophy*. New York: Oxford University Press.

1991. "Maimonides on Metaphysical Knowledge," *Maimonidean Studies* 3: 49–103.

1992. *Alfarabi, Avicenna and Averroes on Intellect*. New York: Oxford University Press.

1992–3. "Maimonides on Metaphysical Knowledge," *Maimonidean Studies* 3: 137–56.

1997. "Maimonides' Putative Position as Official Head of the Egyptian Jewish Community," in *Hazon Nahum: Studies Presented to Dr. Norman Lamm in Honor of His Seventieth Birthday*, ed. Yaakov Elman and Jeffrey S. Gurock. New York: Yeshiva University Press, pp. 115–28.

2000. "Further on a Problematic Passage in *Guide for the Perplexed* 2.24," *Maimonidean Studies* 4: 1–13.

2001. "The Authenticity of Works Attributed to Maimonides," in Fleischer et al. 2001.

Dienstag, Jacob 1975. *Studies in Maimonides and St. Thomas Aquinas*. New York: Ktav.

Dienstag, Jacob 1986. "The Relationship of Spinoza to the Philosophy of Maimonides: An Annotated Bibliography, *Studia Spinozana* 2: 375–416.

Diesendruck, Z. 1936. "Samuel and Moses Ibn Tibbon on Maimonides' Theory of Providence," *Hebrew Union College Annual* 11: 341–65.

Dobbs-Weinstein, Idit 1995. *Maimonides and St. Thomas on the Limits of Reason*. Albany, NY: State University of New York Press.

Duhem, Pierre 1969. *To Save the Phenomena. An Essay on the Idea of Physical Theory from Plato to Galileo*, trans. E. Dolan and C. Maschler. Chicago: University of Chicago Press.

Dunlop, D. M. 1957. "Al-Farabi's Introductory *Risālah* on Logic," *Islamic Quarterly* 3: 224–35.

Efros, I., ed. and trans. 1938. *Maimonides' Treatise on Logic*. New York: American Academy for Jewish Research.

Eisen, Robert 1999. "Samuel Ibn Tibbon on the Book of Job," *Association for Jewish Studies Review* 24: 263–300.

Emden, Jacov 1970. *Miṭpaḥat Sefarim*. Jerusalem: Makor.

Eshbili, Yom Tov 1983. *Sefer Zikharon*. Jerusalem: Mossad Ha Rav Kook.

Fackenheim, E. 1946/7. "The Possibility of the Universe in Al-Farabi, Ibn Sina, and Maimonides," *Proceedings of the American Academy for Jewish Research* 16: 39–70.

Fakhry, Majid, ed., 1985. *Avicenna: Kitāb al-Najāt*. Beirut: Dar al-ifāg al-jadīdan.

Faur, J. 1978. *Iyyunim be-Mishneh Torah le-ha-Rambam*. Jerusalem: Mosad ha-Rav Kook.

Fazzo, Silvia and Mauro Zonta, ed. and trans. 1999. *Alessandro di Afrodisia, La Providenza.* Milano: Bibliotecca Universale Rizzoli.

Feldman, Seymour 1980. "The Theory of Eternal Creation in Hasdai Crescas and Some of His Predecessors," *Viator* 11: 289–320.

1982. "Crescas' Theological Determinism," *Da'at* 9: 3–28.

1984. "A Debate Concerning Determinism in Late Medieval Jewish Philosophy," *Proceedings of the American Academy for Jewish Research* 5: 15–54.

1985. "The Binding of Isaac: A Test-Case of Divine Foreknowledge," in *Divine Omniscience and Omnipotence in Medieval Philosophy*, ed. T. Rudavsky. Dordrecht: Reidel, 105–134.

1986. "The End of the Universe in Medieval Jewish Philosophy," *Association for Jewish Studies Review* 11: 53–78.

1990. "Abravanel on Maimonides' Critique of the Kalam Arguments for Creation," *Maimonidean Studies* 1: 5–25.

1998. "Prophecy and Perception in Isaac Abravanel," in *Perspectives on Jewish Thought and Mysticism*, ed. A. Ivry, E. Wolfson, and A. Arkus. Amsterdam: Harwood Academic.

2000. "An Averroist Solution to a Maimonidean Perplexity," *Maimonidean Studies* 4: 15–30.

Fenton, Paul 1981. *Treatise of the Pool*. London: Octagon.

1982. "A Meeting with Maimonides." *Bulletin of the School of Oriental and African Studies* 45: 1–4.

1987. *De traitès de mystique juive*. Lagrasse, France: Verdier.

Fierro, M. 1996. "Bāṭinism in Al-Andalus," *Studia Islamica* 64: 87–112.

Fine, L., ed. 2001. *Judaism in Practice*. Princeton: Princeton Univ. Press.

Fleischer, E., G. Blidstein, C. Horowitz, and B. Septimus, eds. 2001. *Me'ah She'arim: Studies in Medieval Jewish Spiritual Life in Memory of Isadore Twersky*. Jerusalem: Magnes Press.

Fixler, D. 1999. "Astronomy and Astrology in Maimonides' Thought," *Tehumin* 19: 439–47.

Fotinis, A. P., trans. 1979. *The De Anima of Alexander of Aphrodisias*, Washington, DC: University Press of America.

Fox, Marvin 1965. "The Guide of the Perplexed by Moses Maimonides." Review of the 1963 translation of S. Pines. *Journal of the History of Philosophy* 3: 265–74.

1990. *Interpreting Maimonides*. Chicago: University of Chicago Press.

Fraenkel, C. 2002. *From Maimonides to Samuel Ibn Tibbon: The Transformation of the Dalālat al-ḥā'irīn into the Moreh ha-Nevukhim*. Ph.D. Dissertation. Jerusalem: The Hebrew University.

Frank, D., ed. 1995. *The Jews of Medieval Islam: Community, Society, and Identity*. Proceedings of an International Conference held by the Institute of Jewish Studies, University College London, 1992. Leiden, The Netherlands: Brill.

Frank, Daniel 1985. "The End of the Guide: Maimonides on the Best Life for Man," *Judaism* 34: 485–95.

1989. "Humility As a Virtue: A Maimonidean Critique of Aristotle's Ethics," in Ormsby 1989, pp. 89–99.

1990. "Anger As a Vice: A Maimonidean Critique of Aristotle's Ethics," *History of Philosophy Quarterly* 7: 269–81.

Freimann, A. 1936. "The Genealogy of Moses Maimonides' Family" [in Hebrew], *Alumma*, 9–32, Addenda et corrigenda, 137–8. Appendix: "Table of Genealogy of Maimonides' Family."

Freud, S. 1937. *Mourning and Melancholia*, The Standard Edition, trans. under the general editorship of James Strachey. London: Hogarth P. Institute of Psycho-Analysis, 1953–1974, Vol. 14, pp. 243–58.

Freudenthal, Gad 1988. "Maimonides' *Guide of the Perplexed* and the Transmission of the Mathematical Tract 'On Two Asymptotic Lines' in the Arabic, Latin, and Hebrew Medieval Traditions," *Vivarium* 26: 113–40. (Reprinted in *Maimonides and the Sciences*, ed. Robert S. Cohen and H. Levine. Dordrecht, The Netherlands: Kluwer, 1999, pp. 35–56.)

1993. "Maimonides' Stance on Astrology in Context: Cosmology, Physics, Medicine, and Providence," in *Moses Maimonides – Physician, Scientist, and Philosopher*, ed. Samuel Kottek and Fred Rosner. Northvale, NJ: Jason Aronson, pp. 77–90.

1995. "Science in the Medieval Jewish Culture of Southern France," *History of Science* 33: 23–58.

1996. "Levi ben Gershom (Gersonides), 1288–1344," in *The Routledge History of Islamic Philosophy*, ed. S. H. Nasr and O. Leaman. London/New York: Routledge, pp. 739–54.

2001. "Between Holiness and Defilement: The Ambivalence in the Perception of Philosophy by Its Opponents in the Early Fourteenth Century," in *Gli Ebrei e le Science. The Jews and the Sciences* (= *Micrologus* IX). Florence: Sismel/Edizioni del Galluzo, pp. 169–93.

2003. " 'Instrumentalism' and 'Realism' as Categories in the History of Astronomy: Duhem vs. Popper, Maimonides vs. Gersonides," *Centaurus* 45: 96–117.

Freudenthal, Jacob 1887. "Spinoza und die Scholastik," in *Philosophische Aufsätze zu Eduard Zeller*. Leipzig, Germany: pp. 85–138.

Friedman, M. A. 1987. "Social Realities in Egypt and Maimonides' Rulings on Family Law," in *Maimonides As Codifier of Jewish Law*, N. Rakover, ed. Jerusalem: Jewish Legal Heritage Society, pp. 225–36.

1988–9. "Moses ben Maimon in Legal Documents from the Geniza" [in Hebrew], *Shenaton ha-Mishpaṭ ha-ʿIvri* 14–15: 177–88.

1993. "A Student's Notes" [in Hebrew], *Tarbiz* 62: 325–85.

2001. "Two Maimonidean Letters: From Maimonides to R. Samuel the Sage to Maimonides on his Marriage" [in Hebrew], in Fleischer et al. 2001, pp. 191–240.

2002. *Maimonides, The Yemenite Messiah and Apostasy* [in Hebrew]. Jerusalem: Ben-Zvi Institute and The Hebrew University.

Funkenstein, Amos 1977. "Maimonides: Political Theory and Realistic Messianism," *Miscellanea Medieavalia* 9: 81–103.

1983. *Maimonides: Nature, History and Messianic Beliefs* [in Hebrew]. Tel Aviv: The Israeli Ministry of Defense.

Gadamer, Hans-Georg 1989. *Truth and Method*, 2nd rev. ed., trans. revised by Joel Weinsheimer and Donald G. Marshall. London: Sheed & Ward.

Gafni, I. M. and A. Ravitzky 1992. *Sanctity of Life and Martyrdom: Studies in Memory of Amir Yekutiel* [in Hebrew]. Jerusalem: Zalman Shazar Center.

Galston, Miriam 1978. "Philosopher-King v. Prophet," *Israel Oriental Studies* 8: 204–18.

1978–9. "The Purpose of the Law According to Maimonides," *Jewish Quarterly Review* 69: 27–51.

1990. *Politics and Excellence: The Political Philosophy of Alfarabi*. Princeton, NJ: Princeton University Press.

Gauthier, Léon 1909. "Une réforme du système astronomique de Ptolémée, tentée par les philosophes arabes du XIIe siècle," *Journal Asiatique* 11: 483–510.

Gellman, Jerome 1989. "Freedom and Determinism in Maimonides' Philosophy," in Ormsby 1989.

Genequand, Charles, trans. 1984. *Ibn Rushd's Metaphysics*. Leiden, The Netherlands: Brill.

Ghosh, A. 1992. "The Slave of MS. H6," *Subaltern Studies* 7: 159–220.

1993. *In an Antique Land*. New York: Alfred A. Knopf.

Gil, M. and E. Fleischer 2001. *Yehuda Ha-Levi and His Circle*. Jerusalem: World Union of Jewish Studies.

Gileadi, A. 1984. "A Short Note on the Possible Origin of the Title "Moreh Ha-Nevukhim," *Le Muséon* 97: 159–61.

Giora, Z. 1988. "The Magical Number Seven," in *Occident and Orient: A Tribute to the Memory of A. Scheiber*. Budapest/Leiden, The Netherlands: Brill, pp. 171–8.

Goitein, S. D. 1966. "The Life of Maimonides in the Light of New Finds from the Cairo Geniza" [in Hebrew], *Peraqim* 4: 29–42.

1967–93. *A Mediterranean Society: The Jewish Communities in the Arab World as Portrayed in the Documents of the Cairo Geniza*, 6 vols. Berkeley/Los Angeles/London: University of California Press.

1973. *Letters of Medieval Jewish Traders*. Princeton, NJ: Princeton University Press.

1980."Moses Maimonides, Man of Action: A Revision of the Master's Biography in Light of the Geniza Documents," in *Hommage à Georges Vajda*, ed. G. Nahon and Ch. Touati. Leuven, Belgium: Peeters, pp. 155–67.

1999, with M. A. Friedman, "Abraham Ben Yiju, A Jewish Trader in India" [in Hebrew], *Teudah* 15: 259–92.

Goldman, Eliezer 1968. "The Worship Peculiar to Those Who Have Apprehended True Realities" [in Hebrew], *Bar-Ilan Annual* 6: 287–313.

Goodman, Lenn 1980. "Maimonides and Leibniz," *Journal of Jewish Studies* 31: 214–36.

Grossman, A. 1992. "The Roots of Sanctification of the Name in Early Ashkenaz," in Gafni and Ravitzky 1992, pp. 99–130.

Gueroult, Martial 1968. *Spinoza: Ethique 1: Dieu*. Hildesheim, Germany: G. Olms.

Hadot, P. 1995. *Philosophy As a Way of Life*, ed. A. I. Davidson, trans. M. Chase. Oxford/Cambridge, MA: Blackwell.

Halbertal, Moshe and Margalit, Avishai 1992. *Idolatry*. Cambridge, MA: Harvard University Press.

2001. *Concealment and Revelation: The Secret and Its Boundaries in Medieval Jewish Tradition* [in Hebrew]. Jerusalem: Orna Hess.

Halkin, A. S. 1953. "Le-toldot ha-shemad bime al-muwaḥḥidin," in *The Joshua Starr Memorial Volume*. New York: Jewish Social Studies Publications, No. 5, pp. 101–10.

Hampshire, Stuart 1971. "A Kind of Materialism," in *Freedom of Mind and Other Essays*, Princeton: Princeton University Press, 210–31.

Hartman, David 1976. *Maimonides: Torah and Philosophic Quest*. Philadelphia: Jewish Publication Society.

1982–3. "Rabbenu Mosheh ben Maimon's *'Iggeret ha-Shemad,'*" *Jerusalem Studies in Jewish Thought* 2: 362–403.

1988. "Philosophy and Halakhah As Alternative Challenges to Idolatry in Maimonides (Hebrew)," *Jerusalem Studies in Jewish Thought* 7: 319–33.

Harvey, S. 1992. "Did Maimonides' Letter to Samuel ibn Tibbon Determine Which Philosophers Would Be Studied by Later Jewish Thinkers?" *Jewish Quarterly Review* 83: 51–70.

1997. "The Meaning of Terms Designating Love in Judaeo-Arabic Thought and Some Remarks on the Judaeo-Arabic Interpretation of

Maimonides," in *Judaeo-Arabic Studies*, ed. N. Golb. Amsterdam: Harwood Academic, pp. 175–96.

Harvey, Warren Zev 1973. *Ḥasdai Crescas' Critique of the Theory of the Acquired Intellect*. Unpublished dissertation, Columbia University.

1977. "Holiness: A Command to Imitatio Dei," *Tradition* 16: 7–28.

1979. "Maimonides and Spinoza on the Knowledge of Good and Evil" [in Hebrew]. *Iyyun* 28: 167–85.

1980. "Political Philosophy and Halakhah in Maimonides" [in Hebrew], *Iyyun*, 29: 198–212.

1981a. "A Third Approach to Maimonides' Cosmology Prophetology Puzzle," *Harvard Theological Review* 74: 287–301.

1981b. "A Portrait of Spinoza as a Maimonidean," *Journal of the History of Philosophy* 19: 151–71.

1989. "Averroes and Maimonides on the Obligation of Philosophic Contemplation" [in Hebrew], *Tarbiz* 58: 75–83.

1990. "Maimonides on Human Perfection, Awe, and Politics," in *The Thought of Moses Maimonides*, ed. Ira Robinson, Lawrence Kaplan, and Julien Baur. Lewistown, NY: Edwin Mellon.

1994. "Political Philosophy and Halakhah in Maimonides," in *Jewish Intellectual History in the Middle Ages*, ed. Joseph Dan. Westport, CT: Praeger.

1997. "Maimonides' First Commandment, Physics, and Doubt," in *Hazon Nahum: Studies in Jewish Law, Thought, and History, Present to Dr. Norman Lamm*, ed. Y. Elman and J. S. Gurock. New York: Yeshiva University Press.

1998a. "Ibn Rushd and Maimonides on the Obligation of Philosophical Contemplation (*iʿtībār*)," *Tarbiz* 58: 75–83.

1998b. *Physics and Metaphysics in Ḥasdai Crescas*. Amsterdam: J. C. Gieben.

2000. *Maimonides' Political Philosophy and Its Relevance for the State of Israel*, The Dean Ernest Schwartz Memorial Lecture. New York: City University of New York.

2001. "How Did Leo Strauss Paralyze the 20th Century Study of the *Guide of the Perplexed*?" [in Hebrew], *Iyyun* 50: 387–96.

Havlin, S. Z. 1972. "Mosheh ben Maimon," in *Hebrew Encyclopaedia*, Vol. 24, pp. 536–42.

1985. "Le-Toledot ha-Rambam," *Daʿat* 15: 67–79.

Hayoun, Maurice 1989. *La Philosophie et la Théologie de Moïse de Narbonne*. Tübingen, Germany: J. C. Mohr.

Helbig, A. H. 1908. *Al-Qāḍī al-Fāḍil, der Wezīr Saladin's: Eine Biographie*. Leipzig, Germany: Druck von W. Drugulin.

Hill, B. S. 1985. "Une Liste de Manuscrits: Préliminaire a une nouvelle édition du *Dalalat al-Hayryn*," in *Sobre la vida y obra de Maimónides*: Vol. I, Congreso Internacional Ediciones. Cordoba, Spain: El Almendro.

Hirschberg, H. Z. (J. W.) 1974. *A History of the Jews in North Africa*, 2 vols., 2nd rev. ed., translated from the Hebrew. Leiden, The Netherlands: E. J. Brill.

Hogendijk, J. P. 1986. "Discovery of an 11th Century Geometrical Compilation: The Istikmāl of Yūsuf al-Mu'tamar ibn Hūd, King of Saragossa," *Historia Mathematica* 13: 43–52.

Hopkins, S. 2001. *Maimonides's Commentary on Tractate Shabbat*. Jerusalem: Yad Izhak Ben-Zvi and The Hebrew University.

Hourani, George F., trans. 1967. *Averroes: On the Harmony of Religion and Philosophy*. London: Luzac.

Hyman, Arthur 1967. "Maimonides' 'Thirteen Principles,'" in *Jewish Medieval and Renaissance Studies*, ed. A. Altmann. Cambridge, MA: Harvard University Press, pp. 119–45.

1976. "Interpreting Maimonides," *Gesher* 6: 46–59.

1988. "Maimonides on Creation and Emanation," in *Studies in Medieval Philosophy*, ed. J. F. Whipple. Washington, DC: Catholic University of America Press.

1989. "Demonstrative, Dialectical, and Sophistic Arguments in the Philosophy of Moses Maimonides," in Ormsby 1989.

1992. "From What Is One and Simple Only What Is One and Simple Can Come to Be," in *Neoplatonism and Jewish Thought*, ed. Lenn Goodman. Albany, NY: State University of New York Press.

1997. "Aspects of the Medieval Jewish and Islamic Discussion of 'Free Choice,'" in *Freedom and Moral Responsibility*, ed. C. Manekin and M. Kellner. Bethesda, MD: University Press of Maryland.

Idel, Moshe 1991. "Maimonides and Kabbala," in Twersky 1990, pp. 31–81.

Isaacs, H. D. 1993. "An Encounter with Maimonides," in *Moses Maimonides: Physician, Scientist, and Philosopher*. Northvale, NJ/London: J. Aronson, pp. 41–8.

Ishbili, Yom-Tov ben Abraham 1983. *Sefer Zikharon*. Jerusalem: Mossad ha-Rav Kook.

Ivry, Alfred 1967. "Moses of Narbonne's Treatise on the Perfection of the Soul: A Methodological and Conceptual Analysis," *Jewish Quarterly Review* 57: 271–97.

1977. *Moses of Narbonne's Ma'amar Bi-Shelemut ha-Nefesh*. Jerusalem: Israel Academy of Sciences and Humanities.

1985. "Providence, Divine Omniscience, and Possibility: The Case of Maimonides," in *Divine Omniscience and Omnipotence in Medieval Philosophy*, ed. T. Rudavsky. Dordrecht, The Netherlands/Boston: Reidel, pp. 143–59.

1986a. "Maimonides on Creation," in *Creation and the End of Days*, ed. Norbert Samuelson and David Novak. Lanham, MD: University Press of America.

1986b. "Islamic and Greek Influences on Maimonides' Philosophy," in Pines 1986b, pp. 139–56.

1990. "Maimonides on Creation" [in Hebrew], *Jerusalem Studies in Jewish Thought* 9: 115–138.

1991a. "Neoplatonic Currents in Maimonides' Thought," in Kraemer 1991a, pp. 117–26.

1991b. "Leo Strauss on Maimonides," in *Leo Strauss's Thought*, ed. A. Udoff. Boulder, CO: Rienner.

1992. "Strategies of Interpretation in Maimonides' *Guide of the Perplexed*," *Jewish History* 6: 113–30.

1995. "Ismāʿīlī Theology and Maimonides' Philosophy," in *The Jews of Medieval Islam*, ed. Daniel Frank. Leiden, The Netherlands: Brill, pp. 274–6, 281.

1998. "The Logical and Scientific Premises of Maimonides' Thought," in *Perspectives on Jewish Thought and Mysticism*, ed. A. L. Ivry, E. Wolfson, and A. Arkus. Amsterdam: Harwood Academic.

Janssens, Jules 1997. "Creation and Emanation in Ibn Sīna," *Documenti E Studi Sull Tradizione Filosofica Medievale* 8: 455–77.

Kahn, C. H. 1981. "The Role of *Nous* in the Cognition of First Principles in *Posterior Analytics* II.19," in *Aristotle on Science*, ed. E. Berti. Padua, Italy: Antenore, pp. 385–414.

Kaplan, Lawrence 1985. "Maimonides on the Singularity of the Jewish People," *Daʿat* 15: 5–27.

1995. "Rav Kook and the Jewish Philosophical Tradition," in *Rabbi Abraham Isaac Kook and Jewish Spirituality*, eds. L. Kaplan and D. Shatz. New York: New York University Press.

2002. "An Introduction to Maimonides' 'Eight Chapters,'" *Edah Journal*, 2 (available online at www.edah.org).

Kasher, Hannah 1986. "'Talmud Torah' as a Means of Apprehending God in Maimonides' Teachings" [in Hebrew], *Jerusalem Studies in Jewish Thought* 5: 71–82.

Kasher, Hannah 1995. "Maimonides' Interpretation of the Story of the Divine Revelation in the Cleft of the Rock" [in Hebrew], *Daʿat* 35: 29–66.

1998. "'Beloved Is Man for He Was Created in God's Image': Conditional Humanism (Maimonides) Versus Unwilling Humanism (Leibowitz)," *Da'at* 41: 19–29.

Kiener, Ronald 1984. "Jewish Ismāʿīlīsm in Twelfth Century Yemen: R. Nethanel ben al-Fayyūmi," *Jewish Quarterly Review* 74: 249–66.

Kellner, Menachem 1986. *Dogma in Medieval Jewish Thought*. Oxford: Oxford University Press.

1990. *Maimonides on Human Perfection*. Atlanta, GA: Brown Judaic Studies.

1991a. *Maimonides on Judaism and the Jewish People*. Albany, NY: State University of New York Press.

1991b. "On the Status of Astronomy and Physics in Maimonides' *Mishneh Torah* and *Guide of the Perplexed*," *British Journal for the History of Science* 24: 453–63.

1993a. ed. Yizhak Abravanel, *Rosh Amanah*. Ramat Gan, Israel: Bar Ilan University Press.

1993b. "Chosenness, Not Chauvinism: Maimonides on the Chosen People," in *A People Apart: Chosenness and Ritual in Jewish Philosophical Thought*, ed. Daniel H. Frank. Albany, NY: State University of New York Press.

1993c. "Maimonides on the Science of the *Mishneh Torah*: Provisional or Permanent?" *Association for Jewish Studies Review* 18: 169–94.

1996. "On Universalism and Particularism in Judaism," *Daʿat* 36: 5–15.

1999. *Must a Jew Believe Anything?* London: Littman Library of Jewish Civilization.

2000. "Strauss' Maimonides vs. Maimonides' Maimonides," *Le'ela*, December: 29–36.

2001a. "Overcoming Chosenness," in *Revelation and Redemption in Judaism and Mormonism*, eds. Raphael Jospe and Seth Ward. Madison, WI: Farleigh Dickinson University Press.

2001b. "The Literary Character of the Mishneh Torah: On the Art of Writing in Maimonides' Halakhic Works," in Fleischer et al. 2001.

2001c. "Was Maimonides Truly Universalist?" *Trumah*: 14, 3–15.

2002. "Is Maimonides' Ideal Person Austerely Rationalist?" *American Catholic Philosophical Quarterly* 76: 125–143.

Forthcoming. "Maimonides on the Nature of Ritual Purity and Impurity," *Daʿat* 50, to be published.

Klein-Braslavy, Sara 1978. *Maimonides' Interpretation of the Story of Creation*, 2nd ed. [in Hebrew]. Jerusalem: Reuben Mass Press.

1986a. "The Creation of the World and Maimonides' Interpretation of Gen. I–V," in Pines 1986b.

1986b. "Maimonides' Interpretation of the Verb 'Bara' and the Creation of the World" [in Hebrew], *Da'at* 16: 39–55.

1986c. *Maimonides' Interpretation of the Adam Stories in Genesis: A Study in Maimonides' Anthropology* [in Hebrew]. Jerusalem: Reuben Mass Press.

1987. "Maimonides' Interpretation of Jacob's Dream of the Ladder" [in Hebrew], *Annual of Bar-Ilan University: Studies in Judaica and Humanities* 22–23: 329–49.

1996. *King Salomon and Philosophical Esotericism in the Thought of Maimonides* [in Hebrew]. Jerusalem: Magnes Press.

Klever, Wim 1989. "Spinoza and Van den Enden in Borch's Diary in 1661–1662," *Studia Spinozana* 5: 311–27.

1996. "Spinoza's Life and Works," in *The Cambridge Companion to Spinoza*, ed. D. Garrett. New York: Cambridge University Press, pp. 13–60.

Kogan, Barry, S. 1989. "What Can We Know and When Can We Know It?: Maimonides on the Active Intelligence and Human Cognition," in Ormsby 1989.

1990. "Maimonides on the Human Ideal: *Ḥakham or Ḥasid*?" [in Hebrew], *Jerusalem Studies in Jewish Thought* 9: 177–91.

Kraemer, J. L. 1979. "Alfarabi's Opinions of the Virtuous City and Maimonides' Foundations of the Law," in *Studia Orientalia Memoriae D. H. Baneth Dedicata*. Jerusalem: Magnes Press, pp. 107–53.

1984. "On Maimonides' Messianic Posture," in Twersky 1979–2000, Vol. 2, pp. 109–42.

1989. "Maimonides on Aristotle and Scientific Method," in Ormsby 1989, 53–88.

1991a. ed. *Perspectives on Maimonides*. Oxford: Oxford University Press.

1991b. "Maimonides on the Philosophic Sciences in His Treatise on the Art of Logic," in Kramer 1991a, pp. 77–104.

1992. "The Andalusian Mystic Ibn Hūd and the Conversion of the Jews," *Israel Oriental Studies* 12: 59–73.

1999. "Maimonides and the Spanish Aristotelian School," in *Christians, Muslim, and Jews in Medieval and Early Modern Spain*, ed. Mark D. Meyerson and Edward D. English. Notre Dame, IN: University of Notre Dame Press, pp. 40–68.

2000. "Maimonides' Use of (Aristotelian) Dialectic," in *Maimonides and the Sciences*, ed. H. Levine and R. Cohen. Dordrecht, The Netherlands: Kluwer, pp. 111–130.

2001a. "Naturalism and Universalism in Maimonides' Political and Religious Thought," in Fleischer et al. 2001.

2001b. "Maimonides," in *Judaism in Practice*, ed. L. Fine. Princeton, NJ: Princeton University Press, pp. 413–28.

Kraus, P. 1986. *Jābir ibn Ḥayyān: Contribution à l'histoire des idées scientifiques dans l'Islam.* Paris: Les Belles Lettres.

Kreisel, Howard 1991. "Judah Halevi's Influence on Maimonides: A Preliminary Appraisal," *Maimonidean Studies* 2: 95–122.

Kreisel, Howard 1994. "Maimonides' Approach to Astrology," *Proceedings of the Eleventh World Congress of Jewish Studies* 2: 25–32.

1999. *Maimonides' Political Thought.* Albany, NY: State University of New York Press.

2001. *Prophecy: The History of an Idea in Medieval Jewish Philosophy.* Dordrecht, The Netherlands: Kluwer Academic.

Lambert, P., ed. 1994. *Fortifications and the Synagogue: The Fortress of Babylon and the Ben Ezra Synagogue.* Montreal: Canadian Centre for Architecture.

Lamm, Norman 1981. "The Sage and the Saint in the Writings of Maimonides" [in Hebrew], in *Samuel Belkin Memorial Volume*, ed. M. Carmilly and H. Leaf. New York: Erna Michael Colllege of Hebraic Studies.

1992–93. "Maimonides on the Love of God," *Maimonidean Studies* 3: 131–42.

Langermann, Tzvi 1984. "The Mathematical Writings of Maimonides," *Jewish Quarterly Review* 75: 57–65.

1991a. "The True Perplexity: *The Guide of the Perplexed*, Part II, Chapter 24," in Kraemer 1991a, pp. 159–74.

1991b. "Maimonides' Repudiation of Astrology," *Maimonidean Studies* 2: 123–158.

1996. "Some Issues Relating to Astronomy in the Thought of Maimonides" [in Hebrew], *Da'at* 37:107–18.

1999. *The Jews and Sciences in the Middle Ages.* Aldershott, UK: Ashgate.

2000. "Supplementary List of Manuscripts and Fragments of *Dalālat al-ḥa'rīn*," *Maimonidean Studies* 4: 31–7.

2002. "Criticism of Authority in the Writings of Moses Maimonides and Fakhr Al-Dīn Al-Rāzī," *Early Science* and *Medicine* 7, 3: 255–275.

Lazarus-Yafeh, Hava 1975. *Studies in Al-Ghazzālī.* Jerusalem: The Magnes Press.

1997. "Was Maimonides Influenced by Al-Ghazzālī?" in *Tehillah le-Moshe: Biblical and Judaic Studies in Honor of Moshe Greenberg*, ed. M. Cogan, B. L. Eichler, J. H. Tigay, et al. Winona Lake, IN: Eisenbrauns, pp. 163–9.

Lenzner, S. J. 2002. "Author As Educator: Strauss's Twofold Treatment of Maimonides and Machiavelli." The Claremont Institute, available on-line at http://www.claremont.org.

2003. *Leo Strauss and the Problem of Freedom of Thought: The Rediscovery of the Philosophic Arts of Reading and Writing*. Ph.D. Dissertation. Cambridge, MA: Harvard University.

Lerner, Ralph 1963a. "Moses Maimonides," in *History of Political Philosophy*, eds. Leo Strauss and Joseph Cropsey. Chicago: University of Chicago Press.

1963b. "Maimonides: Letter on Astrology," in *Medieval Political Philosophy: A Sourcebook*, ed. R. Lerner and M. Mahdi. New York: Cornell University Press, pp. 227–36.

2000. *Maimonides' Empire of Light*. Chicago: University of Chicago Press.

Le Tourneau, R. 1969. *The Almohad Movement in North Africa in the Twelfth and Thireenth Centuries*. Princeton, NJ: Princeton University Press.

Levenson, J. D. 1988. *Creation and the Persistence of Evil*. Princeton, NJ: Princeton University Press.

Levinger, Jacob 1965. *Maimonides' Techniques of Codification* [in Hebrew]. Jerusalem: Magnes Press.

1989. *Maimonides as Philosopher and Codifier* [in Hebrew]. Jerusalem: Bialik Institute.

1990."Was Maimonides 'Ra'īs al-Yahūd' in Egypt?" in Twersky 1990, pp. 83–94.

Lorberbaum, Menachem 2001. *Politics and the Limits of Law*. Stanford, CA: Stanford University Press.

Lorberbaum, Yair 1999. "Maimonides on *Imago Dei*: Philosophy and Law – The Felony of Murder, the Criminal Procedure, and Capital Punishment" [in Hebrew], *Tarbiz* 68: 533–56.

2000. "Contradictions in the *Guide of the Perplexed*" [in Hebrew], *Tarbiz* 69: 209–37.

2001. "The Parables in the *Guide of the Perplexed*" [in Hebrew], *Tarbiz* 71: 1–46.

2002. "On Contradictions, Rationality, Dialectics and Esotericism in Maimonides' *Guide of the Perplexed*," *The Review of Metaphysics* 55: 711–50.

Lohr, C. H. 1982. "The Medieval Interpretation of Aristotle," in *The Cambridge History of Later Medieval Philosophy*, ed. N. Kretzmann, A. Kenny, and J. Pinberg. Cambridge: Cambridge University Press, pp. 80–98.

Mahdi, Muhsin S. 2001. *Alfarabi and the Foundation of Islamic Political Philosophy*. Chicago: University of Chicago Press.

Maimonides under *Other Works of* 1972. *A Maimonides Reader*, ed. Isadore Twersky. West Orange, NJ: Behrman House.

Maimonides, Moses 1956. *Commentarius in Mischnam*, ed. S. D. Sassoon. Corpus Codicum Hebraicorum Medii Aevi. Pars. I. Copenhagen: E. Munksgaard.

Manekin, Charles 1990. "Belief, Certainty, and Divine Attributes in the *Guide of the Perplexed*," *Maimonidean Studies* 1: 117–41.

1998. "On the Limited-Omniscience Interpretation of Gersonides' Theory of Divine Knowledge," in *Perspectives on Jewish Thought and Mysticism*, ed. A. Ivry, E. Wolfson, and A. Arkush. Amsterdam: Harwood Academic.

Marmura, Michael E., ed. and trans. 1997. *Al-Ghazālī: The Incoherence of the Philosophers*. Provo, UT: Brigham Young University Press.

Marx, A. 1926. "The Correspondence Between the Rabbis of Southern France and Maimonides About Astrology," *Hebrew Union College Annual* 3: 311–57.

Merlan, P. 1963. *Monopsychism, Mysticism, Metaconsciousness: Problems of the Soul in the Neoaristotelian and Neoplatonic Tradition*. The Hague: Martinus Nijhoff.

Morgenbesser, Sidney 1969. "The Realist-Instrumentalist Controversy," in *Essays in Honor of Ernest Nagel. Philosophy, Science, and Method*, ed. Sidney Morgenbesser, Patrick Suppes, and Morton White. New York: St. Martin's Press, pp. 200–18.

Munk, Salomon 1842. "Notice sur Joseph ibn Jehouda," *Journal Asiatique* 14: 5–70.

1851. "Studien von Doctor Abraham Geiger, Rabbiner in Breslau." *Archives Israílites*: 319–35.

Muntner Suessmann 5702 (=1942). *Moshe ben Maimon (Maimonides), Sammey ha-mawet we-ha-refuʾot ke-negdam*, Hebrew translation by R. Moshe Ibn Tibbon. Jerusalem: Rubin Mass.

1957. *Moshe ben Maimon, (Medical) Aphorisms of Moses*, Hebrew translation by R. Nathan Hameati (= *Medical Works*, Vol. 2). Jerusalem: Mosad ha-Rav Kook.

1961. *Moshe ben Maimon* (Maimonides), *Commentary on the Aphorisms of Hippocrates*, Hebrew translation by R. Moshe Ibn Tibbon (= *Medical Works*, Vol. 3). Jerusalem: Mosad ha-Rav Kook.

Nadler, Steven 2001. *Spinoza's Heresy*. New York: Oxford University Press.

Narboni, Moses 1967. "Iggeret Shiʿur. Qoma Moses Narboni's Epistle on Shi'ur Qoma," ed. and English trans. by A. Altmann, in his *Jewish Medieval and Renaissance Studies*, Cambridge MA: Harvard University Press. 225–228.

Nehorai, Michael Zevi 1992. "How a Righteous Gentile Can Merit the World to Come" [in Hebrew], *Tarbiz* 61: 465–87.

Netanyahu, B. 1972. *Don Isaac Abravanel*. Philadelphia: Jewish Publication Society.

Netton, I. R. 1982. *Muslim Neoplatonists: An Introduction to the Thought of the Brethren of Purity*. London: Allen & Unwin.

Neugebauer, O. 1956. "Astronomical Commentary," in Maimonides *Sanctification of the Moon*, pp. 113–49.

1983. *Astronomy and History: Selected Essays*. New York: Springer-Verlag.

Novak, David 1983. *The Image of the Non-Jew in Judaism: An Historical and Constructive Study of the Noahide Laws*. New York/Toronto: Edwin Mellen.

1986. "The Treatment of Islam and Muslims in the Legal Writings of Maimonides," in *Studies in Islamic and Judaic Traditions*, eds. W. Brinner and S. Ricks. Atlanta, GA: Scholars Press.

1990. "Maimonides and the Science of the Law," *Jewish Law Association Studies* 4: 99–134.

1992. *Jewish Social Ethics*. New York: Oxford University Press.

1998. *Natural Law in Judaism*. New York: Cambridge University Press.

Nuriel, Abraham 2000. "Are There Really Maimonidean Elements in the Philosophy of Leibowitz?" [in Hebrew], in *Galui ve-Samui ba-Philosophiah ha-Yehudit bimei ha-Benayim*, ed. A. Nuriel. Jerusalem: Magnes Press.

Nussbaum, M. C. 1982," Saving Aristotle's Appearances," in *Language and Loges*, ed. M. Schofield and M. C. Nussbaum. Cambridge: Cambridge University Press.

Ormsby, E., ed. 1989. *Moses Maimonides and His Time*. Washington, DC: Catholic University of America Press.

Owen, G. E. L. 1961. "*Tithenai ta Phainomena*," in *Aristote et les problemes de methode*, ed. S. Mansion. Louvain: Publications Universitaires.

Owens, J. 1978. *The Doctrine of Being in the Aristotelian Metaphysics*, 3rd rev. ed. Toronto: Pontifical Institute of Mediaeval Studies.

Peters, F. E. 1968. *Aristoteles Arabus. The oriental translations and commentaries of the Aristotelian Corpus*. Leiden, The Netherlands: Brill.

1973. *Allah's Commonwealth*. New York: Simon & Schuster.

Petry, C. F., ed. 1998. *The Cambridge History of Egypt*, Vol. 1, Islamic Egypt, 640–1517. Cambridge: Cambridge University Press.

Pines, Shlomo 1947. "Nathanaël Ben al-Fayyūmī et la Théologie Ismaëlienne," *Révue d'Historie Juive en Egypte* 1: 5–22; in Pines 1997, Vol. V, pp. 317–34.

1960. "Notes on Maimonides' Views Concerning Free Will," *Scripta Hierosolymitana* 20: 195–8.

1963. "The Philosophic Sources of *The Guide of the Perplexed*," in *The Guide of the Perplexed*. Chicago: University of Chicago Press, pp. lvii–cxxxiv.

1968. "Spinoza's Theological-Political Treatise, Maimonides and Kant," *Scripta Hierosolymitana* 20: 3–54.

1979. "The Limitations of Human Knowledge According to Al-Farabi, ibn Bajja, and Maimonides," in Twersky 1979–2000, Vol. 1, pp. 82–109.

1980. "Shī'ite Terms and Conceptions in the *Kuzari*," *Jerusalem Studies in Arabic and Islam* 2: 165–251; in Pines 1997, Vol. V, pp. 219–305.

1983. "On Spinoza's Conception of Human Freedom and Good and Evil," in *Spinoza: His Thought and Work*," ed. N. Rotenstreich and N. Schneider. Jerusalem: Israel Academy of Sciences and Humanities: 147–159.

1986a. "The Philosophic Purport of Maimonides' Halachic Works," in Pines 1986b, pp. 1–14.

1986b, and Y. Yovel, eds. *Maimonides and Philosophy*. Dordrecht, The Netherlands: M. Nijhoff.

1990. "Truth and Falsehood versus Good and Evil," in Twersky 1990, pp. 95–157.

1997. *Collected Works*. Jerusalem: Magnes Press.

Popper, Karl R. 1956/63. "Three Views Concerning Human Knowledge," in *Conjectures and Refutations: The Growth of Scientific Knowledge*. London: Routledge & Kegan Paul, pp. 97–119.

Rashed, R. 1987. "al-Sijzī et Maïmonide: Commentaire mathématique et philosophique de la proposition 11–14 des Coniques d'Apollonius," *Archives Internationales d'Histoire des Sciences* 37: 263–96.

Ravitzky, Aviezer 1966. "The Question of a Created or Primordial World in the Philosophy of Maimonides" [in Hebrew], *Tarbiz* 35: 333–48.

1978–9. "The Possibility of Existence and Its Contingency in the Interpretation of Maimonides in the 13th Century" [in Hebrew], *Da'at* 2–3: 67–97.

1981a. "Samuel Ibn Tibbon and the Esoteric Character of the *Guide of the Perplexed*," *Association for Jewish Studies Review* 6: 87–123.

1981b. "The Sources of Immanuel of Rome's Commentary on Proverbs" [in Hebrew], *Kiryat Sefer* 56: 726–39.

1990a. "The Secrets of Maimonides," in Twersky 1990, pp. 159–207.

1990b. "Aristotle's Meteorology and the Maimonidean Interpretation of the Account of Creation" [in Hebrew], *Jerusalem Studies in Jewish Thought* 9: 225–50.

1991. "'To the Utmost of Human Capacity': Maimonides on the Days of the Messiah," in Kraemer 1991a, pp. 221–56.

1994. "The Image of the Leader in Jewish Thought" [in Hebrew], in *The Real and Ideal Image of the Leader*, The President's Study Group on the

Bible and Sources of Judaism. Jerusalem: The Presidential Residence, pp. 33–46.

1996. *History and Faith: Studies in Jewish Philosophy*. Amsterdam: J. C. Gieben.

2002. "The Binding of Isaac and the Covenant" [in Hebrew], in *The Faith of Abraham*, ed. Moshe Halamish, Hannah Kasher, and Yohanan Silman. Ramat Gan, Israel: Bar Ilan University Press, pp. 11–38.

Reif, S. C. 2000. *A Jewish Archive from Old Cairo: The History of Cambridge University's Genizah's Collection.* Richmond, UK: Curzon.

Reines, Alvin 1970a. *Maimonides and Abravanel on Prophecy.* Cincinnati: Hebrew Union College.

1970b. "Maimonides' Concept of Mosaic Prophecy," *Hebrew Union College Annual* 40: 325–62.

Revah, I. S. 1959. *Spinoza et le docteur Juan de Prado*. The Hague: Mouton.

Rigo, Caterina 1998. "Human Substance and Eternal Life in the Philosophy of R. Judah Romano" [in Hebrew], *Jerusalem Studies in Jewish Thought* 14: 181–222.

Rosenberg, Shalom 1981. "On Biblical Exegesis in the *Guide*" [in Hebrew], *Jerusalem Studies in Jewish Thought* 1: 85–157.

1983. "Ve-Halakhta Be-Derakhav" (in Hebrew) Philosphiah Yisraelit. Ed. Asa Kasher and Moshe Hallamish. Tel Aviv, pp. 79–92.

Rosenthal, F. 1981. "Maimonides and a Discussion of Muslim Speculative Theology," in *Jewish Tradition in the Diaspora: Studies in Memory of Professor Walter J. Fischel,* ed. M. Maswari Caspi. Berkeley, CA: Judah L. Magnes Memorial Museum, pp. 109–11.

Roth, Norman 1978. "The 'Theft of Philosophy' by the Greeks from the Jews," *Classical Folia* 32: 53–67.

Sabra, A. I. 1980. "Avicenna on the Subject Matter of Logic," *Journal of Philosophy* 77: 746–64.

1984. "The Andalusian Revolt Against Ptolemaic Astronomy," in *Transformation and Tradition in the Sciences,* ed. Everett Mendelsohn. Cambridge, MA: Harvard University Press, pp. 133–53.

1998. "Configuring the Universe: Aporetic, Problem Solving, and Kinematic Modeling as Themes of Arabic Astronomy," *Perspectives on Science* 6: 288–330.

Saliba, George 1999. "Critiques of Ptolemaic Astronomy in Spain," *Al-Qantara* 20: 3–25.

Samuelson, Norbert 1991. "Maimonides' Doctrine of Creation," *Harvard Theological Review* 84: 249–71.

Sanders, P. 1998. *The Fātimid State, 969–1171* in Petry 1998, pp. 151–74.

Schachter, J. J. 1988. "Rabbi Jacob Emden's *Iggeret Purim,*" in Twersky 1979–2000, Vol. 2, pp. 441–6.

Schimmel, A. 1993. *The Mystery of Numbers.* Oxford: Oxford University Press.

Schneersohn, Menachem Mendel (Rabbi of Lubavitch) 5740 (=1980). *Torah u-madda*ʿ. Kefar Habbad, Israel: Makhon Loubavitch.

Scholem, Gershom 1935. "The Kabbalist's Legend Concerning Maimonides" [in Hebrew], *Tarbiz* 6: 342–34.

Schwartz, Dov 1999. "Did the Sun Stand Still for Joshua? On the Doctrine of Miracles, as Mirrored in Jewish Medieval Thought" [in Hebrew], *Da*ʿ*at* 42: 33–62.

2002. *Contradiction and Concealment in Medieval Jewish Thought* [in Hebrew]. Ramat Gan, Israel: Bar Ilan University Press.

Schwarz, Michael 1991. "Who Were Maimonides' Mutakallimun? Some Remarks on *Guide of the Perplexed* Part 1 Chapter 73," *Maimonidean Studies* 2: 159–209.

1992–3: "Who Were Maimonides' Mutakallimun? Some Remarks on *Guide of the Perplexed* Part 1 Chapter 73," *Maimonidean Studies* 3: 143–172.

Schwarzschild, Steven S. 1962. "Do Noachites Have to Believe in Revelation?" *Jewish Quarterly Review* 52: 297–365.

1977. "Moral Radicalism and 'Middlingness,' in The Ethics of Maimonides," *Studies in Medieval Culture* 11: 65–94.

Seeskin, Kenneth 1991. *A Guide for Today's Perplexed.* West Orange, NJ: Behrman House.

1996. "Holiness As an Ethical Ideal," *Journal of Jewish Thought and Philosophy* 5: 191–203.

2000. *Searching for a Distant God: The Legacy of Maimonides.* New York: Oxford University Press.

Sela, Shlomo 2001a. "Abraham Ibn Ezra's Astrological Cosmological Exegesis" [in Hebrew], *Da*ʿ*at* 47: 5–34.

2001b. "The Fuzzy Borders Between Astronomy and Astrology in the Thought and Work of Three Twelfth-Century Jewish Intellectuals," *Aleph* 1: 59–100.

Septimus, Bernard 2001. "What Did Maimonides Mean by *Madda*ʿ?" in Fleischer et al. 2001.

Sermoneta, Joseph 1965. "La dottrina dell'intelletto e la "fede filosophica" di Jehudah e Immanuel Romano," *Studi Medievali*, Ser. 6, No. 2: 3–78.

Sermoneta, Joseph 1976. "Pour une Histoire du Thomisme Juif," in *Aquinas and the Problems of His Time*, ed. G Verbeke and D. Verhelst. Leuven, Belgium: Leuven University Press.

1980. "Jehudah ben Mosheh ben Daniel Romano, Traducteur de Saint Thomas," in *Hommage a Georges Vajda*, ed. G. Nahon and C. Touati. Louvain: Peters: pp. 235–262.

1984. "Prophecy in the Writings of R. Yehuda Romano," in Twersky 1979–2000, Vol. 2.

1990. "'Thine Ointments Have a Goodly Fragrance': R. Judah Romano and the Open Text Method," *Jerusalem Studies in Jewish Thought* 9: 77–114.

Shailat, Yishaq 5748 (=1988). *Letters and Essays by Moses Maimonides* [in Hebrew]. Maaleh Adumim, Israel: Maʿaliyot Press.

5752 (=1992). *Hakdamot ha-Rambam la-Mishnah* [Maimonides' Introductions to the *Mishnah*]. Jerusalem: Hotsaʾat Maʿalīyot.

Shapira, Chaim Elazar 1933. *Divrei Torah*, Vol. 5. Muncakz: n.p.

Shatz, David 1990. "Worship, Corporeality and Human Perfection: A Reading of *Guide* 3:54," in *The Thought of Moses Maimonides*, ed. Ira Robinson, Lawrence Kaplan, and Julien Baur. Lewiston, NY: Edwin Mellon, pp. 77–129.

Shmidman, Michael 1984. "On Maimonides' Conversion to Kabbala," in Twersky 1979–2000, Vol. 2, pp. 375–86.

Sirat, Colette 1990. *A History of Jewish Philosophy in the Middle Ages*. New York: Cambridge University Press.

2000. "Une Liste de Manuscrits: Préliminaire à une nouvelle édition du *Dalālat al-ḥaʾirīn*," *Maimonidean Studies* 4: 31–7.

Silman, Yochanan 1986. "Halakhic Determinations of a Nominalistic and Realistic Nature: Legal and Philosophical Considerations" [in Hebrew], *Dine Israel* 12: 249–66.

1993. "Introduction to the Philosophical Analysis of the Normative-Ontological Tension in the Halakha," *Daʿat* 31: 5–20.

Soloveitchik, H. 1980. "Maimonides' *ʿIggeret Ha-Shemad:* Law and Rhetoric," in *Joseph H. Lookstein Memorial Volume*. New York: Ktav, pp. 281–318.

Sorabji, Richard 1983. *Time, Creation and the Continuum*. Ithaca, NY: Cornell University Press.

Stern, J. 1989. "Logical Syntax As a Key to a Secret of the *Guide of the Perplexed*" [in Hebrew], *Iyyun* 38: 137–66.

1997. "Maimonides' Conceptions of Freedom and the Sense of Shame," in *Human Freedom and Moral Responsibility: General and Jewish Perspectives*, ed. C. Manekin and M. Kellner. College Park, MD: University Press of Maryland, pp. 217–66.

1998. *Problems and Parables of Law: Maimonides and Nahmanides on Reasons for the Commandments*. Albany, NY: State University of New York Press.

2000."Maimonides on Language and the Science of Language," in *Maimonides and the Sciences* (*Boston Studies in the Philosophy of Science*

211), ed. R. S. Cohen and H. Levine. Dordrecht, The Netherlands: Kluwer, pp. 173–226.

2001. "Maimonides' Demonstrations: Principles and Practice," *Medieval Philosophy and Theology* 10: 47–84.

2004. "Maimonides on the Growth of Knowledge and the Limitations of the Intellect," to appear in *Maimonide: Traditions philosophiques et scientifiques médievales arabe, hébraique, latine*, ed. Tony Levy and Roshdi Rashed. Leuven, Belgium: Peeters.

Forthcoming. *The Matter and Form of Maimonides' Guide*. Cambridge, MA: Harvard University Press.

Stern, S. 2001. *Calendar and Community*. Oxford: Oxford University Press.

Stern, S. M. 1962. "A Collection of Treatises by 'Abd al-Laṭīf al-Baghdādī" *Islamic Studies* 1: 53–70; reprinted in *Medieval Arabic and Hebrew Thought*, ed. F. W. Zimmermann. London: Variorum, 1983, no. xviii.

1983. *Studies in Early Ismāʿīlism*. Leiden, The Netherlands/Jerusalem: Brill/Magnes Press.

Strauss, Leo 1935. *Philosophie und Gesetz*. Berlin: Schocken.

1936. "Quelques remarques sur la science politique de Maïmonide et de Farabi," *Revue des Etudes Juives* 100: 1–37.

1948/1991. *On Tyranny*. New York: Free Press.

1952. "The Literary Character of *The Guide of the Perplexed*," in *Persecution and the Art of Writing*. Glencoe, IL: Free Press.

1953. "Maimonides' Statement on Political Science," *Proceedings of the American Academy for Jewish Research* 22:115–30; reprinted in Strauss 1959.

1958. *Thoughts on Machiavelli*. Glencoe, IL: Free Press.

1959. *What Is Political Philosophy? And Other Studies*. Glencoe, IL: Free Press.

1963. "How to Begin to Study *The Guide of the Perplexed*," Introduction to Shlomo Pines' English Translation of the *Guide*. Chicago: University of Chicago Press, pp. xi–lvi.

1964. *The City and Man*. Chicago: Rand McNally.

1967. "Notes on Maimonides' Book of Knowledge," in *Studies in Mysticism and Religion Presented to Gershom Scholem*, ed. E. Urbach. Jerusalem: Magnes Press.

1982. *Spinoza's Critique of Religion*. New York: Schocken Books.

1983. *Studies in Platonic Political Philosophy*. Chicago: University of Chicago Press.

1987. *Philosophy and Law*, trans. Fred Baumann. Philadelphia: Jewish Publication Society.

1997. *Gesammelte Schriften*, 3rd., ed. H. Meier. Stuttgart/Weimar, Germany: Metzler.

Stroumsa, S. 1999. *The Beginnings of the Maimonidean Controversy in the East, Yosef Ibn Shim'on's Silencing Epistle Concerning the Resurrection of the Dead*. Jerusalem: Ben-Zvi Institute and the Hebrew University.

Talmage, Frank 1986. "Apples of Gold: The Inner Meaning of Sacred Texts in Medieval Judaism," in *Jewish Spirituality: From the Bible through the Middle Ages*, ed. Arthur Green. London: Crossroad.

Tanenbaum, A. 1996. "Nine Spheres or Ten? A Medieval Gloss on Moses Ibn Ezra's 'Be Shem El Asher Amar,'" *Journal of Jewish Studies* 47: 294–310.

Touati, Charles 1954. "Dieu et le Monde selon Moise Narboni," *Archives d'histoire littéraire et doctrinale du Moyen Age* 21: 193–205.

1973. *La Pensée Philosophique et Théologique de Gersonide*. Paris: Mouton.

1974. "Hasdai Crescas et ses paradoxes sur la liberte," in *Melanges d'histoire des religions offerts a Henri-Charles Puech*. Paris: Presses Universitaires de France, pp. 573–8.

Twersky, Isadore 1967. "Some Non-Halakhic Aspects of the Mishneh Torah," in *Jewish Medieval and Renaissance Studies*, ed. Alexander Altmann. Cambridge, MA: Harvard University Press, pp. 95–118.

1979–2000. ed. *Studies in Medieval Jewish History and Literature*, 3 vols. Cambridge, MA: Harvard University Press.

1980. *Introduction to the Code of Maimonides*. New Haven, CT: Yale University Press.

1990. ed. *Studies in Maimonides*. Cambridge, MA: Harvard University, Center for Jewish Studies.

Urmson, J. O. 1980. "Aristotle's Doctrine of the Mean." Reprinted in *Essays on Aristotle's Ethics*, ed. Amelie Oksenberg Rorty. Berkeley, CA: University of California Press.

Urvoy, D. 1998. *Averroès: Les ambitions d'un intellectuel musulman*. Paris: Flammarion.

Vajda, Georges 1960. *Isaac Albalag: Averroiste Juif, Traducteur et Annotateur d'Al Ghazali*. Paris: Vrin.

Van Ess, J. 1968. "Skepticism in Islamic Religious Thought," *Al-Abhath* 21: 1–18.

Walker, P. 1998, "The Ismā'īlī Da'wa and the Fāṭimid Caliphate" in Petry 1998, pp. 120–50.

Wallace, W. A. 1972. *Causality and Scientific Explanation*, 2 vols. Ann Arbor, MI: University of Michigan Press.

Walzer, Richard 1962. *Greek into Arabic*. Oxford: Bruno Cassirer.

1985. "Galen, 'On Medical Experience,'" in *Three Treatises on the Nature of Science*, trans. Michael Frede and R. Walzer. Indianapolis, IN: Hackett.

Wegner, J. 1982. "Islamic and Talmudic Jurisprudence: The Four Roots of Islamic Law and Their Talmudic Counterparts," *American Journal of Legal History* 26: 25–72.

Weil, R. and S. Gerstenkorn, eds. and trans. 1988. *Lettre de Maïmonide sur le calendrier hébraïque*. n.p.

Weiss, Raymond L. 1991. *Maimonides' Ethics*. Chicago/London: University of Chicago Press.

Weiss, Roslyn 1992–1993. "Maimonides on the End of the World," *Maimonidean Studies* 3: 195–218.

Wolfson, Harry 1929. *Crescas' Critique of Aristotle*. Cambridge, MA: Harvard University Press.

1969. *The Philosophy of Spinoza*, 2 vols. New York: Schocken Books.

1973. *Studies in the History of Philosophy and Religion*, ed. Isadore Twersky and George H. Williams. Cambridge, MA: Harvard University Press.

Yahalom, Y. 1997. "Sayeth Tuviya ben Zidkiyah': The *Maqama* of Joseph ben Simeon in Honor of Maimonides" [in Hebrew], *Tarbiz* 66: 543–78.

Ziai, H. 1992. "The Source and Nature of Authority: A Study of al-Suhrawardī's Illuminationist Political Doctrine," in *The Political Aspects of Islamic Philosophy*, ed. C. Butterworth. Cambridge, MA: Harvard University Press, pp. 294–334.

Zimmermann, F. W. 1981. *Al-Farabi's Commentary and Short Treatise on Aristotle's De Interpretatione*. Oxford: Oxford University Press.

Index